Revenue Administration Handbook

Raúl Félix Junquera-Varela and Cristian Óliver Lucas-Mas

WORLD BANK GROUP

Contents

Boxes

Figures

Tables

Foreword

Revenue administration is a major point of contact between the government and the people. Recognizing this, and in line with the broader digital government transformation process, today, the focus has expanded from one centered on making it more effective and easier from the perspective of the government to collect revenue to one that also aims to improve citizens' lives by facilitating their interactions with the government. Broadening the focus means building from the foundational revenue management approaches to develop easy-to-use, citizen-centered services that leverage rapidly advancing digital technologies coordinated as a part of a whole-of-government approach.

Experience has demonstrated that the main challenges to this process are often not about the technology itself but rather about change management. It is not merely about digitalizing existing revenue administration processes, but rather about fundamentally reconceptualizing how the public sector, and the revenue administration within it, goes about its work and how citizens and businesses interact with it. This requires addressing key governance issues—such as making sure that different agencies across the government act in a coordinated way and have the needed skills—while continuing to strengthen the foundational tax administration practices with which many of us are familiar.

From a personal perspective, this is a topic that is of great interest to me. Over the course of my career, I have been responsible for leading two tax administration agencies—one at the subnational level and another at the national level. While doing so, when questions arose—as they always do—I would have loved to have a comprehensive and easy-to-read reference that offered practical guidance to me as a policy maker and practitioner.

This guidance is what we have in this handbook today. Offering clear guidance, best practices, real cases, and success stories and lessons from World Bank engagements, it draws from the Governance Global Practice in the Equitable Growth, Finance, and Institutions Practice Group Vice Presidency's extensive experience in partnering with countries to support their tax administration.

This *Revenue Administration Handbook* is not a theoretical exercise—quite the opposite; it distills practical experiences from the different jurisdictions where the World Bank is supporting revenue administrations. It aims to strike a balance between tax policy and tax administrative issues, serving as a timely and comprehensive resource for clients that can motivate them to carry reforms forward, especially in the area of tax digitalization, as well as for World Bank teams engaged in work to improve the quality of tax operations. While some areas might be beyond the scope of some tax administrations' current stage of the reform process, it is never too early to start thinking about the digital transformation journey and exploring opportunities to leapfrog the process by building upon the experience of others and rapidly advancing technological capabilities.

To make a big leap forward in improving tax compliance and boosting revenue collection, the digitalization of revenue administration should not be limited to digitization of taxpayer services; it requires a revision of tax policy, rethinking and reforming traditional revenue administration practices and core functions, enhancing strategic planning, and strengthening analytical capacity. This handbook, which focuses on clearly and concisely discussing the most critical aspects of this process, is intended to support governments and development partners working in the area of revenue administration as they think through these changes and push for deeper and transformational reforms of tax and customs administrations.

The following chapters connect the dots between the choices linked to policy trade-offs on complexity and the associated administrative arrangements. Recognizing that there is no one-size-fits-all answer to policy choices on tax issues, the chapters instead lay out the advantages and disadvantages of different options and the factors to consider based on good international practices.

As we navigate a world shaped by overlapping crises and tightening fiscal space, the importance of these topics will only grow. I hope *Revenue Administration Handbook* can play a part in supporting this process.

Arturo Herrera Gutiérrez
Global Director, Governance Global Practice
World Bank

Preface

Revenue Administration Handbook aims to provide a comprehensive and systematic description of the structure and management of not only tax administrations but also the often-neglected customs administrations. This publication comprises research in the areas of tax policy design considerations that impact tax administration, institutional setup and strategic planning, analytical capacities and maturity models, core business processes, tax sanctions, digital transformation of revenue administrations, and how to build data science capabilities.

In recent years, the adoption of technologies by revenue administrations has contributed to the better provision of e-services to taxpayers and the strengthening of tax compliance control mechanisms that can contribute to the increased collection of tax revenue. However, such technologies have not been developed by all countries, and many tax authorities still rely on burdensome, paper-based, and lengthy core business processes. As these authorities look to navigate this transition within a context of increased digitalization of the economy and society, a different model of tax and customs administrations is needed.

How then do we unlock the full potential of these new technologies to transform tax and customs administrations? How do we ensure that they allow revenue administrations to administer taxes more effectively and efficiently, enhance service delivery, and reduce administration costs and taxpayers' costs of compliance, thereby improving the business climate? With all the choices available to tax and customs administrations today, how do we select technologies that are most relevant and will support the achievement of stated objectives with acceptable return on investment? Most probably, tax and customs administrations of tomorrow will look very different from those of today. How do we prepare for that?

Drawing extensively on examples from actual World Bank projects, the handbook presents pioneering work in the field of digital transformation, including a roadmap for policy makers and tax officials on how to incorporate and manage disruptive technologies, such as machine learning, into building modern revenue administrations. Altogether, this handbook offers a holistic view of the appropriate technology to be applied by tax and customs administrations, taking into account their respective maturity levels. It is intended to be helpful not only for policy makers and tax officials but also for information technology experts and information and communication technology providers who need to understand the needs of tax and customs administrations to better design and implement the most appropriate technology solutions.

Acknowledgments

This handbook is a product of the Governance Global Practice in the Equitable Growth, Finance, and Institutions Practice Group Vice Presidency. It draws on a range of the World Bank's operational engagements in the areas of tax policy and administration.

First, the authors would like to dedicate this handbook to the memory of their friend and mentor, Professor Richard M. Bird, for his guidance and wholehearted support throughout their careers.

The authors want to acknowledge Ivan Krsul and Vladimir Omar Calderon Yksic for generously contributing their work and research in the key area of data science capabilities in tax and customs administration.

The authors are very grateful to peer reviewers Viet Anh Nguyen, Maya Gusarova, Bernard James Haven, Charles Victor Blanco, Moses Sabuni Wasike, Jeffrey Owens, Pratheep Ponraj, and Ana Cebreiro Gómez for valuable contributions and noteworthy technical advice.

They thank Salma Lemkhente El Bounaamani, Mayra Mas Echevarría, and José Lucas Carrasco for providing assistance in reviewing the research literature and for sharing their extensive knowledge throughout the drafting process; Asli Senkal and Adrienne Elizabeth Hathaway-Nuton for insightful comments and technical observations that improved the quality of this work; and Bertin Lopez for providing timely operational support.

They are also appreciative of the encouragement and guidance provided during rehearsal sessions by the members of the Tashkent A Cappella Choir: Ana Patricia Solis García Barbón, Juan Miguel Márquez, Alberto García Carregal, Isabel García Araquistaín, Gonzalo Fournier Conde, Alejandra García, Jose Carlos Giménez, and Lola Vico López.

They commend the professional work and valuable editorial contributions made by Richard Crabbe.

The authors would like to express special gratitude to Serdar Yilmaz for his inestimable support and leadership that ultimately made possible the publication of this handbook. Finally, they also thank Pablo Saavedra, Aart C. Kraay, and Arturo Herrera Gutiérrez for overall management and direction.

About the Authors

Raúl Félix Junquera-Varela is global lead on domestic resource mobilization at the World Bank. He has more than 40 years of experience in public sector reform, with a particular focus on tax administration and customs. He held senior positions at the Spanish Revenue Agency from 1984 to 1998, including as director of a regional Tax and Customs Office and senior national tax auditor in the Large Taxpayer Office. He headed the Spanish Diplomatic Mission at the Inter-American Centre of Tax Administration and served as public finance counselor to the Spanish Embassy in Panama from 1998 until 2004. In 2005, he joined the International Monetary Fund as technical assistance adviser in the Revenue Administration Division of the Fiscal Affairs Department. In 2009, he joined the World Bank as senior public sector specialist in the Public Sector Governance Department. His research interests include institution building and operational reform of revenue administrations, and he has authored numerous publications on these topics. He is an economist, a lawyer, and a certified public accountant. From 1990 until 1992, he was professor of tax law at the University of Oviedo, Spain. From 2005 until 2015, he was professor of the Master of Public Finance program of the Institute for Fiscal Studies of Spain.

Cristian Óliver Lucas-Mas is a senior economist specializing in tax policy and administration at the World Bank, where he has provided technical assistance and tax advice to more than 30 countries since 2016. He has more than 20 years of experience in international taxation as an attorney-at-law, economist, consultant, researcher, and university professor. He was admitted to practice law in New York and Spain, where he started his career in a leading law firm and later opened his own private legal practice, specializing in international tax planning. In academia, he has held various teaching positions at universities in Spain, the United States, and the Democratic People's Republic of Korea and has published extensively in international tax journals. As a consultant, he has worked as a tax policy adviser for the International Monetary Fund and as an adviser for the General Authority of Zakat and Tax of Saudi Arabia. He holds a PhD in tax law and public finance from the University of Barcelona, an LLM from Harvard Law School, an MPA from the Harvard Kennedy School, and an MBA from the Massachusetts Institute of Technology; he is a graduate of the International Tax Program at Harvard Law School. In 2000, he received the First Prize of the National Awards for Academic Excellence in Legal Studies from the government of Spain, and the Harvard Kennedy School named him a Public Service Fellow in 2007.

Executive Summary

Revenue Administration Handbook aims to provide a comprehensive view of all aspects involving tax and customs administrations, starting from tax policy considerations that affect administrative functions (chapter 1). There is a broad consensus on the existence of strong linkages between tax policy and tax administration. The best tax design needs to be implemented to achieve a fair and consistent application of tax laws. Conversely, a modern and effective tax administration needs a coherent and consistent set of laws to achieve its goals. Among the topics covered in the first chapter and its appendixes, taxpayer segmentation is vital to allocate the scarce resources of revenue bodies more efficiently and to effectively control compliance. Similarly, presumptive taxation may prove useful when the treatment and analysis of the real tax base entail a high degree of complexity. This involves an interesting question that consists of establishing the extent to which presumptions can contribute to the simplification of tax administration without fundamentally altering or substituting the essence of their respective tax bases and the original nature of the tax itself. This chapter concludes with a discussion of nontechnical drivers, reflecting the fact that before designing tax reform and a tax project to support the reform, it is important to understand the political economy context, the institutional environment, and taxpayer morale.

The handbook also covers the overall institutional framework of revenue administrations, paying special attention to institutional arrangements, degree of autonomy of administrations, responsibilities of the tax administration, and external oversight (chapter 2). Special emphasis is given to the extent to which the tax administration is granted autonomous or semiautonomous powers to administer the tax system. The rationale behind the establishment of semiautonomous revenue bodies points to less political interference to conduct their operations; more responsibility and accountability for managers to achieve their objectives; and more management capacity, especially in terms of budgeting decisions and human resource policies. These governance structures allow tax administrations to be free from rigid bureaucratic structures and to apply private sector management principles. Likewise, the creation of specialized large taxpayer units is mostly motivated by efficiency considerations rather than organizational needs. Large taxpayers, who are in proportion much fewer in number, still contribute the majority of tax revenue collections, something that, from an efficiency perspective, calls for a dedicated tax administration system, especially as related to certain functions that are specific to the features of this taxpayer segment. It is also important that tax administration leaders implement a holistic compliance risk management method that spans the full revenue administration cycle and systematically identifies compliance risks within the taxpayer population to determine how to mitigate and treat them in the most effective and efficient way.

In addition, it is important to build a model that assesses the general level of maturity of revenue administrations and customs so that plans for improvement are tailored to a given context (chapter 3). This is especially relevant in low-capacity environments and more effective than a benchmarking exercise. Maturity models do not assess revenue administrations by their distance from the "really good practice frontier" but in the form of constraints to achieve comprehensive functionality appropriate to the level of maturity—identify taxpayers; assess taxes; collect, investigate, and audit; manage disputes; report; and offer transparency and accountability in a manner that imposes reasonable cost for taxpayers and revenue administration. Chapter 3 presents the four-level models and assesses the level of maturity of tax administrations and customs in terms of their current capabilities. The usual practices at lower levels of maturity are also described so that plans for improvement can be made. By using the maturity models, revenue administrations can monitor their progress, practice by practice, to better identify how to sustain improvement and performance across areas and functions. Also, such models help leverage existing systems, processes, and tools in designing strategies to overcome the gap in tax administration and customs capacity.

This handbook also presents the entire cycle of tax administration, covering all functions from registration to appeals, with special emphasis on voluntary compliance mechanisms and strategies, as well as on understanding how the different elements align with one another (chapter 4). A comprehensive system of taxpayer registration and identification is critical for the effective operation of a tax system. Similarly, the tax assessment function is important for maintaining high levels of voluntary compliance and citizens' confidence in the tax system; the same applies for dispute prevention and resolution, which are essential mechanisms. For example, improved reliability and accuracy of tax administration data—including the identity of registered taxpayers, efficient taxpayer account management and respective guidelines, and strong established links between information management and core business processes of tax administration—are conducive to strengthening tax administration and improving control of compliance and collection enforcement mechanisms.

However, in the absence of voluntary compliance, tax enforcement would not be possible without institutional mechanisms that make noncompliance costly—tax sanctions (chapter 5). Some altruistic taxpayers may have a high motivation to voluntarily comply with their tax obligations. The broader reality is that the motivation for voluntary tax compliance is correlated to the threat of being caught—effective enforcement—and being punished at the administrative or criminal level, depending on the tax violation. Therefore, when taxpayers do not fulfill their tax obligations, it is necessary to enforce the appropriate institutional mechanisms that help ensure that they assume the consequences of their violation. Such mechanisms are known as *tax sanctions* and comprise different types of instruments. The function or objective of these tools is to impose a cost on the noncompliant taxpayer by being punitive, deterring, and/or compensatory. Chapter 5 reviews the framework governing tax sanctions and provides some basic guidelines on best practices for their design. As a starting point, it analyzes the challenges and misconstructions of tax sanctions systems, as well as addresses those features that are desirable. For example, an excessively strict and complex tax sanctions system may discourage tax compliance with the consequent negative effect on the tax base of a country. Therefore, any reform of a tax sanctions system must aim at achieving greater levels of uniformity, coherence, publicity, consistency, proportionality, progressivity, and balance in the application of tax penalties, surcharges, and interests. To this end, it is essential to clearly define the notion, nature, and purposes of penalties, surcharges, and interests to prevent any misconceptions and properly align tax offenses and sanctions.

The last two chapters provide fresh and in-depth guidance regarding the digital transformation of tax and customs administrations and building data science capabilities. The handbook focuses on data analytics and information management, as well as the role of digitalization as a strategic tool for domestic resource mobilization (chapter 6). Digitalization results in improvements in the efficiency of tax collection, cost reductions, and a more efficient fight against corruption, fostering transparency and tracking and tracing operations. The digitalization of tax and customs administrations allows them to evolve into a new role and find the balance between facilitating tax compliance and maintaining effective control of taxpayers' obligations. Technological change affects organizational structure, business processes, and human resource policies. Beyond the adoption of new tools and technologies, real digitalization of the tax administration involves a comprehensive legal and institutional transformation. This process encompasses all required adjustments to traditional operational models with the purposes of achieving long-term and sustainable efficiencies, offering new and improved services to taxpayers, and developing new capabilities in key areas such as digital invoicing, tax payments, digital fiscalization, advanced data analytics, and value chains and factoring. Such developments allow tax administrations to process huge volumes of information and increase the reliability, accuracy, and timeliness of the information processed, which altogether reduce administration costs. Nowadays, tax administration is essentially a business of information management. These elements are strongly supported by the use of information and communication technology (ICT). Today, the use of ICT is not a choice; it is a necessity.

Finally, data science is typically used in revenue administrations to make sense of the vast amounts of available data, so that organization can become smarter, faster, and more efficient. Of particular interest is the field of machine learning, a subset of data science that can be used to solve difficult problems that arise from the inability of a tax or customs administration to process massive amounts of data efficiently (chapter 7). The field of machine learning includes applications such as identifying fraudulent operations, automatically answering questions posed by taxpayers, identifying illegal goods via x-rays, predicting the cost of interventions, identifying the code of a given article in the harmonized system, and identifying potential errors or inconsistencies in declarations or tax returns. These techniques can improve the efficiency of a revenue administration significantly, but processes and protocols must ensure an acceptable level of confidence in data and support a culture of innovation. This is examined in chapter 7, which explores what a digital roadmap for building data science capabilities would look like and how to determine the appropriate technology to be applied by tax and customs administrations, taking into account their maturity level. This chapter explores questions such as: What should be the sequence of automation and institutional reforms? How does one get the right mix between tactical taxpayer service and long-term strategic process and approach to change? How can an administration deal with legacy systems and nonstandard transactions? What are some of the best practices in this area?

This handbook is intended to serve as a reference work to facilitate the modernization of revenue administrations across the globe and to reach different audiences, including tax experts and policy makers, nontax government officials, businesses and academic communities, and even the general public, all of whom play an active role in day-to-day revenue administration operations.

Abbreviations

APA	advance pricing arrangement
BDT	business domain team
CADE	corporate average data center efficiency
CIAT	Inter-American Center of Tax Administrations
CIF	cost, insurance, and freight
CIP	compliance improvement plan
CIT	corporate income tax
CRM	compliance risk management
DApp	decentralized application
DIAMOND	Development Implementation and Monitoring Directives
DRM	domestic resource mobilization
ECtHR	European Court of Human Rights
EU	European Union
GDP	gross domestic product
HIC	high-income country
HR	human resources
HRM	human resource management
HQ	headquarters
HTS	Harmonized Tariff Schedule
ICT	information and communication technology
IT	information technology
KPI	key performance indicator
LIC	low-income country
LMICs	low- and middle-income countries

LTU	large taxpayer unit
MIS	management information system
MNE	multinational enterprise
MOF	Ministry of Finance
MSME	micro, small, and medium enterprises
MTU	medium taxpayer unit
NFT	nonfungible token
NSWS	national single window system
OCR	optical character recognition
OECD	Organisation for Economic Co-operation and Development
PCA	postclearance audit
PFM	public financial management
PIT	personal income tax
PUE	power usage effectiveness
RMS	risk management system
SME	small and medium enterprises
SRA	Systems Readiness Assessment
SSCs	social security contributions
STU	small taxpayer unit
TA	technical assistance
TIN	Taxpayer Identification Number
TR	trouble report
USAID	United States Agency for International Development
VAT	value added tax

CHAPTER 1

Tax policy design considerations that impact the tax administration

Certainty and simplicity

Richard M. Bird said, "policy change without administrative change is nothing," and that it is critical to ensure that "changes in tax policy are compatible with administrative capacity." Along the same lines, Milka Casanegra de Jantscher believed that "tax administration is tax policy" in developing countries (Bird and Casanegra de Jantscher 1992). Their views are nowadays more relevant than ever before. This chapter analyzes certainty and simplicity, taxpayer segmentation, presumptive taxation, and tax morale and other nontechnical drivers.

Tax policy per se, no matter how well designed, cannot be effective without a modern and efficient tax administration that implements it. Tax policy and tax administration work symbiotically. The actual working of the tax law depends a lot on how it is administered, especially in countries with a weak and uncertain rule of law (Bird and Oldman 1995). Also, improvement of tax administration often requires revised policies and procedural authority in the law. Efficient collection and administration of the value added tax (VAT) and income taxes, in particular, need policy reforms to eliminate exemptions and zero-rating clauses and simplify complex rate structures, which otherwise become avenues for evasion and make tax calculations more difficult even for honest taxpayers.

Hence, there is a broad consensus on the existence of strong linkages between tax policy and tax administration. The best tax policy design needs to be implemented to achieve a fair and consistent application of tax laws (Bird 2010b). This also works the other way around in the sense that a modern and effective tax administration needs a coherent and consistent set of laws to achieve its goals. This section focuses on capacity constraints or impediments imposed by deficient or incomplete tax systems, including substantive and complex laws and complementary regulations, also referred to as procedural features.

The legal and regulatory powers vested in the tax administration by all tax legislation—for example, tax procedure code and complementary regulations—can facilitate administering tax laws in an efficient way or, on the contrary, can impose significant constraints and impediments to the operational performance of tax administration (Faria and Yücelik 1995).

Some countries have a tax procedure code that encompasses the powers granted to the tax administration agency to administer the tax system, taxpayers' rights and obligations, and the elements and key features of the basic processes of tax administration such as collection, registration, tax audit, tax disputes, tax rulings, and collection enforcement of tax debts (Lucas-Carrasco 1997). They also include the penalties to apply in case of noncompliance with tax laws and regulations. These codes need to strike a balance between the powers granted to the tax administration agency and taxpayers' rights to promote a fair application of the tax system (box 1.1).

Furthermore, tax systems should provide a fair and predictable business climate with a view to promoting trade and attracting investment, including foreign direct investment. Certainty in tax policy, along with its positive impact transmitted in business environment, leads to increased transparency and integrity of revenue systems. However, empirical evidence suggests that tax policy is more volatile in developing countries than in advanced countries in the sense that developing countries change their tax rates, which is a powerful policy instrument, by larger amounts than advanced economies (Vegh and Vuletin 2015). With the exception of corporate tax rates, the percentage change in tax rates is much higher, about 50 percent, for developing countries than advanced ones. Furthermore, taxes should have broad bases and low rates to minimize negative economic effects on prices and to reduce the potential for administrative corruption and tax evasion (Lucas-Carrasco 1997). An important corollary of the "broad-based, low-rate" proposition is to minimize distortionary tax concessions and to evaluate the tax relief framework from a cost–benefit analysis perspective.

Tax reform must be revenue neutral, and lowering rates should only be done to the extent that a significant broadening of the tax base occurs, specifically through abolishing and phasing out of profit-based tax incentives. Also, no new exemptions should be introduced without conducting a prior cost–benefit analysis, and any tax reform should focus on establishing a transparent process to grant incentives (Bird and Oldman 1977). Besides, preference should be given to replacing profit-based incentives with cost-based incentives, abolishing excessive and outdated VAT exemptions, introducing sunset clauses to periodically review existing tax incentives and exemptions, and using the same phasing-out approach to all profit-based tax incentives.

BOX 1.1   Assessment of procedural features in tax laws and regulations

1. Does a tax procedure code exist?

2. Is the tax administration responsible for all tax administration functions assessment: collection, data processing, audit, recovery of tax arrears, and taxpayer service and claim investigations?

3. Is the tax administration provided by law with sufficient powers to efficiently undertake all its statutory responsibilities?

4. Examination of collection enforcement powers granted to the tax administration, such as seizing bank accounts, movable assets, and property; imposing administrative sanctions for noncompliance; and adopting precautionary measures to ensure collection of tax debts.

5. Information sharing: legal restrictions to request tax-related information from third parties, including bank and financial institution secrecy.

6. Complaint-handling mechanisms and tax administration oversight bodies: independent and dedicated bodies to handle tax administration–related complaints, for example, tax ombudsman or an organizational unit within the tax administration agency, separate and independent oversight bodies, and developed tax appeals and tax dispute procedures.

7. Participation of the tax administration in the formulation of tax legislation and fiscal policy. Is the tax administration responsible for or does it participate in the formulation of laws concerning the assessment, collection, and enforcement of taxes?

In this context, a domestic resource mobilization (DRM) strategy is important to attain the objective of improving the vertical and horizontal equity of the tax system and to improve fairness in administering it. The DRM strategy should provide a conceptual framework to address key shortcomings in the resource mobilization systems of low- and middle-income countries (LMICs). It should seek to facilitate increased tax collection to provide countries with a stable and predictable fiscal environment and to promote growth, equity, and development (Junquera-Varela et al. 2017). Achieving this objective requires putting in place tax systems that are broad, simple, and equitable and that facilitate taxpayer compliance.

The proposed strategy hinges on three pillars: enhancing the quality of tax systems—increasing tax collection but also minimizing economic distortions and reducing inequality; strengthening the operational capacity of tax administrations in terms of administrative and policy aspects; and fostering social acceptance and legitimacy of the tax system, while improving public accountability (Bagchi, Bird, and Das-Gupta 1994). Steps to take in this direction include simplifying taxes, strengthening tax administrations, and enhancing the role of subnational governments. Tax administration is part of the equation as far as it guarantees fair implementation of the tax system and, as a result, ensures that everybody pays their fair share of tax revenue. Tax reforms should therefore aim to strengthen governance, improve the business environment, and support formalization of the economy (Awasthi and Engelschalk 2018). These reforms should also extend to subnational and local governments and seek to generate more revenue at these levels.

Another important issue is legal stability, which requires systemizing the principles regarding interpretation and application of various tax laws, and codifying the principles that courts have developed throughout the application of tax norms (Ferreiro-Lapatza 1996). Also, it is necessary to promote the administrative processes for the legal stability of taxpayers, which include the implementation of binding tax rulings and a clear and efficient procedure to request and obtain such rulings. The complexity of tax laws and tax procedures hinders voluntary compliance and increases compliance costs that are regressive to low-income taxpayers who cannot afford professional assistance from tax preparers (Dom et al. 2022). On the other hand, such complexity benefits those other taxpayers who can engage in tax planning or tax evasion schemes. Therefore, any tax analysis must take into consideration the complexity that impacts its administration, because it can have a negative effect on equity (box 1.2). Increased equity in the application of tax laws should also be a key priority for tax administration. Reducing inequality in tax burden rather than focusing on maximizing collections results in higher levels of legitimacy of the tax administration and the political system as a whole (Burgess and Stern 1993).

Tax incentives and tax expenditures

Tax expenditures are the revenue losses from exclusions, exemptions, deductions, tax credits, preferential tax rates, and deferrals. In a way, tax expenditures are very similar to direct spending through the budget (Kaldor 1955). Tax expenditures are measured relative to the normal tax system. The fact or even the general perception that well-connected groups of individuals or companies are receiving preferential treatment under the tax laws severely jeopardizes the integrity and effectiveness of a tax system.

Economists have long argued that tax incentives are poor instruments for attracting investments, even in theory, and are highly abused in practice (Surrey 1973). But governments argue that they are obliged to give tax incentives because their neighbors are giving them, and there is some truth in this contention—the "race to the bottom." Although there is no systematic way to bring all

BOX 1.2   Assessment of the level of complexity of the tax system that may negatively impact tax administration and voluntary compliance

1. Degree of complexity of tax laws and tax procedures to avoid rising compliance and administrative costs and the proliferation of tax planning or tax evasion mechanisms.

2. Examine the most significant complexities involved in the tax system to identify possible loopholes that can lead to tax evasion or tax avoidance.

3. Tax provisions contained in nontax laws and the level of complexity they impose to administering tax laws.

4. Number of taxes in the tax system and their level of compliance and revenues.

5. Constraints and impediments imposed on tax administration by tax laws and complementary regulations in terms of their ability to gather information relevant for administering the tax system.

6. Presence of exemptions, incentives, and tax relief clauses in the tax laws, including bilateral agreements outside the tax code. Impact on revenue and administrative burden and compliance costs.

7. Total number of taxpayers and its impact on administrative costs. Rate of growth of taxpayer population by type of taxes and legal thresholds in value added tax (VAT), personal income taxes (PITs), and corporate income taxes (CITs), if any.

8. Social acceptance of the tax system, paying special attention to tax education programs, if any.

9. In case tax policy reforms or tax administration reforms have taken place over the past years, examine if they have gone hand in hand or have occurred at different times.

10. Possibility of determining compliance costs and administration costs, including transition costs from a prereform situation to a postreform situation, in case some reforms have previously taken place.

11. Does a tax code comprising all substantive tax laws exist?

12. Is there a presumptive taxation regime for small and medium taxpayers? If it exists, what are its main characteristics?

13. What are the VAT withholding mechanisms provided by law, if they exist?

14. How frequently are the tax laws and rules changed? Specify the number of laws and their main amendments to assess the level of legal stability.

15. Has the government granted tax amnesties over the past few years? How many and what are their main characteristics?

16. Analyze if the domestic legal framework is aligned with internationally agreed standards on tax transparency and exchange of information in terms of availability of information, ability of the tax administration to obtain it, and mechanisms in place to effectively exchange information between countries.

17. Is there in place a transfer pricing legislation aligned with internationally agreed transfer pricing guidelines? Is there adequate capacity to implement these rules to ensure that multinational enterprises (MNEs) pay their fair share of tax revenue? In particular, examine whether or not there is a dedicated international taxation unit and staff trained with the necessary skills to apply the abovementioned rules.

18. Assess the overall effectiveness of the judiciary process in its interactions with both the government and the taxpayers in key aspects, such as verification, collection, enforcement of criminal sanctions, and protection of taxpayers' rights. How do tax courts procedurally handle the tax matters brought about by the government and the taxpayers in terms of fairness and timing?

19. Evaluate the institutional relationship between tax authorities of different levels of government—central and subnational—and its potential effect on mutual collaboration and assistance to protect their tax bases.

---

of these countries around a table and make them agree to a basic norm of providing or not providing tax incentives, some LMICs are now realizing the poor choice they made when granting tax incentives and have started to rationalize and even eliminate them. In addition, some progress is being made in the regional harmonization of tax incentives, for example, in East Africa (Gray 2001).

Although tax incentives are still widespread in many LMICs, at the very least, there should be transparency around tax expenditures, including those generated by tax incentives. At present, most low-income countries (LICs) cannot or simply do not publish a list of recipients or the estimated revenues forgone. This lack of transparency leads to discretionary concessions, backdoor dealings, outright corruption, and other abuses and helps to legalize tax avoidance by well-connected firms (Wadhawan and Gray 1998; Gray 2001). Even if a more detailed and sophisticated analysis of tax expenditures by most LMICs is not feasible, an industry and regional inventory of recipient businesses, with a simple accounting of revenue lost, would go a long way toward improving tax administration and compliance.

The next step is to publish tax expenditures as a line item in the annual budget so that they receive the same level of scrutiny as direct spending programs through line ministries and government agencies. Including tax expenditures in the budget does not imply any value judgment about their merits or effectiveness. It is primarily meant to increase the transparency of the tax system and to allow the legislature to debate and review the provisions annually and get a sense of the revenue loss involved (Junquera-Varela 2011). The good news is that estimating tax expenditures from direct tax instruments is relatively straightforward and is becoming more prevalent in LMICs. Tax expenditure accounts are now routinely produced not only by high-income countries (HICs) but also by Latin American countries (USAID 2013; CIAT 2019) and some African and Asian countries as well (ADB 2018).

The process is time and data intensive at least in the initial years, but once the database is created and the exercise is undertaken as part of annual budget making, it becomes less arduous (Le et al. 2016). It pays rich dividends eventually and has the potential to enhance the tax to gross domestic product (GDP) ratio by 2–3 percentage points, depending on the country. Estimating expenditures clearly is vital in the context of DRM, particularly in LICs.

Resource mobilization at the subnational government level

Decentralization is an ongoing international trend that focuses on creating strong local governments. Decentralization helps to improve efficiency in service delivery, enhance political and fiscal accountability, and change the process of entering into a fiscal contract with the government (Bird 2010a). Local government taxes contribute significantly to the DRM agenda in LICs and, at the same time, support the provision of local services that affect people the most. Since it has the potential to engage taxpayers, decentralization also ensures better use of funds by the local government, as people take more interest in how what they pay locally is spent and in what they can see. But the absence of an effective property tax, one of the most important subnational taxes, is an important weakness in the tax systems of LMICs (Junquera-Varela et al. 2017). It involves significant revenue losses and adversely affects redistribution of wealth in society, as property is one of the assets owned by richer segments of the population. Additionally, an appropriate tax on land can be instrumental in promoting more efficient use of land.

Decentralization includes the assignment of service delivery functions and expenditure responsibilities as well as the assignment of revenue: delegation of "function," followed by devolution of "finance." Revenues at the local government level come from own taxes and fees plus fiscal transfers from the central government supplemented by borrowing, debt, and capital finance. To develop own revenues for local government, it is necessary to decompose tax bases vertically between the center and subnational levels and to identify revenue sources with low mobility within the local jurisdiction. Transfers are usually required for correcting regional imbalances.

Local taxes are defined as those that satisfy the following criteria (Junquera-Varela et al. 2017). Local governments can (a) decide whether to levy the tax; (b) determine the precise base of the tax; (c) decide on the tax rate; (d) in the case of "direct" taxes (income taxes), assess the tax imposed on any particular taxpayer, individual, or business; (e) administer the tax; and (f) keep all collections. Box 1.3 shows the types of revenue allocation available at the subnational level.

More concretely, some revenue instruments are used at subnational and local levels, as shown in box 1.4.

Property taxes can be based on annual rental value, capital value of land and improvements, capital or rental value of land, or land or improvement area. Within these general categories, there are many variations. The property tax meets the "good tax" argument because it (a) has significant revenue potential; (b) is quite visible, as it is clearly linked to local government services and

---

BOX 1.3   Models of local government taxation

- **Independent subnational taxes**. Legislation, administration, and revenue are under the control of regional governments, often under broad guidelines from the central government (property tax).

- **Centrally assisted subnational taxes (coadministration)**. Legislation and revenue are directly under the control of regional governments, but the administration could be shared with the central government—for example, property tax with central valuation.

- **Surcharges (piggybacking)**. Administration is under central control, while policy discretion is given to regional governments to set a rate on the nationally determined tax base. Revenue is given back to the regions on the basis of the tax rate, origin of revenues, residence of taxpayers, or some formula—for example, income taxes and value added tax (VAT) in Canada.

- **Tax sharing (transfer)**. All policy and administration are under central government control. A portion of revenue is given to regional governments on the basis of origin, residence, or some formula—for example, VAT in China and transitional economies of the former Soviet Union.

- **Revenue sharing (transfers and grants)**. All policy, administration, and revenue are under central government control. Revenue can then be given back to the regional governments through revenue sharing based on a formula.

BOX 1.4   Revenue instruments used at the subnational and local levels

- **Asset taxes**, including taxes on immovable property (land and building), machinery and equipment, motor and other vehicles (aircrafts, boats, bicycles), and natural resource taxes and charges

- **User charges** for specific services that are rivals in consumption and where exclusion of nonpayers is possible, focusing on the benefit principle

- **Consumption taxes**, including excises, sales taxes, and value added tax

- **Income taxes** on individuals (personal income taxes) and businesses (corporate income taxes) and payroll taxes on employers

- **Local business taxes**, including business permit or regulatory fees and licenses

---

strengthens public accountability; (c) meets the equity test in terms of ability to pay, since assessed value is correlated with the property owners' capacity to pay the tax bill; (d) is less distortive than other local taxes because it is a tax on land and buildings, which are comparatively immobile; and (e) has the potential to be transparent (Junquera-Varela et al. 2017).

There are four basic approaches to determining property value and assessing the tax base:

- **Rental value system**. Many countries, including India, Malaysia, Nigeria, and Trinidad and Tobago, use the annual rental value of properties as the tax base.
- **Capital value system**. The capital value system is the main form of property tax base valuation used in Organisation for Economic Co-operation and Development (OECD) countries. The tax base is the market value adjusted by an assessment ratio.
- **Land value or site value systems**. The tax base is the market value of land, including improvements, such as clearing, grading, and installation of utilities—examples can be found in Australia, Denmark, Estonia, Jamaica, Kenya, New Zealand, and South Africa.
- **Area-based systems**. The area-based systems approach is used in many countries of Central and Eastern Europe as well as in China and Vietnam. Each parcel is taxed at a specific rate per area unit of land and per area unit of structure(s).

Many different tax rate structures are used in LMICs. It is best to choose a simple rate structure that is easy to administer, minimizes cost of administration, and promotes compliance. A good valuation usually addresses differences in ability to pay, so differential tax rates are not necessary for equity reasons and might complicate the administration. Sometimes local governments set the property tax rate, sometimes they are only permitted to choose a rate within a prescribed range, and sometimes the rate is set by a higher-level government.

The four key components of property tax administration are (a) identifying all properties, (b) keeping the records and updating the tax roll (cadaster), (c) valuing and revaluing properties, and (d) handling tax collections, enforcement, and appeals.

Taxes on property transfers are widely used for immovable property. Property taxes satisfy most of the "good tax" characteristics: they are efficient, because they do not distort investment decisions, and they fall on those who have the ability to pay. Yet they are underused around the world. This is especially true in LMICs; they particularly fail to tax the property sector efficiently, indicating administrative inefficiencies and the underdeveloped state of their economies.

The main reason for the underutilization of property taxes is the lack of political will and poor administration at the local government level. These taxes fall mostly on well-to-do people who are politically influential and manage to get the tax diluted or neglected. Since local authorities administer the taxes, local elites are able to influence their administration as well (Junquera-Varela et al. 2017). Thus, notwithstanding the fact that the tax is in place, it is generally ineffective. Valuation, which is at the core of this tax, is mostly neglected due to bureaucratic inefficiency and political inertia; even if a property tax is in force, it raises negligible amounts of revenue. As a result, subnational governments often have to depend on central government subventions, especially in LICs.

Recently, more emphasis has been placed on user charges because of their dual role in promoting economic efficiency and generating revenue. User-charge financing is more attractive due to the greater share of benefits accruing to direct users. Ideally, user charges should be determined using marginal cost pricing; however, in practice, some form of average cost pricing may be necessary. Another approach is to use "average incremental cost," which is widely used in aid-funded projects. Exemption from user fees should be an exception and not a rule and should be well justified. For equity reasons, basic needs services may be free of user charges. Equity concerns may be left for other public policies like progressivity of property taxes or, better still, the expenditure route.

Income and consumption taxes are used if more subnational "own-source" revenue is required, either to expand the size of subnational activities or to make them more self-sufficient. Local income taxes are generally levied at a flat rate, are locally determined, and have the same tax base as the national income tax collected by the central government or by the state government, depending on the latter's administrative capability (Bird 2010a). They are more feasible in HICs; in LMICs, even central governments have trouble collecting revenue from the personal incomes taxes (PITs), so income taxes are less likely to be a major source of revenue for local governments. Similar issues arise with the corporate incomes taxes (CITs).

A strong economic and administrative case can be made for regional and even local excises with respect to vehicle-related taxes: fuel tax, toll roads, annual automobile registration, and driver's license fees. Sales tax is common in HICs and in LMICs. Local governments can also apply a sales tax or have it piggyback on the state or national tax. At subnational levels, VAT is quite hard to design, especially in federal structures. Sometimes, an origin-based VAT may have to be used. Subnational business taxes are popular with local governments. They are essentially a production origin–based VAT applied on income rather than consumption (destination). Business licenses may be an effective method of taxing the informal sector at the local government level, as done in Kenya.

Taxpayer segmentation

Tax administrations have scarce resources to ensure compliance. As a result, taxpayer segmentation is vital to allocate these scarce resources more efficiently. Moreover, segmentation of taxpayers is at the heart of tax administration strategy to effectively control compliance. To manage compliance risks effectively, the revenue agency needs to analyze and develop knowledge for each group of taxpayers—main characteristics, key sectors of the economy, types of risk, and needs.

Market segmentation may be based on type of tax, size, type of activity (industry or sector), or type of risk. As part of the process, tax administrations need to incorporate criteria to classify taxpayers in the different segments. This kind of analysis is very useful to implement strategies that are tailored to the unique characteristics and compliance issues presented by each group of taxpayers—for example, develop risk management approaches to tax audit or adjust compliance control to taxpayer risk profiles (World Bank Group 2007).

Since audit resources should be directed at cases exhibiting highest risk to revenue, it is essential to assess market segmentation strategies of the tax administration and risk profiling approaches. Based on findings, the next step would be to analyze the appropriateness of control of compliance strategies. This should also be an element to take into consideration when it comes to assessing the efficiency of tax administrations.

In case large taxpayers' share in revenue receipts is very high, special emphasis should be put on reinforcing control mechanisms to avoid sudden drops in revenue as a consequence of lack of control of this segment, which concentrates a significant amount of tax revenue both directly and via withholding arrangements. Table 1.1 shows the key features of segments of large and medium-size taxpayers, as identified by the authors.

TABLE 1.1 Main characteristics of large and medium-size taxpayers

Key features	Large taxpayers	Medium-size taxpayers
Revenue generation.	High	Medium
Business structure.	• Entities and corporate groups, which in many cases have subsidiaries abroad. It may also include state-owned enterprises. • A small number of entities that account for a substantial amount of revenue generated from direct and indirect taxes.	• Incorporated businesses that spread across manufacturing activities, construction, or services. • A moderate number of taxpayers that accounts for a significant amount of tax revenue.
Noncompliance	• Complexities involved in noncompliance result in a substantial amount of revenue at stake. Usually, legal interpretations are the key issue in tax audit. • Tax avoidance in the form of tax planning is very common.	• Noncompliance comes mainly from underreporting of sources of income and overclaiming of tax credits and deductions. • Tax evasion and tax avoidance through tax planning are common.
Tax audit.	• Comprehensive tax audits. • High audit coverage. • A significant amount of tax disputes.	• Different types of audits that include comprehensive tax audits and issue-oriented audits. • Moderate audit coverage. • Cross-check of third-party information through mass audits is being increasingly used.
Taxpayer assistance.	• Personalized • Emphasis on prevention.	• General programs. • Online services through virtual offices and call centers.
Submission of tax returns.	• E-filing and e-payment are widely used. • In some countries, it is mandatory for large taxpayers to file tax returns electronically.	E-filing and e-payment are increasingly used.
Collection of tax arrears.	• Complex issue. • Need to establish dedicated units to deal with large taxpayers' tax debts.	Medium-intensity collection mechanisms.

Source: Original table for this publication.

Knowing the growth rate of the taxpayer population over the past years is important to facilitate a better allocation of resources. Tables that break down taxpayer population by size covering a significant number of years can be very useful for this purpose (Le et al. 2016). More detailed information could enable incorporating the distribution of taxpayer population by provinces or regions. And an examination of the workload of tax offices would be an important complement to this analysis.

Informal sector taxation

All countries face the problem of taxing micro, small, and medium enterprises (MSMEs), but the size and nature of the problem vary across countries. The share of the informal sector in GDP and employment varies between 10 and 20 percent in HICs but could be as high as 50 percent of GDP and around 90 percent of employment in LMICs. Traders in the informal sector, including not only MSMEs but also larger taxpayers engaged in informal activities, compete unfairly with formal sector businesses, including foreign investors, and this unfair competition can become a major hurdle to economic growth (Junquera-Varela et al. 2017).

Two main issues are involved in taxation of informal businesses. First, taxing small businesses is important to promote equity—not generate revenue—and to ensure that normal taxpayers do not hide under the cloak of informality (Awasthi and Engelschalk 2018). Taxing them is also important for resource mobilization in the sense that most citizens are willing to pay taxes if others are paying their fair share too. It may be difficult to improve taxation of small businesses as well as enforce local taxes because costs to the government can be very high, including loss of political support, relative to the revenue gains. At the same time, it is important to protect some minimum level of income from taxation. Direct taxation of income is generally difficult to apply to small businesses.

Second, for the sake of cost-effectiveness, the administrative and compliance costs must not exceed revenues. Tax administrations in LMICs are often severely constrained with regard to both resources and skills. They often have to choose between improving the compliance of medium- and large-scale firms already in the tax net, where potential revenue payback is higher, and bringing smaller firms into the tax net, where the potential reward is lower.

Taxation is essentially an information game. By definition, informality is weakly documented by the authorities. For formal businesses, the people who have information are the owners or shareholders, business managers, third parties such as financiers and bankers, buyers of outputs or suppliers of inputs, external accountants or auditors, and the government regulatory, audit, or service agencies or tax agency (Junquera-Varela et al. 2017). The problem with informality is that information is concentrated in the owner-manager only; most of the other sources of information do not apply to informal business activities.

In HICs, taxpayers may have the capacity to pay taxes but be unwilling to pay them, giving rise to tax avoidance. In LMICs, lack of compliance capacity is an added problem. And even if informal taxpayers are willing to pay taxes, they may lack the necessary skills and means to do so. This requires exempting businesses, taxing them indirectly, simplifying the tax, or upgrading the compliance capacity of taxpayers.

Administrative strategies that focus on MSMEs are also possible. For example, the use of third-party information, improved external audits and investigations, appropriate penalties, and improved education and services for taxpayers may lower compliance costs (World Bank Group 2007). Financial and other positive incentives for moving into the formal sector, such as the provision of institutional finance, may be successfully used. For instance, informal firms are well aware of the costs of informality and the potential benefits of becoming formal. Often, bureaucratic complexities, not taxation, are the biggest barriers to formalization. The first step is to reduce the costs of formalization and to provide visible benefits of doing so, such as access to banking finances, ability to compete for government contracts, and protection from harassment by local government employees and the police. If the business registration process and the subsequent regulatory measures could be simplified and tax compliance could be made easier, many informal firms would become formal (Junquera-Varela et al. 2017).

Another alternative is using an annual lump-sum tax or a single business permit. The tax is applied to all businesses, not just those below the VAT threshold. The tax rate is scaled to location, market size, sector, and business size—small, medium, and large—using simple criteria such as floor space, number of hotel rooms or beds, and restaurant capacity. It is a highly simplified tax in which all kinds of business license fees are replaced with one annual lump-sum tax. The effective tax rate declines with business size so that the actual rate is low for businesses that may also be paying VAT and income taxes.

Having local governments administer informal business taxes is more efficient and cost-effective, as they provide many facilities and services to these businesses (Bird 2010a). Complementary functions by local governments lower costs and increase the effectiveness of identifying, registering, and assessing businesses in the tax base—for instance, business registration; application of land use regulation, including street vendors; property taxation; utility, waste disposal, and other services to business properties; and management of public markets, taxi stands, and bus stations.

The labor costs for local tax officials are also low, making local administration more cost-effective since tax yield per business is low in these cases. In contrast, engaging highly paid professionals of the central revenue authority is more suitable for the taxation of formal businesses.

Special tax regimes for the micro and small taxpayers: risks and opportunities

Special tax regimes for the micro and small taxpayer segment may facilitate administration of the tax system and may also result in decreasing compliance costs, which are regressive in this segment (World Bank Group 2007). However, they raise questions about the rationale behind its establishment and its consistency with the objective of having a simple, easy-to-administer, and fair tax system as well as widely agreed principles of a good tax administration.

From a revenue standpoint, taxation of this segment has been traditionally neglected by developing countries, which have primarily focused on the large taxpayer segment that accounts for the bulk of tax collection. In addition, the costs to administer this segment are comparatively high, especially in view of its small contribution to revenue. This trade-off can be summarized as follows: tax administrations in developing and transitional countries are generally severely constrained in terms of resources and skills and must often choose whether to go after the larger firms already in the tax net, where the potential tax revenue payback may be higher, or pursue instead the less lucrative smaller taxpayers who are largely outside that net (Bird and Wallace 2003). What, then, is the key driver for the establishment of these special tax regimes? These authors point to widespread tax evasion at the lower end of the economic scale, together with the obvious expense and difficulty startup enterprises may have in complying with complex tax laws, as the main reason some countries have adopted specific tax regimes to deal with the "hard-to-tax" problem.

From the tax administration perspective, an overarching objective is to facilitate administration of the tax system. It is mostly a matter of efficiency in the allocation of scarce resources, especially in the case of developing countries, which also face capacity constraints. In this regard, efficiency calls for directing tax audit resources to those taxpayers who have a bigger contribution to revenue and, as a result, pose a higher risk to the integrity of tax collection (Junquera-Varela 2013).

Not doing that leads to a very low coverage of tax audits in relation to the universe of taxpayers. In fact, special tax regimes, especially if they are based on indicators or presumptions—which will be addressed in the next section—allow tax administrations to rely on verification and indirect methods to control this segment, which broadens tax audit coverage and results in a better allocation of resources (Gaitero-Fortes 1988).

From the taxpayer perspective, these tax regimes aim at decreasing compliance costs, including simplifying requirements to comply with bookkeeping and accounting standards. When the private sector perspective is taken into consideration, spurring formalization and growth of this segment becomes the key goal. So, a good tax regime for small firms is a key policy tool to pave their way out of the informal sector, which is characterized by low growth, limited access to markets, and exclusion from formal financial services.

But achieving this objective is very challenging, and there are a variety of technical options in terms of design. Experience shows that the design of these tax regimes should be guided by the country context and particularly by the level of capacity of the tax administration (Grapperhaus 1997). It is vital for the tax administration to understand the key features and characteristics of this segment. Strong emphasis should be put on removing barriers to formalization and establishing a graduated path to the standard tax regime, including aligning the latter with these special tax regimes to avoid the creation of parallel tax systems.[1]

Moreover, policy makers encounter significant difficulties to reconcile the objectives of simplicity of administration, equality in implementation, and efficiency (Kaplow 1996). Choosing the right instruments usually boils down to having to choose between simplicity and fairness. Putting in place a simple and easy-to-administer tax regime is often achieved at the expense of fairness in the application of the tax system. When these systems evolve to try to better tailor their content to the ability-to-pay principle, this results in increased complexity and consequently higher compliance and administrative costs.

Overall, special tax regimes can be an effective tool in dealing with the micro and small taxpayer segment by facilitating tax administration and reducing the compliance costs. In particular, they can play a key role in developing countries where tax evasion and informality is a predominant feature of economic sectors included in this category of businesses (Junquera-Varela 2013).

Why, then, are these regimes not attaining their objectives? Is it due to bad or poor design or a lack of regulations regarding when these regimes should end? There are many explanations for this observed poor performance in implementing these systems, which mostly seems to derive from difficulties involved in reconciling different goals. At the end of the day, a parallel system is created that undermines good administration of the entire tax system. To avoid this, one important feature these regimes should contain is a provision of when these regimes should end. This means establishing a seamless graduated path to the standard tax system, which is not always the case with current special tax systems for micro and small taxpayers.

The key conclusions are the following: taxation of this segment should not be viewed only from a revenue perspective; key goals are to widen the tax base by providing an incentive to small business to formalize and keep to a minimum administrative and compliance costs; and there is a need to rethink tax audit strategies and heavily lean on verification checks and cross-check of third-party information, thereby freeing tax audit resources (Junquera-Varela and Vostroknutova 2015). The latter will be enhanced by digital transformation, which will reduce compliance and administration costs. Briefly, these regimes involve a lot of risks and challenges, but perhaps they are the most realistic option available for dealing with a complex and dynamic segment.[2]

Market segmentation as a central plank of a tax administration strategy to control compliance and provide services to taxpayers

Micro and small businesses comprise a majority of taxpayers that contribute little to revenue. It is a very dynamic sector with widespread informality and low levels of recordkeeping. This segment includes numerous businesses that vary in size, and its key characteristic is heterogeneity, which makes it difficult to have a unique definition of what a micro and small business is (Junquera-Varela and Vostroknutova 2015). Table 1.2 provides a summary of main characteristics of this segment. It highlights low audit coverage, which reflects how little attention tax administrations pay to this segment, especially in developing countries where resources have been primarily directed to large taxpayers out of revenue mobilization considerations.

Size is the most common criterion to allocate the universe of taxpayers to different segments, resulting in three main size-related segments: large taxpayers, medium-size taxpayers, and small taxpayers. Taxpayers can also be grouped according to nonsize criteria such as business type and international taxation issues. When it comes to size, there are different criteria to segment taxpayer populations, including turnover, business assets, number of employees, and taxes paid (Gale 2001).

All of these criteria have advantages and disadvantages, but there is a broad consensus on considering turnover as the best measure of size. According to this criterion, large taxpayers would be situated above a previously defined high turnover threshold while micro and small taxpayers would be placed below the VAT threshold, where it exists, or below a presumptive one as defined by the small and medium enterprises (SME) regime in place. Medium-size taxpayers would be placed in between. In case a presumptive tax regime has been established—which will be analyzed in the next section—it is recommended to establish a lower tax-free threshold for subsistence activities (micro taxpayers). This tax-free threshold should ideally be the PIT exemption threshold. The use of turnover, and consequently thresholds, to delineate segments and particularly to determine application of standard and special tax regimes poses challenges to tax administration. For example, it is difficult to define the tax-free threshold for subsistence-level activities in connection with the PIT exemption threshold (Junquera-Varela 2011). VAT thresholds should strike a balance between revenue generation and tax administration and compliance capacity. It should be noted that turnover is a variable that is difficult to control and tends to be underreported by businesses.

In practice, companies above the presumptive threshold established for the special or presumptive tax regime have the incentive to split their operations or underreport their sales to benefit from a lower tax burden and simplified bookkeeping and tax filing requirements. The same happens with large taxpayers that have the incentive to get around the scrutiny of large taxpayer units (Tanzi and Casanegra de Jantscher 1987). Therefore, one recurrent challenge when designing systems for

TABLE 1.2 Key characteristics of micro and small taxpayers' segment

Key characteristics	Micro and small taxpayers
Revenue generation.	Low
Business structure.	• Micro businesses and self-employed professionals and entrepreneurs. • This segment consists of a large number of companies that encompass a wide range of activities (mostly retail) that account for a small part of revenue collected by the tax administration.
Noncompliance	Significant presence of informal economy.
Tax audit.	• Low level of audit coverage. • Verification activities and cross-check of third-party information.
Taxpayer assistance.	Online services.
Submission of tax returns.	Tax administration assists taxpayers in preparation of tax returns. In most cases, paper is still used.
Collection of tax arrears.	Low-intensity administrative mechanisms to collect tax revenue, such as phone calls or issuance of reminders.

Source: Original table for this publication.

small taxpayers is to impede attempts by medium or large taxpayers to unduly benefit from advantages of these regimes; increasing digitalization may help address this challenge.

Heterogeneity poses difficulties in the design of tax regimes. It is difficult to cater these special regimes to the characteristics of different groups of small taxpayers, which range from small artisans to small agricultural businesses to professionals. Trying to take into account different characteristics increases the complexity of the system and, as a result, administrative and compliance costs. Maintaining the simplicity of the system is always at the expense of fairness in administering the tax system.

Why establish special regimes for taxing micro and small taxpayers?

Taxing micro and small taxpayers seems to be not a good idea. While the cost of administering taxation of small companies is high, they contribute little to revenue. Additionally, compliance costs are high, and this is an important barrier to formalization, inducing these companies to stay out of the formal economy (Malik 1970). Bringing small taxpayers into the tax net is not exclusively a revenue issue; it is mainly a development and growth issue.

Once one considers these regimes from the broader perspective, the policy objectives of establishing these special tax regimes make sense: simplify the tax system (reduction of administrative and compliance costs), spur formalization and growth of informal businesses, reduce tax evasion, strengthen the social contract between citizens and the state and increase accountability and transparency through widening the tax base, increase perceived fairness in application of the tax system, and collect revenue (Lapidoth 1977). As for the latter, expectations have to be managed since this is not the only purpose of establishing these tax regimes. Moreover, an inequitable design that overtaxes specific sectors may lead to undermining of these regimes and declining tax revenues, let alone fairness considerations.

Main categories of special tax regimes for micro and small taxpayers

Countries have two options to deal with this segment, namely, to put in place a simplified version of the standard tax systems or to create a special tax regime. The first approach is most suitable for developed countries, while the second one is more recommended in countries with widespread informality to deal with the hard-to-tax sectors (Bird and Wallace 2003). Simplifying the application of the general tax system usually relates to reduced tax rates and simplification of tax forms, bookkeeping and accounting requirements, and simplified filing and payment process, including reduced frequency of filing and payment obligations. As for special regimes, they are based primarily on presumptions—presumptive tax regimes that usually replace income tax and VAT, which are analyzed in the next section. As indicated above, there is also a trade-off between different objectives of a tax system in terms of simplicity, economic efficiency, and fairness (Thuronyi 2000). The more special tax regimes systems evolve to be aligned with the ability-to-pay principle, the less they attain goals of neutrality and equity.

There are many options for countries to choose when it comes to implementing presumptive tax regimes for the SMEs. In this regard, it is useful to differentiate between micro and small enterprises (Tanzi and Casanegra de Jantscher 1986). It is recommended not to tax micro businesses below the level of subsistence. In case they are taxed, a small annual fee (patent) would suffice. Companies or individuals operating at a subsistence level do not have an incentive to formalize as opposed to other SMEs. On the other hand, a turnover-based system could be the most appropriate option for companies below the VAT threshold, while for SMEs above the VAT threshold, indicator-based systems could be more adequate for segments with particular risk of turnover evasion (Bulutoglu 1995). Other SMEs above VAT thresholds would apply the standard tax regime but with simplified bookkeeping and filing requirements. It should be noted that an adequate VAT threshold leads to a decrease in the tax burden and compliance costs of small business as well as administration costs. Simplified formal requirements for companies above the VAT threshold may facilitate transition into the standard regime.

It is also worth mentioning that the use of indicators—usually physical indicators that translate into an average profit—or a turnover tax with a single rate produces some distortions. Some taxpayers are undertaxed. As a result, they are unperturbed and have no incentive to transition to the standard tax system. Other taxpayers are overtaxed, providing them with the incentive to move toward informality. Solutions proposed range from differentiating tax rates by sectors —for example, trade and services—to taking into account different profit margins. In many cases, this means increasing the complexity of the regime, with the consequences already known. An indicator-based system includes a number of parameters such as number of employees, number of self-employed persons, energy consumption, or vehicles, which leads to an estimate of profits (Taube and Tadesse 1996). As a result, taxes due are determined based on physical data. Out of fairness considerations, some adjustments may be introduced to better match these regimes with the ability-to-pay principle, which may include depreciation of assets or weight of salaries in a company's expenses. All of these adjustments may result in increasing the complexity of the system and undermining revenue collection while increasing administration and compliance costs.

Guidelines for tax design of special tax regimes for micro and small taxpayers

As already noted, the micro and small taxpayer segment is characterized by its heterogeneity. It is a diverse group whose members range from subsistence agriculture, small trade or service business, or professionals. It is challenging to design a good special tax system for this segment (Thuronyi 1998). As a result, a first broad recommendation is to take into account the specific features of this group and match the design of these special tax regimes to small taxpayers' capacity. Box 1.5 summarizes several recommendations that can guide tax design of special tax regimes for micro and small taxpayers. This is not an exhaustive list, and it is important to recognize that some of these guidelines are not universally accepted.

BOX 1.5 Guidelines and recommendations for tax design of special tax regimes for micro and small taxpayers

1. Desirable features of these systems are simplicity, low administration and compliance costs, and fairness. Rates should be low enough to not discourage formality but not excessively low to provide incentives to abuse the system.

2. There is a need to strike a balance between simplicity and fairness in administration.

3. The key objective of these systems is not revenue collection, but rather the encouragement of growth and formalization of small business since taxes are viewed as an important barrier to formalization.

4. A turnover-based presumptive system is preferable to an indicator-based system, although turnover is a variable difficult to control, using withholding taxes to mitigate this issue.

5. Indicator-based systems are appropriate for some contexts, given several caveats, since their design and implementation are more complex. However, control of compliance is simpler than occurs in the case of turnover-based presumptive systems.

6. A multiple-rate turnover-based presumptive system is fairer than a single-rate system since it takes into account different average profit margins in different sectors.

7. A path to formality must be established to facilitate business growth and formalization. It has to be a real graduated path to the standard regime, with real incentives to progress through and out of the special tax regime.

8. The system has to put provisions in place to avoid abuse of the systems and contamination of the general tax system.

9. There should be only a presumptive tax regime for value added tax (VAT) and income tax.

10. The taxpayer has to be given the option to opt in to VAT and income tax general tax regimes.

11. Micro enterprises should be exempt when they operate at a subsistence level or be taxed with a small annual fee (patent).

12. A cash accounting system is more appropriate than accrual accounting, which is too complex and costly. These systems require basic accounting rules.

13. Simplicity should also apply to compliance oversight. These systems should rely on spot checks and systematic cross-checks of third-party information. Traditional tax audit methods are more costly and less adequate for controlling this segment.

BOX 1.6   Advantages and disadvantages of special tax regimes for micro and small taxpayers

Advantages
- Lower compliance costs
- Tax liability more predictable
- Less interaction with tax administration
- Generally lower tax burden

Disadvantages
- No incentive to improve bookkeeping
- No relief in case of tax losses
- Potential disincentive to grow
- Risk of abuse
- Fairness concerns

Possible advantages and disadvantages of these tax regimes are summarized in box 1.6. Regarding the risk of abuse, special attention is to be paid to medium-size companies or large taxpayers who may split operations or underreport turnover to fall under the thresholds of these regimes. One important thing to consider, then, is to avoid that taxpayers unduly benefit from these special tax regimes (Wallace 2002). Another key concern is how to prevent the use of these special tax regimes for purposes of money laundering, especially when they are based on indicators or physical data to determine tax liability.

Presumptive taxation

To establish a tax, the law, apart from defining the taxable event, must quantify the tax obligation. The valuation may consist of a directly determined amount to be paid (fixed taxes), or it may be set based on two elements, namely, the tax base and the type of tax (variable taxes). Thus, the tax base is the quantification element of the taxable event, which can be expressed in both monetary and nonmonetary units and which functions to measure the economic capacity of each taxpayer. That capacity is revealed in the objective element of the taxable event from which it is derived, as an interdependence between the base and the taxable event (Calero-García 1996). Consequently, the tax rate sets the amount of the tax benefit, so there is a close relationship between both tax concepts, since the first serves as support for the application of the rate (Cazorla-Prieto 2002). In addition, for taxes with progressive rates, the amount of the base determines the rate to be applied.

But, when the treatment and analysis of the real tax base entail a high degree of complexity, presumptive taxation proves to be very useful. In turn, this involves an interesting question consisting of establishing the extent to which presumptions can contribute to the simplification of tax administration, without fundamentally altering or substituting the essence of their respective tax bases, and the original nature of the tax itself (Lucas-Mas 2004). This and other issues of interest will be analyzed throughout this section.

Background and rationale for tax bases' simplification

Over the last two centuries, income taxation has undergone an evolution that can be summarized in the following trends and changes. On the one hand, there has been a transition from tax estimation to an attempt to measure the income actually received by the taxpayer. There has also been a tendency toward global income taxation (Bird and Oldman 1977), as opposed to separate taxation of the different categories and components thereof, as a reflection of the need to achieve greater progressivity. The use of self-assessment has been generalized, and it must be the taxpayer who quantifies and declares their own tax debt, and there is a propensity to use the withholding tax system.

This desire for tax equity led to tax systems based on the taxation of personal income, which conceptual delimitation entailed great difficulties by aspiring to a definition as exact and complete as possible. It included income from sources as diverse as goodwill to capital gains, passing through the estimation of business and professional income, the application of complex exemptions, innumerable deductions, and personal and family minimums (Musgrave 1986, 1990). Another series of complexities derived from the use of the tax system as an instrument of fiscal policy were the exemptions of capital gains in case of reinvestment; the varied and flexible existing amortization systems; the special treatment granted to part of the undistributed profits; the various ways of financing investments, differentiating by activity sectors; and many other manifestations of regulatory casuistry (Zolt 1996). As can be seen, trying to combine the principles of tax justice and regulatory simplicity with their practical implementation in reality becomes a very challenging task.

Regarding the administrative perspective, it is worth mentioning that in many jurisdictions, especially in developing countries, the difficulty involved in determining the current income of taxpayers far outweighs the benefits derived from it. This, together with tax fraud and the shortage of material resources and qualified personnel on the part of the tax administration, makes the applicability and effective compliance of tax regulations very difficult, if not impossible (Rajaraman 1995). Given this outlook, there are only two possible solutions: (a) modify the theoretical conception of what is understood by taxable income to simplify the tax system and make it more practicable, thus increasing compliance and efficiency, or (b) carry out significant efforts to modernize and increase the operational capacity of the tax administration. Both options are addressed in the handbook, but this section focuses on the former.

In the field of legislative technique and its simplification, it should be noted that the tax law must establish the taxable event and its quantification, a requirement that derives from the *ex lege* nature of the tax obligation (Oh and Kim 2008). As stated earlier, setting the amount can be done either directly—as in fixed taxes—or by establishing the quantification elements of such amount, mainly the tax base and the type of tax, as in variable taxes.

The normative measurement of tax bases can be carried out in accordance with real magnitudes or with average or potential magnitudes. Examples of real magnitudes are the profit or net income of a company or natural person, the price actually paid in a transaction, and the volume of imported or manufactured merchandise, the use of which results in directly measurable bases referring to determined and individualizable subjects. Average or potential magnitudes comprise elements among those that serve to directly measure the tax base (sales, salaries), signs or indexes unrelated to it (number of workers, installed power), or even the taxpayers themselves (as industry average returns) (Tanzi 1986). The base measurement procedure that is most faithful to the principle of capacity is the one based on real magnitudes (Kaplow and Shavell 2002). Despite this, management and collection costs, indirect tax pressure, tax evasion, the complexity of the tax system, and the lack of qualified personnel and insufficient material and personal resources on the part of the tax administration justify the persistence of taxes on presumed or potential average returns—known as presumptive taxation (Shome 1992; Avi-Yonah 1997).

Tax assessment versus tax estimate

In its strictly technical-legal sense, the regimes for quantifying the tax base can be defined as the set of rules through which the tax base abstractly defined by law is set at a specific amount and in relation to a certain tax assumption (Clavijo-Hernández 2001). In other words, the regimes constitute a legal concept, in the sense that they are a set of legal-material norms that regulate the method, the means, and the procedure.

As for the terms *determination* and *estimate*, it should be noted that both refer to regimes for quantifying tax bases, although the essential difference is that the determination, specification of the direct method, involves an exact assessment, while the estimate—the practical application of the indicative method—corresponds to an assessment that is as close as possible to reality or replaces it. For this reason, these are to be treated as independent and well-differentiated concepts, since depending on the method applied, the following is obtained: the tax base, if direct determination is applied, or alternative tax bases, if estimate is used (Sáinz de Bujanda 1970).

The "direct method" aims to assess the base with certainty, so that it is a true reflection of the fact that it indicates economic capacity, which is why it is said that it aims to achieve the greatest possible accuracy at all times. For this, it uses means of an analytical nature, that is to say, *direct*. Fundamentally, this is what the French doctrine calls the controlled declaration, based on the fact that the treasury obliges those who know the amount of the taxable matter to declare its true amount, as well as the data used for its quantification (Lapidoth 1977). But it also uses means of proof, including assumptions, which can undermine the purity of this method.

Regarding the "indicative method," it only aspires to an assessment that is close to the true or (definitely) true or replaces it, renouncing accuracy in advance (Calero-García 1996). For these purposes, it uses means of a synthetic nature, that is, indirect means, such as external signs, *forfait*, coefficients, and indexes. All the same, within the indicative method, two basic regimes can be clearly differentiated: the real estimate and the presumed estimate.

The "real estimate" constitutes a system for estimating alternative tax bases characterized by aspiring to estimate the actual income or what is actually received by the taxpayer, and which is applied as a sanction and on a subsidiary basis, in the event of legally incorrect conduct of the taxpayer that does not allow the tax administration to know the necessary data for the direct determination of the tax bases or yields (Lapidoth 1977).

A defining and distinctive feature of this regime compared to the presumed estimate is that the real estimate is based on the application of a rebuttable presumption or *iuris tantum*, which admits proof to the contrary, in principle only by the taxpayer. On the other hand, the "presumptive estimate" consists of an income quantification system based on the substitution of the determination of all or part of the factual elements established in the regulations that define the tax base by the result of the application of a series of presumptions, fictions, and other indexes (Lapidoth 1977). With this, the simplification of the liquidation process and the reduction of costs, both of management and collection, as well as those derived from the indirect fiscal pressure on the body of taxpayers, are pursued. Given that this regime assumes the character of a "pact" or "agreement" between the tax administration and the taxpayer regarding the estimation of the average or potentially received income, thus renouncing the exact determination of the current income, evidence to the contrary is not admitted, and therefore it is an irrebuttable presumption or *iuris et de iure*.

The distinction that some authors have made, in the field of presumed estimation, between the concepts of "average or normal income" (Einaudi 1963; Giannini 1957; Ullastres-Calvo 1943) and "potential income" (Sadka and Tanzi 1993) must be clarified. The first of these, normal income, consists of the average applicable and common to a group of taxpayers, therefore of a collective nature, and is calculated based on a series of basic premises, namely, an average level of effort, an average number of hours of work, the assumption of an average risk, and the use of a technology with average characteristics. On the other hand, the notion of potential income is a concept that requires an individualized application to each taxpayer, since it consists of the income that each taxpayer can obtain if they make the maximum possible effort according to their particular conditions, keeping the remaining variables constant. Evidently, the calculation of potential income requires an individualized estimate, not a collective one, while normal or average income can be estimated both collectively and individually by taking average values of all the factors common to all members of the population to which it applies.

Appendix A provides additional analysis on design options for presumptive taxes.

Advantages and incentives

Presumptive taxation offers a series of advantages, the most important of which will now be analyzed. First, by limiting the discretion of the tax official regarding the interpretation of the accounts, the potential scope of corruption and abuse by tax administration officials, as well as fraud by taxpayers, is reduced. Second, presumptive taxation enables the taxation of those groups of taxpayers that lack accounting, or keep it irregularly or incompletely, or even results in implausible information (Bird and Wallace 2003). Likewise, tax estimates offer incentives in terms of economic efficiency, given that a taxpayer who obtains higher productivity or results than those resulting from applying the indicators—in the sense that they obtain more sales or income than the presumed according to the estimation formula applied—will not have to pay more taxes. In short, the marginal rate applicable to any excess over estimated income is zero.

Special emphasis should be placed on simplicity and convenience, which justifies presumptive taxation. Even so, this can be detrimental in some cases, depending on the precision with which the estimation mechanism has been designed. However, if the taxpayer has the option of choosing between the direct method and the indicative method, the aforementioned risk is mitigated, and the taxpayer acquires a position of advantage. The main virtue of tax estimation is that it is possibly the only effective way of taxing small businesses in developing countries (Surrey 1958; Lucas-Mas 2004). Given that small businesses make up practically the entire business fabric, this can lead to a substantial increase in the number of taxpayers.

Another noteworthy advantage is the fact of facilitating the mobility of small taxpayers, from the informal economy sector to the formal level, which translates into greater availability of information, helping to control and reduce tax fraud. But this may apparently contradict another effect of presumptive taxation—the monetization of the subsistence sector—specifically with respect to the figure of the tax on the potential gross product applied to the field of agriculture (Bird 1974).

There is also the possibility that the presumptive tax could increase tax collection in relative, not absolute, terms if both the explicit and implicit costs associated with the quantification, assessment, compliance, and verification are factored into the tax in a realistic manner. In other words, presumptive taxation can result in a decrease in management costs and indirect tax pressure, which in turn translates into an increase in collection in relative terms, despite an apparent decrease in revenue in absolute terms (Erbas 1993).

Finally, presumptive taxation offers a high degree of effectiveness and efficiency in terms of reducing costs and time in the audit process, especially in countries with high illiteracy (Gillis 1989). Moreover, this decrease also affects the indirect fiscal pressure, given that taxpayers are the ones who bear to a greater extent the costs derived from the assessment and collection of taxes.

Disadvantages and difficulties

Various authors have criticized the use of presumptive taxation (Bird and Casanegra de Jantscher 1992; Bulutoglu 1995) and have pointed out a series of difficulties and inconveniences that its application may entail. Below are those negative judgments and contrary reasoning that have had the greatest acceptance.

The aforementioned authors believe that no effort or attempt should be made to use presumptive taxation, since serious difficulties are generated when selecting the indicators on which the preliminary assessment is based—for example, whether to take gross sales, property value, number of employees, or stock. Likewise, the tax estimate can become an entry barrier, in an economic sense, of access to the market for small businesses, compared to its nonexistence in the absence of any tax. This, in turn, can cause companies to assume greater risks and, consequently, decide to subsume in the informal economy (Bulutoglu 1995). These inconveniences on small businesses justify the moderate use of the index methods and the need for them to vary according to the potential level of income of the taxpayers.

Another drawback is the more than probable transfer of the presumptive tax in an arbitrary and dangerous way, especially if taken into account that it is not a true tax on net income, but rather a tax on the factors that serve as indicators and basis for calculating the estimate. In some countries, presumptive taxes are deliberately established with a punitive or sanctioning nature, to force taxpayers to avail themselves of self-assessment in accordance with the ordinary rules for determining tax bases (Bulutoglu 1995). In this regard, it should be stated that experience has shown the failure of this scheme and its respective approach by generating a migration of registered taxpayers to the informal economy sector.

Another negative consequence derived from the use of presumptive taxation is the possibility that it may generate a disincentive for keeping accounts and other records. In this same sense, tax estimates, when applied mainly to natural persons and sole traders, may create a disincentive for the incorporation of companies, given that it is assumed that companies and other legal entities have the obligation and the capacity to keep adequate accounting.

Also of serious importance is the eroding effect of the self-assessed tax base that the estimate may have through the widespread use of false invoices. Experience shows that companies subject to the determination regime employ companies subject to the estimation regime as their providers of false invoices, with the aim of inflating their expenses (Bulutoglu 1995). To avoid this unpleasant consequence, the only solution is an exhaustive control by the tax administration of the invoices and receipts issued by these latter companies. This obviously reduces the savings in terms of enforcement costs that were previously advocated as an advantage of presumptive taxation.

Functions and effects

Tax estimation offers the possibility of expanding the tax base in developing countries, taking into account their economic structure, as well as the information gap that tax administrations must face (Avi-Yonah 1997). In addition, the limited resources and talent of tax administrations are better used in the design and elaboration of presumptive norms applicable to those who do not declare or do so incompletely, which will exceed the requirements of justice and equity, rather than in the prosecution and verification of each entity, without having the necessary guidelines.

Tax estimation can play an important role in reducing tax evasion, as well as tax avoidance. Also, it allows controlling that sector of fraud that originates as a consequence of the high costs of verification and detection by the tax administration, as well as of the high enforcement costs (Dastur 1997). And it helps to alleviate the difficulties in complying with the tax obligations derived, either from the activity in question or from the ignorance of the procedures by those taxpayers belonging to low-income sectors.

In the same way, the presumptive taxation tends to be used as an instrument against tax evasion in those cases in which related transactions are not carried out at market conditions. Given that it is difficult to verify the veracity of the data provided by the parties involved in the transaction(s), the tax administration may not pay attention to the amount for which the parties actually claim to have contracted and replace it with the valuation resulting from the tax estimate, which will be based on the market value of the transaction. In this line of argument, several countries have tried to minimize tax fraud, resorting to the use of minimum taxes and other methods and variants of tax estimation. According to the latter, and as they are currently being used in a large number of countries, the tax administration assigns taxpayers a certain income based on their standard of living, the value of their home, and that of other elements of their assets that reflect their quality of life—for example, cars, pleasure boats, and second homes.

Likewise, it is possible to estimate the added value of companies based on their sales statistics or other indicators such as employees or area. There is also the possibility that a company or individual's minimum tax may be based on their gross assets (Sadka and Tanzi 1993; Stotsky 1995). Moreover, presumptive taxation can restrict the scope of tax avoidance by covering those legal gaps and dysfunctions that the tax system suffers, thus achieving greater coherence and completeness of the tax system in its application.

Furthermore, presumptive taxation can improve both the horizontal and vertical equity of the tax system in which it is integrated. Horizontal equity is enhanced by facilitating the taxation of self-employed professionals and small entrepreneurs who operate outside the official economy, both groups that often escape the reach of the tax system or contribute insufficiently (Musgrave 1986; Kaplow 1989). Regarding vertical equity, this would be improved to the extent that tax estimates allow professionals with high incomes to be taxed based on objective indicators, such as years of experience, which makes it difficult to underreport their tax debt.

Three necessary requirements can be established for the sake of a correct application of the presumptive tax: (a) the tax administration must have the necessary technical resources to carry out studies and statistics of profitability by type of activity, (b) an adequate number of tax auditors is required for the effective control and verification of the information provided by taxpayers in relation to the characteristics of their businesses, and (c) because some indicative methods involve conversations and discussions between tax officials and taxpayers regarding the level of income, tax administration officials must be closely supervised and adequately paid; otherwise, the system creates important incentives for corruption (Lucas-Mas 2004). In other words, presumptive regimes need to be jointly implemented with specific risk-based audits.

Permanent or transitory solution?

A decisive issue is the determination of the temporary scope of application of the presumptive taxation. Should it be considered a supplement, a substitute for the traditional tax system, or simply a merely transitional phase until the tax administration is able to collect the taxes without resorting to presumptions?

Presumptive taxation, beyond being a simple substitute, can offer a very valuable instrument for the achievement of diverse fiscal policy objectives, such as those that have already been mentioned throughout this section. The idea underlying the circumstantial regulations is that small merchants, whose businesses are almost never organized as a legal entity, generally do not have adequate accounting for tax parameters, if they have any at all. In this situation, for the tax authorities, it is too costly and hopeless to try to know or obtain the facts and real data, so they resort to the tax estimate for more efficient collection. If the economic structure of the country is such that there is a high number of small companies and few medium or large companies, which normally occurs in developing countries, the presumptive tax is revealed as the ideal solution, being the rule rather than the exception (Avi-Yonah 1997).

Still, the opposite position has been defended by some authors (Lapidoth 1977), who consider that the estimation methods should be used only as transitory techniques, without a vocation for permanence, during a transitory period until the necessary accounting level is reached. Once this phase is completed, the use of presumptive taxation should be limited exclusively by legal means to those taxpayers incapable of proper accounting, such as small businesses.

For this category of taxpayers subject to the special presumptive regime, there should be no place for any legally incorporated business in the form of a company, since in these cases, record-keeping will be deemed mandatory. On the other hand, those taxpayers who cannot comply with the general accounting system should not be released from the minimum documentary obligation of a simplified record of their operations, even if it is in a basic and imperfect format; the tax administration should insist on this. Therefore, since it may not be possible to determine the tax base according to accounting criteria, recourse to presumptive taxation will be inevitable. A mechanism sometimes used to force taxpayers to transition out from a presumptive regime is not updating the thresholds of application of such regime (Junquera-Varela 2011).

In this context, it is important to mention that there are generally two thresholds: (a) the one that determines the subjection or not to taxation, and exceeding it to the special regime, and (b) the other that establishes the separation between applicability of the special regime and the general (the latter in case to exceed it). This reality raises a series of considerations, for example, the need for their careful establishment and, in principle, their periodic updating. Not doing so can generate dysfunctions with respect to the spectrum of taxpayers that will be subject to taxation and also with respect to the assignment to one regime or another of the subjects.

Likewise, it is important to encourage the transition of those taxpayers subject to the special taxation regime to the general one; otherwise, a stagnation occurs (Junquera-Varela 2013). This can be achieved either by not updating the thresholds or by establishing a maximum period of subjection to the special regime. The only exception to the need for indexing or updating are those thresholds set in physical terms or with respect to gross income.

Another interesting method used to promote the transition toward an eventual subjection to the general regime is to condition the granting of passports, various licenses, and other documentation necessary for certain activities that demonstrate the existence of sufficient economic capacity to pay taxes under the general regime—for example, enjoy pleasure boats and luxury vehicles, hunting, trips abroad, dressage of horses—upon presentation of "tax compliance certificates" issued by the tax administration, establishing that the taxpayer is subject to the general tax regime and up to date with payment of their tax obligations.

Guidelines for tax design of presumptive tax regimes

Presumptive taxation inherently implies injustice, since it entails an abandonment of the traditional accounting methods used to determine the tax base (Thuronyi 2000). This can generate unfair situations such as that taxpayers without any real income are taxed based on their estimated income by applying an irrefutable presumption. On the other hand, presumptive taxation facilitates the collection of taxes from taxpayers who otherwise would not contribute to sustaining public spending because they are benefiting, sometimes in an abusive and unjustified manner, from economic circumstances such as inflation that allows companies to claim losses and tax benefits like deductions, credits, or bonuses, reducing their taxation to zero and escaping monitoring by and obligation to the tax system. Thus, presumptive taxation, and specifically a tax such as the one that is levied on assets, can be instrumentalized as a minimum tax (Stotsky 1995).

However, and despite the fact that a minimum, not final, presumptive tax is better for the purposes of granting tax credits by countries where parent companies reside that have branches or subsidiaries in other countries subject to this type of tax, such characterization may undermine the incentives that the presumptive tax provides in terms of economic efficiency, as formulated by Luigi Einaudi (1963). This is because if the estimated tax is not final, but minimal, any excess income over it is taxed at progressive marginal rates, different from zero, which is precisely the incentive offered by the taxation of average returns or optimal tax defended by Einaudi (Giannini 1957; Einaudi 1963).

Of vital importance is the ability of the tax administration to handle and apply presumptive tax methods. For example, when civil servant corruption is a serious problem, an approach like the French contractual method—*forfait* taxation, or expenditure-based taxation—will be bound to fail. Another sample would be the Israeli *tachshiv*, which requires a detailed study and prior preparation, and so will only be effective if the basic work has been done beforehand. In addition, if taxpayers can hide the factors or indicators on which the estimate is based as simply as the income to be estimated, said presumption will not be of any use, nor will it offer any comparative advantage (Thuronyi 2000).

Another element to consider when evaluating which presumptive method should be applied is whether it grants tax benefits and incentives. This means that depending on how a presumption is established and applied, it can result in the reduction of the tax burden for certain (groups of) taxpayers. It must also be recognized that each presumptive tax method has its own incentive and collection effects, its own redistributive consequences, its own levels of complexity, and its own legislative and administrative implications. This makes it dangerous to generalize about presumptive taxation (Lucas-Mas 2004).

Increasingly, developing countries are adopting some form of asset tax, either as a supplement to income tax or as a way to improve their ability to collect income tax from taxpayers with significant business income. In addition, practice has shown that said tax on assets fulfills more of a function of a minimum income tax, rather than a final tax. The tax on assets presents as one of its main drawbacks that it is accrued even in those periods in which the business has had a bad financial year. On the other hand, despite being burdensome for companies, it is very supportive for the government, since it provides a constant and predictable source of income (Avi-Yonah 1997). This is particularly important for countries that lack advanced procedures in terms of budget activity.

But when the alternative minimum tax on assets is based on gross assets, businesses cannot reduce their tax by accumulating debt. This aspect of the asset tax prevents the erosion of the tax base (Bulutoglu 1995), since the tax liability cannot be reduced below a certain level. In short, this tax sets significant limits to taxpayer activity aimed at reducing their tax burden through inadequate tax planning and manipulation of information. Regarding the choice between net and gross assets as the tax base, it should be noted that gross assets seem to be the most recommended option, since it allows a lower tax rate, is easier to administer and enforce, and makes tax evasion and avoidance more difficult. As already established, income taxes do not necessarily have to be applied to precisely measured and well-defined income concepts; in fact, in many countries, this is not the case.

A presumptive tax that is the result of good design can result in a tax system that, in some of its aspects, is superior—at least from the point of view of economic efficiency—to one that is based on the determination of actual income (Tanzi and Casanegra de Jantscher 1987). The reason for this statement is very simple: when taxpayers are taxed on the basis of average returns, any excess derived from their effort above the average will be implicitly taxed at a rate of zero percent.

If it is assumed that individuals respond to incentives of this kind, the conclusion must be to ensure the existence of benefits in terms of efficiency derived from the application of presumptive taxation. By their nature, presumptive taxes require a large amount of work and previous resources by the tax administration to be able to base themselves on realistic and objective criteria. Additionally, a balanced and sustainable presumptive tax system requires a gradual adoption and consolidation over time, focusing efforts and giving priority to those sectors of the population most affected by tax fraud (Lucas-Mas 2004). If this introduction of the system and its subsequent consolidation are achieved, the benefits are innumerable. Its costs are also insignificant relative to the increase in collection and available resources derived from the reduction in tax management and verification costs and indirect fiscal pressure.

A priori, it might be thought that the application of the concept of potential income entails too great administrative difficulties. But a distinction must be made in this respect between developing countries and advanced countries. To say that the concept of potential income is difficult to apply does not necessarily mean that this concept is more difficult to apply than that of effective income. It should be remembered that effective income taxation in developing countries has not been successful (Rajaraman 1995). In these countries, measuring actual income from many activities can be as difficult as quantifying potential income, if not more so. Therefore, at least in developing countries, administrative considerations alone do not automatically constitute an argument against the use of potential income and in favor of effective income.

The more rigid and unsophisticated the methods used, the more arbitrary they and their application will be. The less adaptable they are to the special circumstances of a specific taxpayer whose income must be taxed, the more they will tend to lose their nature and characterization as substitutes for income tax; they will become taxes independent of the one they supposedly replace (Lapidoth 1977). Already in the specific field of methods, it is important to state that the bases set according to assets seem preferable to those that take net wealth as a reference point. This is justified because asset-based bases disincentivize financing through the use of debt, therefore preventing base erosion and profit elimination via interest deduction, which occurs in the traditional CIT, unless it is reformed for that purpose. However, with net wealth as the indicator, the problem of detecting fraudulent debt persists. Also, a base on assets has the inconvenience of double taxation in loan transactions between companies, making it inadvisable for the financial sector (Rajaraman 1995).

Presumptive taxation would enable uprooting from the inception of the tax laws the accursed vice arising from reciprocal envy between one taxpayer and another, a manifest vice in the absurd search for the absolute tax "truth"—immaculate and immanent—and replace it with the gift of practical "truth," which tries to make each one pay what they owe to the state because of the work carried out by the state to create the legal and collective environment within which each one is called to work (Einaudi 1963).

Appendix B provides a detailed taxonomy of methods of presumptive taxation.

Tax morale and other nontechnical drivers

Accurately analyzing the nontechnical drivers of tax administration reform is crucial to its ultimate success and sustainability. Generally, effective tax reform requires political will to overcome vested interests that benefit from the status quo distribution of taxes. Indeed, the intent and intensity of local officials to implement reforms are the primary factors of change—according to World Bank research on public financial management (PFM) reforms (Fritz, Verhoeven, and Avenia 2017; World Bank 2017)—even compared to potential technical drivers such as the size of external assistance or fiscal or budgetary pressures, and other nontechnical drivers such as domestic demands from citizens or civil society or the institutional balance between the executive and parliament. And the same dynamic observed with spending resources is likely to apply to collecting resources.

Therefore, tax administration reform is likely to be feasible and sustainable only if it is associated with enhanced governance through improved rule of law, accountability, and transparency standards (Müller, Spengel, and Vay 2020). However, taxpayers are unlikely to cooperate with increased tax collection efforts unless they have a better view of their government, confidence in its legitimacy, and trust in how the taxes would be spent; this leads to the analysis of tax morale.

Tax morale

There are three components in the implementation of a tax system—the law, the tax administration, and the taxpayers—which are influenced by their economic, political, social, and cultural environment, notwithstanding international influences. This section focuses on a country's body of taxpayers, particularly on their philosophy and the different types and characteristics that identify them.

The important role that the culture of taxpayers plays in the design of a tax system is noteworthy. It is understood as the habits of the population, the degree of internalization of the duty of tax compliance, the usual practices in the management of their businesses and accounts, the degree of literacy and training that enables a correct understanding and access to tax regulations and the legal system in general, the material means and resources available to the population, the history and evolution of habits of taxpayers in their relations with the tax administration, and, especially, popular perception about the degree of tax justice in the country, which will directly determine and be associated with levels of tax evasion, concealment, and attempted tax fraud (Mellon et al. 2021). This culture of taxpayers also plays a decisive role in the budgetary process of estimating the variation in revenue derived from a legislative change in fiscal matters. It is therefore essential to consider the response and attitude that taxpayers are likely to adopt in the face of a change in the tax laws applied to them, if one wishes to obtain a realistic estimate of the effects of a tax reform.

The taxpayer's ideology is highly influenced by the other two elements—the law and the tax administration. For example, it is not the same to be subject to a tax regulation that sanctions fraud with a pecuniary fine as it is to be subject to another that sanctions it with the death penalty; nor is it the same to deal with a tax administration that is known to be corruptible, which supposes an incentive for noncompliance, as to deal with another characterized by scrupulous compliance with the law.

Likewise, and here the tax estimate comes into play, the attitude of the tax administration, specified in that of its officials, will depend on the type and design adopted in the preparation of the tax regulation. This is because a system based on mechanical application will hinder the appearance of corrupt practices in the tax administration, compared to another contractual system that grants greater discretionary power to the official at the time of negotiating the tax debt, such as the *forfait* system. And the type of regulations that can be approved must be related to the material means and human resources available to each tax administration at the time of applying and enforcing them.

In this context, it is important to highlight the role of a new field: tax morale, which focuses on the attitude and acceptance by the taxpayer body of the regulations as well as of the administrative practices for its application (Torgler 2011). In this line of reasoning, and connecting with the dimension of tax justice, it would be worthwhile to reflect on the degree of equity involved in the adoption of estimative or presumptive methods only for certain sectors of the population and, based on different factors, the indexes and indicators used.

As pointed out before, when the legislation resorts to presumptive taxation, what it is really being done is taxing something totally different from real or even potential income, which, taken one step further, means that different sectors of the population are taxed according to different variables or factors. Different yardsticks are applied, and this entails problems of acceptance by the taxpayer population, unless a convincing explanation can be offered for said differential treatment (Lucas-Mas 2004). It is true that if the tax estimate were infallible and there was no possibility of fraud, the aforementioned considerations could perhaps be ignored, if analyzed from a point of view focused exclusively on tax compliance. Even so, the question of acceptance by taxpayers of the said system of rules would remain pending, which is a completely different issue.

As everyone knows, doing something because we want to is not the same as being forced to do it. Therefore, it must be taken into account that there is no better tax system than the one that is fully accepted by the body of taxpayers, which is directly related to the study of tax morale. Likewise, it is relevant to assess the effects of presumptive taxation on taxpayers, the degree of acceptance, the level of tax compliance in the different settings where it has been applied, and what has caused its success or failure. It is necessary to guarantee, therefore, that the use of any notion of potential income is not perceived by the taxpayer as a violation of the principle of tax justice. This may be more a matter of fairness within, than between, professions.

Developing countries show a wide variety of levels of tax compliance, reflected not only in the effectiveness of their respective tax administrations but also in the attitudes of taxpayers in relation to taxation and the government, and to other factors. Attitudes are formed in a social context and are the product of factors such as the perceived level of fraud, the perceived fairness of the tax system,[3] its complexity and stability, the way it is administered, the value associated with the activities of the government, and the legitimacy of the latter. Attitudes affect intentions, and intentions and feelings determine behavior. Therefore, government policies that affect any of the aforementioned factors may, indirectly, influence the attitudes of taxpayers and, as a consequence, the degree of tax compliance (Dom et al. 2022). In this sense, there is sufficient agreement regarding the potential importance of social norms on tax compliance conduct. Compliance is intimately conditioned by the force and responsibility that the social norm of compliance evokes and generates on the taxpayer.

Thus, the following conclusions emerge from the literature review. First, those companies that comply with their tax obligations perceive tax fraud as something immoral. Second, the degree of compliance is higher if the government appeals to the morale of the taxpayer. Third, the poor reputation and social prestige derived from being a fraudster can be an important repulsive. Fourth, individuals who have tax evaders among their friends probably can defraud themselves or already do. And fifth, the level of compliance is higher in those communities that have a more developed social feeling of cohesion. Likewise, it turns out that people will not pay their taxes if they do not like the way in which the income derived from them is spent or the purposes to which they are destined. They may also not pay their taxes if they consider that they have no capacity to intervene in this regard, if they feel that the government ignores and is oblivious to their requests and wishes, or if they consider that they are unfairly treated by the government.

To fully understand the differences in voluntary compliance behavior between different cultures, it is necessary to understand not only the differences in social norms and the attitudes of citizens toward the governments of their respective countries but also the differences regarding the tax administration. Thus, if tax evasion is considered acceptable behavior, the courts will not favor the imposition of sanction. On the other hand, if the level of compliance is generally high, any fraudsters who are detected will receive little sympathy from the judicial bodies and the public. Therefore, the role of administrative institutions is essential in this process.

Social institutions, such as the social norm of compliance and the existence of an effective tax administration, are essential for better understanding of tax compliance in transition and developing countries. In summary, for transition and developing countries, it seems equally important to consolidate and strengthen social compliance standards as it is to modernize and improve the operational capacity of tax and customs administrations.

Nontechnical drivers of tax administration reform

Both technical and nontechnical drivers interact in determining the ultimate outcome of tax reform efforts, and the relative significance of each specific factor may depend on the context. Technical factors are quantifiable variables, such as income levels or wealth inequality, which can affect the likelihood of policy reform. These drivers can facilitate or impede reform, because it may be easier, for instance, to change the distribution of costs and benefits from a particular policy when many are well off or in the same socioeconomic category.

In contrast to technical drivers, nontechnical factors are qualitative measures, such as institutions, interests, and ideas. This tripartite framework (Hall 1997; Przeworski 2004), although applicable to policy reform generally, usefully captures the salient features of any policy process and provides a valuable structure for analysis for tax administration reform efforts.

World Bank research on PFM reforms (World Bank 2017) demonstrated the primary importance of two nontechnical factors in explaining the success of reforms: intent and intensity of local officials to implement reforms. Unsurprisingly, policy change does not occur unless the relevant officials support it. Moreover, support occurs with varying degrees: from strong, deep, and long-lasting to weak, superficial, or short-lived. It is noteworthy, however, that these two drivers stood out in terms of relative importance compared to other potential technical and nontechnical drivers.

For instance, research showed that "strong commitment to governance reforms" in both Georgia and the Philippines explained PFM progress in those two countries (Diokno 2005). Moreover, the intensity of commitment can be signaled by embedding specific reform within wider governance reform. For example, PFM reform can form part of an anticorruption drive or improving service delivery. Other nontechnical factors, such as the institutional balance between the executive and parliament, were also important to PFM reform. Legislatures can be important sources of oversight but can also serve as areas of policy deadlock. Likewise, divisions between federal and regional institutional structures can affect the prospects of policy reform. Notably, other nontechnical drivers such as domestic demands from citizens or civil society were less significant in explaining PFM reform (Junquera-Varela 2011).

Moreover, the importance of political economy analysis applied to tax reform will continue to grow both as an area of research and in its practical application. While political commitment is widely held as key to reform, recent research has been able to map in greater detail how it affects reform. See appendix C, which addresses political economy considerations for tax reform.

Institutions: formal and informal

Any political and economic system is structured by its institutions: the organizations—governmental ministries, legislatures, courts, media, nongovernmental organizations—as well as the formal and informal rules, norms, expectations, and customary practices that structure the policy process. Institutions define the basic rules of the road under which actors pursue their objectives. Depending on the context, different institutions will have varying relative weights of influence on a policy process, a dynamic that in practice may be known only ex post, rather than assessed theoretically ex ante. Sometimes, it is difficult to assess the full picture of a particular policy process, as various actors may have insight only into parts of the proverbial elephant.[4] Institutions and their relative influence can change, evolve, or reform but are likely to do so at a slower pace than specific policies. New agencies can be established, constitutions amended, and fundamental practices altered, but these changes take more time than altering policies within an existing institutional structure.

Tax administration reform needs to be customized to the local context, rather than homogeneously applied based on a uniform set of programs. The old adage that all politics is local applies to taxes as well. And given that local actors will often have the most accurate insight into the internal distribution of power, institutional dynamics, and informal customs, tax reform programs need to be designed in light of this local knowledge (Junquera-Varela 2011).

The broader institutional context shapes the environment in which different actors pursue their interests. As such, analysis of nontechnical drivers involves an effort to understand how institutions shape support for, or opposition to, reform. Analysis needs to consider, at a minimum, aspects of the national political environment, the character of the relationship between the tax administration and other branches of government, and the organization of the tax administration itself.

Given the centrality of high-level political leadership to reform efforts, understanding electoral dynamics and the political foundations of leading political parties is essential. Historically, tax reform has been common after changes in government, reflecting both the political demands unleashed by elections and the destabilization of entrenched interests opposed to reform. But whether changes in government lead to reform depends on the particular salience of tax considerations to ongoing political debates.

It is equally important to understand how the tax administration is linked to the rest of government, and particularly to the Ministry of Finance (MOF). Leadership for reform may come from the MOF, the Executive Branch, or the leadership of the tax administration itself, depending on the nature of both formal and informal institutional linkages. Leadership from the MOF is often critical to tax reform. However, in other contexts, power may be centralized in the Executive Branch, or the tax administration itself may exercise significant reform leadership. Understanding these dynamics in the local context is critical to ascertaining where reform leadership is needed and which interests are likely to be most important to shaping reform efforts.

Institutional structures are likely to shape not only the influence wielded by the tax administration itself but also the extent of support for reform among civil servants. For example, where tax administrations are relatively fragmented, there may be strong resistance to reform that threatens the autonomy of individual administrative units. Similarly, rules governing recruitment and promotion, and who controls the processes, may profoundly shape the interests of different groups. In assessing the institutional landscape in a particular country, a technical assessment team should conduct a previsit survey. See box 1.7 for a list of questions to investigate based on the analysis above to guide the team's interactions with local authorities and stakeholders.

BOX 1.7   Institutional landscape assessment survey a list of questions

1. What is the nature of the relationship between the Executive Branch (president or prime minister) and the tax administration? Does the executive influence policymaking, hiring, or day-to-day activities within the tax administration?

2. What is the nature of the relationship between the Ministry of Finance (MOF) and the tax administration? Does the MOF influence policymaking, hiring, or day-to-day activities within the tax administration?

3. What is the relationship between the government and the parliament? Are there oversight committees or bodies available in the parliament to monitor reforms? How active are they?

4. Are there any other related public sector reform programs that could reinforce or detract from the proposed reform program?

5. Are there any other international development partners working on similar or related reform programs in the country?

6. What international or domestic monitoring mechanisms are available to track progress of reforms?

7. Are reform efforts—related both to the tax policy and to tax administration—driven primarily by the president/prime minister, the minister of finance, other ministers, or officials inside the tax administration (for example, a tax policy unit)?

8. What political factors and constituencies are most influential in shaping engagement by the president or prime minister and the minister of finance?

9. Do specific actors within the government, the MOF, or the tax administration exercise effective veto power over reform efforts? Where are these "veto points"?

Interests, actors, and support for reform

Within the institutional landscape assessed above, various actors pursue their interests, with positive or negative impact on reform. Interests are specific objectives sought by various actors that affect the policy process—government officials, parliamentarians, civil servants, civil society, and taxpayers—typically as reflected through their expressed preferences, for example, through public statements or policy documents.

Generally, individuals and groups are more likely to mobilize and form coalitions to pursue their interests if their costs or benefits due to a policy are concentrated, rather than diffused. In the case of taxes, costs are frequently concentrated to specific groups of taxpayers who are often well organized, but the benefits in terms of public spending facilitated by taxes are frequently dispersed; this dynamic underpins the difficulty of tax reform (Diokno 2005). Interests range across a preference ordering for a specific policy option—for example, A > B > C—as well as in terms of intensity (high versus low).

Furthermore, tax reform packages should be presented as a critical component of a comprehensive governance reform program. Such a program should highlight the government's efforts to improve public sector efficiency, transparency, and accountability. Tax reform programs tend to be adopted at the beginning of a new administration. The early days of a new administration provide a window of opportunity to garner political capital to enact a comprehensive tax reform (Thirsk 1991). Still, the most successful tax reforms have benefited from detailed planning and preparation as well as close monitoring during and after their implementation.

Tax reform, much like PFM reform, will be driven by high-level or leadership commitment. Although real commitment is sometimes difficult to ascertain, it can be identified through the following:

- *Nature of government's reform platform during elections.* Promises can sometimes be exaggerated, but they create expectations and constraints within which the elected government operates.
- *Strength of government's electoral mandate.* A strong and clear victory can provide a government with space for policy reform, whereas a weak mandate or lack of majority in the parliament can lead to policy deadlock.
- *Capability of government to implement reform.* Prior reform experience or demonstrated ability of key government officials can accelerate reform, and lack of it can delay reforms.

Countries that demonstrated strong indicators on all of these three dimensions had the best performance in terms of PFM reform. In contrast, countries that showed weak political commitment across the three indicators had the worst performance in terms of PFM reform.

With tax reform, as with public finance management, local politics will predominate over external incentives or pressure. Research shows that internationally driven reform without local support can result in superficial copying without a real intent to achieve improvement. Such "isomorphic mimicry" may accomplish the immediate objective of international development programs but fail to achieve any real change on the ground. Instead, "politically smart" reform programs need to be designed to reach the underlying goals.

Assessing the alignment of political support for reform by determining the specific interests of groups who are politically influential in relation to particular reform objectives is a useful starting point for analyzing nontechnical drivers. This can provide a preliminary picture of whether reform objectives are consistent with existing political dynamics and how reform may be designed or pursued in order to minimize political opposition. However, such analysis must be conducted with care, as resistance to tax reform often occurs behind closed doors or through informal mechanisms, centered on large taxpayers and senior government officials.

Political resistance to tax reform frequently comes from multiple sources, and it is essential to consider these multiple possible sources of resistance. The most obvious source of opposition is taxpayers, who tend to be instinctively resistant to increased taxation and wary of broader changes in tax systems. While many taxpayers may, in principle, benefit from increased public spending and service provision, they are often skeptical that governments will use additional revenue productively. Moreover, taxation presents a severe collective action problem, as taxpayers have strong incentives to "free-ride" on the tax payments of others and are unlikely to support new taxation unless they are confident that all taxpayers will pay their fair share. Taxpayers rarely express this confidence in the comparatively weak control environment that characterizes many, but not all, developing country tax administrations.

Behind these general messages frequently lie important differences between particular groups of taxpayers with potentially very different interests. Efforts to reform PITs are likely to confront very different opposition than efforts aimed at reforming CITs. In similar fashion, tax reforms affecting businesses are likely to elicit resistance from some businesses and support from others. Differences may, for example, exist between small and large businesses, or between businesses that enjoy preferential tax treatment and those that do not. Understanding these divisions among taxpayers can help in refining reform strategies and mobilizing support for reform.

While resistance among taxpayers is crucial, it is essential to equally focus on the incentives and interests of civil servants and of political leaders. Resistance to reform by tax administration officials has often been an important, but overlooked, challenge. Officials at every level may feel that proposed reform programs threaten their discretion and autonomy. They may also fear that major reorganization or greater reliance on information technology (IT) may undermine their seniority, opportunities for advancement within the civil service, and maybe their jobs. This may be reflected in overt resistance to reform efforts but may equally be reflected in day-to-day resistance through a conscious failure to implement unpopular reform objectives. Similar concerns may be apparent among other branches of the public service that are essential to effective tax reform, including the judiciary, police, and business registration departments.

Attention must also be paid to the incentives of the senior political leadership, who may in some cases rely on discretionary tax reforms to dispense patronage and reinforce existing political coalitions. Successful reforms frequently depend on high-level leadership. Where the political strategies of political leaders are intertwined with existing incentives, exemptions, and weaknesses in the tax system, reform leadership is far less likely.

In assessing the key actors, their interests, and support for reform in a particular country, a technical assessment team should conduct a previsit survey. See box 1.8 for a list of questions to investigate based on the analysis above to guide the team's interactions with local authorities and stakeholders.

BOX 1.8 Interests, actors, and support for reform assessment survey—a list of questions

Support and opposition

1. Which institutions and officials support reform? What are the primary interests and objectives of supporters?

2. Which institutions and officials oppose reform? What are the primary interests and concerns of opponents?

3. What do local officials perceive as the main objectives of reform?

(continued)

BOX 1.8 Interests, actors, and support for reform assessment survey—a list of questions (*Continued*)

4. What do local officials perceive as their core challenges or obstacles to reform? What are the main perceived bottlenecks?

5. What is the benchmark of successful reform as perceived by local officials? What is the likelihood of success? How do these assessments compare to benchmarks and assessments of international actors?

6. What is the view and commitment of subnational governments and stakeholders?

7. Besides the Ministry of Finance and the Central Bank, who are the other relevant stakeholders who can support or oppose reform?

8. What is the expected timeline for reform?

Politics within the tax administration and civil service

1. Are public service unions generally influential? Are tax officials politically organized and influential?

2. Is authority within the tax administration centralized or fragmented across different divisions? How do these patterns shape support for, or resistance to, reform?

3. To what extent are senior tax officials political appointees with strong ties to the political party in power, and to what extent are tax officials relatively independent of political influence?

4. Are internal hiring and promotion processes relatively merit based, or do senior officials exercise significant discretion? If the latter, does this contribute to resistance to reform?

5. To what extent are relevant related agencies, such as the judiciary, police, and business registry, supportive of reform efforts?

Business actors and civil society

1. How influential is the business community in shaping the potential for tax reform?

2. Which business actors are most influential? Do they operate through business associations or lobby government bilaterally?

3. What are the sources of business influence—for example, financial contributions to political parties or the potential for mass mobilization?

4. Are there significant divisions between different groups of business actors in relation to tax reform proposals?

5. Are there any civil society groups—nonprofit organizations, advocacy groups, academic institutions, private actors—that exercise influence on tax policy and tax administration? What are their interests and objectives? How supportive are they of the intended reforms?

Public and media engagement

1. Is there significant public attention to tax reform issues, including attention from the media, or are tax discussions largely limited to policymakers and large taxpayers? Have tax issues been a significant electoral issue?

2. Is the public supportive of reform or generally distrustful of government proposals? Is there potential to bring the public or media on board as supporters of reform? If so, how? What are some of the key messages that can encourage support for reform?

Ideas and the potential for change

Having identified the institutional landscape and the key actors and their interests, a technical assessment team can then develop potential ideas for tax administration reform. Ideas are policy options and recommendations derived from descriptive research and normative values—what is and what ought to be. Ideas can be introduced by any actor within the policy process, and often by policy experts and policy entrepreneurs within the government, civil society, and international community. Networks of policy experts in international institutions and academia can be valuable sources of analysis and innovation for policy ideas.

International best practices need to be blended with local input to develop policy ideas tailored to the country of assessment. Analysis of the nontechnical drivers of the kind described so far is very helpful at explaining the status quo, as it highlights the sources of political resistance to as well as support for reform, and the institutional foundations of existing interests. However, such analysis is frequently static, thus providing limited guidance for future reform strategies. The goal of analyzing nontechnical drivers must thus be to develop a dynamic perspective on the politics of reform.

Analysis should focus on how and when a realignment of political forces may open new opportunities for reform. Historical experience of tax reform has frequently depended on the appearance of windows of opportunity for reform, often resulting from fiscal crises or political transitions that disrupt existing antireform coalitions. The history of economic reform has been punctuated by these moments in which political interests suddenly realign, thus opening the door to previously impossible reform. Because the interests of different constituencies are frequently interconnected, change in the position of one set of actors may prompt broader realignment, as those previously opposed to reform instead seek to positively influence reform that is now viewed as inevitable. As such, reformers should seek to respond to such windows of opportunity and, to the extent possible, to anticipate potential reform openings.

Equally important, analysis should also aim to understand what reformers might do in the short term to shift the balance of political interests in favor of reform. Major reform is most likely during periods of economic and political transition, but reform is about more than simply waiting for crisis. Thus, for example, small changes in institutional relationships within the tax administration, or in relevant civil service hiring practices, may create an environment more amenable to reform when reform openings emerge. Similarly, small steps aimed at increasing engagement with key stakeholders, particularly in the business community, may provide a stronger foundation for future reform efforts.

In developing specific ideas for policy reform in a particular country, a technical assessment team should conduct a previsit survey. See box 1.9 for a list of questions to investigate based on the analysis above to guide the team's interactions with local authorities and stakeholders.

BOX 1.9   Assessment survey to develop ideas for policy reform—a list of questions

1. Has the proposed tax reform been proposed in the past? If so, what role did the political climate during that time play in the failure of the reform, and how has the political context changed?

2. What obstacles or challenges occurred with prior reform efforts? Why were prior attempts at reform unsuccessful or only partially successful?

3. Were prior reform programs customized for the specific country or standardized, based on international best practices?

4. Did prior reform programs involve one-off international assistance or periodic international assistance over time?

5. Is the current reform effort led primarily by domestic actors, or is the international community significantly involved in trying to advance or design reform?

6. Given the alignment of political forces, what types of reform may face comparatively little political resistance? Are there opportunities for small-scale reforms that may nonetheless contribute to building support for subsequent larger reforms?

7. How has the tax reform effort been framed? Has this framing been effective in minimizing opposition and mobilizing support? How might changing the framing affect political and public support for reform?

8. Are there major political or economic events on the horizon (elections, fiscal crises), or is there the prospect of major political changes? If so, might these changes open up new space for pursuing tax reform?

9. Are there any questions the local officials deem important that have not been asked?

Notes

1 | It is important to differentiate between a regime designed for a specific taxpayer segment (tax policy) and a special process and procedures to facilitate the compliance of this segment under the general regime (tax administration).

2 | Tax administrations also face the challenge of effectively identifying businesses that are incorrectly hiding under special tax regimes for the micro and small taxpayer segment. Moving toward digitalization should also enable the use of other sources of data to identify these areas of noncompliance. Some examples of how digitalization can change the landscape are provided in chapter 7, like how machine learning could help identify potentially unregistered taxpayers.

3 | The perception of fairness is closely linked to tax compliance. Hence, if a well-implemented regime for professionals is applied—for example, with cross-data analysis—it may be more effective in taxing them than the general regime, and it will be perceived as fairer.

4 | "Several blind men approached an elephant and each touched the animal in an effort to discover what the beast looked like. Each blind man, however, touched a different part of the large animal, and each concluded that the elephant had the appearance of the part he had touched. Hence, the blind man who felt the animal's trunk concluded that an elephant must be tall and slender, while the fellow who touched the beast's ear concluded that an elephant must be oblong and flat. Others of course reached different conclusions. The total result was that no man arrived at a very accurate description of the elephant. Yet each man had gained enough evidence from his own experience to disbelieve his fellows and to maintain a lively debate about the nature of the beast" (Puchala 1972).

Bibliography

ADB (Asian Development Bank). 2018. *A Comparative Analysis of Tax Administration in Asia and the Pacific: 2018 Edition*. Manila, Philippines: ADB. https://www.adb.org/publications/comparative-analysis-tax-administration-asia-pacific.

Ahmad, Ehtisham, and Nicholas Stern. 1991. *The Theory and Practice of Tax Reform in Developing Countries*. Cambridge, UK: Cambridge University Press.

Avi-Yonah, Reuven, ed. 1997. *Presumptive Income Taxation*. Proceedings of a Seminar held in New Delhi in 1997 during the 51st Congress of the International Fiscal Association. The Hague, Netherlands: Kluwer Law International.

Awasthi, Rajul, and Michael Engelschalk. 2018. "Taxation and the Shadow Economy: How the Tax System Can Stimulate and Enforce the Formalization of Business Activities." Policy Research Working Paper 8391, World Bank, Washington, DC.

Bagchi, Amaresh, Richard Bird, and Arindam Das-Gupta. 1994. "An Economic Approach to Tax Administration Reform." Unpublished, World Bank, Washington, DC.

Barreix, Alberto, Jerónimo Roca, and Fernando Velayos. 2016. "A Brief History of Tax Transparency." Discussion Paper No. IDB-DP-453, Inter-American Development Bank, Washington, DC.

Berry, R. Albert. 1972. "Presumptive Income Tax on Agricultural Land: The Case of Colombia." *National Tax Journal* 25 (2): 169–181. https://doi.org/10.1086/NTJ41791789.

Bird, Richard. 1974. *Taxing Agricultural Land in Developing Countries*. Cambridge, MA: Harvard University Press.

Bird, Richard. 2010a. "Taxation and Decentralization." *Economic Premise* No. 38, November, World Bank, Washington, DC.

Bird, Richard. 2010b. "Taxation and Development." *Economic Premise* No. 34, October, World Bank, Washington, DC.

Bird, Richard, and Milka Casanegra de Jantscher, eds. 1992. *Improving Tax Administration in Developing Countries*. Washington, DC: International Monetary Fund.

Bird, Richard, and Oliver Oldman. 1977. "The Transition to a Global Income Tax: A Comparative Analysis." *Bulletin for International Fiscal Documentation* 31 (10): 439–454.

Bird, Richard, and Oliver Oldman, eds. 1995. *Taxation in Developing Countries*, 5th ed. Baltimore, MD: Johns Hopkins University Press.

Bird, Richard, and Sally Wallace. 2003. "Is It Really So Hard to Tax the Hard-to-Tax? The Context and Role of Presumptive Taxes." Paper prepared for "Conference on the Hard-to-Tax Sector," Georgia State University's Andrew Young School of Policy Studies, International Studies Program, May 15–16, 2003.

Blank, Joshua. 2017. "The Timing of Tax Transparency." *Southern California Law Review* 90: 449–528.

Bulutoglu, Kenan. 1994. "An Intermediate Tax Technology: Presumptive Taxation." Unpublished, International Monetary Fund, Washington, DC.

Bulutoglu, Kenan. 1995. "Presumptive Taxation." In *Tax Policy Handbook*, edited by Parthasarathi Shome, 258–262. Washington, DC: IMF. https://doi.org/10.5089/9781557754905.071.

Burgess, Robin, and Nicholas Stern. 1993. "Taxation and Development." *Journal of Economic Literature* 31 (2): 762–830. https://www.jstor.org/stable/2728515.

Byrne, Peter. 1994. "The Business Assets Tax in Latin America—No Credit Where It Is Due." Development Discussion Paper No. 506, Harvard Institute for International Development, Cambridge, MA.

Calero-García, María Luz. 1996. "La Base Imponible en el Derecho Tributario General" (The Tax Base in the General Tax Law). *Cuaderno de Estudios Empresariales* 6: 67–87. Universidad Complutense de Madrid.

Cazorla-Prieto, Luis María. 1981. "Poder Tributario y Estado Contemporáneo" (Taxing Power and Contemporary State). Instituto de Estudios Fiscales. Madrid: Ministerio de Hacienda.

Cazorla-Prieto, Luis María. 2002. *El Derecho Financiero y Tributario en la Ciencia Jurídica* (The Finance and Tax Law in the Juridical Science). Madrid: Editorial Aranzadi.

CIAT (Inter-American Center of Tax Administrations). 2019. "Marco de Referencia para el Aseguramiento de la Integridad y los Valores en las Administraciones Tributarias" (Frame of Reference for Ensuring Integrity and Values in the Tax Administrations). Grupo de Trabajo sobre "Control Interno," Abril 2018. https://www.ciat.org/Biblioteca/Papeles_Trabajo/Etica/2019/PT_02_2019.pdf.

Clavijo-Hernández, Francisco. 2001. "Los regímenes de Determinación de la Base Imponible (Una Reflexión a la Luz de los Trabajos de Sáinz de Bujanda y Palao Taboada)" (The Tax Base Assessment Regimes [A Reflection in Light of the Works of Sáinz de Bujanda and Palao Taboada]). *Revista Técnica Tributaria* 52: 21–31. Asociación Española de Asesores Fiscales, Enero-Marzo.

Cubero-Truyo, Antonio Manuel. 1997. "La Simplificación del Ordenamiento Tributario" (The Simplification of the Tax System) (Desde la Perspectiva Constitucional). Madrid: Marcial Pons.

Dastur, Sohrab Erach. 1997. "The Indian Methodology." In *Presumptive Income Taxation: Proceedings of a Seminar Held in New Delhi in 1997 during the 51st Congress of the International Fiscal Association*, edited by Reuven S. Avi-Yonah, Vol. 22d. The Hague, Netherlands: Kluwer Law International.

Del Vecchio, Giorgio. 1908. "Sull'idea di una scienza del diritto universale comparato" (On the Idea of a Science of Comparative Universal Law). *Rivista Italiana per le Scienza Giuridiche* 173.

Del Vecchio, Giorgio. 1953. "La Unidad del Espíritu Humano Como Base Para el Estudio Comparativo del Derecho" (The Unity of the Human Spirit as a Basis for the Comparative Study of Law) (Spanish translation by E. Galán y Gutiérrez). *Revista general de legislación y jurisprudencia* 195 (5): 523–533.

Díaz-Álvarez, Amelia. 1987. "Teoría General de la Imposición" (General Theory of Taxation), Monograph 53, Instituto de Estudios Fiscales, Madrid, Spain.

Diokno, Benjamin. 2005. "Reforming the Philippine Tax System: Lessons from Two Tax Reform Programs." University of the Philippines School of Economics Discussion Paper No. 0502, University of the Philippines, Manila.

Dom, Roel, Anna Custers, Stephen Davenport, and Wilson Prichard. 2022. *Innovations in Tax Compliance: Building Trust, Navigating Politics, and Tailoring Reform*. Washington, DC: World Bank.

Einaudi, Luigi. 1963. "La Scienza Italiana e la Imposta Ottima" (Italian Science and the Optimum Tax). Original work published in 1924. In *Miti e Paradossi della Giustizia Tributaria*, chapter X, Giulio Einaudi (editor). Torino, Italia, 1938. Spanish translation: "Mitos y Paradojas de la Justicia Tributaria." Barcelona: Ediciones Ariel.

Erbas, S. Nuri. 1993. "Presumptive Taxation: Revenue and Automatic Stabilizer Aspects." FAD WP/93/69. Unpublished, IMF, Washington, DC.

Eseverri, Ernesto. 1980. "La Estimación Objetiva Singular de Bases Imponibles" (The Singular Objective Estimate of Taxable Bases). *Hacienda Pública Española* 62: 225–254.

Faria, Angelo, and M. Zühtü Yücelik. 1995. "The Interrelationship Between Tax Policy and Tax Administration." In *Tax Policy Handbook*, edited by Parthasarathi Shome, 267–270. Washington, DC: IMF.

Ferreiro-Lapatza, José Juan. 1996. "El Principio de Legalidad" (The Principle of Legality). Las Facultades de la Administración en Materia de Determinación de Tributos. Ponencia presentada en las XVIII Jornadas Latinoamericanas de Derecho Tributario, Montevideo, ILADT, Diciembre.

Ferreiro-Lapatza, José Juan, ed. 2003. *La Justicia Tributaria en España. Informe sobre las Relaciones entre la Administración y los Contribuyentes y la Resolución de Conflictos entre Ellos* (The Tax Justice in Spain. Report on the Relationships between the Tax Administration and the Taxpayers and the Conflict Resolution amongst them). Grupo Investigador del Proyecto sobre "Justicia Tributaria" del Ministerio de Educación y Ciencia del Gobierno Español, Madrid.

Fritz, Verena, Marijn Verhoeven, and Ambra Avenia. 2017. *Political Economy of Public Financial Management Reforms: Experiences and Implications for Dialogue and Operational Engagement*. Washington, DC: World Bank. https://documents1.worldbank.org/curated/en/596281510894572778/pdf/121436-REVISED-PUBLIC-PE-of-PFM-Reforms-Report-Web.pdf.

Gaitero-Fortes, Jaime. 1988. "Simplification of Administrative Procedures: Audit Procedures." In *Tax Simplification. Technical Papers and Reports of the 20th General Assembly of the Inter-American Center of Tax Administrators (CIAT)*, Buenos Aires, Argentina, 7–11 April 1986. Amsterdam: International Bureau of Fiscal Documentation.

Gale, William. 2001. "Tax Simplification: Issues and Options." Paper based on testimony submitted to Congress of the United States on July 17, 2001. Unpublished. Brookings Institution, Washington, DC.

García-Novoa, César. 2002. "Los Métodos de Simplificación Fiscal en la Experiencia Latinoamericana. Referencia Comparativa a los Casos Brasileños y Argentino" (Tax Simplification Methods in the Latin American Experience. Compared Reference to the Brazilian and Argentinean Cases). Informe Interno del Proyecto sobre "Justicia Tributaria" del Gobierno Español, Barcelona.

Génova-Galván, Alberto. 1986. "Los Regímenes de Determinación de la Base Imponible" (The Tax Base Assessment Regimes). *Revista de Derecho Financiero y Hacienda Pública* 36 (181): 13–56.

Giannini, Achille Donato. 1957. *Instituciones de Derecho Tributario* (Tax Law Institutions) (translation by D. Fernando Sáinz de Bujanda). Madrid: Editorial De Derecho Financiero.

Gillis, Malcolm. 1989. *Tax Reform in Developing Countries*. Durham, NC: Duke University Press.

Graetz, Michael, and Emil Sunley. 1988. "Minimum Taxes and Comprehensive Tax Reform." In *Uneasy Compromise: Problems of a Hybrid Income-Consumption Tax*, edited by Henry J. Aaron, Harvey Galper, and Joseph A Pechman. Washington, DC: Brookings Institution.

Grapperhaus, Ferdinand. 1997. "The Trade-Off Between Accuracy and Administrability." In *Presumptive Income Taxation: Proceedings of a Seminar Held in New Delhi in 1997 during the 51st Congress of the International Fiscal Association*, edited by Reuven S. Avi-Yonah, vol. 22. The Hague, Netherlands: Kluwer Law International.

Gray, Clive. 2001. "Enhancing Transparency in Tax Administration in Madagascar and Tanzania." African Economic Policy Discussion Paper No. 77, USAID, Bureau for Africa, Washington, DC, https://pdf.usaid.gov/pdf_docs/Pnacm656.pdf.

Hall, Peter. 1997. "The Role of Interests, Institutions, and Ideas in the Comparative Political Economy of the Industrialized Nations." In *Comparative Politics: Rationality, Culture, and Structure*, edited by Mark Lichbach and Alan Zuckerman, 174–207. Cambridge, UK: Cambridge University Press.

Hinrichs, Harley. 1966. *A General Theory of Tax Structure Change during Economic Development.* Cambridge, MA: Harvard University Press.

Independent Evaluation Group. 2017. *Tax Revenue Mobilization: Lessons from World Bank Group Support for Tax Reform.* Washington, DC: World Bank.

IMF (International Monetary Fund) and OECD (Organisation for Economic Co-operation and Development). 2017. "Tax Certainty: IMF/OECD Report for the G20 Finance Ministers." https://www.imf.org/external/np/g20/pdf/2017/031817.pdf.

Junquera-Varela, Raúl Félix. 2011. "An Integrated Assessment Model for Tax Administration: The Diagnostic Tool." Unpublished, World Bank Poverty Reduction and Economic Management, Public Sector and Governance Group, Washington, DC.

Junquera-Varela, Raúl Félix. 2013. "Special Tax Regimes for the Micro and Small Taxpayers." Unpublished, World Bank, Washington, DC.

Junquera-Varela, Raúl Félix, Marijn Verhoeven, Gangadhar P. Shukla, Bernard Haven, Rajul Awasthi, and Blanca Moreno-Dodson. 2017. *Strengthening Domestic Resource Mobilization: Moving from Theory to Practice in Low- and Middle-Income Countries.* Directions in Development, Public Sector Governance. Washington, DC: World Bank.

Junquera-Varela, Raúl Félix, and Ekaterina Vostroknutova. 2015. *Peru—Selected Issues in Fiscal Policy: Taxation and Equity.* Washington, DC: World Bank. https://documents1.worldbank.org/curated/en/378471630384987203/pdf/Peru-Selected-Issues-in-Fiscal-Policy-Taxation-and-Equity.pdf.

Kaldor, Nicholas. 1955. *An Expenditure Tax.* London: George Allen & Unwin.

Kaplow, Louis. 1989. "Horizontal Equity: Measures in Search of a Principle." *National Tax Journal* 42 (2): 139–154. https://doi.org/10.1086/NTJ41788784.

Kaplow, Louis. 1990. "Optimal Taxation with Costly Enforcement and Evasion." *Journal of Public Economics* 43 (2): 221–236. https://doi.org/10.1016/0047-2727(90)90031-C.

Kaplow, Louis. 1996. "How Tax Complexity and Enforcement Affect the Equity and Efficiency of the Income Tax." Discussion Paper No. 174, Harvard Law School, Cambridge, MA.

Kaplow, Louis, and Steven Shavell. 2002. *Fairness versus Welfare.* Cambridge, MA: Harvard University Press.

Khadka, Rup. 2001. "Presumptive Taxes: Assessing Origin & Its Practice." *The Rising Nepal*, February 22, 2001.

Lapidoth, Arye. 1977. *The Use of Estimation for the Assessment of Taxable Business Income: With Special Emphasis on the Problems of Taxing Small Business.* Vol. 4 of *Selected Monographs on Taxation.* Amsterdam: International Bureau of Fiscal Documentation.

Le, Tuan Minh, Leif Jensen, Gangadhar Shukla, and Nataliya Biletska. 2016. "Assessing Domestic Revenue Mobilization: Analytical Tools and Techniques." MFM Discussion Paper 15, World Bank, Washington, DC.

Lipin, Ilya. 2012. "Failing Corporate Tax Transparency and the Immediate Need to Reduce Overburdening Duplicative Tax Reporting Requirements." *Akron Tax Journal* 27: 119–152.

Lucas-Carrasco, José. 1997. "Requisitos Urgentes para Incrementar la Eficacia y Eficiencia de la Inspección de Hacienda ante el Fraude Fiscal" (Urgent Requirements to Increase the Effectiveness and Efficiency of the Tax Audit Department to Tackle Tax Evasion). Unpublished, Informe interno de la Administración Estatal de la Administración Tributaria. Madrid: Ministerio de Economía y Hacienda.

Lucas-Mas, Cristian Óliver. 2002. "The Cuban Tax System Through History." *Tax Notes International* 27 (5): 609–630. https://www.taxnotes.com/tax-notes-today-international/corporate-taxation/cuban-tax-system-through-history/2002/07/29/1b95m?highlight=lucas-mas.

Lucas-Mas, Cristian Óliver. 2004. "General Tax Theory on Simplified Methods for the Assessment of Tax Bases: A Study on Presumptive Taxation." Doctoral dissertation, University of Barcelona, Spain. Unpublished.

Malik, I. A. 1970. "Text of Discussion Paper on Use of Presumptive Techniques in Taxation of Small Traders and Other Categories of Self-Employed Individuals." FISC Working Paper 15, United Nations, Economic Commission for Africa, Training Course in Tax Policy, Legislation and Administration, Addis Ababa, October 8–27, 1973.

Malik, I. A. 1979. "Use of Presumptive Tax Assessment Techniques in Taxation of Small Traders and Professionals in Africa." *Bulletin for International Fiscal Documentation* 33 (4): 162–178.

Mellon, Jonathan, Tiago Peixoto, Fredrik Sjoberg, and Varun Gauri. 2021. "Trickle Down Tax Morale: A Cross-Country Survey Experiment." Policy Research Working Paper 9507, World Bank, Washington, DC. http://hdl.handle.net/10986/35013.

Mikesell, John. 1999. "The Unified Tax on Imputed Income in the Russian Federation: Problems with an Alternative Tax Scheme." *Tax Notes International.* https://www.taxnotes.com/tax-notes-international/unified-tax-imputed-income-russian-federation-problems-alternative-tax-scheme/1999/12/27/1tr2m.

Moller, Lars Christian, Raúl Félix Junquera-Varela, and Daniel Álvarez. 2012. *El Gasto Tributario en Colombia: Una propuesta de evaluación integral y sistemática de este instrumento de política pública* (Tax Expenditure in Colombia: A Proposal for a Comprehensive and Systematic Evaluation of this Public Policy Instrument). Washington, DC: World Bank. http://documents.worldbank.org/curated/en/945121468022751656/El-Gasto-Tributario-en-Colombia-una-propuesta-de-evaluacion-integral-y-sistematica-de-este-instrumento-de-politica-publica.

Müller, Raphael, Christoph Spengel, and Heiko Vay. 2020. "On the Determinants and Effects of Corporate Tax Transparency: Review of an Emerging Literature." ZEW (Centre for European Economic Research) Discussion Paper 20-063, ZEW, Mannheim, Germany.

Musgrave, Richard. 1969. *Fiscal Systems*. New Haven, CT: Yale University Press.

Musgrave, Richard. 1986. "The Nature of Horizontal Equity and the Principle of Broad-Based Taxation: A Friendly Critique." In *Public Finance in a Democratic Society Volume III: The Foundations of Taxation and Expenditure*, edited by Richard Musgrave, 150–166. Cheltenham, UK: Edward Elgar.

Musgrave, Richard. 1990. "Income Taxation of the Hard to Tax Groups." In *Taxation in Developing Countries*, edited by Richard Bird and Oliver Oldman, 299–309. Baltimore, MD: Johns Hopkins University Press.

OECD (Organisation for Economic Co-operation and Development). 2012. "Working Smarter in Structuring the Administration, in Compliance, and Through Legislation." Forum on Tax Administration, Information Note, OECD, Paris.

OECD (Organisation for Economic Co-operation and Development). 2013. *Managing Service Demand: A Practical Guide to Help Revenue Bodies Better Meet Taxpayers' Service Expectations*. Paris: OECD Publishing.

OECD (Organisation for Economic Co-operation and Development). 2014a. *Tax Compliance by Design: Achieving Improved SME Tax Compliance by Adopting a System Perspective*. Paris: OECD Publishing. doi:10.1787/9789264200821-en.

OECD (Organisation for Economic Co-operation and Development). 2014b. *Measures of Tax Compliance Outcomes: A Practical Guide*. Paris: OECD Publishing. https://doi.org/10.1787/9789264223233-en.

OECD (Organisation for Economic Co-operation and Development). 2015. *Building Tax Culture, Compliance and Citizenship: A Global Source Book on Taxpayer Education*. Paris: OECD Publishing. https://doi.org/10.1787/9789264205154-en.

OECD (Organisation for Economic Co-operation and Development). 2016. *Co-operative Tax Compliance: Building Better Tax Control Frameworks*. Paris: OECD Publishing. https://doi.org/10.1787/9789264253384-en.

OECD (Organisation for Economic Co-operation and Development). 2019a. *Tax Administration 2019: Comparative Information on OECD and Other Advanced and Emerging Economies*. Paris: OECD Publishing. https://doi.org/10.1787/74d162b6-en.

OECD (Organisation for Economic Co-operation and Development). 2019b. *Tax Policy Reforms 2019: OECD and Selected Partner Economies*. Paris: OECD Publishing. https://doi.org/10.1787/da56c295-en.

OECD (Organisation for Economic Co-operation and Development). 2020. *Tax Policy Reforms 2020: OECD and Selected Partner Economies*. Paris: OECD Publishing. https://doi.org/10.1787/7af51916-en.

OECD (Organisation for Economic Co-operation and Development). 2021. *Tax Policy Reforms 2021: Special Edition on Tax Policy during the COVID-19 Pandemic*. Paris: OECD Publishing. https://doi.org/10.1787/427d2616-en.

OECD (Organisation for Economic Co-operation and Development). 2022. *Tax Morale II: Building Trust between Tax Administrations and Large Businesses*. Paris: OECD Publishing. https://doi.org/10.1787/7587f25c-en.

Oldman, Oliver, and Jennifer Brooks. 1987. "The Unitary Method and the Less Developed Countries: Preliminary Thoughts." *International Business Law Journal* 45 (1): 45–61.

Ortega, Luis. 1991. "La Nacionalización del Suelo en Gran Bretaña (The Community Land Act 1975)." *Revista Española de Derecho Administrativo* 14: 459–478.

Owens, Jeffrey (Coord.). 2022. "The Impact of Technologies on Emerging Tax Policy Issues." Informal Summary of Discussions. Digital Economy Taxation Network (DET) Conference hosted by WU Global Tax Policy Center at Vienna University of Economics and Business, December 12–13, 2022. *Review of International and European Economic Law* 2 (3): 1–25. https://www.rieel.com/index.php/rieel/article/view/68.

Przeworski, Adam. 2004. "Institutions Matter?" *Government and Opposition* 39 (4): 527–540. https://doi.org/10.1111/j.1477-7053.2004.00134.x.

Puchala, Donald. 1972. "Of Blind Men, Elephants and International Integration." *Journal of Common Market Studies* 10 (3): 267–284. https://doi.org/10.1111/j.1468-5965.1972.tb00903.x.

Rajaraman, Indira. 1995. "Presumptive Direct Taxation. Lessons from Experience in Developing Countries." *Economic and Political Weekly* 30 (18–19): 1103–1124. http://www.jstor.org/stable/4402735.

Sabine, B. E. V. 1966. *A History of Income Tax*. London: George Allen & Unwin.

Sadka, Efraim, and Vito Tanzi. 1993. "A Tax on Gross Assets of Enterprises as a Form of Presumptive Taxation." Working Paper 1992/016, IMF, Washington, DC. https://www.imf.org/en/Publications/WP/Issues/2016/12/30/A-Taxon-Gross-Assets-of-Enterprises-as-a-Form-of-Presumptive-Taxation-767.

Sáinz de Bujanda, Fernando. 1970. "Los métodos de determinación de las bases imponibles y su proyección sobre la estructura del sistema tributario" (The Taxable Base Assessment Methods and their Projection on the Structure of the Tax System). Speech at the Royal Academy of Jurisprudence and Legislation, Madrid, February 16, 1970.

Shome, Parthasarathi. 1992. "Trends and Future Directions in Tax Policy Reform: A Latin American Perspective." Working Paper 1992/043, IMF, Washington, DC. https://doi.org/10.5089/9781451846263.001.

Shome, Parthasarathi. 1993. "The Taxation of High Income Earners." IMF Paper on Policy Analysis and Assessment PPAA/93/19, IMF, Washington, DC.

Stotsky, Janet. 1995. "Minimum Taxes." In *Tax Policy Handbook*, edited by Parthasarathi Shome, 263–266. Washington, DC: IMF.

Surrey, Stanley. 1958. "Tax Administration in Underdeveloped Countries." *University of Miami Law Review* 12 (2): 158–188. https://repository.law.miami.edu/umlr/vol12/iss2/3.

Surrey, Stanley. 1973. "Tax Policy and Tax Administration." In *Tax Policy and Tax Reform: 1961-1969/Selected Speeches and Testimony of Stanley S. Surrey*, edited by William Hellmuth and Ockleford Oldman. Chicago: Commerce Clearing House.

Tanzi, Vito. 1986. "Potential Income as a Tax Base in Theory and in Practice." *Hacienda Pública Española* 100. Madrid: Ministerio de Hacienda.

Tanzi, Vito, and Milka Casanegra de Jantscher. 1986. "The Use of Presumptive Income in Modern Income Tax Systems." In *Change in Revenue Structures: Proceedings of the 42nd Annual Congress of the International Institute of Public Finance*, Athens, Greece, 1986, edited by Also Chiancone and Kenneth Messere. Detroit, MI: Wayne State University Press.

Tanzi, Vito, and Milka Casanegra de Jantscher. 1987. "Presumptive Income Taxation: Administrative, Efficiency, and Equity Aspects." IMF Working Paper 1987/054, IMF, Washington, DC.

Taube, Günther, and Helaway Tadesse. 1996. "Presumptive Taxation in Sub-Saharan Africa: Experiences and Prospects." IMF Working Paper 96/5, IMF, Washington, DC.

Thirsk, Wayne. 1991. "Lessons from Tax Reform: An Overview." Policy, Research, and External Affairs Working Paper Series No. 576, World Bank, Washington, DC.

Thuronyi, Victor, ed. 1996. *Tax Law Design and Drafting, Vol. 1*. Washington, DC: IMF.

Thuronyi, Victor, ed. 1998. *Tax Law Design and Drafting, Vol. 2*. Washington, DC: IMF.

Thuronyi, Victor. 2000. "Presumptive Taxation." In *Tax Law Design and Drafting*, edited by Victor Thuronyi, 401–433. The Hague, Netherlands: Kluwer Law International.

Tideman, Nicolaus, ed. 1994. *Land and Taxation*. Georgist Paradigm Series. London: Shepheard-Walwyn Ltd.

Torgler, Benno. 2011. "Tax Morale and Compliance: Review of Evidence and Case Studies for Europe." Policy Research Working Paper WPS 5922, World Bank, Washington, DC.

Tulacek, Michal. 2019. "Legal Aspects of Tax Administration Electronisation." In *European Financial Law in Times of Crisis of the European Union*, edited by Gábor Hulkó and Roman Vybíral, 577–584. Budapest, Hungary: Dialóg Campus.

Ullastres-Calvo, Alberto. 1943. "La Renta Media como Criterio para la Imposición Fiscal" (Average Income as Tax Criterion). *Revista de Estudios Políticos, Suplemento de Información Económica* 3: 273–308.

USAID (United States Agency for International Development). 2013. *Detailed Guidelines for Improved Tax Administration in Latin America and the Caribbean*. USAID's Leadership in Public Financial Management. Washington, DC: USAID.

Valdés-Costa, R. 1996. *Curso de Derecho Tributario* (Course on Taxation Law). Depalma-Temis-Marcial Pons, Buenos Aires, Santa Fe de Bogotá: Brazil.

Vegh, Carlos, and Guillermo Vuletin. 2015. "How Is Tax Policy Conducted over the Business Cycle?" *American Economic Journal: Economic Policy* 7 (3): 327–370. https://doi.org/10.1257/pol.20120218.

Wadhawan, Satish, and Clive Gray. 1998. "Enhancing Transparency in Tax Administration: A Survey." *Journal of African Development* 4 (1): 65–101. https://econpapers.repec.org/RePEc:afe:journl:v:4:y:2001:i:1:p:65-101.

Wald, Haskell, and Joseph Froomkin, eds. 1954. "Papers and Proceedings of the Conference on Agricultural Taxation and Economic Development." International Program in Taxation, Harvard Law School, Cambridge, MA.

Wallace, Sally. 2002. "Imputed and Presumptive Taxes: International Experiences and Lessons for Russia." Working Paper 02–03, Andrew Young School of Policy Studies, International Studies Program, Georgia State University.

Warren, Alvin. 1980. "Would a Consumption Tax Be Fairer Than an Income Tax?" *The Yale Law Journal* 89 (6): 1081–1124. https://doi.org/10.2307/796024.

Wilkenfeld, Harold. 1973. *Taxes and People in Israel*. Cambridge, MA: Harvard University Press.

World Bank. 2017. *World Development Report 2017: Governance and the Law*. Washington, DC: World Bank.

World Bank Group. 2007. *Designing a Tax System for Micro and Small Businesses. Guide for Practitioners*. Washington, DC: International Finance Corporation. https://documents1.worldbank.org/curated/en/980291468158071984/pdf/424350TaxSystem01PUBLIC1.pdf.

Zodrow, George, and Charles McLure, Jr. 1991. "Implementing Direct Consumption Taxes in Developing Countries." Policy, Planning, and Research Working Paper WPS 131, World Bank, Washington, DC. https://documents1.worldbank.org/curated/en/231021468740958491/pdf/multi-page.pdf.

Zolt, Eric. 1996. "The Uneasy Case for Uniform Taxation." *Virginia Tax Review* 16 (1): 39–109.

Zolt, Eric, and Richard Bird. 2008. "Technology and Taxation in Developing Countries: From Hand to Mouse." *National Tax Journal* 61 (4): 791–821. https://www.journals.uchicago.edu/doi/abs/10.17310/ntj.2008.4S.02.

CHAPTER 2

Institutional setup and strategic planning of revenue administrations

Institutional arrangements

This chapter covers aspects of the overall institutional framework of revenue administrations, paying particular attention to institutional arrangements, degree of autonomy, responsibilities of the tax administration, and external oversight. Special emphasis is given to the extent to which the tax administration is granted autonomous or semiautonomous powers to administer the tax system. These responsibilities may range from the possibility of allocating or reallocating budget expenditures, establishing the tax administration's organizational structure, or managing human resource policies, to participating in tax policy design or having the responsibility for designing and developing strategic and business plans. This chapter analyzes institutional arrangements, organizational structure, strategic management, risk management, and performance management.

In discussing reform, it is vital to put current institutional arrangements into context by considering the influence of political and economic variables and public sector practices or traditions.

An important issue is whether or not customs and tax operations have been merged under a single revenue body and institutional arrangements are in place for the tax administration to collect social security contributions (SSCs). Merging tax and customs operations and integrating tax and social security contributions are not trendy, but many countries have adopted this approach with mixed results.

Later in this section, the outsourcing of specific functions of tax administration to external providers is briefly analyzed to show the pros and cons of this approach, and issues to take into consideration to obtain the full potential of these arrangements in case a tax administration opts for following this path. Nontax roles of tax administration would be highlighted, including valuation of properties, collection of nontax debts, and payment of social benefits.

Merging customs, tax administration, and SSC collection in a single revenue body

By including tax and customs operations within a single management structure, countries are merging two separate organizations. The rationale for the alignment of tax and customs operations lies behind a number of factors, which include similarity in tax functions of both administrations: synergies with customs that collect value added tax (VAT) on imports, perceived economies of scale by combining operational functions in revenue collection (e.g., human resources [HR] and information technology [IT] functions), lower taxpayer compliance costs, lower administrative costs, and the improvement of competitiveness of domestic firms. But the most important reason for merging tax and customs administration is the goal of enhancing effectiveness through integrated revenue collections and services, because such integration not only improves the government's ability to keep track of taxpayer information but also alleviates the compliance burden on business taxpayers (CIAT 2000).

In the case of SSCs, some countries have opted for integrating SSC activities into their revenue administrations. For example, Canada and the United States have always integrated SSCs with general revenue collections. Under this institutional arrangement, social security agencies keep their responsibilities in terms of administering benefits. The main motive for integrating the collection of SSCs with tax collections operations is the fact that revenue administrations and social security agencies share common core processes in the collection of tax and SSCs. The collection of SSCs would therefore benefit from the tax administration's core collection capacity and its compliance-based processes. This process of integrating SSCs into the revenue administration also leads to economies of scale and lower compliance and administrative costs (Barrand, Ross, and Harrison 2004).

Level of integration

As international experience shows, the degree of integration between customs and tax operations ranges from merely sharing a unified management structure and common support departments, such as in Colombia and Portugal, to an intense operational integration in core business processes, as in Brazil, the Netherlands, and Spain (CIAT 2000).

Deepening the integration process so as to achieve not only efficiency gains by sharing common resources but also enhanced operational capacity faces significant obstacles. The most important relates to the different nature and scope of tax and customs operations. First, customs plays a key role in collecting taxes such as tariffs, excises, and VAT on imports, and it also performs nonrevenue border services/nontax functions, including regulation of trade flows, trade facilitation, and environmental, health, and border security controls. This issue is highly dependent on the context and relevance of customs in a given country. For example, countries where the land and sea borders do not pose a significant challenge may view the border control role of customs as less important (CIAT, SII, and IMF 2022). Second, customs tax functions are inherently "real time," compared to tax administration operations, and much emphasis is put on physical controls and control of cross-border transactions.

It also has to be recognized that the approach to tax compliance controls in customs has evolved over time due to the role customs is playing in facilitating legitimate trade. Customs is increasingly moving away from physical controls to postrelease audits and tax audits at taxpayers' premises, which results in increased similarities with tax administration control procedures and processes. To reach the best decision about the degree of integration, special consideration should be given to the Canadian approach, according to which only tax functions are integrated, while nontax functions such as border control, protection, or security are attributed to a dedicated border security agency. This approach has been followed by other revenue administrations in the Czech Republic and the United Kingdom. Indeed, several Organisation for Economic Co-operation and Development (OECD) member countries, including Estonia, Hungary, and Spain, and non-OECD countries such as Bhutan and Saudi Arabia have aligned the tax and customs operations within a single agency.

Also, in Sub-Saharan Africa (i.e., Ghana, South Africa), many unified semiautonomous revenue bodies administer both tax and customs.

As for SSCs, due to the similarities between the collection of taxes and SSCs, it all mainly comes down to expanding systems used for the tax administration's collection function to include SSC collection (Junquera-Varela 2011). Complexities involved include compatibility of IT systems, the need for big information and communication technology (ICT) investments, assessment of current procedures and forms, compatibilities of registries, and HR policies.

The implementation process

Once a decision about the level of integration has been made, a carefully planned implementation process is of essence to avoid rolling back the integration effort—as happened in Colombia in the 1990s (Moller, Junquera-Varela, and Álvarez 2012). Achieving greater effectiveness or greater efficiency through integration invariably requires some level of modernization of revenue administration. If, at present, functions and institutions being considered for integration are not all modern, as defined in box 2.1, they should be modernized in the integration process (World Bank 2010).

Other key things to take into account include the different culture of the integrated organizations; timetable; steps of the process—in this regard, a step-by-step approach is suggested; internal and external communication to overcome entrenched interests; leadership; HR policies; and ICT solutions (Verhorn and Brondolo 1999). Recent experiences regarding merging of tax and customs administrations also call for putting both organizations on an equal footing before initiating the process to ensure the success of the initiative. This can be done by making sure that both organizations have comparable IT and HR capabilities, that their work cultures are aligned, and that their work processes are compatible and can be integrated.

The same considerations apply to integration of collection of SSCs, albeit to a lesser extent in many cases. Key priorities in this process are ICT solutions and the need to implement new HR policies to ensure a smooth integration of personnel. In effect, an issue that affects both processes is the need to establish a new HR framework to facilitate integration of personnel from other organizations and usually with different organizational and work culture and skills. This factor has

---

BOX 2.1   Key features of a modernized revenue agency

A modernized revenue agency has at least the following features:

- A modern organizational structure that is function based and not territorial

- A performance-based management system

- Segmentation by type of revenue payers

- A high level of specialization for each of the key functions

- Fully automated business processes

- A single national identification number

- A risk-based compliance and enforcement program

- A one-stop service "window," mostly via the use of call centers, for every client

- An integrated IT system

- The capacity for speedy coordination among government agencies

- Skilled and professional staff acting with fairness, honesty, and transparency

Source: World Bank 2010.

proved to be very relevant in many of the cases studied. Integrating IT systems and reengineering business processes also pose significant challenges.

Revenue authorities or semiautonomous bodies

The rationale behind the establishment of semiautonomous revenue bodies points to less political interference to conduct their operations, more responsibility and accountability for managers to achieve their objectives, and more management capacity, especially in terms of budgeting decisions and HR policies. These governance structures allow tax administrations freedom from rigid bureaucratic structures and to apply private sector management principles (Kidd and Crandall 2006). The autonomy granted to the revenue bodies must be balanced against a high degree of accountability for the outcomes. It should be stressed that this autonomy does not mean that these semiautonomous bodies are independent from the government and cease to be part of the public sector. On the contrary, external control and oversight on the part of the minister of finance and external audit bodies have to be strengthened.

One cannot pretend that establishing a revenue authority or a semiautonomous revenue body will translate in the short or medium term into increased revenues and improved operational capacity of the tax administration. Its establishment needs to be complemented with improvements in core business processes, organizational reforms, and investment in ICT. Political commitment and willingness to implement the necessary changes are also of the essence in view of the fact that comprehensive tax administration reforms are complex and could take much time to mature and yield outcomes (Junquera-Varela et al. 2019). Many countries that have established this governance model view it as a catalyst for tax reform and improved performance. They signal that there is a strong perception held by those countries that have adopted the revenue authority concept that this particular governance model has made a significant contribution to reform and improved performance.

Outsourcing

In some cases, tax administrations outsource some of their functions to external providers. The reasons for doing this include better controlling costs and benefits, developing new processes at lesser costs, facilitating access to new IT and new methodologies in a cost-effective way, and mitigating the lack of expertise or personnel in specific areas. Outsourcing also enables responding better to significant increases in taxpayers' demands during certain periods of the year due to seasonality of certain activities of the tax administration, provides access to external experience and knowhow in core business processes, facilitates standardizing procedures to gain efficiency and service delivery, increases productivity, and encourages acquisition, deployment, and sharing of new technologies and resources.

Some caveats apply when it comes to assessing whether or not it would be convenient or efficient for an organization to outsource some of its areas of business or functions. This is especially important in the case of tax administrations because of the vital role these organizations play in collecting necessary revenues to fund public services. In this regard, there is a broad consensus (Junquera-Varela et al. 2019) that strategic functions of core business processes of the tax administration, such as taxpayer registration, tax audit, and revenue arrears management, should never be outsourced. The same applies to strategic or vital information for administering the tax system. As a result, outsourcing by the tax administration should be confined to supporting functions such as IT systems or specific arrangements regarding the provision of services to taxpayers, such as data-processing centers and call centers (Castro et al. 2009). Receipt of tax payments by banks can also be considered an outsourcing arrangement or a sort of privatization of a tax administration function.

Obtaining the full potential of outsourcing requires paying special attention to the following issues:

- The tax administration needs to clearly define the intended goals and expected benefits from the planned outsourcing arrangements. Prioritization is the key.
- Outsourced companies should not have access to vital information such as tax returns, asset declaration forms, transaction activity information, and invoice lists to administer the tax system.
- The contract should include a sound contractual framework governing relationships between the outsourcer and the tax administration. The contractual framework should specify inter alia the duration of the outsourcing contract, minimum service levels and standards—including confidentiality agreements—that the contractor has to comply with and penalties in case it does not meet these minimum standards; a series of milestones covering goals to achieve over the entire life of the contract; mechanisms to allow the tax administration to regularly monitor compliance with services levels and established goals; and a light organizational structure to control the contracted company.
- Due to rapid changes in technology and business context, contracts need to be flexible to adapt to changes in the operating environment.
- All contracts should foresee how to transition from outsourcing to in-house arrangements when the contract terminates. Particularly, all contracts should provide for transfer of relevant knowhow to the tax administration to ensure continuity of business processes.

Nontax functions of revenue administrations

In some countries, revenue administrations have the responsibility for managing nontax functions, which are mostly welfare-related functions, such as the payment of social welfare benefits or the administration of retirement policies. In some cases, these nontax functions deal with collecting nontax debts or administering taxes from property valuation.

Organizational structure

Organizational structures of tax administration can be mainly based on three main criteria: type of taxes collected, functions performed, and segments of taxpayers; in addition, a hybrid model is possible. Over the past decades, tax administrations have evolved from a type-of-tax model to a functional model, which is dominant nowadays (Junquera-Varela et al. 2019). The taxpayer segment model, which has been established by a number of advanced tax administrations, organizes taxpayer services and enforcement activities principally around segments of taxpayers—for example, large businesses, small and medium taxpayers, individuals—with a view to better tailoring tax administration processes to their characteristics.

Another approach is the process-oriented tax administration, where dedicated process-oriented centers are established to deal with massive processes that apply to all taxpayers, such as tax return processing, primary checks to all tax returns, and basic information services. Other processes target different taxpayer segments and are tailored to their specific characteristics (Junquera-Varela et al. 2013). The latter include taxpayer assistance and information, control of compliance, and revenue arrears management.

In practice, organizational structures of most tax administrations are a mix of the different features and characteristics of models available, which is called the "hybrid" model. In this regard, while practically all tax administrations' organizational structures are based on the functional model, the majority of them have established a large taxpayer unit (LTU). Some forms of the type-of-tax oriented tax administration have also survived in many of them. For example, in some countries, customs administer excise taxes even after they have been merged with the tax administration's operations.

Taxpayer segmentation: Large taxpayer units

The creation of specialized LTUs is mostly motivated by efficiency reasons, rather than by organizational needs. It is established that large taxpayers, though relatively low in number, still contribute the majority of tax revenue collections. From an efficiency perspective, this supports calls for a dedicated tax administration system, especially as regards certain functions that are specific to the features of this taxpayer segment.

Criteria to guide selection into the segment of large taxpayers may include taxes actually paid, turnover, physical assets, consolidated group, or staff employed by the company; normally, the allocation of taxpayers to this segment is based on a combination of different criteria paying special attention to turnover. Increased focus on the large taxpayer segment has become a key characteristic of modern tax administration given (a) their importance from a revenue perspective—on average, large taxpayers can secure 60 to 80 percent of domestic taxes and even more in island economies; (b) their engagement in large-scale, complex, specialized, and often international operations; (c) associated high revenue compliance risks; and (d) their role as a significant source of third-party information and tax withholding. The importance of tightening control over this segment derives not only from the amount of revenue that is collected, directly and indirectly, through withholding arrangements but also from the significant amount of third-party information that it receives and transmits to the tax administration (IMF 2002). This information provides the foundation for the compliance risk management system on which all tax audit strategy should be based.

All these considerations have greatly contributed to the spread of LTUs in many developed and developing countries. Traditionally, LTUs had been conceived as full-fledged offices, which encompassed all relevant core business processes of tax administration such as data processing and taxpayer assistance, tax collection, tax audit, legal services, and tax debt management. However, in recent years, due to technological improvements, certain tax functions, including taxpayer assistance, tax collection, and simple tax debt management, have been standardized across taxpayer segments, and there is no need to replicate their management systems throughout specialized units. This trend is not based so much on organizational reasons but instead on efficiency considerations, because in the case of LTUs, those standardized functions can be managed like those of other taxpayer segments.

On the other hand, LTUs should still retain certain dedicated functions, such as specialized tax audit tailored to the characteristics and schemes used by large taxpayers, complex tax debt management, specific risk assessment criteria and mechanisms, and any other tax services that require a special approach given the nature of the activity of the large taxpayer segment. The remaining functions would be covered by the general tax administration units. Hence, the tax administration adopts a functional model that benefits all segments of taxpayers, and specialized units focus only on auditing and a few other tasks that are specific to each taxpayer segment. Any other option could become very complex and burdensome, and extremely inefficient in terms of resource allocation. It is highly discouraged to replicate all tax functions for each type of taxpayer segment and within each specialized unit. The main objective is to achieve synergies in all those functions that can be managed jointly.

While tax administration may benefit from adopting taxpayer segmentation, such a strategy should neither cover nor replicate all functions; otherwise, the organization would shift de facto from a functional model to a taxpayer-type-based model, which is not efficient. It is acceptable, as mentioned already, to incorporate within certain units some specialized functions, but not all of them, since it creates serious risks of duplicities and also disconnects between different departments and units conducting the same functions within the organization. The tax audit and complex tax debt management functions may require such specialization given the special features of large taxpayers, but most importantly to control tax revenue collection.

LTUs need a stronger knowledge and skills base to handle this segment and adequate IT equipment. The characteristics of this segment, which covers companies and taxpayers with very complex tax issues, may even involve international taxation and call for a significant degree of specialization of staff and business processes. In this regard, industry/sectoral specialization should be strongly promoted with a view to improving audit effectiveness (Hashim 2014). In particular, it is recommended to establish dedicated units within the LTUs to deal with international taxation issues, natural resource taxation, or the financial sector. Peculiar difficulties arise when there is a group of companies consisting of a parent company and a series of affiliates or subsidiaries normally operating in different countries. These may be transfer pricing issues, hybrid mismatches, abusive tax avoidance schemes, intragroup services and lending operations that erode the tax base, and artificial avoidance of permanent establishment status. Control of consolidated groups is therefore crucial for managing this segment to avoid fragmentation of companies resulting in many companies being subject to a lesser degree of control.

A common practice in many countries going through a major tax administration reform is to pilot key processes and organizational changes in these units before later implementing these improvements in other areas and segments of tax administration. For example, some countries have extended their LTU approach to establish medium taxpayer units (MTUs) to deal with medium-sized enterprises and small taxpayer units (STUs) to deal with micro and small taxpayers (Bird and Casanegra de Jantscher 1992). However, this approach must be highly discouraged because it creates complex matrix-type organizational structures where functions and taxpayer segments are intertwined, which hinders coordination while lacking the efficiency rationale that justifies LTUs. In other words, taxpayer segmentation should be limited to LTUs for efficiency reasons, but it should not be adopted as a tax administration–wide strategy for small or medium taxpayer segments, since their tax functions do not usually require any special treatment. Yet this approach does not undermine the need in certain cases for simplified regimes for some taxpayer segments—for example, micro and small taxpayers—whose administration can be managed by the general functional organization without duplicating resources or increasing complexity (Bird 2013).

A set of minimum requirements needs to be fulfilled so LTUs can work properly for expected benefits to materialize (IMF 2002):

- A sound legal framework
- Application of clear and simple criteria for identifying large taxpayers, which vary from country to country
- Standard and transparent procedures
- The administration of all large taxpayers by the LTU
- The administration of all national-level domestic taxes by the LTU
- LTU performance of all core tax administration functions
- Clear reporting lines between the LTU and the headquarters (HQ) office

- Appropriate job grading and remuneration of LTU staff
- Effective LTU staff training
- Identification and regular compilation of key performance indicators

Most observers have found LTUs in developing countries to be useful. However, a review of LTUs' experiences conducted by the International Monetary Fund (IMF) found that while they improved tax collections, there was only mixed success in generating positive spillovers to other areas of tax administration. Despite significant benefits from adopting a strong LTU strategy of administrative organizational reform, it may produce unintended consequences in the absence of significant efforts to improve the tax compliance of small and medium-size businesses.

Box 2.2 summarizes some aspects and relevant issues, including taxpayer segmentation, that strongly influence tax administration (Junquera-Varela 2011) and should be examined in the course of a tax administration diagnosis to assess the organizational structure.

BOX 2.2 Assessment of aspects and issues of organizational structure, including taxpayer segmentation, that influence tax administration

1. *Criteria used to organize tax administration.* "Type of tax," "functional," or "taxpayer segment."

2. *Tax administration's organizational structure, including number and location of autonomous and regional-level offices.* Does the organizational structure of the tax administration provide for the decentralization of responsibilities and sufficient flexibility, so that decisions concerning the taxpayers are made at the most appropriate level?

3. *Management of reform process.* If the tax administration is going through a tax administration modernization process, how is the reform process being managed, and is there a change management team or a project implementation unit?

4. *Organization of field offices.* Have the roles and responsibilities of each function and of employees working at all levels within each function been clearly defined?

5. *Mechanisms in place to ensure coordination within and between organizational units in both HQ and regional/local offices, as well as between HQ and regional/local offices.*

6. *Organizational chart of the tax audit function at HQ and at regional/local levels.* Indicate human resources devoted to audit function as a percentage of total staff resources, and distinguish between those who actually conduct tax audits and those who provide support to audit activities (in relative terms). Specify responsibilities of HQ and territorial offices.

7. *Organizational chart of the debt collection function at HQ and at regional and local levels.* Specify responsibilities of HQ and territorial offices and indicate the human resources devoted to this function as a percentage of total staff resources.

8. *Organizational chart of the taxpayer assistance function at HQ and at regional and local levels.* Specify responsibilities of HQ and territorial offices and indicate the human resources devoted to this function as a percentage of total staff resources.

9. *Workload of different offices.* Assess according to agreed criteria. This can be relevant information for managers when undertaking major changes in the organizational structure or when developing the strategic and business plans of the revenue body.

10. *Does a LTU exist?* If so, describe its mandate, the scope of its activities, organizational structure, and criteria to assign taxpayers to this unit.

11. *Number and location of LTUs, staff assigned, and budget.*

12. *Establishment of LTU, MTU, and STU, and main criteria used to assign taxpayers to each segment.*

13. *Legal provision for the segment of small taxpayers and control strategy in place, IT equipment, and functions covered by LTUs or MTUs.*

14. *"Field intelligence."* Develop knowledge for each group of taxpayers, particularly for hard-to-tax sectors—for example, understanding the nature and main characteristics of the taxpayer population, key sectors in which they are operating, identifying key compliance risks and how they arise—from weak laws and regulations, administrative capacities, and so on. It is important to determine how much revenue in percentages is collected by the LTU.

15. *International taxation issues.* Is there any dedicated unit to deal with such issues included in the organizational structure of the LTU?

16. *Taxation of natural resources.* Is there any dedicated unit to deal with this included in the organizational structure of the LTU?

Note: HQ = headquarter; IT = information technology; LTU = large taxpayer unit; MTU = medium taxpayer unit; STU = small taxpayer unit.

Decentralization: subnational government level and local taxes

The creation of a semiautonomous agency at the subnational level should be considered a medium-term objective of the tax reform agenda. The rationale behind the establishment of semiautonomous revenue bodies points to less political interference in conducting their operations, more responsibility and accountability for managers to achieve their objectives, and more management capacity, especially in terms of budgeting decisions and HR policies. In this context, box 2.3 differentiates between the issue of administration and the revenue assignment issue.

Some policy options may involve operating subnational-level taxes on an agency basis, for example, piggybacked options for the personal income tax and surcharges on excises. By doing this, subnational governments would have a strong incentive to expand the bases of these taxes and improve availability of information to control them. This would also improve the exchange of information between national and subnational authorities (Bird 2013). The suggested approach to improve overall efficiency levels through a relative centralization of tax administration vis-à-vis assignment of tax powers at different levels of government may raise concerns about rooted federalism at the outset.

Piggybacking on the federal personal income tax has the potential of providing subnational (state) governments with a stable and elastic source of revenue collected by the federal tax authority under substantial economies of scale. Taxpayers are required to file a unified (federal and state) tax return and calculate the state tax as a percentage of their federal tax base. In addition, each state would have the authority to set its own tax rate within an agreed range of values. For budgeting purposes, the federal government could project an annual amount to states based on the previous year's collection and thereafter provide a final reconciliation after all tax returns have been received. State tax administrations would enforce compliance following annual audit plans with the collaboration of federal tax authorities and other state governments. Importantly, this proposal would endow state governments with a critical mass of taxpayer registrations with lots of potential applicability to enforce compliance regarding other sources of revenue such as wage taxes through cross-verification of transactions.

To maintain the accountability principle of the fiscal federalism framework prevailing in some jurisdictions, subnational governments should be responsible for setting tax rates to harmonized subnational tax bases. What matters for accountability is not so much who receives the bulk of the

---

BOX 2.3   Administering local taxes

The key characteristic of a "local" tax, in terms of accountability, is that the local (or regional) government should be politically responsible for the tax imposed. That usually requires that the local government be able, perhaps within limits, to set the tax rate. However, neither this nor any other assignment principle requires that local taxes be administered by the local government.

Thus, the issue of administration can be considered apart from the revenue assignment issue. Many different ways of organizing subnational tax administration exist in different countries. In the United States, at one extreme, each local government may be responsible for administering its own taxes. At the other extreme, there may be only one tax authority responsible for administering

the taxes at all levels of government. Although no country appears to go quite that far, Canada has moved a long way down this path with respect to provincial taxes, and countries such as Denmark have both an integrated information system and strong operational synergies between levels of government. In some cases, the "national" tax authority may be directed by a board that includes significant representation from subnational governments. There are countries in which subnational governments may even be responsible for much of the administrative work involved in administering some national taxes. In others (often regarding the property tax, for example), one level of government may establish the tax base (the cadastre) while another level (or levels) sets rates, and both collect and enforce the tax.

Source: Bird 2010.

revenues or who administers the tax but who bears the political responsibility for it, and the simplest and clearest evidence of accountability in this sense is who determines the tax rate (Junquera-Varela et al. 2019). For example, a surcharge on a federal tax is a subnational tax even though it is imposed on a federal tax base and collected by a federal authority. This option provides a powerful incentive for subnational governments to provide information to federal authorities to expand the tax base.

Additionally, a unique taxpayer identification number at a national level, together with a unified taxpayer registry and a single taxpayer account, are essential elements of improving tax administration. This should be a central plank of a strategy aimed at better exploiting information for control of compliance. Other initiatives, such as creating a semiautonomous agency at the subnational level or an independent cadastre at the subnational level, would also be instrumental in unifying administration of taxes and centralizing processes and information (De Cesare 2012). The process of creating a unique identification number for taxpayers should start by unifying identification numbers both at federal and subnational levels. This identification number should be mandatory for all tax-related transactions, which would be instrumental in improving reliability and accuracy of information.

Furthermore, harmonizing the federal and subnational tax bases is an important element in facilitating tax compliance and achieving efficiency gains in revenue collection. Some countries, such as Canada and the United States, have opted for integrating SSCs into their revenue administrations, while the social security agencies keep their responsibilities in terms of administering benefits. This is because revenue administrations and social security agencies share common core processes in the collection of tax and SSCs. The collection of SSCs would then benefit from the tax administration's core collection capacity and its compliance-based processes (Barrand, Ross, and Harrison 2004). This process of integrating SSCs into the revenue authority also leads to economies of scale and lower compliance and administrative costs. But a key step is the harmonization of the tax bases.

Regarding management of the arrangement, the inclusion of representatives from subnational authorities on the board of directors of the federal tax administration can provide the needed institutional bridge to strength collaboration and coordination for the administration of a state's sources of revenue on an agency basis. From an efficiency perspective, federal authorities could further exploit the economies of scale to administer the collection of state-level revenues—mainly but not exclusively the personal income tax piggybacked surcharge—on behalf of and/or in collaboration with the state governments. At the same time, the integration of the federal board of directors could provide the executive institutional arrangement for state governments to ensure the quality and reliability of collection figures and distribution among states, as well as to influence core strategic decisions within the federal government—audit plans—with particular relevance for the administration of subnational tax sources (Farvacque-Vitkovic and Kopanyi 2014).

A similar interinstitutional arrangement could be established between state and municipal governments for an agency model to undertake the collection of municipal revenue sources, with the collaboration of the federal government. This approach could pave the way to strengthen the fiscal collaboration between both levels of government to enhance the administration of municipal tax sources, especially property tax and other local taxes.

Efficiently administering a tax system is primarily about information management. A change in the tax structure that aims at closing loopholes in major taxes and facilitating administration of the tax system will increase availability of information, reduce its current fragmentation that results in proliferation of information silos, and increase information flows among local, regional, and national authorities (IFC, World Bank, and MIGA 2011). It is therefore crucial that both subnational and national agencies make the necessary investments in IT infrastructure and human capital to fully exploit the additional information (box 2.4).

BOX 2.4   Efficient information management in tax administration at national and subnational levels

Efficient information management in tax administration requires an integrated database that incorporates all taxpayer-related transactions administered by the revenue agency. This results in the need for a single taxpayer account that registers and manages the agency's transactions with each taxpayer. Complexities involved in this task include the following: (a) establish a unified taxpayer register for taxpayers subject to all taxes; (b) for the subnational level, especially when it comes to the property tax, connect the unique Tax Identification Number to property owners, thereby linking taxpayers subject to the property tax with their properties; and (c) design and implement an accounting system that will support the registration of these transactions (Rozner 2009).

It is then vital to integrate taxpayers' account information, taxes, and collection data into a unified database. This will allow the tax administration to establish a single taxpayer account that is automatically updated by incorporating the impact of administrative decisions, such as assessments, penalties, appeals, and refunds, on a taxpayer's liabilities. The single taxpayer account will contribute to improving taxpayer services

and to the accuracy of tax assessment. Moreover, it will facilitate effective risk management.

In the case of subnational tax administrations, managing efficiently the property tax database is highly dependent on the quality of data of other registries and databases, particularly the property registry. Therefore, special emphasis is put on strengthening linkages between the cadastre and the property registry. A significant challenge for subnational tax administration is the weak connection between the cadastre and the property registry, with the effect that a substantial portion of the properties registered in the cadastre lack up-to-date ownership information (Bahl and Martínez-Vázquez 2007). Another challenge is that often only a small percentage of taxpayers registered in the property tax registry have their properties correctly assigned to them (Bahl 2009). This results in unreliable information and additional administration costs. To address these issues, it is crucial to define the kind of taxpayer information to be included in the taxpayer registry and to promote information exchange and data synchronization with other external institutions such as the federal tax administration, civil registry, and property registry.

Strategic management

To achieve the mission of maximizing voluntary compliance, tax administration agencies need a strategic planning process. This process will set the course for improved operational performance and will facilitate adequate allocation of the tax administration agency's scarce resources to the areas that pose greater compliance risks. This process covers all core business activities of tax administration and takes into account the context and environment in which the tax administration operates and internal factors, with a view to achieving tax administration objectives.

Advanced tax administrations use risk management approaches to select their long-term objectives, which in turn would allow tax administration agencies to better anticipate risks and achieve greater effectiveness in compliance control (CIAT, SII, and IMF 2022). These goals permeate throughout the entire organization to ensure staff engagement in a tax administration agency's overarching objectives. They are also communicated to civil society and relevant stakeholders, and channels of communication are established to ensure their active involvement. A management information system (MIS) monitors performance of the tax administration agency and the degree of its compliance with objectives. Implementing this entire system is labeled as a strategic management process.

Strategic plans play an important role in a changing environment since they provide tax administrators with the necessary tools to rapidly react to threats and opportunities. In this context, this process ensures that the tax administration agency's mission and its strategic objectives will be implemented in a coherent and systematic way. It also ensures that tax administration business processes address key institutional priorities in a context of efficient allocation of resources (European Commission 2006).

These plans typically span several years and are complemented with annual business plans that implement the key principles and objectives set in the strategic plan in a systematic way. Within this framework, strategic objectives aim at achieving specific results, which translate into measurable

47

outputs and outcomes. Performance measurement involves qualitative and quantitative indicators that will provide managers with information about the timeliness, effectiveness, and efficiency of tax administration in delivering on its mandate (Brondolo et al. 2022). The result of this process will be a vital input for the strategic planning process and will facilitate further refining and improvement of the strategic plan and associated business plans.

As the OECD indicates, all modern tax administration agencies have developed a strategic management system to (a) assist them to manage emerging organizational risks, (b) ensure that they continuously improve their performance, and (c) implement multiyear developments effectively and without being overtaken by immediate imperatives. While strategic management differs among organizations, certain themes are common to most approaches (OECD 2004).

The key steps, which generally comprise a complete strategic management system, may be summarized as follows (Spencer and Spencer 1993):

- Develop foundation statements such as mission, vision, and value statements
- Conduct environmental analysis
- State broad strategies
- Develop action plans and projects
- Monitor and analyze performance against plan
- Establish feedback mechanisms

The strategic cycle is very similar in most countries. It usually encompasses the following stages: establish mission, values, vision, and principles; put in place strategic objectives or strategic goals; evaluate strategies; set up priorities and allocate resources; plan activities; and execute programs. There are two feedback mechanisms: program evaluation and submission of implementation reports, and monitoring of the programs (Whyte 2022).

Box 2.5 summarizes some relevant aspects of the strategic management process that influence tax administration, which should be examined in the course of a tax administration diagnosis.

BOX 2.5   Assessment of strategic management issues that influence tax administration

1. Does the tax administration have a multiyear strategic plan and associated business plans? If yes, provide the last strategic plan as well as the last business plan.

2. Provide a summary of key elements of a tax administration's strategic plan in terms of context, mission, vision, and values; key focus areas or strategic objectives; and corresponding performance indicators to measure achievement of goals.

3. Are these plans made public and accessible?

4. How is the tax administration's vision and mission reflected in day-to-day functioning and modernization plans?

5. Describe the key elements of the strategic cycle and the stages that it encompasses.

6. What are the strategic objectives or key goals that the tax administration must meet as outlined in the strategic plan?

7. Is there any mechanism in place for stakeholders to have a say in setting the objectives of the tax administration and evaluating its performance?

8. Does the tax administration regularly conduct surveys to get taxpayers' views on effectiveness, efficiency, and fairness in administering the tax system?

9. Do the results of these surveys feed into the strategic plans of the tax administration?

10. Are there performance indicators to measure achievement of objectives?

11. Is there a proper reporting or management information system (MIS) to ensure delivery of performance reports to the management?

12. In case an MIS exists, is it fully automated, or at least is manual input kept to a minimum?

13. Does the tax administration issue an annual report on its performance? Provide the most recent annual report, if available.

14. Are there any mechanisms in place for getting feedback from interested parties? How are they compiled and taken into consideration, particularly by management and the relevant departments?

Risk management

Revenue administrations face numerous risks that have the potential to adversely affect revenue and tax and customs administration operations. These can be classified as compliance risks and institutional risks. Risk management is essential to effective revenue administration, and it involves a structured approach to identifying, assessing, prioritizing, and mitigating risks. It is an integral part of multiyear strategic and annual operational planning.

Institutional risk

Institutional risks refer to where tax administration functions may be interrupted if certain external or internal events occur, such as natural disasters, sabotage, loss or destruction of physical assets, failure of IT system hardware or software, or strike action by employees. Another problem issue is administrative breaches—leakage of confidential taxpayer information that results in loss of community confidence and trust in the tax administration.

Good practices in institutional risk management include the following (TADAT Secretariat 2015):

- Having a risk register—a central repository of identified institutional risks that potentially pose a threat to the continuity of tax administration operations. Risk registers vary from organization to organization but typically include, as a minimum, the following information: short description of the risk, date identified, likelihood of occurrence, severity of effect, mitigation measures, name of risk owner, the person responsible for ensuring that risk is addressed, and risk status.
- Having a plan for continuity of tax administration operations in the event of a disaster that destroys part or all of the administration's assets and resources, including HR, buildings, IT and other equipment, data, and other records. Plans of this kind, commonly referred to as *business continuity plans* or *disaster recovery plans*, typically:

  ° Assess the likelihood and consequences of natural disasters (e.g., flood, fire, and earthquake) and humanmade events—sabotage, theft, civil unrest, and internal fraud.
  ° Outline steps to be taken in the event of disaster to maintain revenue collections, provide taxpayer services, ensure safety of staff, and preserve confidentiality of taxpayer records.

- Training staff in disaster recovery procedures—for example, through disaster simulation exercises.
- Taking preventive measures such as offsite backup of data and implementing internal controls to protect tax administration systems from fraud and error.
- Having effective internal and external oversight to detect and deter unwanted events.

Also, regarding customs, the implementation of comprehensive risk management should include the identification, analysis, and treatment of key institutional risks, which have a direct or indirect impact on the ability of customs to manage compliance risks (CIAT, SII, and IMF 2022).

A proper diagnostic should analyze the control processes before, during, and after dispatch under the following six key elements: (a) the regulatory framework, (b) the processes, (c) the information, (d) the infrastructure, (e) the computer and telecommunications systems, and (f) human capital. Based on this classification, the following are the main recommendations for institutional risk management in customs (CIAT, SII, and IMF 2022):

(a) Regulatory framework:

- Ensure clarity and complementarity between the competencies and functions performed by different departments and areas related to risk management

- Have legal initiatives to strengthen powers and improve the sanctioning framework
- Have legal powers for obtaining electronic information from various government entities

(b) Processes:
- Foster continuous improvement culture to keep processes up to date
- Conduct risk analysis during prior control, and follow a systematic process
- Update handbooks and operational guidelines
- Introduce processes to analyze data quality
- Adopt processes to address risks related to export operations—particularly those arising from simulation exercises—by extraction or overassessment of goods
- Follow a structured process for the analysis of selectivity criteria or rules

(c) Information:
- Improve the quality of information received from the tax administration, so as to perform timely electronic validations and mass data analysis
- Enable the means to receive information from other government departments, such as trade, economic development, health, and agriculture, in electronic form to facilitate risk management

(d) Infrastructure:
- Improve the infrastructure at most international borders to implement effective controls and facilitate legal trade
- Provide border infrastructure and clarity on how to handle operational, maintenance, and improvement costs
- Provide sea and air entry facilities with scales in optimal condition
- Implement use of nonintrusive screening equipment, linked to customs computer systems and a risk management strategy
- Install adequate laboratory material and equipment for sample collection and analysis

(e) Computer systems and telecommunications:
- Expand the scope of the risk module beyond mere control during dispatch, and improve the analysis and update of selectivity criteria
- Reconcile manifests, bills of lading, and customs returns
- Program the risk module used during the dispatch of goods to provide for automatic generation of a risk indicator, information on actions to be taken, and feedback
- Ensure that the information provided by computer systems to customs officials is sufficient and timely

(f) Human capital:
- Ensure adequate staffing through recruitment plans aligned with the strategic management process
- Create an administrative career path that allows for stability and continuous staff development
- Strengthen basic technical skills (classification, origin, and assessment) and those relating to personnel management
- Establish a customs school for the continuing education of staff
- Fully implement training plans that correspond to the strategic objectives of the customs administration

Compliance risk management

Taxes are a critical domestic revenue source that provides governments with the funds needed to support social development and inclusive growth. Tax administration leaders implement compliance risk management (CRM) to ensure optimization of revenue collections by improving taxpayer compliance across the four basic tax obligations: registration, timely filing, timely payment, and correct reporting (Whyte 2022). It is a methodology used to systematically identify compliance risks within the taxpayer population and determine how to mitigate and treat them in the most effective and efficient way.

The importance and relevance of adopting a holistic approach to CRM must be highlighted, driven by a compliance improvement plan (CIP), which spans the full cycle of a taxpayer–revenue administration interaction, from registration to appeals. This approach is reflected in the IMF CRM framework (Brondolo et al. 2022), which illustrates how CRM affects virtually every part of tax administration and how the results from the CRM process drive the operational workloads of the administration. It is based on international risk management good practice and the OECD CRM process (OECD 2004). The CRM framework has two dimensions: the horizontal dimension shows the necessary inputs to, and the resulting outputs from, the CRM, and the vertical dimension shows the governance, CRM processes, planning, and performance evaluation, as shown in figure 2.1.

FIGURE 2.1   CRM framework

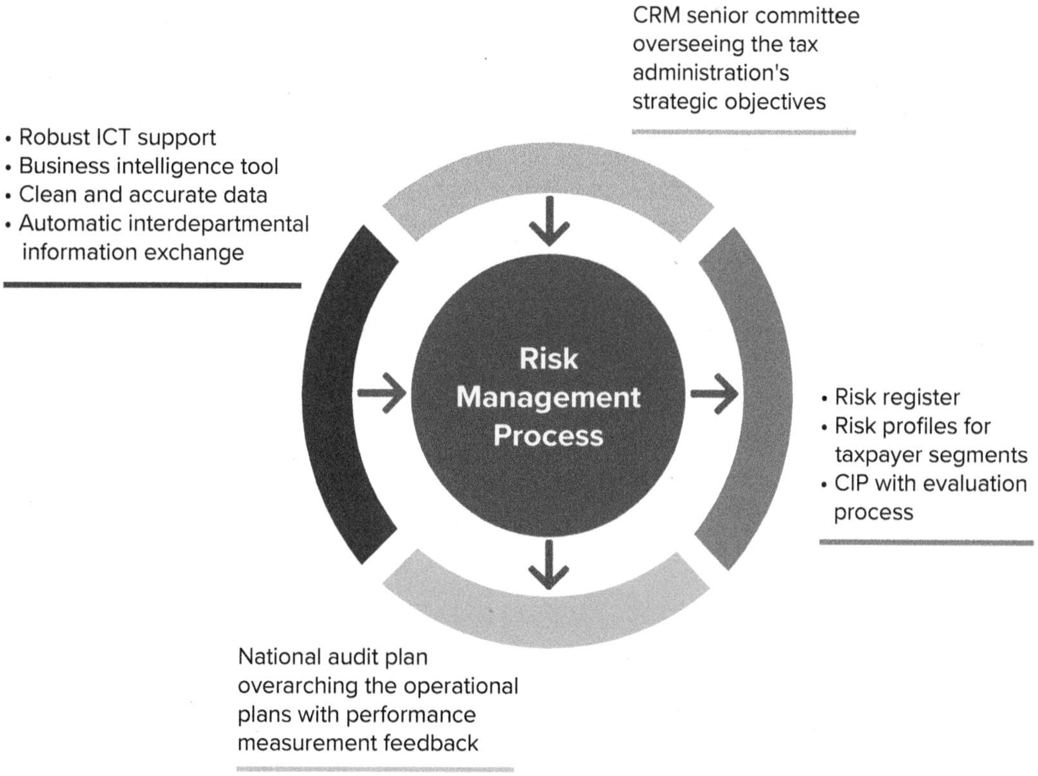

Source: Original figure for this publication.
Note: CIP = compliance improvement plan; CRM = compliance risk management; ICT = information and communication technology.

Central to the risk management process is the operational context, which can be defined as the "environments" in which the tax administration operates. A wide variety of environmental and organizational factors have to be considered. Context can be viewed as the playing field together with the rules of the game. This is the framework that risk management is applied within. The objectives describe the purpose of the game and what to achieve. The strategy describes how to play the game to reach the objectives. Within this framework, risk management is used to decide what to do to reach the objectives. There are any number of external and internal contexts in which the administration works; some are economic, some are at governmental level, and others are at national and regional levels (Brondolo et al. 2022).

Regarding the holistic view of CRM, taxpayer registration is key to effective management of compliance risks. To this end, the revenue body needs to analyze and develop knowledge for each group of taxpayers—main characteristics, key sectors of economy, type of risks, and needs. Also, good taxpayer services play a key role in the CRM process that aims at minimizing the tax gap (prevention measures).

Taxpayer services are an important element in preventing noncompliance risks and may have a significant impact on compliance trends (Betts 2022). Facilitating compliance therefore requires improving both the efficiency and quality of taxpayer services. The importance of the link between better tax services and tax compliance is widely accepted among tax experts and is a regular feature of tax reform programs. Aiming at fostering this linkage, as emphasized by the *OECD Model on Compliance Risk Management* and the more recent EU *Compliance Risk Management Capability Maturity Model*, many revenue bodies have developed taxpayers' service strategies. The EU model enables tax administrations to assess and understand their current CRM capability maturity levels, define what level they want to achieve, identify the gaps, set objectives, and identify and prioritize actions for key improvements, all with the aim of increasing taxpayer compliance and preventing noncompliance (European Commission 2021). Figure 2.2 shows what is involved in performing an effective CRM.

In addition to providing taxpayers with services to help them comply with the tax law, tax administrations have to put in place strategies to respond to taxpayers' noncompliance schemes. While recognizing that promoting voluntary compliance is the most cost-effective way of collecting tax revenues, tax administrations have to tackle levels of noncompliance to ensure that they are kept to a minimum level. Triggering control of compliance mechanisms is very costly, and that is why advanced tax administrations adopt a risk management approach to direct resources to taxpayers posing a higher risk to revenue (Barber 2021).

In this scenario, it is vital to understand taxpayer attitudes with a view to better identifying underlying factors of noncompliance. In effect, in some cases, compliance strategies will focus on prevention, on assisting taxpayers to comply with tax laws. In other cases, and depending on attitudes to compliance, the tax administration will prioritize "soft" forms of control aimed at deterring noncompliance and thereby promoting voluntary compliance. Only in the most severe cases will deployment of the complete set of enforcement powers available to tax administrations be the most appropriate choice. As a result, compliance strategies are implemented in the most cost-efficient way.

Likewise, audit strategies need to be developed within a context of the CRM process, which, as seen, is a structural process for the systematic identification, assessment, ranking, and treatment of tax compliance risks (Barber 2021). On the one hand, the tax administration should be seeking to maximize the number of taxpayers who choose to voluntarily comply through taxpayer assistance and education programs. On the other hand, it must have effective enforcement-related strategies to deter, detect, and address noncompliance.

FIGURE 2.2   Setting an effective CRM model

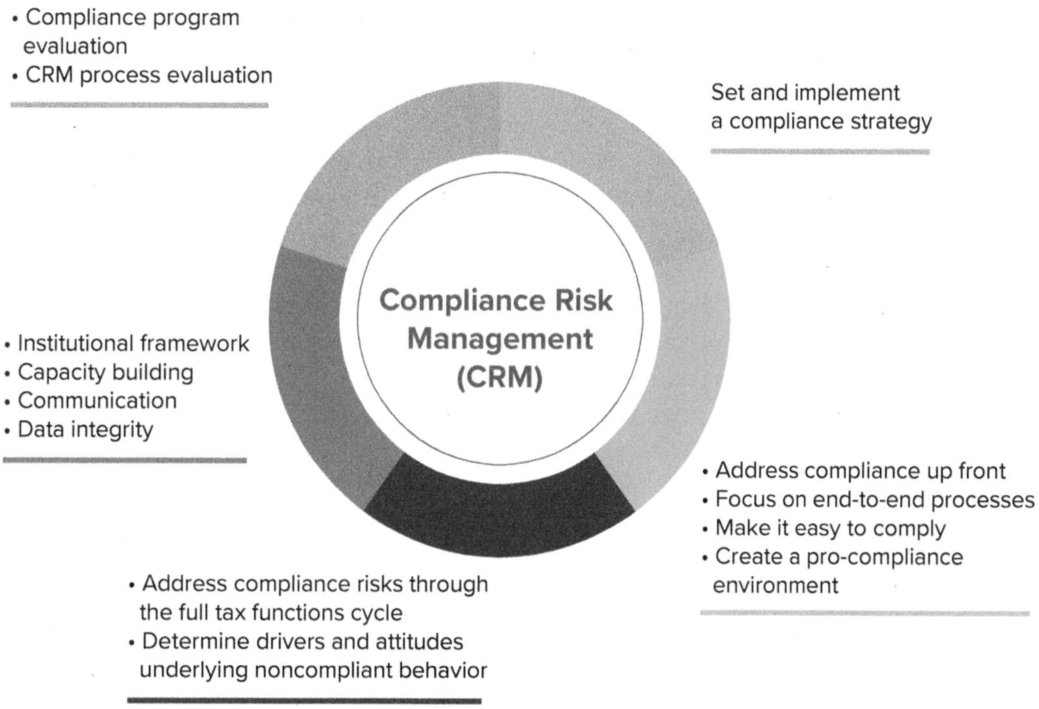

- Compliance program
  evaluation
- CRM process evaluation

Set and implement
a compliance strategy

**Compliance Risk
Management
(CRM)**

- Institutional framework
- Capacity building
- Communication
- Data integrity

- Address compliance up front
- Focus on end-to-end processes
- Make it easy to comply
- Create a pro-compliance
  environment

- Address compliance risks through
  the full tax functions cycle
- Determine drivers and attitudes
  underlying noncompliant behavior

Source: Original figure for this publication.

Moreover, it is highly recommended to establish a tax intelligence unit in the tax administration, considering the key role it would play in helping the tax administration to develop a sound strategic framework for enforcing tax compliance. In addition, this unit would be better placed to receive feedback from tax audits conducted in the field, thereby better evaluating the accuracy and reliability of risk identification and enhancing risk assessment analysis. It is also recommended to develop an antifraud plan as a companion of the strategic plan of the tax administration based on analysis and studies of tax compliance trends and fraud patterns. The outcomes of implementing this antifraud plan would feed into the strategic plan and specifically into the CRM processes of the revenue administration, as already seen in the previous section.

Furthermore, by automating manual functions, the tax administration can move to a CRM model that systematically identifies, assesses, ranks, and treats tax compliance risks so that the tax administration can effectively deploy its limited resources (Krsul 2021). The necessary capabilities for improving recovery of arrears and tax debt, supporting intelligence and fraud detection, and identifying tax gaps are therefore created. Hence, effective implementation of IT systems for a tax administration has the potential to significantly increase its efficiency.

To conclude, an effective approach to managing and improving tax compliance is to follow a structured risk management process that involves (a) continuously monitoring the operating context of the authority and taxpayer activity; (b) identifying, assessing, and prioritizing risks to the revenue, the taxation system as a whole, and the reputation of the authority in the community; (c) understanding the factors underlying taxpayer behavior that drive any noncompliance; (d) addressing noncompliant behavior; and (e) evaluating the success of any intervention (European Commission 2021).

Performance management

Budget management

Analysis of the magnitude of expenditure of a tax administration can provide useful information about its efficiency and effectiveness in collecting revenue. Revenue administrations often suffer from underresourcing and misallocation with rigid and legislatively mandated financing.

In assessing the efficiency and effectiveness in collecting revenues, tax administrations usually apply the cost-to-collection ratio by which the administration costs, excluding compliance costs, are compared with net tax revenue collected (Hashim 2014). However, this ratio has some limitations when it comes to assessing efficiency of tax administration, mainly because there are a series of factors that have a strong influence on the tax system. Moreover, the ratio cannot be considered a measure of efficiency since it only provides information about how much it costs the tax administration to collect revenue, not how effectively this task has been done. Indeed, tax gap analysis is more appropriate in measuring the effectiveness.

There are also limitations when this ratio is used to make comparisons between countries. There are many factors to consider, ranging from different institutional arrangements in tax administrations, such as the scope of taxes collected by the tax administration, to measurement of data or to the presence of nontax functions (Hashim 2014). In addition, "hidden costs" in some tax administrations do not appear in their budgets, such as remuneration to banks for receiving tax payment via "floating" arrangements, or cases in which some functions have been outsourced to private companies—for example, customs in preshipment verification services, or valuation services.

The cost-to-collection ratio could be used to assess efficiency of one country across time, but not across countries. Moreover, it could be viewed as a partial measure of efficiency. In this context, a downward trend of this ratio for a given tax administration over a number of years, once the possible impact of relevant factors is isolated, may lead one to conclude that this tax administration has increased levels of efficiency in administering the tax system. It is also advisable to differentiate between operational and investment costs, since using only operational cost to calculate this ratio can provide a more accurate picture of performance of a given tax administration in terms of efficiency (Junquera-Varela et al. 2013).

Another ratio that can serve the purpose of measuring relative levels of efficiency of a given tax administration is the ratio of an administration's costs to gross domestic product (GDP). By comparing tax administration expenditure with GDP, this measure avoids some of the problems of the cost-to-collection ratio in terms of impact of tax policy changes or macroeconomic context. However, it can provide a distorted picture when the tax administration is going through significant investment programs. This can be solved by computing only operational costs in calculations of this ratio.

To examine the total costs of administering a tax system, one should take into account not only administrative costs but also costs of compliance. Compliance costs incurred by taxpayers encompass costs resulting from complying with tax laws and from designing tax avoidance schemes as well as legal and illegal payments, as in the case of bribes paid to tax administration officials. Legal payments include money paid to tax preparers, costs involved in keeping accounting books or tax books required by a country's laws, submission to tax authorities of third-party information, time spent to prepare and pay tax returns, or purchases of specialized software. In some cases, costs are borne by companies or external parties to whom tax laws impose specific obligations related to collecting taxes; an example is the banks when they receive tax returns or payments from taxpayers or withholding agents (Junquera-Varela 2011). Therefore, it is advisable for a tax administration to conduct estimates of tax compliance costs to assess, together with administrative costs, the magnitude of the total costs involved in administering the tax system.

Box 2.6 summarizes some budget management issues that influence tax administration, which should be examined in the course of any tax administration diagnosis.

BOX 2.6   Assessment of budget management issues that influence tax administration

1. What is the current annual budget of the tax administration in absolute terms and as a percentage of tax collection? Is the given budget sufficient to ensure the efficient implementation of its policies and achievement of its objectives? The following outcome/measures/indicators may be used by the team in this regard:

   - The timeliness of service delivery.

   - The trend of taxpayer satisfaction with the services provided measured by surveys over time.

   - Rates of taxpayers' compliance achieved—for example, for filing, reporting, and payment for major taxes, and their trend over time.

   - Perception of employee engagement/satisfaction and their trend over time, measured by staff survey.

2. Examine the level of investment of the tax administration over a number of years. Is the investment expenditure sufficient to ensure that the tax administration has a level of infrastructure necessary to implement its strategic plan? Has there been some abnormal expenditure, for example, relating to ICT in some of the years examined by the team?

3. Is the tax administration permitted to retain any part of its collection, for example, a percentage of collection exceeding its revenue target, for its own use?

4. Examine the cost-to-collection ratio, differentiating operating costs from investment costs.

5. Examine the ratio of administrative expenditure to GDP, differentiating operational costs from investment expenditure.

Note: ICT = information and communication technology.

Human resources management

Staff constitute the most valuable asset of a tax administration. The complexities involved in administering the tax systems require trained and skilled staff, especially in core business areas such as tax audit or tax arrears management. Modernizing the HR function is a key objective of any tax administration reform program with a view to providing the HR function with tools needed to improve HR management, enhancing the staff development aspects of HR, overhauling HR policies and procedures, and providing the tax administration with an HR management and information system (Junquera-Varela 2011). A good starting point is to put in place a manual describing job positions, including an inventory of required skills and salary levels for each position.

An HR strategy is needed to manage HR in a coordinated and structured way to improve the overall HR environment. This strategy would aim at hiring and retaining skilled staff within the tax administration to improve its operational capacity. Issues to consider include recruitment policies, salary regime, staff development plans, IT support, training programs, and jobs description and skills inventories.[1]

An analysis of the salary levels when compared with similar jobs/positions in the private sector may be of use in terms of explaining retention problems. Low salaries may also be a critical factor when it comes to recruiting staff. The comparison may lead to a salary policy that attempts to bridge the gap in certain core functions such as a tax audit or the IT area where retention proves to be more difficult (Spencer and Spencer 1993). For certain categories of staff, it may be necessary to expand salary bands to pay more to staff with more technical expertise in challenging and critical areas—for example, tax auditors working on international taxation issues.

The salary regime is not the only factor influencing recruitment, retention, motivation, and performance, but it is an important element to take into account when designing HR policies. For instance, paying for performance policy, which is increasingly used in public administration of OECD countries, has produced surprising results: staff are less motivated than might have been expected by the prospect of more money for working better. But performance-related pay can help improve performance when it is applied in the right managerial context and within a comprehensive and well-designed HR policy.

Another key aspect is the allocation of employees to the different functions with a special focus on control of tax compliance (that is, tax auditing, taxpayer services, collection of revenue, tax appeals, and management of tax arrears). However, special care has to be taken when comparing among tax administrations or in determining the ideal levels of staff for the different functions. It should be noted that there are differences between tax administrations with regard to the content/scope of some functions. For example, some administrations carry out mass compliance checks through cross-checking of third-party information with information contained in tax returns that are not under the responsibility of the audit function. In the same vein, some factors may have an impact on the results; these include specific institutional arrangements of a given tax administration, number of offices, level of automation, or degree of outsourcing.

Box 2.7 summarizes some HR management issues that influence tax administration (Junquera-Varela 2011), which should be examined in the course of a tax administration diagnosis.

Training human resources for machine learning

A revenue administration that wants to delve into machine learning needs to have highly qualified data scientists who can curate and apply a range of techniques to these data, including visualization, predictive analysis, clustering, classification, and machine learning, to identify trends, patterns, and classes of behaviors from vast quantities of data with a high number of variables (Krsul 2021). The level of complexity of machine learning solutions for revenue administrations is high, and the learning curve very steep, since machine learning is a full-blown profession that requires intensive training and experience, and no single individual is likely to master all the techniques and tools that make up the machine learning landscape.

It is possible to hire qualified data scientists who are already trained and can quickly produce significant results for the revenue administration. But skilled and experienced data scientists are in short supply, and their scarcity will likely be a limiting factor in initiatives. This is especially true in

---

BOX 2.7   Assessment of HR management issues that impact tax administration

1. Has the tax administration developed and published a human resource management strategy?

2. If the response to the previous question is positive, what topics are included in this strategy? Examples include recruitment and appointment policies, remuneration, training plans, or staff satisfaction.

3. Has the tax administration put in place a strategic human resource planning system to predict and meet its future employment requirements?

4. Does the tax administration have a staff development program aimed at enhancing staff skills?

5. Does the tax administration provide systematic on-the-job training and off-the-job training courses in-house or externally?

6. Has the tax administration outsourced some functions to the private sector? Examples include call center operations, data-processing operations, or collections enforcement of tax arrears. It also includes collection of tax revenues through banks, which is a general trend in all modern tax administrations. If the answer is positive, describe the nature of the tax functions outsourced.

7. Does the tax administration conduct surveys to measure staff satisfaction and motivation on a regular basis?

If the answer is positive, are the results of these surveys published and shared with staff or not? Do the outcomes of these surveys feed into the HR management strategy of the tax administration or HR policies of the institution?

8. Is there a manual or equivalent document comprising all job positions with their profiles, responsibilities, selection criteria, and remunerations levels?

9. To what extent does the tax administration have autonomy in recruiting and appointing staff?

10. Does the tax administration evaluate staff performance on a regular basis?

11. Does the performance management system, in case it exists, establish performance goals for each staff member, unit, or department?

12. Does the tax administration have flexibility to remunerate staff according to performance? In particular, has the tax administration put in place bonus schemes or variable payments tied to performance? How would the wage base of the tax administration staff be positioned in comparison with the private sector?

13. Is the tax administration planning future reductions, increases, or changes in the allocation of its personnel?

Note: HR = human resources.

tax (revenue) administration, where deep subject matter expertise is required and where the best data science experts are those who are also experts in the domain. These are people who understand the organization, the processes, and the data. With extensive background in both data science and the subject, they will create the most adequate solutions to the hardest problems (Krsul 2021).

Many revenue administrations are building their capabilities in data science by developing partnerships with leading university computer science departments to identify future engineers who can participate in internships in the organization and to conduct targeted research and development, since the revenue administration has the most important resource for any learning project: data. Hence, the tax administration is encouraged to create an internship program and to identify within its ranks experienced analysts who can be trained in the management of data and the application of learning algorithms. Training in data science is available through third-party specialists, such as academic centers, IT institutes, universities, or software firms, and is generally free or relatively inexpensive (Krsul 2021). A person who has the necessary background can expect to complete basic training in machine learning or data science in about 12 months for basic proficiencies and 24 months for advanced qualifications.

It is possible to advocate for a more effective manpower planning strategy that is aligned to the digitalization transformation strategy. The number of staff needed as well as the required skill sets are changing more rapidly than ever, so administrations must be forward looking regarding potential requirements.

Note

1 | Having a competency framework for tax-related jobs is good practice in modern tax administration. In addition to technical skills requirements, competencies include a set of characteristics—motives, traits, self-concepts, attitudes, values, content knowledge, or cognitive and behavioral skills—that lead to successful performance in a specific role (Spencer and Spencer 1993).

Bibliography

ADB (Asian Development Bank). 2018. *A Comparative Analysis of Tax Administration in Asia and the Pacific: 2018 Edition*. Manila, The Philippines: ADB. http://doi.org/10.22617/TCS189264.

Awasthi, Rajul, Hyung Chul Lee, Peter Poulin, Jin Gyu Choi, Woo Cheol Kim, Owen Jae Lee, Myung Jae Sung, and Sun Young Chang. 2019. *The Benefits of Electronic Tax Administration in Developing Economies: A Korean Case Study and Discussion of Key Challenges*. Report. Washington, DC: World Bank. https://documents1.worldbank.org/curated/en/246061561388336942/pdf/The-Benefits-of -Electronic-Tax-Administration-in-Developing-Economies-A-Korean-Case-Study-and-Discussion-of-Key-Challenges.pdf.

Bahl, Roy. 2009. "Property Tax Reform in Developing and Transition Countries." USAID, Washington, DC. https://pdf.usaid.gov /pdf_docs/PNADW480.pdf.

Bahl, Roy, and Jorge Martínez-Vázquez. 2007. "The Property Tax in Developing Countries: Current Practice and Prospects." Working Paper, Lincoln Institute of Land Policy, Cambridge, MA. https://www.lincolninst.edu/sites/default/files/pubfiles/1256_Bahl%20Final.pdf.

Barber, Jon. 2021. *Toolkit for Performance Management, Risk Management and Internal Audit*. Centre of Expertise for Good Governance. Strasbourg, France: Council of Europe Publishing. https://rm.coe.int/toolkit-on-performance-management-/168070c09f.

Barrand, Peter, Stanford Ross, and Graham Harrison. 2004. "Integrating a Unified Revenue Administration for Tax and Social Contribution Collections: Experiences of Central and Eastern European Countries." IMF Working Paper 04/237, IMF, Washington, DC. https://www.imf.org/external/pubs/ft/wp/2004/wp04237.pdf.

Betts, Susan. 2022. "Revenue Administration: Compliance Risk Management Framework to Drive Revenue Performance." IMF Technical Notes and Manuals (TNM/2022/005), IMF, Washington, DC. https://www.imf.org/en/Publications/TNM/Issues/2022/08/26 /Revenue-Administration-Compliance-Risk-Management-Overarching-Framework-to-Drive-Revenue-520479.

Bird, Richard. 2010. "*Taxation and Decentralization*." Economic Premise No. 38, November 2010. Washington, DC: World Bank Group. http://documents.worldbank.org/curated/en/221831468153883993/Taxation-and-decentralization.

Bird, Richard. 2013. "Subnational Taxation in Developing Countries: A Review of the Literature." Policy Research Working Paper, World Bank, Washington, DC. https://doi.org/10.1596/1813-9450-5450.

Bird, Richard, and Milka Casanegra de Jantscher, eds. 1992. *Improving Tax Administration in Developing Countries*. Washington, DC: IMF. https://doi.org/10.5089/9781557753175.071.

Brondolo, John, Annette Chooi, Trevor Schloss, and Anthony Siouclis. 2022. "Compliance Risk Management: Developing Compliance Improvement Plans." Technical Notes and Manuals. IMF, Washington, DC. https://www.imf.org/en/Publications/TNM /Issues/2022/03/18/Compliance-Risk-Management-Developing-Compliance-Improvement-Plans-515263.

Castro, Patricio, Raúl Félix Junquera-Varela, Osvaldo Schenone, and Antonio Teixeira. 2009. *Evaluation of Reforms in Tax Policy and Administration in Mozambique and Related TA 1994-2007*. Washington, DC: IMF. https://www.imf.org/external/np/pp /eng/2009/090109b.pdf.

CIAT (Inter-American Center of Tax Administrations). 2000. *Handbook for Tax Administrations: Organizational Structure and Management of Tax Administrations*. Panama City, Panama: CIAT. https://www.ciat.org/Biblioteca/DocumentosTecnicos /Ingles/2000_handbook_for_ta_netherlands_ciat.pdf.

CIAT, SII (Servicio de Impuestos Internos de Chile), and IMF (International Monetary Fund). 2022. *Handbook on Compliance Risk Management for Tax Administrations*. Original Spanish version published in 2020. Panama City, Panama: CIAT. https://www.ciat.org/Biblioteca/DocumentosTecnicos/Ingles/2022-Handbook-Compliance-Risk.pdf.

De Cesare, Cláudia M. 2012. *Improving the Performance of the Property Tax in Latin America*. Policy Focus Report. Cambridge, MA: Lincoln Institute of Land Policy. https://www.lincolninst.edu/publications/policy-focus-reports/improving-performance -property-tax-in-latin-america.

European Commission. 2006. *Risk Management Guide for Tax Administrations*. Fiscalis Risk Analysis Project Group. Brussels, Belgium: Directorate-General, Taxation and Customs Union, European Commission. https://taxation-customs.ec.europa.eu /system/files/2016-09/risk_management_guide_for_tax_administrations_en.pdf.

European Commission. 2021. *Compliance Risk Management Capability Maturity Model*. Fiscalis Risk Analysis Project Group. Brussels, Belgium: Directorate-General, Taxation and Customs Union, European Commission. https://taxation-customs.ec.europa.eu /system/files/2023-01/Compliance%20Risk%20Management%20Capability%20Maturity%20Model_2021.pdf.

Farvacque-Vitkovic, Catherine, and Mihaly Kopanyi. 2014. *Municipal Finances: A Handbook for Local Governments*. Washington, DC: World Bank. http://hdl.handle.net/10986/18725.

Hashim, Ali. 2014. *A Handbook on Financial Management Information Systems for Government: A Practitioners Guide for Setting Reform Priorities, Systems Design and Implementation*. Washington, DC: World Bank. http://hdl.handle.net/10986/23025.

IFC (International Finance Corporation), World Bank, and MIGA (Multilateral Investment Guarantee Agency). 2011. *Avoiding the Fiscal Pitfalls of Subnational Regulation: How to Optimize Local Regulatory Fees to Encourage Growth*. Washington, DC: World Bank. http://hdl.handle.net/10986/27217.

IMF (International Monetary Fund). 2002. "Improving Large Taxpayers' Compliance: A Review of Country Experience." Occasional Paper 215, IMF, Washington, DC. https://www.imf.org/external/pubs/nft/op/215/.

IMF. 2022. "Compliance Risk Management for Tax Administration Leaders: Recognizing the Importance of CRM in Modern Tax Administration." IMF Technical Note, IMF, Washington, DC. https://www.imf.org/-/media/Files/Topics/Fiscal/Revenue -Portal/compliance-risk-management-for-tax-administration-leaders.ashx#:~:text=It%20is%20a%20methodology%20 used,most%20effective%20and%20efficient%20way.

ITC (International Tax Compact) and KfW (KfW Development Bank). 2015. *Information Technology in Tax Administration in Developing Countries*. Frankfurt am Main: KfW Development Bank. https://www.taxcompact.net/sites/default/files /resources/2015-07-ITC-IT-Tax-Administration.pdf.

Junquera-Varela, Raúl Félix. 2011. "An Integrated Assessment Model for Tax Administration. The Diagnostic Tool." Poverty Reduction and Economic Management. Unpublished draft. World Bank, Washington, DC.

Junquera-Varela, Raúl Félix, Rajul Awasthi, Oleksii Balabushko, and Alma Nurshaikhova. 2019. "Thinking Strategically about Revenue Administration Reform: The Creation of Integrated Autonomous Revenue Bodies." Policy Note. Governance Discussion Paper 4, World Bank, Washington, DC. doi: 10.1596/33079.

Junquera-Varela, Raúl Félix, Karina Ramírez, Daniel Álvarez, Calvin Zebaze, Erwin Tiongson, Tania Díaz, Ehtisham Ahmad, Giorgio Brosio, Caroline Pöschl, and Roberto Zanola. 2013. *Mexico: Tax Reforms for Sustainable Growth and Accountability*. Mexico Country Management Unit, Latin America and the Caribbean Region, Internal Report. Washington, DC: World Bank.

Kidd, Maureen, and William Crandall. 2006. "Revenue Authorities: Issues and Problems in Evaluating Their Success." IMF Working Paper 06/240, IMF, Washington, DC. https://www.imf.org/en/Publications/WP/Issues/2016/12/31/Revenue-Authorities -Issues-and-Problems-in-Evaluating-their-Success-19814.

Krsul, Ivan. 2021. "Building Data Science Capabilities in a Tax Administration. Vol. 7." Working Paper, Unpublished, World Bank, Washington, DC.

Moller, Lars Christian, Raúl Félix Junquera-Varela, and Daniel Álvarez. 2012. *El Gasto Tributario en Colombia: Una propuesta de evaluación integral y sistemática de este instrumento de política pública* (Tax Expenditure in Colombia: A Proposal for a Comprehensive and Systematic Evaluation of this Public Policy Instrument). Washington, DC: World Bank. http:// documents.worldbank.org/curated/en/945121468022751656/El-Gasto-Tributario-en-Colombia-una-propuesta-de -evaluacion-integral-y-sistematica-de-este-instrumento-de-politica-publica.

OECD (Organisation for Economic Co-operation and Development). 2004. *Compliance Risk Management: Managing and Improving Tax Compliance*. Paris: OECD Publishing. https://www.oecd.org/tax/administration/33818656.pdf.

OECD. 2009. *Tax Administration in OECD and Selected Non-OECD Countries: Comparative Information Series (2008)*. Paris: OECD Publishing. https://www.oecd.org/ctp/administration/CIS-2008.pdf.

OECD. 2012. "Working Smarter in Structuring the Administration, in Compliance, and Through Legislation." Forum on Tax Administration, Information Note, OECD Publishing, Paris. https://www.oecd.org/tax/forum-on-tax-administration/publications-and-products/49428209.pdf.

OECD. 2013. *Tax Administration 2013: Comparative Information on OECD and Other Advanced and Emerging Economies.* Paris: OECD Publishing. https://www.oecd.org/ctp/administration/tax-administration-2013.htm.

OECD. 2015. *Tax Administration 2015: Comparative Information on OECD and Other Advanced and Emerging Economies.* Paris: OECD Publishing. https://www.oecd-ilibrary.org/taxation/tax-administration-2015_tax_admin-2015-en.

OECD. 2016. *Tax Administrations and Capacity Building: A Collective Challenge.* Paris: OECD Publishing. https://doi.org/10.1787/9789264256637-en.

OECD. 2017a. *Tax Administration 2017: Comparative Information on OECD and Other Advanced and Emerging Economies.* Paris: OECD Publishing. doi:10.1787/tax_admin-2017-en.

OECD. 2017b. *Shining Light on the Shadow Economy: Opportunities and Threats.* Paris: OECD Publishing. https://www.oecd.org/tax/crime/shining-light-on-the-shadow-economy-opportunities-and-threats.pdf.

OECD. 2019. *Tax Administration 2019: Comparative Information on OECD and Other Advanced and Emerging Economies.* Paris: OECD Publishing. https://doi.org/10.1787/74d162b6-en.

OECD. 2021. *Tax Administration 2021: Comparative Information on OECD and Other Advanced and Emerging Economies.* Paris: OECD Publishing. https://doi.org/10.1787/cef472b9-en.

Rozner, Steve. 2009. "Best Practices in Fiscal Reform and Economic Governance: Implementing Property Tax Reform." Best Practice Note, USAID, Washington, DC.

Spencer, Lyle, and Signe Spencer. 1993. *Competence at Work: Models for Superior Performance.* New York: John Wiley & Sons.

TADAT Secretariat. 2015. *Tax Administration Diagnostic and Assessment Tool: Field Guide.* TADAT Secretariat. https://www.tadat.org/assets/files/IMF_TADAT-FieldGuide_web.pdf.

Verhorn, Charles, and John Brondolo. 1999. "Organizational Options for Tax Administration." *Bulletin for International Taxation* 53 (11): 499–512. https://www.ibfd.org/shop/journal/organizational-options-tax-administration.

Whyte, Graham. 2022. "Compliance Risk Management for Tax Administration Leaders: Recognizing the Importance of CRM in Modern Tax Administration." IMF Technical Note, International Monetary Fund, Washington, DC.

World Bank. 2010. *Integration of Revenue Administration: A Comparative Study of International Experience.* Washington, DC: World Bank. http://hdl.handle.net/10986/13529.

CHAPTER 3

Maturity models for tax and customs administrations

Rationale and methodological considerations

Maturity models do not assess revenue administrations by the distance from the "really good practice frontier" but in the form of constraints to achieve comprehensive functionality appropriate to the level of maturity—identify taxpayers, assess taxes, collect, investigate and audit, manage disputes, report, and offer transparency and accountability in a manner that imposes reasonable cost for taxpayers and revenue administration (Junquera-Varela 2011). Hence, a maturity model assessment will determine the level of compliance of the organization with the practices at each level. Recommendations are typically provided to help the organization develop first with controlled operations, then with efficient operations, and finally with sustainable operations. This chapter addresses maturity models applied to tax and customs administrations, as well as digital maturity. This chapter analyzes rationale and methodological considerations, and maturity models for tax administrations, customs administrations, and information technology.

It is important to build a model that assesses the general level of maturity of revenue administrations and customs so that plans for improvement are tailored to a given context. This is especially relevant in low-capacity environments and is more effective than a benchmarking exercise.

A key goal of any maturity model is to enable moving away from the present model, which suggests that moving consistently toward functionality configurations from advanced countries is the appropriate reform path. The problem with this is twofold: the focus is on building maturity and modern functionalities that may not be sustainable and are often implemented in a piecemeal manner that shortcuts actual functional improvement (Junquera-Varela et al. 2022). For immediate results and sustainability, one should start assessing what is the binding constraint to achieving a level of functionality that matches the level of capacity and maturity.

In specific cases of low capacity, the priority should be to identify binding constraints to achieving comprehensive functionality, which acknowledges the limited performance that may come with that. Lower priority can be assigned to building maturity in other areas; they can be done at the same time but should clearly fit into the model. Maturity building may take time, and it is important to take advantage of reform opportunities (Dener et al. 2021).

Maturity models do not assess revenue administrations by the distance from the "really good practice frontier" but in the form of constraints to achieve comprehensive functionality appropriate to the level of maturity—identify taxpayers, assess taxes, collect, investigate and audit, manage disputes, report, and offer transparency and accountability in a manner that imposes reasonable cost for taxpayers and revenue administration (Junquera-Varela 2011). That does not mean tax administrations do not push for the maturity dimension, but maturity development should not be pursued for its own sake or because there is a belief that, over time, everything will work perfectly if the authorities forge ahead.

One should start by delineating the broad contours of a four-level model to assess the levels of maturity of revenue and customs administrations. This is the approach of the United States Agency for International Development (USAID), that is, relying on the "rules of thumb" to assess the strengths and weaknesses of key functions of revenue administrations. USAID published in 2013 a report on *Detailed Guidelines for Improved Tax Administration in Latin America and the Caribbean*, which compiles key benchmarks to evaluate tax administration performance by areas, functions, and operations. This section is inspired by that report (USAID 2013) and draws on some of the maturity models developed therein. The World Bank–developed web-based Development Implementation and Monitoring Directives (DIAMOND)[1] diagnostic tool adopts the same approach, which incorporates a four-level model for the progressive application of good practices.[2]

Subsequently, the World Bank team developed in Colombia a more robust methodology to allocate standards, good practices, and indicators to the different levels (Moller et al. 2012). Strong emphasis was also placed on better describing the different levels and relevant variables, considering the various situations of limited maturity of revenue administrations. In Colombia, the World Bank team also analyzed how this level-of-maturity model plays out in terms of designing technical assistance programs that aim to achieve comprehensive functionality of revenue bodies and improve overall performance. In this context, maturity models reflect a series of good practices, and every practice belongs to a certain maturity level (see figure 3.1).

FIGURE 3.1 Levels of maturity of a revenue administration

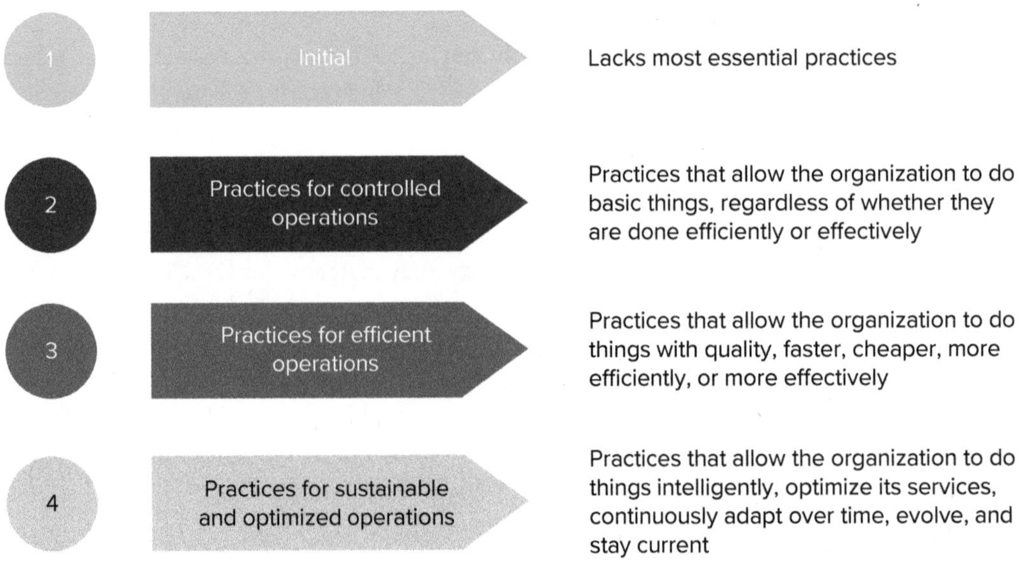

Source: World Bank 2019.

It is important to clarify that the term "optimized operations" in level 4 does not mean the same as the term "efficient" in level 3. Optimized goes beyond mere efficiency; it pertains to making the design and operation of a system or process as good as possible in a defined sense, whereas efficiency is mostly about using resources reasonably well. In terms of the natural order on the progressive implementation of the practices, as shown in figure 3.2, level 2 corresponds to the basic practices that should be implemented first in an organization. Level 3 concerns intermediate practices that are typically implemented once the basic practices are consolidated, and level 4 relates to advanced practices that require a consolidated and relatively mature organization that has appropriately implemented solid foundations that are necessary for implementing the most advanced practices.

In general, good practices are implemented sequentially in an organization, although there is no requirement that one must implement the practices in order. But it is generally difficult to make a practice efficient if the fundamentals are not implemented, and it is difficult to sustain the practice if the operations are not efficient.

Hence, a maturity model assessment will determine the level of compliance of the organization with the practices at each level. Recommendations are typically provided to help the organization develop first with controlled operations, then with efficient operations, and finally with sustainable operations. Table 3.1 describes the characteristics of a revenue administration's levels of maturity.

The next subsections present the four-level model and assess the level of maturity of tax administrations and customs in terms of their current capabilities. The usual practices at lower levels of maturity are also described so that plans for improvement can be made. By using the maturity models, revenue administrations can monitor their progress, practice by practice, to better identify how to sustain improvement and performance across areas and functions. Also, such a model helps to leverage existing systems, processes, and tools in designing strategies to overcome the gap in tax administration and customs capacity (Junquera-Varela et al. 2022).

FIGURE 3.2 Progressive implementation of the practices

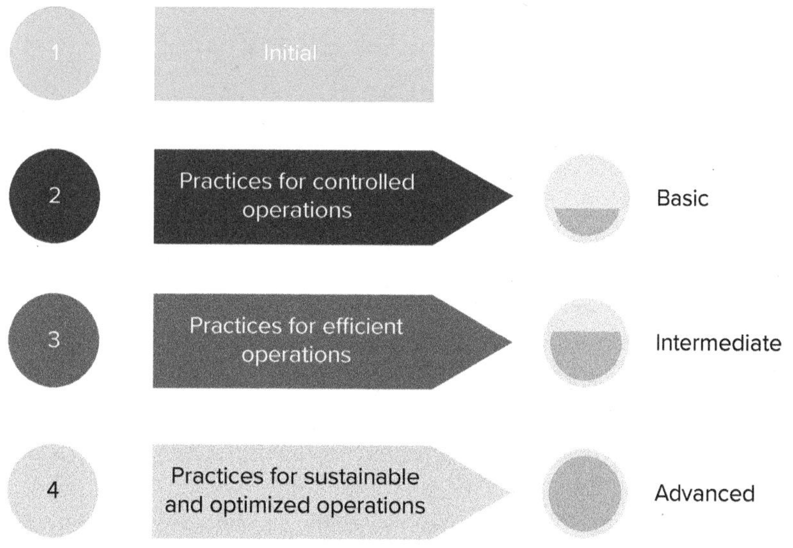

Source: World Bank 2019.

TABLE 3.1 Characteristics of the levels of maturity of a revenue administration

Maturity level	Operations	Processes	Organization	Technology
Level 1: Initial.	• Ad hoc. • Operations are informal, sporadic, and ever changing.	• Disintegrated, chaotic processes. • Results are not consistently achieved. • Variability in achieving results. • Emergencies are very common.	• Fragmented • High frustration or complacency. • Functional silos. • Low participation and commitment.	• Rudimentary • Low level of technology adoption. • Technological tools, when present and implemented, are not correctly used.
Level 2: Basic (Practices for controlled operations).	• Formalized • Operations are formalized, evidenced by regular practice or documentation.	• Reactive processes. • High costs involved in achieving results. • Still variability in achieving results. • Low visibility.	• Compliant • Clear roles and responsibilities. • Reward and punishment mechanisms have been established and implemented.	• Structured • Information and data are structured using technological solutions. • Technology is used to have a perception of control.
Level 3: Intermediate (Practices for efficient operations).	• Integrated • Policies, programs, processes, and tools are consistent.	• Stable and predictable. • Controlled, planned, balanced, and monitored processes. • Results are consistently achieved. • Budget and costs are controlled. • Performance management system is in place. • Compliance with forecasts and plans. • Variability is controlled.	• Performance oriented and collaborative. • Leadership, teamwork, and accountability. • Effective performance management systems are in place. • Competencies are aligned with existing job profiles. • Career streams are in place.	• Deterministic • Systems and applications use and transform the organization's data. However, these applications conform to a very well-defined process or algorithm.
Level 4: Advanced (Practices for sustainable and optimized operations).	• Strategic • Organization strategy and performance goals filter through all levels.	• Optimal • Existing processes are stable, flexible, and adaptable. • Minimal variability. • Continuous improvement and innovation.	• Intelligently-led tax administration. • Smart tax administration. • Continuous innovation. • Knowledge sharing.	• Intelligent • Implemented tools and solutions use existing data as feedback to enhance the current applications. • Organizations provide intelligent services.

Source: Junquera-Varela et al. 2022.

Maturity model for tax administrations

The main functional features and level-specific practices[3] that characterize the different maturity levels of a tax administration can be classified as follows:

Maturity level 1: Initial

- There is a lack of adequate legal framework—legal/regulatory institutions, modern tax policy, civil service rules and regulations for attracting and retaining qualified staff, international accounting and professional standards, and modern financial and banking standards and institutions.
- There is an absence of policies and procedures in place to guide staff.
- There is a lack of tax administration control regarding the taxpayer population.
- There are no provisions in the tax laws for self-assessments.
- There is an ineffective and inefficient taxpayer registry.
- There is a lack of a well-functioning taxpayer account.
- There are no compliance strategies in place.
- There is a potential for corruption.

- Voluntary compliance is not a concept practiced by the revenue administration.
- Informal economy is widespread and impacts tax administration functioning.
- Taxpayer services are largely nonexistent.
- Relations between tax administration and taxpayers are confrontational.
- There is no segmentation of taxpayers to tailor processes and strategies to its distinctive features.
- There are no lines of communication with public and private sector institutions.
- Technology is not available or is available on a limited scale. Hence, work is mostly conducted manually.

Maturity level 2: Basic (Practices for Controlled Operations)

- A formal process to register taxpayers exists but usually with unreliable Taxpayer Identification Numbers.
- Taxpayer accounts are largely unreliable.
- Segmentation of taxpayers has begun, but well-defined criteria for inclusion in different segments are nonexistent.
- Progress is made in the incorporation of provision in the law for self-assessment and in the development of the concept of voluntary compliance and its inclusion in tax administration strategies.
- Development of an anticorruption strategy limits opportunities for corruption.
- Taxpayer service program exists but is poorly organized and understaffed.
- Ill-conceived compliance strategies do not focus on high-risk segments.
- Long-term strategic plans for the overall tax administration do not exist.
- Annual operational plans of the departments are independent of each other and not coordinated.
- Some technology is available but is usually outdated; most of the work is still done manually.
- Procedure manuals are minimal, and institutionalization of procedures varies across departments.
- Skills of the staff vary across departments.
- Some contacts with public and private sector groups have started, but there is lack of coherence and sustainability.
- There is a substantial lack of legal framework.

Maturity level 3: Intermediate (Practices for Efficient Operations)

- Provisions in the law enable self-assessment.
- Limited opportunities for corruption.
- Voluntary compliance by a high percentage of taxpayers—more than 75 percent.
- Registration of taxpayers has been completed, supported by a good system of Taxpayer Identification Numbers.
- Taxpayer accounts are usually accurate.
- A segmentation process backed by good criteria exists to facilitate identifying different segments.
- Compliance strategies focus on high-risk taxpayers.
- Strategic plans for the tax administration exist, and these plans coordinate annual operational plans of core functions. There is still a greater focus on short- and medium-term objectives and a lack of focus on long-term direction.
- Policy and procedure manuals are available for all the core functions, but they are not updated.
- Good relationships with public and private sector groups with some exceptions.
- Modern technology and equipment are available, but there is often a shortage in specific departments.

- The tax administration has begun embracing many technological advances used in the private sector.
- Legal and regulatory institutions, modern tax policy, and civil service rules to support operations exist.

Maturity level 4: Advanced (Practices for Sustainable and Optimized Operations)

- A strong presence of legal and regulatory institutions, modern tax policy, and civil services rules exists.
- Provisions in the tax law for self-assessment have been implemented for several years.
- Concise online policy and procedure manuals are available for all tax administration functions.
- Registration of taxpayers is accurate, and the taxpayer registry consists mostly of active taxpayers.
- Voluntary compliance by more than 90 percent of taxpayers.
- Taxpayer accounts are rarely inaccurate.
- Cases of corruption are rare.
- Segmentation of taxpayers is a dynamic process with well-defined criteria.
- Compliance programs tailored to different risks posed by segment of taxpayers are in place.
- Extensive use of third-party information to broaden the coverage and effectiveness of compliance programs.
- Strategic plans are focused on long-term objectives that guide the development and implementation of annual work plans.
- Relationships with public and private sector groups are very positive.
- The tax administration has reliable information systems supported by the latest technology.
- The tax administration has already embraced and implemented many technological advances used in the private sector.

Maturity model for customs administrations

In general, maturity levels for customs should be assessed in the context of the overall maturity level identified for the tax administration. This will allow for a balanced and sensible allocation of resources and development efforts to move both revenue agencies from a "bad" equilibrium to a "good" equilibrium scenario. Extracted from the technical assistance programs and good practices compiled throughout the World Bank missions, the main functional features and level-specific practices that characterize the different maturity levels for customs can be classified as follows:

Maturity level 1: Initial

- Most of the processes are manually performed.
- Basic core, nonintegrated information system exists in combination with a high number of physical examinations for imports.
- Use of warehouses is mandatory, and most of them are publicly owned.
- Ad hoc risk management system with no feedback mechanisms from operations and private stakeholders.
- Use of customs brokers is mandatory.
- Duties and taxes are paid in cash.
- Customs valuation is the main driver for tax collection and is based on discretionary decisions from customs officials, creating room for integrity issues.

- Weak or nonexistent human resource management (HRM) system.
- Customs budget depends on the decisions of the Ministry of Finance.
- Highly centralized organization wherein all decisions depend on the chair.
- No systematic feedback from main stakeholders.
- Lack of strategic thinking.
- No exchange of information with the tax administration.

Maturity level 2: Basic (Practices for Controlled Operations)

- Imports and exports are managed by a core information system.
- High level of physical and documentary examinations.
- Some warehouses are licensed to the private sector, but no systematic audits are performed to renew licenses, and their use is still mandatory.
- Risk management is only linked to the harmonized system codes that are considered sensitive.
- Selective system is preponderantly random based.
- Minor imports do not need a customs broker.
- Some duties and taxes can be paid electronically through traders' current accounts held by customs.
- Customs valuation is the main driver for revenue purposes and uses a valuation database for adjusting declared values.
- Incipient HRM systems are introduced.
- Some procurement capabilities exist for procuring information and communication technology (ICT) equipment.
- Decision-making process remains centralized.
- Sporadic meetings with private stakeholders take place, but no systematic follow-up happens.
- Lack of strategic thinking.
- Limited coordination with border agencies happens for security purposes.
- Per-case-based exchange of information with the tax administration.

Maturity level 3: Intermediate (Practices for Efficient Operations)

- Core business processes (imports, exports, warehousing, and transit) are managed by an integrated information system.
- Between 10 percent and 30 percent of the imports are physically and documentarily examined.
- Incipient advance declarations are allowed.
- Formally, the use of warehouses is not mandatory, but in practice, importers have few alternative options.
- Use of customs brokers is not mandatory, but collusion between customs and brokers discourages the traders to use this option.
- Risk management on traders' risk profiles is introduced only for importers and exporters, combined with risk profiles for sensitive Harmonized System codes.
- Selectivity system frequently uses random-based criteria.
- A transactional postclearance audit (PCA) is introduced but without links to the central risk management system (RMS).
- Duties and taxes can be paid at authorized banks and electronically.
- HRM systems exist and are operational, but no systematic review and update processes are in place.
- Customs administration has a strategic plan, but it is not regularly updated or used for driving the organization.

- The country has introduced a basic national single window system (NSWS).
- Regular exchange of information with the tax administration.
- Meetings with the private sector are regular and documented; most of the agreements are fulfilled, although with some important delay.

Maturity level 4: Advanced (Practices for Sustainable and Optimized Operations)

- All business processes, including the administrative ones, are managed through an integrated information system.
- Preclearance and prearrival inspections are operational and represent an important part of the operations.
- Use of warehouses is completely voluntary.
- Use of customs brokers is completely voluntary.
- A trustee trader program exists and is operational.
- Only 1 percent to 5 percent of imports declarations are physically and documentarily examined.
- An entity-based PCA program exists, and it is operational and linked to the central RMS, focusing on customs valuation.
- Joint audits are performed together with the tax administration.
- Complete risk profiles for authorized operators, with inputs from the tax administration and the financial system.
- Advance ruling on classification and valuation exists and is operational.
- An integrated tariff system exists and is operational and publicly available.
- The RMS is centralized and fully integrated into the core information system with systematic feedback from operations.
- The annual audit plan is risk based and integrates all operational risks; it is reviewed and updated formally by the risk management committee.
- Electronic payment is available for duties, fees, and taxes.
- Use of warehouses is voluntary.
- Use of customs brokers is voluntary.
- Decentralized and semiautonomous organization.
- HRM systems are complete and updated systematically.
- Meetings with the private sector are systematic, and agreements are fulfilled promptly and effectively.
- The strategic plan drives the development of the organization.
- A mature NSWS exists together with an integrated border management.

Maturity model for information technology

Digitalization is the key enabler for revenue authorities. Digital maturity refers to the level of digitalization of the tax procedures of tax authorities. A digital maturity index aims to evaluate, in a standardized form, the efforts of tax and customs administrations in transforming themselves into digitalized institutions. It takes into account not only the technology itself but also the potential combination of available technologies and the system's integration that result in the most appropriate resource allocation. What are the factors taken into account when evaluating the digital maturity of tax and customs administrations? What metrics can we use to assess the progress in tax administration in digitalization efforts? How does the digital maturity level of tax administrations relate to the starting point in implementing a digital roadmap? The following section addresses these questions.

Digitalization of tax and customs administrations should be adapted to the environment available in each country and to the maturity level of each revenue administration (Junquera-Varela et al. 2022). It is important to note that the pacing of each tax and customs administration varies. The key question is how to properly sequence upgrading the information technology (IT) infrastructure with the institutional reform needed to make digitalization happen. Governments must take a strategic rather than an opportunistic perspective and make digitalization an integral part of their internal strategy with clear policy objectives. A modular approach should be adopted to facilitate the act of "plugging something in," seeing how it works, and then removing or improving it. Talent management is key because information should not be lost as we move toward digitalization (Ihnatisinova 2021). Likewise, trust with private sector vendors should be established and sustained through the reform process. Hence, it is important that a roadmap has a clear vision of how tax and customs administrations should look in the near future. In defining a useful baseline and benchmark mechanisms to accurately identify the actual digital maturity level of a tax administration, it is important to keep in mind that the primary objective is not to follow the latest trend or hype in the industry. Instead, the institution should have a healthy and comprehensive long-term strategy on how to deal with the ever-evolving technological landscape (Rosario and Chavali 2020).

The tax administration, in general, has two options in fulfilling its IT requirements (Respati 2020): (a) off-the-shelf solutions or (b) in-house software development. In practice, most of the time, a combined scheme is applied. The institution must be equipped with the necessary knowledge, processes, and resources to adequately evaluate, acquire, and integrate the existing products and to engage in productive and effective development when required (World Bank 2021b). Still, regardless of the option taken, the tax administration must have an ICT unit that is robust enough to provide continuity and sustainability to the technological solutions and avoid falling as a client captive of some external company. It is of paramount importance for the tax administration to clearly understand that technology can provide better tools, but even a very good tool is not a complete solution on its own. A good solution involves careful consideration, design, and evaluation. It must start with a clear definition of the problem and the mechanics required to measure the gained efficiencies objectively and quantifiably (Twesige et al. 2020).

Innovation is not obtained by purchasing the latest digital technology. Instead, innovation must become an integral part of the organization's culture. To this end, it must become a permanent goal aimed at the taxpayers' (client) needs—aligning them to institutional priorities, improving and refining existing processes to simplify and facilitate compliance, and constantly evaluating and responsibly adopting new technological advancements to enhance the institution's level of maturity and functionality (World Bank 2021a).

The main functional features and level-specific practices[4] that characterize the different maturity levels for information technology can be classified as detailed below.

Maturity level 1: Initial

- No official IT department in the institution; the little available maturity is scattered and dependent on individual knowledge or skills.
- No standard or properly documented procedures are in place, for the most part.
- Work is mostly conducted manually.
- Technology is not available, or it is available on a limited scale.
- No personnel performance measurement mechanisms have been established.
- Much of the information obtained or produced by the administration is still paper based.
- Signatures and other similar approval mechanisms are still manual.

- Adequate training in IT is not available for the personnel.
- No formal mechanisms of information exchange exist among the areas inside the institution or with external entities.
- Innovation and technology-related topics are nonexistent in the institutional strategy.
- No formal procedure is in place to identify functionality gaps and how to address them.
- Technological infrastructure is almost nonexistent or presents severe deficiencies.
- Procurement of tools and software is done following subjective "by boss" authorization, without a comprehensive evaluation process.
- No mechanisms to collect and analyze the taxpayer satisfaction level or feedback are in place.
- No performance monitoring and reporting tools are in place, although digital systems are available.
- Transparency-related efforts are nonexistent.

Maturity level 2: Basic (Practices for Controlled Operations)

- An official IT department exists in the institution but is viewed merely as a support group.
- The IT area has no strategic or long-term vision; it dedicates most of its resources to solving day-to-day problems as they arise.
- Personnel receive sporadic training, but it is not necessarily designed to address specific institutional needs.
- Investment in infrastructure is improving but is done without following a detailed needs analysis.
- Systems are in place for most of the more important areas in the institution, but very few present a full coverage of at least the core functions.
- The institution implements off-the-shelf tools, but there are no measures in place to avoid provider lock-in and ensure sustainability or proper integration.
- Some efforts are being done in software development, but there is no formal and effective methodology in place to cover all the stages involved from planning to production.
- Software procurement and development efforts are not aligned to solve institutional maturity or functionality gaps.
- Some information being consumed or produced by the institution is digital, but it is usually in unstructured formats.
- There are efforts to digitalize and systematize work in most areas, but there are still no standard and properly documented procedures in some of them.
- Information exchange between areas inside the institution exists but is very limited and often done manually.
- Several independent systems appear in different areas of the institution, and new problems of interoperability arise too.
- Performance measurement mechanisms exist but are usually limited to monitoring downtime—they measure the availability but not the actual performance.
- There are efforts to collect user feedback, but the information gathered is not used in any way to improve the overall IT or institutional strategy.
- Limited transparency efforts.

Maturity level 3: Intermediate (Practices for Efficient Operations)

- The IT department is well established inside the organization, usually at the same level as other functional areas and under the direct supervision of the highest authority figure.
- The IT department has a long-term strategic vision that is well aligned with institutional goals and priorities.

- Day-to-day problem solving still takes a good share of IT personnel's time and resources, but it is combined with activities for continuous development and improvement.
- Training is regular and usually prioritized according to institutional needs and an individual's career track.
- Investment in infrastructure is done following a long-term plan based on identified and measured requirements.
- Properly documented procedures are deployed for all core tasks in the institution's functional areas, with a constant emphasis to digitalize and systematize the work being done.
- Systems in place present full coverage of, at least, the core functions in the most relevant areas in the institution.
- Measures are in place to avoid provider lock-in when opting to implement off-the-shelf tools and ensure long-term sustainability and proper integration with existing systems.
- There are personnel dedicated fully to software development, which follows in-house defined methodologies to cover all the stages, from planning to deployment of products.
- Structured formats are preferred to facilitate the tasks of further processing and analysis when consuming or producing digital information.
- Digital information exchange between areas inside the institution is partially automated.
- Some integration with external information sources exists but is usually limited to specific application cases.
- Interoperability problems still exist, but some efforts are being done to integrate the systems used in different areas of the institution, usually in the form of shared data sources.
- Performance measurement mechanisms are more sophisticated and are used to monitor some interesting metrics like response time, errors occurring, and unauthorized access attempts. However, there is no clear high-level policy on what to do with the collected information.
- User feedback and satisfaction level is gathered and understood as a key metric of the system's performance, but there is a need to link this information with the strategic long-term vision within the organization.
- Transparency efforts are spread and generalized in the institution, and usually, reports produced from collected data are published on the website.

Maturity level 4: Advanced (Practices for Sustainable and Optimized Operations)

- The IT department is an established technostructure supporting the organization. It provides guidelines, standards, and tools for the rest of the business areas.
- Innovation and technological development are fundamental in the organization's long-term strategic vision and are translated in appropriate institutional goals and priorities.
- Day-to-day problem solving takes a minimal share of IT personnel's time and resources. The main priority in the department is continuous development and improvement.
- Regular training is seen as a hard requirement and is always prioritized according to institutional needs, individuals' career track, and new demands arising from future goals and challenges.
- Investment in infrastructure is carefully done following a long-term strategy based on the institutional requirements; where applicable, new trends like cloud computing and software-as-a-service solutions are applied to maximize efficiency.
- No paper-based processes exist. All information consumed and generated by the organization is managed in digital formats.
- Signatures and other similar approval mechanisms are all generated electronically. No manual signatures are required in any process.

- Systems in place present full coverage of all functions in the most relevant areas in the institution, with a well-defined methodology and calendar of new releases development.
- Data are mostly managed in digital structured formats that facilitate the tasks of processing and analysis; the results obtained are used to improve the decision-making process in all business areas in the institution.
- When opting to implement off-the-shelf tools, there is a regular process to search and evaluate open-source solutions available before opting for third-party commercial products. When using commercial alternatives, measures are in place to avoid provider lock-in and ensure long-term sustainability and adequate integration with existing systems.
- There is a dedicated software development team, which follows professional and well-established methodologies to cover all the stages, from planning to deployment of products. Even when not developing large systems in-house, this team's expertise is used when evaluating and deploying third-party tools.
- Procurement (off-the-shelf solutions) and development (in-house solutions) efforts are designed to mitigate or solve institutional maturity or functionality gaps.
- Digital information exchange between areas inside the institution is completely automated. All areas publish a standard catalog of all available data resources to facilitate discovery and consumption—for example, following the Data Catalog Vocabulary open standard.
- Integration with external information sources is a continuous effort that is not limited to specific application cases. The tax administration's goal is to ensure access to as many information sources as possible, allowing the flexibility required for all business areas to decide the best ways to integrate them in its functions.
- Interoperability problems are avoided by focusing on producing and maintaining solid protocols and standards that can be adopted by all systems used in different areas of the institution. Consistency is ensured by providing proper communication mechanisms rather than using shared data sources that can produce functional and security problems.
- Performance measurement mechanisms are very sophisticated and used to collect some metrics like response time, errors occurring, and unauthorized access attempts. All the gathered data are used to produce comprehensive reports that improve the decision-making process and allow for better root-cause analysis of problems.
- User feedback and satisfaction level are gathered and understood as a key metric of institutional performance. This information helps improve the strategic long-term vision of the organization.
- Transparency efforts are spread and generalized in the institution. Information is published using automated and standards-based systems that facilitate discoverability and consumption by entities both inside and outside the organization.
- There is a continuous and healthy pilot-based research program that formalizes the allocation of resources to evaluate and test new technological advancements, resulting in new tools or knowledge for the institution.

This maturity model for IT must be put in context to fully understand the implications of progressing from one level to the next. In this respect, the rapid development of ICT in recent decades has allowed tax administrations to administer the tax system more efficiently and to deal with a great number of the taxpayer population. Increasingly, cheaper access to this technology has resulted in decreasing administration costs that include the investment in ICT and the operational costs associated with supporting these systems, better data processing, and more accurate and reliable information (Krsul 2021). On the taxpayer side, a wide array of electronic services has been provided, which has a significant impact on the reduction of tax compliance burden.

Increased use of ICT has also influenced the way tax administrations organize themselves and how core business processes, which include the delivery of taxpayers' services, are managed (Bentley 2019). In effect, regional and local offices have gone through significant changes, and in many countries, flatter management arrangements in tax administration organizational structure are in place as a result of eliminating intermediate or regional layers. In this vein, many tax administrations are centralizing key functions—such as tax returns and tax payments processes or taxpayers' services, tax audit, and some routine processes related to collection enforcement—while local offices are losing relevance. Technology has changed the way of delivering services to taxpayers and demands less interaction between taxpayers and tax administrations (Junquera-Varela et al. 2022).

This new paradigm has a significant impact on human resources (HR) policies when it comes to allocating staff to different offices and different functions. In effect, changes in the workload of local offices should be reflected in reallocation of personnel. Intensive use of IT for routine processes requires putting in place programs that provide training to support staff who are no longer needed in their current assignments. New technologies demand new staff skills due to dramatic changes in the way tax administration does business nowadays. There are often challenges in attracting strong IT skills to the public sector, compared with the private sector, due to pay scale limits or other factors (Krsul 2021). Thanks to IT technologies, tax and customs administrations are now able to manage great amounts of third-party information, enabling them to massively cross-check this information with the content of tax returns and customs declarations. In addition, IT-based compliance risk management processes result in a better identification of compliance issues across all core tax administration functions—for example, to prioritize collection of debt and selection of cases for audit.

Consequently, the maturity model for the IT area becomes a key element in assessing the IT performance gap and in designing an action plan. This helps build the data science capabilities needed to advance to the next maturity level, which is part of the digital transformation of tax and customs administrations. Based on the maturity levels in IT, and with reference to best practices in IT system implementation, chapter 7 examines how to build data science capabilities in revenue administrations, focusing on data management and data science tools, the creation of machine learning capabilities and their application, and the feasibility on the use of blockchain initiatives.

Notes

1 | The DIAMOND tool is an integrated assessment tool for measuring tax and customs administrations' performance. The assessment tool allows the collection of data and information for different functions, units, and departments and subsequently does the measurements, which provide the organization an overall description about how it is operating and delivering services. Measurements are condensed in a set of key indicators organized in a flexible and adaptable manner to reflect the local context under which the organization operates. This customization process enables more accurate and meaningful measurements. With these, the tool can be used to evaluate the relative strengths and weaknesses of any tax and customs administration and compare them to good practices. The distinctive feature of the DIAMOND tool is that all data are objectively verifiable and comparable across countries and across time periods.

2 | The DIAMOND tool enables governments to conduct a tax administration functional review, evaluate and determine their infrastructure investment needs, assess the ICT landscape of their tax administration and customs, and improve their methodologies for business process reengineering and business process mapping. In-depth assessments are also available for the functional areas of HR, international taxation, tax audit, tax gap and revenue forecasting, domestic tax evasion, and offshore tax evasion. Moreover, the DIAMOND modules assess the overall performance of tax administrations and customs functions by measuring the gap between actual performance and good practices and standards (external benchmarking). By using specific dimensions, the tool facilitates prioritizing plans for improvement and delineates a technical assistance program and action plan aimed at addressing identified performance gaps.

3 | These practices are extracted from the DIAMOND tax administration functional evaluation and the business process mapping modules.

4 | These practices are extracted from the DIAMOND IT assessment modules that evaluate core ICT governance functions and infrastructure investment needs.

Bibliography

Barnay, Aurélie, Jonathan Davis, Jonathan Dimson, Emma Gibbs, and Daniel Korn. 2018. "Four Innovations Reshaping Tax Administration." McKinsey & Company, January 29, 2018. https://www.mckinsey.com/industries/public-sector/our-insights/four-innovations-reshaping-tax-administration.

Bentley, Duncan. 2019. "Timeless Principles of Taxpayer Protection: How They Adapt to Digital Disruption." *eJournal of Tax Research* 16 (3): 679–713. http://www.austlii.edu.au/au/journals/eJTR/2019/19.pdf.

Dener, Cem, Hubert Nii-Aponsah, Love E. Ghunney, and Kimberly D. Johns. 2021. *GovTech Maturity Index: The State of Public Sector Digital Transformation*. International Development in Focus. Washington, DC: World Bank. http://hdl.handle.net/10986/36233.

Ihnatisinova, Denisa. 2021. "Digitalization of Tax Administration Communication under the Effect of Global Megatrends of the Digital Age." SHS Web of Conferences No. 92, Globalization and Its Socio-Economic Consequences. https://doi.org/10.1051/shsconf/20219202022.

Junquera-Varela, Raúl Félix. 2011. "An Integrated Assessment Model for Tax Administration: The Diagnostic Tool." Poverty Reduction and Economic Management, Public Sector and Governance Group. Unpublished draft, World Bank, Washington, DC.

Junquera-Varela, Raul Felix, Cristian Óliver Lucas-Mas, Ivan Krsul, Vladimir Calderon, and Paola Arce. 2022. "Digital Transformation of Tax and Customs Administrations." Equitable Growth, Finance & Institutions Insight. World Bank, Washington, DC. http://hdl.handle.net/10986/37629.

Krsul, Ivan. 2021. "Building Data Science Capabilities in a Tax Administration. Vol. 7." Working Paper, Unpublished, World Bank, Washington, DC.

Moller, Lars Christian, Raúl Félix, Junquera-Varela, and Daniel Álvarez. 2012. *El Gasto Tributario en Colombia: Una propuesta de evaluación integral y sistemática de este instrumento de política pública*. Washington, DC: World Bank. http://documents.worldbank.org/curated/en/945121468022751656/El-Gasto-Tributario-en-Colombia-una-propuesta-de-evaluacion-integral-y-sistematica-de-este-instrumento-de-politica-publica.

OECD. 2016. *Technologies for Better Tax Administration: A Practical Guide for Revenue Bodies*. Paris: OECD Publishing. https://doi.org/10.1787/9789264256439-en.

OECD. 2017. *Technology Tools to Tackle Tax Evasion and Tax Fraud*. Paris: OECD Publishing. https://www.oecd.org/tax/crime/technology-tools-to-tackle-tax-evasion-and-tax-fraud.htm.

OECD. 2019a. "Tax Compliance Burden Maturity Model." OECD Tax Administration Maturity Model Series, OECD Publishing, Paris. https://www.oecd.org/tax/forum-on-tax-administration/publications-and-products/tax-compliance-burden-maturity-model.pdf.

OECD. 2019b. "Tax Debt Management Maturity Model." OECD Tax Administration Maturity Model Series, OECD Publishing, Paris. https://www.oecd.org/tax/forum-on-tax-administration/publications-and-products/tax-debt-management-maturity-model.pdf.

OECD. 2019c. "Introducing a Commercial Off-the-Shelf Software Solution." OECD Publishing, Paris. https://www.oecd.org/tax/forum-on-tax-administration/publications-and-products/introducing-a-commercial-off-the-shelf-software-solution.pdf.

OECD. 2019d. "Implementing Online Cash Registers: Benefits, Considerations and Guidance." OECD Publishing. https://www.oecd.org/ctp/implementing-online-cash-registers-benefits-considerations-and-guidance.htm.

OECD. 2019e. *Unlocking the Digital Economy–A Guide to Implementing Application Programme Interfaces in Government*. OECD Publishing, Paris. https://www.oecd.org/ctp/unlocking-the-digital-economy-guide-to-implementing-application-programming-interfaces-in-government.htm.

OECD. 2021. *Enterprise Risk Management Maturity Model*. OECD Tax Administration Maturity Model Series. OECD Publishing, Paris. https://www.oecd.org/tax/forum-on-tax-administration/publications-and-products/enterprise-risk-management-maturity-model.htm.

Respati, Nugroho Dian. 2020. "The Adoption of E-Government in the Tax Administration: A Scoping Review." *Scientax, Jurnal Kajian Ilmiah Perpajakan Indonesia* 1 (2): 109–130. https://doi.org/10.52869/st.v1i2.38.

Rosario, Shireen, and Kavita Chavali. 2020. "Digitization of Taxation in the Changing Business Environment & Base Erosion & Profit Shifting (BEPS): Special Reference to India." *European Scientific Journal* 16 (1): 61–74. http://dx.doi.org/10.19044/esj.2020.v16n1p61.

Twesige, Daniel, Faustin Gsheja, Uzziel Hategikimana, Raymond Philippe Ndikubwimana, Yvette Mwiza, and Innocent Hitayezu. 2020. "Smart Taxation (4Taxation): Effect of Fourth Industrial Revolution (4IR) on Tax Compliance in Rwanda." *Journal of Business and Administrative Studies* 12 (1): 1–27. https://doi.org/10.20372/jbas.v12i1.4235.

USAID (United States Agency for International Development). 2013. *Detailed Guidelines for Improved Tax Administration in Latin America and the Caribbean*. USAID's Leadership in Public Financial Management. https://pdf.usaid.gov/pdf_docs/PNAED062.pdf.

World Bank. 2019. "Guidelines for the Development of Tax Diamond Assessments." Unpublished draft for internal review.

World Bank. 2021a. *World Bank Guidebook for Accessible GovTech*. Equitable Growth, Finance & Institutions Insight-Governance. Washington, DC: World Bank. https://thedocs.worldbank.org/en/doc/3fcff7a44bd530a0413e23245ace2f03-0350012021 /related/EFI-Insight-Accessible-GovTech-4-1.pdf.

World Bank. 2021b. *Disruptive Technologies in Public Procurement*. Equitable Growth, Finance & Institutions Insight-Governance. Washington, DC: World Bank. http://documents.worldbank.org/curated/en/522181612428427520/Disruptive-Technologies -in-Public-Procurement.

CHAPTER 4

Selected core business processes of revenue administrations

Taxpayer registration and risk profiling

A comprehensive system of taxpayer registration and identification is critical for the effective operation of a tax system. Similarly, the tax assessment function, which includes all activities related to processing tax returns and payments, and the collection of outstanding returns and payments is important for maintaining high levels of voluntary compliance and citizens' confidence in the tax system. Also, dispute prevention and resolution are essential features of tax systems. All core business processes are equally important and need to be fully aligned; none is more or less important than another. This chapter comments on some of these issues that are of significance for the performance of revenue administrations in discharging their primary role of collecting taxes. This chapter analyzes taxpayer registration and risk profiling; assessment, filing, and revenue collections systems; taxpayer services; tax audit function; and revenue arrears management and tax disputes.

The taxpayer register is the bedrock of a tax administration. Comprehensive systems of taxpayer registration and numbering are a critical feature of the tax administration arrangements in most countries, supporting tax administration processes and underpinning all return filing, collection, and assessment activities. Lack of accuracy and reliability of the taxpayer register will lead to deficiencies in collection and enforcement processes and, subsequently, increases in administrative and compliance costs (Junquera-Varela 2011).

Identification of taxpayers is therefore vital to effectively undertake the spectrum of functions that a tax administration has to perform, including detection of stop-filers, control of compliance, and tax arrears management. Consequently, it is imperative for the tax administration to know its client base, and with a unique Taxpayer Identification Number (TIN) assigned to taxpayers to ensure correct identification in the taxpayer register. Implementation of a unique taxpayer identifier across all tax types, as opposed to multiple TINs, is generally considered good practice. The TIN forms the basic building block for the overall revenue administration information technology (IT) systems, particularly a computerized taxpayer register, as it allows connecting taxpayers to their returns, payments, and major taxable transactions with third parties.

In some countries, tax regulations provide for mandatory use of a unique TIN for all tax-related transactions. This forces taxpayers to register with the revenue administration, and the assigned TIN must be used for all declarations, payments, and correspondence with the tax administration, and in major potentially taxable transactions, it provides all information needed for taxpayers (OECD 2015). Broadening the tax base by registering potential taxpayers and lowering the underreported base require the taxpayer register to be accurate and to include mechanisms for periodic updating. To enforce compliance and reduce evasion, the tax administration needs to understand the extent and nature of the potential tax base. In developing countries, the potentially reachable tax base constitutes a smaller portion of total economic activity because of the (a) informal (shadow economy), which is significant and outside the formal tax structure, and (b) underreported tax base where many taxpayers who are in the tax system are substantially underreporting (Borgne and Baer 2008).

Keeping the database of registered small business taxpayers and other hard-to-tax sectors up to date is extremely difficult due to the high "death rate," but it is necessary and highly recommended, despite limited revenue potential. Small businesses are a highly heterogeneous group, from micro businesses—street traders, subsistence farmers—with limited ability to pay in both fairness and practical terms, to professionals and businesses with many employees. The tax treatment and accurate registration of small businesses have importance beyond revenue generation, as they are often considered important in generating employment and productivity-enhancing innovations. Additionally, bringing small businesses into the tax net can help to secure their participation in the political process and improve government accountability, thus contributing to the overall state-building process.

A unique TIN may also help to build linkages between tax administration and other areas of government. For instance, in Latin America, a unique TIN was introduced initially for tax administration alone, but other government agencies quickly began to make use of it to improve information sharing, leading to broad improvements in performance and data management. In some countries, the TIN is used by various agencies that interact directly with the tax administration, including municipal governments, the civil and company registry, and private banks.

Adopting a TIN system is also recommended in the international context. Globalization and greater international mobility of economic activities, coupled with sophisticated financial systems, increase the ease with which funds may cross international borders to escape taxes. In fact, since 1997, the use of an international TIN has been highly recommended to enhance exchange of information among tax administrations and facilitate processing of information received automatically from a treaty partner (OECD 2004).

There are some key principles to consider when designing a TIN. First, the TIN should consist of a sequential number plus a check-digit for security reasons and to eliminate errors in data processing. Only numbers should be used since alphabetic characters may in some cases lead to confusion—for example, the use of 0 (zero) and the letter O. A second key principle is that only one unique TIN be assigned to each taxpayer, which includes businesses. Duplication of TINs can be a significant problem for some tax administrations because it undermines the taxpayer register, thus adversely affecting the effectiveness of tax administration core processes. Third, only the tax administration should have the responsibility of assigning TINs and managing the taxpayer register database.

Any diagnostic study needs to carefully analyze levels of registration, taking into account specific tax arrangements such as the value added tax (VAT) threshold or final withholding regimes that exempt a significant number of employees from submitting income tax annual returns (box 4.1).

The main functional features and level-specific practices that characterize the different maturity levels of a tax administration (as presented in chapter 3) in terms of taxpayer registration can be classified as follows (USAID 2013):

BOX 4.1   Assessment of the taxpayer registration system of a tax administration

1. Is the taxpayer registry fully computerized?

2. What taxpayer attributes are stored in the registry: date of formation, entity type, economic activity, or other key attributes? (Please enumerate.)

3. Does the tax administration use a single Taxpayer Identification Number (TIN)?

4. Is it mandatory by law to use the TIN for all tax-related transactions, including customs?

5. Is only one TIN assigned to each taxpayer? Are there registration controls in place to avoid duplicate TINs or duplicate registrations of the same taxpayer?

6. Is the tax administration the only body responsible for assigning TINs?

7. Are there electronic forms on the tax administration website to facilitate taxpayers complying with their registration obligations?

8. In case of noncompliance with registration requirements, does a sanctions regime exist?

9. Are taxpayers obliged to inform the tax administration about changes in data contained in the taxpayer registry?

10. Do legal provisions allow the tax administration to correct inaccurate data in the taxpayer's information in the register?

11. Does the tax administration periodically update the taxpayer registry? If so, what is the frequency of this process?

12. Does the tax administration periodically clean up the taxpayer registery of inactive taxpayers?

13. Does the tax administration routinely and systematically carry out checks to detect and bring to the tax net unregistered taxpayers?

14. Has the administration developed a general taxpayer compliance strategy that aims at promoting voluntary compliance? One of the elements of this strategy is to control compliance of taxpayers with registration and/or register obligations. In case of noncompliance with registration requirements, does a sanctions regime exist?

15. If so, could you please describe the procedures, its frequency, and outcomes?

16. Assess the growth rate of the taxpayer population over the past years, and break it down by taxpayer's size.

Note: TIN = Taxpayer Identification Number.

Maturity level 1: Initial

- Limited registration information is recorded. Information for third-party data matching, for example, business registry numbers, or information needed for good planning, such as expected turnover, is not included.
- Required written policies and procedures for registration staff do not exist, and staff act independently, inconsistently, and erratically.
- Tax file numbers are issued by different entities and are not controlled by the tax administration. Taxpayers identify themselves by name and may be unaware of their assigned file number, which may change from year to year.
- There are separate registration forms and procedures for each type of tax. Registration requires visits to multiple tax offices and the approval of tax officials.
- Registration information (the taxpayer register) is not properly maintained—for example, to cater to business reorganization or liquidation, and it contains taxpayers that are no longer in operation.
- The tax administration does not use third-party information to track noncompliance.
- Registration systems are manual, with little modern technology and equipment available.

Maturity level 2: Basic (Practices for Controlled Operations)

- Some basic registration information is recorded: taxpayer name, contact, responsible parties, and so on; however, information for third-party data matching (business registry numbers) or information needed for good planning, such as expected turnover, is not included.
- Issuance of new file numbers is done solely by the tax administration, but taxpayers continue to identify themselves by name.

- There are separate registration forms for each type of tax, although registration procedures may be similar. Registration requires a visit to a single tax office and, still, the approval of a tax official.
- Some parts of the registration process have written instructions, but there is inconsistency in application across the tax administration's field offices.
- Registration information is not properly maintained, for example, to record business reorganization or liquidation, and it contains taxpayers that are no longer in operation.
- The tax administration does not use third-party information to track noncompliance.
- Most registration work is still done manually, with little modern technology and equipment available. What little computerization equipment is available is supported by outdated technology.

Maturity level 3: Intermediate (Practices for Efficient Operations)

- Almost all registration information is recorded, including information for third-party data matching, for example, business registry numbers. However, information needed for good planning, such as expected turnover, is not available.
- TINs are issued by the tax administration and used by taxpayers to identify themselves. TINs are not sufficiently well controlled by the tax administration to ensure uniqueness.
- Registration is integrated across taxes with a single form and a single facility to register for all tax obligations. No tax administration official's approval is needed, but taxpayers still experience delays.
- Step-by-step operational procedures for the registration process are available and are consistently applied across the organization.
- Registration information is maintained through occasional ad hoc programs but not in a timely manner. Maintenance includes adding new registrants as well as removing taxpayers who are no longer active. It does not include updating information upon taxpayer reorganization.
- The tax administration uses third-party information to track noncompliance but does so in an ad hoc manner and irregularly.
- Modern technology and equipment are available for registration, but there are often ongoing maintenance issues, and funds for the purchase of new equipment or supplies are often limited.

Maturity level 4: Advanced (Practices for Sustainable and Optimized Operations)

- All necessary basic taxpayer information is recorded, including information that allows third-party data matching, for example, business registry numbers, and information that allows for good planning, such as expected turnover.
- Unique TINs are issued and controlled by the tax administration and used by taxpayers to identify themselves.
- Registration is integrated across tax types with a single form and a single facility to register for all tax obligations. Registration is automated and expedited.
- Operational procedures are integrated with the IT tax administration system, with as many steps as possible being automated.
- Registration information is maintained regularly and in a timely manner, not only by adding new registrants but also by removing taxpayers who are no longer active and by updating information upon taxpayer reorganization.
- The tax administration regularly uses third-party information to track noncompliance.

Taxpayer segmentation as a core strategy of a modern tax administration

Taxpayer registration is key to managing compliance risks effectively. To this end, the revenue body needs to analyze and develop knowledge for each group of taxpayers: main characteristics, key sectors of economy, type of risks, and needs. "Market segmentation" may be based on type of tax, size of organization, type of activity (industry/sector), or type of risk. This analysis is very useful in developing strategies that are tailored to the unique characteristics and compliance issues presented by each group of taxpayers. For example, information obtained in the analysis can help in developing risk management approaches to tax auditing and to tailor control of compliance to taxpayer risk profiles. An overall taxpayer segmentation strategy must include as well as evaluate market segmentation strategies of the tax administration, strengths and weaknesses of large taxpayer units (LTUs), whether or not there are specific offices to handle the medium taxpayers segment, criteria to classify taxpayers in the different segments, legal provision for the segment of small taxpayers, control processes in place, and IT equipment and functions covered by LTUs and medium taxpayer units (MTUs) (Junquera-Varela 2011).

Since enforcement or compliance resources for issues including monitoring taxpayers that have escaped registration requirements, on-time filing and payment compliance, and inaccurate reporting should be directed at cases exhibiting the highest risk to revenue, it is essential to assess market segmentation strategies of the tax administration, evaluate risk-profiling approaches, and analyze in the light of this the appropriateness of control of compliance strategies. This should also be an element to consider when it comes to assessing the efficiency of tax administration. If large taxpayers' share in tax revenue receipts is very high, assessors should flag this in the report, putting special emphasis on recommendations aimed at reinforcing control mechanisms. This will help to focus on preventing sudden drops in revenue as a consequence of lack of control of this segment, which concentrates a significant amount of tax revenue directly and via withholding arrangements.

Knowing the growth rate of the taxpayer population over the past years is also important to guide better allocation of resources. Tables that break down taxpayer population by size covering a significant number of years can be very useful in this regard. Additional information could incorporate the distribution of taxpayer population by provinces or regions. Analysis of workload of tax offices can be an important complement to this analysis. Table 4.1 shows the main characteristics of segments of taxpayers, classified by size.

TABLE 4.1 Main characteristics of different groups of taxpayers

Key features	Large taxpayers	Medium-size taxpayers	Micro and small taxpayers
Revenue generation.	High	Medium	Low
Business structure.	• Entities and corporate groups that, in many cases, have subsidiaries abroad. It may also include state-owned enterprises. • A small number of entities that account for a substantial amount of revenue generated from direct and indirect taxes.	• Incorporated businesses across manufacturing activities, construction, or services. • A moderate number of taxpayers that account for a significant amount of tax revenue.	• Micro businesses, self-employed professionals, and entrepreneurs. This segment consists of a large number of companies that encompass a wide range of activities (mostly retail) that account for a small part of revenue collected by the tax administration.
Noncompliance	• Complexities involved result in a substantial amount of revenue at stake. Legal interpretations are often the key issue in a tax audit. • Tax avoidance in the form of tax planning is very common.	• Noncompliance comes mainly from underreporting of sources of income and overclaiming of tax credits and deductions. • Tax evasion and tax avoidance through tax planning are common.	• Significant presence of informal economy.

(continued)

TABLE 4.1 Main characteristics of different groups of taxpayers (*Continued*)

Key features	Large taxpayers	Medium-size taxpayers	Micro and small taxpayers
Tax audit.	• Comprehensive tax audits. • High audit coverage. • A significant amount of tax disputes.	• Different types of audits, including comprehensive tax audits and issue-oriented audits. • Moderate audit coverage. • Cross-check of third-party information through mass audits is being increasingly used.	• Low level of audit coverage. • Verification activities and cross-check of third-party information.
Taxpayer assistance.	• Personalized • Emphasis on prevention.	• General programs. • Online services through virtual offices and call centers.	Online services.
Submission of tax returns.	E-filing and e-payment are widely used. In some countries, it is mandatory for large taxpayers to file tax returns electronically.	E-filing and e-payment are increasingly used.	Tax administration assists taxpayers in preparation of tax returns. In most cases, paper is still used.
Collection of tax arrears.	• Complex issue. • Need to establish dedicated units to deal with large taxpayers' tax debts.	Medium-intensity collection mechanisms.	Low-intensity administrative mechanisms to collect tax revenue, such as phone calls or issuance of reminders.

Source: Original table for this publication.

Assessment, filing, and revenue collection systems

The tax assessment function includes all activities related to processing tax returns, including issuing assessments, refunds, notices, and statements. It also includes the processing and banking of payments.

Determining tax liabilities

The process of determining tax liabilities may be done administratively or through self-assessment procedures. Administrative assessment entails officials from the tax administration examining tax returns prior to issuing assessment to taxpayers. This type of assessment is used with most property taxes. According to the self-assessment principle, taxpayers provide the tax administration with information about their income sources and performed transactions, and calculate tax liabilities accordingly.

An increasing number of tax administrations are relying on self-assessment rather than administrative assessment. This reflects a move toward (a) more comprehensive and targeted approach to providing help and assistance to taxpayers, (b) systematic verification of reported tax liabilities through risk-based desk and field audits, and (c) computerized matching of income reports. For a self-assessment procedure to function properly, seven preconditions must be in place (Ebrill et al. 2001):

1. A simple, clear, stable law
2. A good taxpayer service
3. Simple procedure, such as simplified tax return forms
4. Effective enforcement
5. A reasonable audit
6. Strict penalties
7. A good administrative review system

In recent years, some countries have evolved their systems by increasingly prefilling tax returns with information obtained from third-party sources. Initially, third-party information was made available to taxpayers, preferably online, and prepopulated tax returns were sent to them with the understanding that taxpayers would agree to the calculations, indicate additional sources of income, or provide information that would change the figures. This is a significant change in the tax administration approach to processing tax returns and to controlling compliance. The system of prepopulated tax returns has evolved from prefilling on paper some data to completely automating tax return preparation and assessment.

Electronic filing and electronic payment

Toward the end of the 1980s, a number of revenue bodies implemented arrangements enabling the electronic filing of tax returns by tax return preparers and some individual taxpayers. Since then, the use of electronic filing has increased significantly as internet use has grown among citizens. Electronic filing reduces the costs for taxpayers as well as the administration. Taxpayers spend less time to prepare their returns, resulting in significant reduction in taxpayers' compliance cost (Crotty and Santos 2001). On the other hand, allowing taxpayers to submit the returns electronically significantly reduces administrative costs, especially tax return processing costs. Additionally, the cost of correcting taxpayers' and data entry errors is significantly reduced. Given that, on average, between 10 and 20 percent of the manually prepared forms contain taxpayers' errors and those errors need to be corrected, the tax administration's savings are considerable. Other significant benefits with electronic filing are improvement in the quality of information available to the tax administration and released resources that could be assigned to other tasks to enable the achievement of the ultimate goal of enhancing voluntary compliance.

The following are some additional benefits of electronic filing and electronic payment (USAID 2013):

1. Convenience—returns can accommodate the taxpayer's schedule and be filed at any time, day or night.
2. Saves time, as returns do not require taxpayers making a trip to get a physical return from an office or waiting for the return to arrive by mail.
3. Increased taxpayer and client satisfaction.
4. Certainty of delivery and quick confirmation of receipt, as tax administrations can provide an email confirmation that returns have been received.
5. Fast refunds—allow taxpayers receiving refunds to get them sooner.
6. Ensures taxpayer privacy and security.
7. Online help facilities and user guides can foster self-filing, saving taxpayers time and money that would have been paid to professional tax preparers.
8. Use of online commercial tax preparation software.
9. Eliminates data entry errors and improves data quality.
10. Reduces tax administration operational costs by eliminating the cost of handling paper returns, and staff required for data entry and file maintenance can be reduced.

Overall, e-filing systems significantly reduce the time to prepare and pay taxes, and the likelihood and frequency of visits by tax officials. Since these tax compliance costs are often cited as an impediment to doing business, investing in e-filing can have high returns for firms and the countries where they operate (Kochanova, Hasnain, and Larson 2020). However, these benefits accrue most reliably with e-filing systems that feature an e-payment option, which are more advanced and therefore costlier. Moreover, investments in e-filing can reduce tax evasion in less developed countries, as evidenced by the increase in the ratio of income tax revenue to gross domestic product with the adoption of transactional e-filing systems.

The number of tax returns submitted annually and design of tax return forms are also issues of interest to analyze. It is important to design simple tax return forms to facilitate compliance and reduce both administrative and taxpayer compliance costs, and basic guidelines for tax form design should include the following (USAID 2013):

1. All forms should have a consistent look as part of a corporate identity, and certain information blocks should be standardized.
2. Information requested should be consistent across the whole series of tax returns and other documents.
3. All forms should have a form number and a revision date.
4. Form-making software is available and should be used to prepare all forms to provide a professional appearance.
5. If forms are completed by hand, the response areas should provide sufficient space to accommodate large script.
6. Lines and cells in forms should be numbered. This makes references in instructions easy to follow and navigation in the form simpler.
7. Questions and response areas should follow in a logical progression.
8. Statutory references should be absent or should be included as footnotes to any explanatory notes or instructions.
9. All forms available to the public should be accessible online through the tax administration website, either for download or to be filled out online and submitted.
10. Clear instructions with examples should be provided.
11. In cases where minimal information is captured and a large number of forms need to be processed, the tax administration should consider the use of forms that can be processed using optical character recognition technology.
12. Some tax administrations have implemented preprinted forms, where some information, mainly identification information, is printed on forms that are sent to taxpayers. This process relies on a well-established and efficient mailing infrastructure.
13. With the increase in the amount of electronic data being collected for audit and other purposes, tax administrations have the ability to prepopulate tax forms for taxpayers in some cases. For example, the use of electronic invoices and information from customs facilitates the preparation of a prepopulated form for the monthly VAT filing.

On-time return filing and on-time payment

While revenue authorities may be successful in bringing more taxpayers into the tax system (increase in number of registered taxpayers), the number of taxpayers who file or those who pay positive amounts of each tax on time or within a specified number of days may be lower. For instance, in some regions, the number of registered taxpayers is impressively high, but the number of taxpayers who file is lower, and the number of taxpayers who pay positive amounts of each tax is even lower. Consequently, once filing requirements are determined, the tax administration needs to define the procedures to deal with stop-filers or nonfilers—those who do not file tax returns even if required to do so. For effective stop-filer control, adequate penalty regimes and imposition procedures need to be in place, a reliable master file created, and procedures instituted to verify that the taxpayers on the master file who are required to file returns have indeed done so

(Crotty and Santos 2001). An important issue to be noted while implementing stop-filer control is related to filing requirements for those with fluctuating incomes near a tax threshold.

To detect nonfilers, stop-filers, and delinquent taxpayers, special emphasis should be placed on frequency, hit rate (results), and linkages to the quality and accuracy of taxpayer registry. Also, it should be noted that on-time filing rates may be expected to improve further as electronic filing and taxpayer services, such as prefiling, continue to grow.

Payment of tax constitutes one of the most common interactions between taxpayers and tax administrations, especially for businesses that are typically required to regularly remit a variety of payments covering both their own tax liabilities and those of their employees. Administrations continue to make progress in increasing the range of e-payment options available to taxpayers and to promote their use. Such progress not only lowers the cost to the administration but can also increase on-time payments and reduce the number of payment arrears cases by providing improved access and a better payment experience.

As shown by OECD country surveys (OECD 2013a, 2015, 2019a), on average, the on-time payments rates for corporate income tax (CIT), VAT, and employer withholding tax are higher than the on-time filing rates, but for personal income tax (PIT), the on-time payment rates are lower than the on-time filing rates. This means businesses are more likely to pay on time than file on time, while individuals are more likely to file on time than pay on time. Indeed, the range of on-time payment shows a significant gap in on-time payment across the main tax types for a number of jurisdictions, in some cases above 50 percentage points. This is similar to what has been observed in relation to on-time filing.

Revenue collection systems

Efficient management of the massive documentation and information flows from tax filings, customs declarations, and payment processes is critical to a revenue collection system. Most countries have automated these processes. In addition, most tax administrations have delegated the task of receiving and processing tax declarations and payments to banks. Taxes are collected by the banks and reported to the national treasury, which passes on the information in electronic form to the tax administration. Banks send collected taxes to the treasury department electronically and inform the tax administration about tax payments received. The tax administration reconciles information received about taxpayer payments with payments credited to treasury accounts. Reliability and timeliness of information processed from banks are vital to detect noncompliance by identifying nonfilers and nonpayers (Crotty and Santos 2001).

Common risks in the payments process are liquidity risk, operational risks, security risks, and legal risks (USAID 2013). To mitigate some of the tax administration's risk, various safeguards should be implemented, including:

- Strong internal and data processing controls on all programs
- Written agreements establishing procedures and risks
- Implementation and periodic review of internal controls that address access control, confidentiality of data, integrity of data, and other information security issues, as appropriate

Box 4.2 summarizes the key critical issues to be examined in the course of a technical assessment of the revenue collection systems and procedures of tax administration (Junquera-Varela 2011), particularly the flow of tax and accounting information among bank accounts, tax administration, and the treasury.

BOX 4.2 Key critical issues of revenue collection systems and procedures of tax administrations

1. Modalities of sending information to the tax administration and treasury, frequency of information submission, and reconciliation

2. Revenue collection and accounting systems and how information is matched against the bank's information and what is contained in tax returns

3. Bank's responsibility to collect taxes and ways of remunerating them

4. Monitoring compliance of banks with their contractual obligations in terms of submitting on time to the treasury the amount of collected taxes and providing quality information to the tax administration—for example, through a dedicated unit within the tax administration

5. Sanction regimes in place in case of the bank's noncompliance with contractual obligations

6. Withholding arrangements and mechanisms for both income tax and value added tax (VAT), considering their importance not only as a way of collecting taxes in advance but also as a vital source of information for the tax administration

7. Third-party information sources available to tax administration and the legal powers granted to tax administration to get information from third-party sources

8. Frequency and mechanisms of cross-checking information collected from third parties against tax returns data

9. Ways and modalities of proving feedback on the results of the cross-checking process

10. Use of new technologies to increase efficiency and effectiveness of collection, with special emphasis on the digitalization process that directly impacts collection systems

The centrality of the taxpayer account

Monitoring compliance requires the establishment and maintenance of taxpayer current accounts and a management information system (MIS) covering ultimate taxpayers and third-party agents such as banks involved in the tax system as well as appropriate and prompt procedures to detect and follow up on nonfilers and delayed payments (Bird 2014). Consequently, a single taxpayer account based on a unified taxpayer register should be established. A well-designed taxpayer account will support the integration of a taxpayer's account information, taxes, and collection data, in addition to third-party information, into a unified database. This will enable automatic updates of taxpayers' accounts by incorporating the impact of administrative decisions such as assessments, penalties, appeals, and refunds regarding a taxpayer's liabilities.

Additionally, improved reliability and accuracy of tax administration data, including the identity of registered taxpayers, efficient taxpayer account management and guidelines, and strong established links between information management and core business processes of tax administration, are conducive to strengthening the tax administration and improving control of compliance and collection enforcement mechanisms.

Furthermore, the integrated taxpayer account would contribute to the following: (a) taxpayer services and accuracy of tax administration could be improved and effective risk management facilitated, (b) automated decision support tools could be developed to improve the efficiency and effectiveness of responses to noncompliance, and (c) additional tools could be developed to allow taxpayers to access their accounts and interact with the tax administration via the internet, resulting in a reduction of compliance costs and promotion of voluntary compliance. The ideal approach is to combine these measures so they could have a maximum effect on compliance.

Box 4.3 provides a summary of all the issues discussed that should be examined in the course of a technical assessment of the tax assessment and revenue collection functions of the tax administration.

BOX 4.3 Assessment of tax assessment and revenue collection of tax administrations

1. Are taxpayers able to submit tax returns electronically or to file returns by post? If the latter is valid, is it backed up with strong legal guarantees and a public relations campaign? (Filing returns by post office or paying through banks is still highly relevant in low-income countries. Both these options have the strong merit of reducing face-to-face contact between taxpayers and tax officials, which is a venue for bribery. Filing by post also needs strong legal guarantees—for example, if a taxpayer sends the tax return by registered mail and has a receipt, they cannot be held liable if the post delivers it later than promised.)

2. Are taxpayers able to make electronic payments or to pay through banks?

3. Examine the revenue collection systems and procedures of the tax administration, especially the flow of tax and accounting information between banks and the tax administration and the treasury accounts. In particular, note how the information is sent to the tax administration and the treasury, frequency of information submission, and reconciliation mechanisms.

4. Examine how this information is matched against the bank's information or third-party information contained in tax returns.

5. Do commercial banks collect tax payments; do they receive tax returns?

6. Examine different services provided from banks to tax administrations in addition to collecting tax payments and receiving tax returns. For example, in some countries, they help taxpayers prepare their declarations.

7. In case commercial banks collect tax payments and/or receive tax returns, how are banks compensated for their services? Under which category does it fall?

8. In case commercial banks collect tax payments and/or receive tax returns, what are banks' tasks and responsibilities?

9. Is there a dedicated unit within the tax administration to monitor banks' compliance with their contractual obligations?

10. Does a sanction regime exist in case of noncompliance with those contractual obligations?

11. Are systems and procedures in place to detect nonfilers, stop-filers, and delinquent taxpayers? If so, it is advisable to have a description of these procedures to try to find possible bottlenecks.

12. Are third-party information sources available to the tax administration? If so, these sources should be described by the tax administration officials and put in a table to find out the capacity of the tax administration to undertake data cross-checking with information contained in tax returns.

13. If information is collected from third parties, is it systematically and routinely cross-checked against tax returns data? If so, the team should request information about the frequency of this process and results obtained.

14. Are there sound and clearly understood systems and procedures for generating and dealing with information exchange requests from other tax administrations, subnational governments, or other areas of the public sector? If so, information about number of requests made to or received from other revenue bodies should be requested.

15. Obtain information about practical implementation problems arising from implementation of exchange of information agreements or implementation of exchange of information and any tax collections request clauses contained in double taxation conventions in place.

Taxpayer services

The taxpayer services division, which generally consumes about 10 percent of a tax administration's human resources, usually has responsibility for developing comprehensive taxpayer services strategies linked to the organization's overall compliance strategy, taking into account taxpayer demands, needs, geography, and service channel options. Most modern taxpayer service functions are the centralized point for providing taxpayer information and educational services, and typically include the following activities (USAID 2013):

1. Registering taxpayers and assigning a unique TIN
2. Maintaining and updating taxpayer registers
3. Interacting with taxpayers who visit, call, or write
4. Providing and staffing taxpayer service counters and call-in operations
5. Responding to general inquiries, including registration, filing, payment requirements, and basic tax law, and ensuring that taxpayers are routed to other departments as appropriate
6. Providing tax returns and instructions

7. Developing informational and educational publications
8. Conducting seminars on changes to tax laws and procedures for targeted business audiences
9. Monitoring subjects of queries to determine the need for additional educational materials for taxpayers, internal tax administration training, and possible internal operational changes
10. Developing and maintaining the content of the tax administration website

As the EU *Risk Management Guide for Tax Administrations* (European Commission 2006) highlights, the primary goal of a tax administration is to collect the taxes payable in accordance with the law and to do this in such a manner that will sustain confidence in the tax system and its administration. Attaining this objective requires a strategy aimed at increasing levels of voluntary compliance that rests on two main pillars: (a) facilitating taxpayers complying with their tax obligations and (b) enforcing noncompliance.

Facilitating compliance requires improving the efficiency and quality of taxpayer services. The importance of the link between better tax services and tax compliance has always been difficult to prove, but it is widely accepted among tax experts and is a regular feature of tax reform programs (LeBaube and Vehorn 1992). Aiming at fostering this linkage, as emphasized by the OECD *Model on Compliance Risk Management* (OECD 2004) and the more recent EU *Compliance Risk Management Capability Maturity Model* (European Commission 2021), many revenue bodies have developed taxpayers' service strategies. Putting in place a sound strategy to provide services to taxpayers is widely considered a good practice. Challenges involved in providing such services include complexities of the tax laws and procedural regulations, degree of literacy and education of the population, the huge number of taxpayers in some taxes such as the income tax, investment in information and communication technology (ICT), and the spread of internet or e-services in a given country. This plan should establish specific objectives and the different modalities of delivering this assistance that should be tailored to different characteristics of different segments of taxpayers. In some countries, authorities publicize a chart of services in which they commit to achieve certain standards of service.

These strategies center on the following (OECD 2007):

1. Reducing taxpayer uncertainty by clarifying legal and procedural ambiguities through outreach and tax education programs
2. Ceasing to change the legal and regulatory framework so often that no one knows what it is about
3. Tailoring taxpayer services and information to respond to different characteristics of taxpayer segments by better understanding taxpayer attitudes to better identify underlying factors of noncompliance
4. Setting service delivery standards and measuring performance against those standards, such as turnaround time to answer taxpayer enquiries, average time to process taxpayer tax refund, and average time to resolve taxpayer disputes and to process CIT returns
5. Making more effective use of service standards and extending service delivery channels available to taxpayers

A taxpayer strategy should be based on market segmentation to better tailor taxpayer services and information to the different characteristics of taxpayer segments. This will enable better allocation of limited resources available to tax administrations. For instance, high-quality services and compliance enforcement strategy to non–large taxpayers emerged with the establishment of medium taxpayer offices in Indonesia and Francophone Africa and some innovative small taxpayer approaches in Algeria, Tanzania, and some Francophone African countries. The strategy should also be based on the broad recognition that good taxpayer services in the form of prevention measures play a key role in the compliance risk management process that aims at minimizing the tax gap (IFC 2011). Taxpayer services are an important element in preventing risks of noncompliance and may have a significant impact on compliance trends.

In addition to providing taxpayers with services to help them comply with the tax law, tax administrations have to address noncompliance issues and establish place strategies to respond to taxpayers' noncompliance schemes (OECD 2016). While recognizing that promoting voluntary compliance is the most cost-effective way of collecting tax revenues, tax administrations have to face levels of noncompliance that should be kept to a minimum level. Triggering control of compliance mechanisms is very costly, and that is why advanced tax administrations adopt a risk management approach to direct resources to taxpayers posing a higher risk to revenue.

It is vital to understand taxpayer attitudes with a view to better identifying the underlying factors for noncompliance. In some cases, compliance strategies will focus on prevention—assisting taxpayers to comply with tax laws. In other cases, and depending on attitudes to compliance, the tax administration will prioritize "soft" forms of control aimed at deterring noncompliance and promoting voluntary compliance (OECD 2014a). Only in the most severe cases will deployment of the complete set of enforcement powers available to tax administration be the most appropriate choice. As a result, compliance strategies are implemented in the most cost-efficient way.

Modern tax administrations are moving toward a client-oriented organization and using an extensive array of services and activities aimed at facilitating voluntary compliance by minimizing the cost of complying with tax obligations. Driven by the objectives of improving both the efficiency and quality of taxpayers' services, many revenue bodies have taken steps to make more effective use of various technology-driven changes in delivering services to taxpayers (OECD 2004), including (a) establishment of customer service units within the tax administration's organizational structure, (b) implementation of an electronic tax filing and collection system through commercial banks, (c) creation of e-tax offices, (d) design and implementation of a set of electronic tools to support taxpayer compliance and interaction with the tax administration, (e) client support programs for filling out and completing income tax returns, (f) establishment of call centers and contact points, (g) introduction of e-invoicing, (h) creation of e-service to electronically pay tax returns, (i) application of information technology to paperless processing imports and exports, and/or (j) implementation of massive virtual training programs through e-based and face-to-face courses.

As indicated above, tax administrations have a variety of channels for delivering services to taxpayers. Each of these channels has different strengths and weaknesses and entails different delivery costs. Therefore, a systematic study of these considerations is needed to arrive at a taxpayer service strategy featuring an optimal mix of service delivery channels in terms of effectiveness and efficiency. This is called the "channel strategy," which should cover technical and physical infrastructure, delivery channels, service content, and administrative processes and culture (OECD 2007).

Successful experiences in tax assistance relate to the establishment of electronic or virtual tax offices. A wide range of services—for example, submit and pay tax returns electronically, register online, submit tax appeals, and request tax installments—is provided through these virtual tax offices. To allow taxpayers to benefit from the use of modern electronic services, it is vital to remove technical complexities. Some developing countries require for every electronic transaction the use of a digital certificate and electronic signature (OECD 2013b). This is considered a major obstacle to the expansion of electronic tax services and to the establishment of a full-fledged virtual tax office. Countries such as Argentina, Brazil, and Chile have reached very high percentages in providing electronic services to taxpayers by using simple identification mechanisms.

Providing a wide range of services to taxpayers and developing service standard charters through a participatory and consultative process are often as or more cost-effective in securing compliance than measures such as audit and penalties that are more directly designed to counter noncompliance. Importantly, service delivery standards should be not only monitored continuously but also published and disseminated widely. Credible service delivery monitoring and reporting systems generally enhance taxpayers' perception of the tax system in terms of fairness, transparency, and accountability (OECD 2014c).

Box 4.4 provides a brief description of recommended tools to assess the effectiveness of a taxpayer assistance strategy. By using these tools, revenue agencies in developing and transition economies would be able to better understand the experiences and perceptions of taxpayers with regard to compliance decisions and costs as well as the overall tax morale in the country.

Generally, efforts to improve taxpayer services focus on tax outreach and education programs and measures to reduce compliance costs, including taxpayer support services. Tax administrations are increasingly recognizing the importance of including tax issues in education plans, starting in schools. Furthermore, experience in a few countries suggests that two other areas may be particularly important to consider: (a) improved monitoring of tax officials to reduce arbitrary behavior and (b) strengthened state–society engagement with tax issues by creating institutionalized channels for consulting with taxpayer groups, business associations, civil society, and other stakeholders. Such strategies can have positive results in terms of improving the investment climate, increasing social acceptance of the tax system, building trust between the tax administration and citizens, and enhancing transparency and accountability (OECD 2016). For a detailed analysis on nontechnical drivers and political economy considerations for tax reform, see the section on "Tax Morale and Other Nontechnical Drivers" in chapter 1 and appendix C.

Providing taxpayers with high-quality services is of paramount importance to increase government's legitimacy and promote social acceptance of the tax system. Social acceptance of the tax system is essential to collect revenue effectively and efficiently. Sociological and political factors, such as cultural norms, history, attitude to government, frequency of granting fiscal amnesty and changing the civil servants, or educational level, therefore play a key role in shaping taxpayers' compliance. For instance, amnesty schemes offering waivers of tax, interest, and penalties, often with "no questions asked," can undermine compliance by creating expectations of more to come and doing a keenly felt injustice to the compliant (Borgne and Baer 2008). Another example is when noncompliance is widespread or perceived as such by taxpayers. In this noncompliance environment, each

---

BOX 4.4   Recommended tools to assess the effectiveness of taxpayer assistance strategy

- Surveys of taxpayers' perception of the quality of services provided by the tax administration are a good practice, albeit it is difficult to feed the outcomes of these surveys into tax administration processes. Numerous surveys attempting to collect information on taxpayer perceptions of tax regimes have been conducted in various developing countries. However, to entirely materialize the benefits from these surveys, two critical issues should be taken into consideration: who designs and who conducts the survey. Questions should be worded neutrally to avoid encouraging favorable responses. Those conducting the survey need to have high credibility in their willingness and ability to protect the confidentiality of all individual respondents.

- Tax perception and compliance cost surveys are important to assess the effectiveness of a taxpayer assistance strategy and its impact on compliance costs. Surveys aimed at capturing perceptions of tax compliance and taxpayer experience with tax compliance costs are

very useful. This would be beneficial to better measure the tax compliance gap and better understand determinants of tax compliance. Tax compliance costs surveys are critical to assessing the efficiency of tax regimes through quantifiable data on the cost of compliance, including the hidden burdens imposed on businesses (in addition to actual tax payments) through the compliance process. These surveys also play a key role in trying to understand general trends in tax compliance.

- Compliance cost surveys are somewhat less common but have been conducted in a few developing countries. Though the number of developing countries where these surveys have been conducted is limited, they have been able to generate substantial knowledge. Their strengths include their ability to capture a broad range of explanatory variables known only to taxpayers, notably their understanding of compliance requirements, relevant values and attitudes, expectations of risks and benefits of noncompliance, and the overall tax morale in the country.

Source: IFC 2011.

individual taxpayer has a strong incentive not to comply. In contrast, when compliance is the social norm, individuals tend to comply more easily, because they fear being identified as dishonest by their peers and because the probability of detection is likely to be high.

Therefore, actions to improve perceptions of tax administrations by taxpayers can include the following: taxpayer education programs, simplified and clear tax laws, simple and streamlined tax procedures, an effective fight against tax fraud, and public expenditure efficiency, effectiveness, and equity. Others are delivery of good taxpayer services facilitating voluntary compliance; external and internal communication channels to disseminate the objective and results achieved by the tax administration; and permanent dialogue with the private sector, other government departments, universities, the judicial power, and other stakeholders (IFC 2011).

It is important not only to take stock of all the different services provided to taxpayers by the tax administration but also to pay special attention to the level of performance achieved. Additionally, consider turnaround time to answer taxpayer enquiries, consistency of interpretation of tax laws, average time to process taxpayer tax refunds, average time to resolve taxpayer disputes, and the range and quality of electronic services provided in specific areas such as taxpayer registration and submission and payment of tax returns. Some tax administrations have committed to complying with service standards—providing charts of services (OECD 2013b). It is advisable to measure actual performance against standards established by the tax administration, if any.

Box 4.5 summarizes some taxpayer services issues that influence tax administration (Junquera-Varela 2011), which should be examined in the course of any tax administration evaluation to diagnose the type of reform needed.

BOX 4.5 Assessment of taxpayer services issues that influence tax administration

1. Is there a strategic plan for the provision of taxpayer services that sets out objectives and targets for performance, including desired levels of service for all product lines?

2. Is there a strategic approach to service delivery that is aligned with the compliance enforcement strategies of the institution?

3. Has the public sector developed a whole-of-government service delivery architecture or put in place an e-government agenda?

4. Describe service delivery channels used by the tax administration or ways of providing information and assistance to taxpayers, such as call centers, telephone help lines, information about the tax system and tax procedures, or assistance to help fill out forms.

5. Has the tax administration set up a one-stop office to assist taxpayers in meeting their tax obligations?

6. Has the tax administration established an e-office? If so, what facilities and services are provided by this virtual office?

7. What is the take-up ratio of electronic services? In particular, provide information about the take-up ratio of electronic submission and payment of tax returns.

8. Has the tax administration provided incentives to taxpayers to increase the use of electronic services? Examples include more expeditious tax refunds in case of e-filing.

9. Is the electronic submission of tax returns mandatory for all or for specific taxpayer segments?

10. Is there a security strategy to maintain confidentiality, integrity, and availability and accessibility of data and systems? How does this strategy address authentication and authorization issues, as well as key aspects such as business continuity in case of system disruption?

11. What are the security requirements necessary to receive electronic service? Are electronic signatures and/or digital certificates mandatory?

12. Does the tax administration regularly conduct taxpayer satisfaction surveys or perception and compliance cost surveys to know taxpayers' views or perceptions on aspects of service delivery, administration of tax laws, and compliance costs? How effective are the feedback systems of the tax administration in this regard? How successfully is feedback used to enhance organizational performance?

13. Are there estimates of tax compliance costs?

14. Has the administration provided a targeted risk-based taxpayer education program? Is any outreach program currently operative?

15. Is there any institutional channel in place for consulting with taxpayer groups, business associations, civil society, and other stakeholders? Please provide examples.

16. Has the tax administration committed to achieving standards of service delivery to taxpayers? Are these "charts of service delivery standards" made public?

17. Does the revenue body publish the results it achieves vis-à-vis its formal service standards?

Tax audit function

Audits are a key tool used by tax administrations to increase compliance. They are used to (a) detect and redress individual cases of noncompliance, (b) promote voluntary compliance by increasing the probability of detection and penalties for noncompliant taxpayers, and (c) gather information on both the health of the tax system and the evasion techniques used by taxpayers. Additionally, audits provide a good opportunity for the tax administration to educate taxpayers on their legal obligations or bookkeeping requirements, thereby improving future compliance.

Modern tax administrations develop audit strategies and plans within a context of compliance management that aims to find the right balance between audit activities and taxpayer assistance as indicated above. On the one hand, the tax department should be seeking to maximize the number of taxpayers who choose to voluntarily comply through taxpayer assistance and education programs. On the other hand, the department must have effective enforcement-related strategies to deter, detect, and address noncompliance. These enforcement strategies should be based on risk management approaches. In this vein, the intensity of audit activity should depend on the level of risk to revenue, which, in turn, is related to the market segments where and when the risks occur (Khwaja, Awasthi, and Loeprick 2011).

There are multiple types of audits available to tax administration, ranging from registration checks, recordkeeping audits, and single-issue audits to comprehensive (full) audits and fraud and criminal investigations. The audit program should also consider the types of audits that are appropriate for specific situations, as presented in box 4.6.

BOX 4.6   Types of tax audits

The types of verifications and checks that a tax authority can perform differ in their intent and thoroughness and can be described as follows:

- **Prima facie desk verifications.** These are used when returns are checked for internal arithmetic consistency, eligibility for deductions claimed, credibility by using norms determined from data mining of past return and audit data, and information provided by the taxpayer across different taxes—for example, value added tax (VAT) income tax, and possibly customs duties. The scope of these verifications will depend on the number of cases typically assigned to an audit officer and the extent of information technology (IT) support to conduct these checks. It is possible for prima facie verifications to be automated, with only returns that fail to pass automated checks being flagged for further attention by audit officers. This is the practice in several developed countries.

- **Education and inspection visits.** These inspections are manpower intensive and are useful mainly for new taxpayers. They consist of visits to a potential business or professional taxpayer's premises to verify the taxpayer's awareness and understanding of tax obligations and also to verify that the taxpayer's books, financial documents, and business forms, such as invoices and receipts, satisfy legal requirements. Such visits should typically be made by prior appointment. While noncompliance should be noted by the tax authority officer for possible future action, these visits are conducted primarily as a service to taxpayers and not

a means to detect noncompliance—unless flagrant abuses are found.

- **Issue-oriented audits.** These are typically desk audits in the tax office, where specific problems identified through prima facie checks are the focus. For consumption taxes, these audits can cover a number of within-year tax returns, if needed. Issue-oriented audits should typically result in a final assessment of the tax due from the taxpayer for the tax period, barring evidence of large-scale unpaid taxes due or fraud becoming known. A special case of such audits, not necessarily linked to prima facie checks, is the refund audit, particularly in the case of new businesses claiming specific deductions or in the case of VAT.

- **Comprehensive desk audits.** These audits may cover several taxes and tax periods. High-risk taxpayers or their tax representatives are asked to produce a wide array of books and records for inspection by the tax office and to provide oral or written answers to the queries of the audit officer or team. Though these audits are practiced in a number of countries, they are relatively ineffective at detecting major tax noncompliance, while imposing high compliance costs on the taxpayer.

- **Comprehensive field audits.** These are typically conducted at the taxpayer's business premises and, with suitable safeguards against abuse by the tax administration, residential premises. These audits may cover several taxes and tax periods. Besides cases deemed to be high risk

(continued)

BOX 4.6 Types of tax audits *(Continued)*

from prima facie checks or issue-based audits, such cases are typically based on careful risk assessment and audit selection. A type of comprehensive audit practiced in some countries is one undertaken to facilitate risk profiling of taxpayers, as done in the United States. For such audits, taxpayers are selected by random sampling from different targeted taxpayer groups or all groups. These visits are also typically made by prior appointment during the taxpayer's business hours. In many cases, such audits may have to be conducted at the residence of taxpayers who are either not engaged in a business or profession or who do not have a separate place of business.

• ***Tax fraud investigations.*** These investigations are typically conducted by special units in the tax administration or even by police-led teams. Such investigations are typically

initiated when evidence of potential criminal activity is found. Verification of fraud typically results in criminal sanctions being imposed on taxpayers by the judicial system. In several developing countries, and in some developed ones, massive underpayment of taxes is almost always associated with tax fraud, with both revealed during comprehensive audits. In such cases, follow-up action for comprehensive audits can typically include civil penalty proceedings as well as a separate criminal prosecution. A special type of tax investigation is the tax raid or search (to be discussed further), which can be undertaken without prior warning to the taxpayer and can result in the seizure of incriminating documents and material. Different countries have different levels of safeguards against misuse of their powers by tax administrations.

Source: IFC 2011.

Different types of audits target different objectives in terms of the level of risks involved in each situation. Desk audits are very useful in carrying out quick checks of the internal consistency of tax returns and analyzing accounts and taxpayer records. In the present digital era, many tax administrations ask taxpayers to submit their records electronically. If further analysis is needed, a partial or a comprehensive audit may take place. As an additional benefit, it should be noted that desk audits can be carried out by lower-level qualified staff. Comprehensive and full audits should then be confined to the most complex cases since they are very costly and require specialized staff.

A trend that is gaining prominence in modern tax administrations is to combine "mass" or automated audits—total oversight—with comprehensive ones to increase audit coverage and the perception of risk as well as to better allocate resources. Higher rates of compliance are achieved when third-party information sources are systematically matched with the information contained in tax returns. Hence, tax administrations should routinely and systematically cross-check the reported information to verify tax returns and detect noncompliance through low-cost and wide-coverage mass audits, which have proven to be very productive. Furthermore, as more data are stored electronically, and the transfer, storage, and integration of data become easier through the application of new techniques and processes, there has been a huge increase in the amount of data available to tax administrations for compliance purposes (OECD 2021c).

At a high level, the audit function should have three elements: (a) taxpayers are selected for audit during audit planning, (b) audits are conducted, and (c) the quality of audits is continually monitored. However, given that it is impossible to audit all taxpayers, especially in the same way, a critical aspect to consider is that the first two elements of the audit function use some form of case selection (OECD 2017a).

Audits are a complex undertaking, and during the entire audit process, the audit function must aim to have a system in place that enables both headquarters (HQ) and district/field office managers to be able to control and monitor each of their responsibilities. The head of the audit division needs to be able to see the status of all the plans and yearly targets on a national and local level to be able to correct, adjust, or take specific action when the process flow reports indicate either national or local problems. This same system must deliver appropriate reports to each manager down the management chain to enable them to take action even before HQ has identified problems.

The annual audit plan sets out the overall number of audit case targets for the year. It takes into account the total number of registered taxpayers, set against the total available resources, and the types of audits considered necessary by the audit division at HQ. As the plan is developed, the targets will be purely numerical and will be used for case selection after the risk-based selection program has been run. At this stage of the exercise, HQ will have decided on average times to be taken for the various types of audit they have chosen.

The annual audit plan includes input from various sources (USAID 2013):

- Previous experience and area-specific knowledge of auditors, particularly knowledge of large taxpayers or specific industries
- Audit area indicating a compliance need
- Recommended overall taxpayer classification: size, industry type, other
- Type of business: industrial, commercial, professional, construction
- Reasons for the recommendation: source of compliance concern, such as prior substantial audit findings, comments from taxpayers or their representatives, feedback from speaking engagements, and so on
- Application of risk-based selection as described below
- Anticipated staff levels in the audit function and the net available time for direct audit work
- Outcomes from the previous year's or years' audit plan
- Estimates of potential revenue per return or per hour

The audit is a powerful tool to be used by the tax administration to control the tax register, and it must be well planned and executed by well-trained professional auditors. As stated earlier, the type of audit will be stipulated by the policy laid down by the audit division at HQ, and the procedures to be carried out during the audit should be available for all staff involved in the audit task. Modern tax administrations have intensive training programs and detailed audit manuals for their auditors, giving them not only knowledge and skills for effective revenue audits but also insight into the activities of the taxpayer. Special manuals may be developed for businesses or activities that have particular difficulties or problems and need specific audit methods outside the general principles.

Once the auditor is satisfied with the compliance of the taxpayer or that the errors discovered do reflect the true liability, the audit must be concluded with the report written up and the assessment(s) issued where necessary. The auditor compiles the audit report without undue delay and while the auditor is still familiar with the case. An audit report should contain a written draft of the audit that the auditor carried out, all relevant information on the basis—legal and procedural—for any conclusions the auditor reaches on the taxpayer's liability, and the proposed measures to be taken because of these conclusions.

The main content of the audit report should include the following (USAID 2013):

- Information on the taxpayer company and general information on its business, including the business sector or industry, and business scope
- Information on the audit, including the date and time, places of business audited, interviews with the taxpayer, whether notification was given to the taxpayer, and whether there was cooperation with the audit team and other authorities
- A description of the taxpayer's accounting and other related systems
- A listing of audited accounting records, tax records, and other materials audited and an indication of the period that the audit covered
- The assessment measures proposed by the auditor on the basis of the audit and a separate justification for each measure, including justification for not proposing any measures

- The contents of the legislation, regulations, instructions, legal cases, and taxation practice relevant to the audit and the content of any expert conclusion that the audit relied upon when justifying assessment measures
- Calculation of the penalty and interest payable, if any
- Any other facts, evidence, and justifications that were of material importance in determining the tax liability of the taxpayer
- Any issues that may be relevant to future audits
- Names and signatures of the auditors that carried out the audit
- Copies of any necessary details that provide clarification regarding the issues on hand, which should be attached to the audit report as appendices and appropriately labeled and numbered so that their connection with the issues presented in the audit report can be linked without difficulty

The functional features and level-specific practices that characterize the different maturity levels of a tax administration in terms of the tax audit function can be classified as follows (USAID 2013):

Maturity level 1: Initial

- There is no audit policy regarding where, when, and how audits are conducted or how to control the tax register, other than to audit all returns and declarations received.
- Direction from tax administration HQ to district and field offices is confusing, contradictory, and short term.
- The lack of an MIS minimizes performance monitoring at any level.
- There is no audit strategy or annual audit plan.
- No audit manuals are ever prepared and auditors are always in a state of confusion and subject to whatever interpretations are made by their local managers.
- The lack of standardized processes and procedures and the absence of an audit manual cause poor-quality audits and chaotic case management.
- The audit target is still set at 100 percent of all returns and declarations filed, causing massive backlogs.
- No risk analysis selection system is in place. Rather, selections are more influenced by tax collection performance, set against the budget estimates, usually ignoring actual declared tax and estimated liabilities.
- Auditors are aggressive and concentrate on identifying misdemeanors for the imposition of fines and penalties, instead of the credibility of returns and declarations.
- No use is made of indirect methods during audits or to reach assessed liability.
- Inconsistencies in interpreting the law contribute to many appeals or delays in finalizing cases.
- Auditor recruitment, training, and retention policy ignore real needs and concentrate on economics and law graduates, with little specialized in-house training.

Maturity level 2: Basic (Practices for Controlled Operations)

- Functional managerial responsibility and accountability start to be considered with a review of the current status compared to leading international practice.
- There is recognition that the policy of 100 percent audit of returns and declarations must be changed if self-assessment and voluntary compliance are to be encouraged. Various actions for different types of audit are being proposed, and even a risk analysis selection program is being considered.
- An audit strategy and plans are prepared but without top management ownership, and commitment to implementation is lacking.

- Managers prepare their own records to try to have some level of control, but little central information is available.
- A review of written regulations, instructions, processes, and procedures produces recommendations for all to be updated and improved. Despite the results, an audit manual is still not considered necessary.
- Auditors are encouraged to be more helpful to taxpayers but at the same time start checking the credibility of declared liabilities, looking for underdeclared tax rather than just misdemeanors.
- Depending on the law, the audit function takes steps either to urge clarification of the powers of indirect methods of assessment or, if they are clear, then to instruct and train auditors on the use of these techniques.

Maturity level 3: Intermediate (Practices for Efficient Operations)

- With roles and responsibilities clearly understood, a management structure is set up, with delegation of powers and authority levels established to facilitate a more effective and efficient implementation of the modernization being undertaken.
- A clear-cut, written audit policy is put in place that identifies various types of audit and provides guidance on how to carry out each type. The policy also indicates that audit selection must be targeted to cases where there is a high potential risk of lost revenue.
- Recognition that the methods of communication within the audit function are not sufficient to meet the needs of the staff leads to a complete review and significant improvements.
- Moves are made to create a computerized, risk-based audit selection system based on the new policies. The system accounts for the types of audit indicated in the policy and the steps required to undertake different types of audit and the resources available.
- An audit strategy is now written using the new policy, and top management is taking ownership. Management shows commitment to the strategy by monitoring and adjusting resources and actions when necessary.
- An annual audit plan is produced that takes the strategy and audit policy into account and gives weight and information to a (computerized) selection system.
- More management information reports are available, but they tend to be on a "one-off" or "on request" basis, and many managers are unaware of what reports can be generated or are available. Little consideration is given to a true MIS as the IT department does not understand that its purpose is to serve and not to dictate operations.
- Recommendations made for rewriting regulations, instructions, processes, and procedures are implemented and the new documents issued. Lack of training for the staff and little management support make the impact less than desired.
- An audit manual is commissioned and is gradually being introduced.
- Auditors are producing better-quality audits using their new techniques, producing more underdeclared tax, and contributing to the self-assessment and voluntary compliance effort.
- Large taxpayers are being identified for special controls, but no national plan is in place.
- The improvements and changes noted above have created a substantial increase in staff training needs. The audit function is ensuring that short-term needs are met, while also reviewing the long-term needs of a modern department.
- The recruitment policy for auditors is reviewed, and more appropriate criteria are proposed.

Maturity level 4: Advanced (Practices for Sustainable and Optimized Operations)

- The tax administration's drive for taxpayer voluntary compliance and self-assessment is at the center of all the audit function's plans and actions.

- The audit function recognizes its role and responsibilities and accepts accountability for the implementation of the law, in addition to instructions, policies, processes, and procedures set out by the tax administration, including the audit division at HQ.
- The management structure within the audit function is clear and well defined. Top management has taken ownership of the delegation and authority levels, ensuring that checks and balances are in place at each stage of the process.
- The roles and responsibilities of the management structure within the function are clearly defined. All managers understand their delegated powers and level of authority and implement their tasks correctly.
- Communication and information flows of the audit function give clear and concise directions and advice to all levels of staff.
- The audit strategy, annual audit plan, and audit policy are all operating well. The targets set are achievable and relevant to available resources, estimated liability due, complexity and perceived risk of taxpayers, and a management that is dedicated to encouraging effective processes and procedures in all tasks. Monitoring, reviews, and staff development are all part of the ongoing tasks undertaken by dedicated sections.
- A five-year audit strategy is developed, and senior managers accept ownership, ensuring regular monitoring, updating, and communication to staff.
- Preparation of the annual audit plan is now a routine process and the division uses expertise and experience to target the highest-risk taxpayers and continually improve the criteria used in the targeting process. Control of the largest taxpayers has become specialized.
- An audit manual has been developed detailing best practices for each type of audit and explaining special techniques to deal with instances where the auditor experiences difficulties in verification of accounts or declarations.
- The well-written regulations, instructions, processes, and procedures of the audit function are implemented in an effective manner and are constantly monitored, developed, and improved by a dedicated section.
- Audit managers and auditors focus on establishing actual liabilities of taxpayers and getting the right tax at the right time.
- Audit techniques detailed in the audit manual, including indirect methods, are being used more, and the quality of audits is becoming much more professional.
- A fully automated, risk-based audit selection system is in place, incorporating a case tracking procedure that informs the annual audit plan and management information reports.
- The management of large traders is routinely monitored and the appropriate regimes put in place to ensure best practice control is maintained.
- A full MIS is in place, giving regular, routine reports of all areas of the audit function's activities, from national down to individual performance. Using the reports, a system of monitoring and inspection is developed to enable managers at each level to ensure fulfillment of their tasks. The reports are used intelligently to adjust focus or methods to improve results.
- The managers, auditors, and audit support staff of the audit function are given the necessary training that equips them to implement the processes and procedures of their tasks and use audit manual techniques. Further dedicated training is also obtained for specialist areas such as computer auditing, international accounting standards, and transfer pricing.
- The recruitment and retention policy incorporates a specification underlining the need for individuals with different educational qualifications and good interpersonal skills who are able to deal with confrontational situations, not just individuals with a degree in law or economics.

In addition, the following are specific quantitative benchmarks based on OECD (Organisation for Economic Co-operation and Development) and other country experiences (OECD 2021a):

- Audit coverage will depend on the resources of the tax administration and the size of the filing population, among other factors. OECD countries audit from less than 1 percent of taxpayers to 5 to 10 percent of taxpayers. Countries in which filing is not universal—not all businesses and persons file—audit a larger portion of returns.
- One hundred percent of large taxpayers should be audited, at least once every two years.
- Approximately 30 to 50 percent of the staff time of the whole tax administration should be devoted to audit and fraud investigations.
- Approximately 2 to 8 percent of net revenues should come from assessments.
- There should be at least around 70 percent success in risk-based audits—positive assessment.

Other important performance measures for the audit function are listed below, but the actual percentage or measure set must depend on local circumstances and the stage of development of the particular tax administration (Khwaja, Awasthi, and Loeprick 2011). The performance measures follow:

- Operating costs of the audit division set against the revenue collected
- Total number of registrants to total number of auditors
- Number of auditors compared to total staff
- Completion of an annual audit plan
- Average time spent per field or desk audit carried out set against additional liability discovered
- Effective field or desk auditing: comparison between total number of audits carried out and total number of audit adjustments made

To conclude, box 4.7 summarizes all the issues discussed that should be examined in the course of a technical assessment of the tax audit function of the tax administration.

BOX 4.7   Assessment of tax audit function of tax administrations

1. Describe the legal basis for tax audits in the tax procedure code and the rules and complementary regulations, paying special attention to the following issues: access to the taxpayer's premises, access to the taxpayer's computer-based systems, limitations on the durations of audits, recordkeeping obligations, notification procedures, confidentiality of information, and the taxpayer's rights.

2. Is there an audit unit in the tax administration HQ with national responsibility for the audit function? Is this department in charge of audit policy, planning, and monitoring at HQ?

3. Does the tax administration have a risk profiling and a risk-based tax audit strategy that determines and prioritizes audits according to agreed risk factors such as the size and complexity of the taxpayers and their compliance records? Has it developed a tax audit plan? Please indicate the agreed risk factors and attach the most recent tax audit plan.

4. Does the risk-based system used for selecting taxpayers for audits build upon a wide range of information

sources—for example, a register of incorporated companies, banks, or financial institutions—and does it provide an overall evaluation based on all relevant tax types?

5. List available sources of information.

6. What is the total budget assigned to the audit function to calculate together with number and results of audits: audits' productivity—for example, revenue yield per audit category, value-for-audit ratio, and cost collection ratio?

7. Is the tax audit information regularly and routinely analyzed and then used to inform and update the strategic risk model?

8. Describe the types of audits that are conducted by the audit department. Does the audit department routinely conduct mass audits?

9. Are there systems in place for monitoring overall levels of tax fraud and tax avoidance? Does the tax administration have an anti–tax fraud plan?

(continued)

BOX 4.7 Assessment of tax audit function of tax administrations *(Continued)*

10. Have the auditors been provided with modern tax audit tools, supported by IT, to control taxpayers' compliance?

11. Has the tax administration developed and implemented a strategy for the prevention of corruption? If so, what are its key elements?

12. Has the tax administration developed and implemented a strategy and procedures to ensure effective internal audit management?

13. Have management systems relating to accountability and authority, monitoring and evaluation, internal control, and integrity been implemented in the tax administration?

14. Does the tax administration have a tax ombudsman who is independent of the tax authority and addresses complaints of corruption against tax officials?

15. Has a code of ethics or a code of conduct been developed and implemented in the tax administration?

16. Does the tax administration meet regularly with taxpayers and their representatives to address issues of corruption and make systematic changes to reduce their incidence?

17. Does the tax administration have an independent department that oversees cases of complaints against its tax officials?

18. Are independent external audits conducted regularly with a view to report on the tax administration's effectiveness and efficiency to the legislature or the president of the country?

19. Has an independent internal audit function been established in the tax administration? If the answer is positive, please describe the main characteristics, competences, tasks, and its place in the organizational chart.

Revenue arrears management and tax disputes

Revenue arrears management

A tax arrears management strategy should be developed to establish priorities for collection of arrears and to set performance targets. Plans should distinguish between different categories of arrears, taking into account the size, nature, and age of the debts, and give priority to large and more recent arrears since the latter are tax debts more likely to be collected. Specialization in collection of arrears needs to be developed, including establishment of a dedicated debt collection function. Additionally, IT applications should be developed to support debtor profiling and to determine optimal collection strategies based on risk assessment. Modern tax administrations use a wide range of progressively more aggressive measures to enforce collection of tax arrears. These measures range from reminder notices, visits at taxpayers' premises, seizure of bank accounts, offsetting of money owed taxpayers from other public departments, issue of third-party demands to major customers, and temporary closure of business to seizure and sale of physical assets of taxpayers (OECD 2004).

There are several ratios to gauge the effectiveness of a tax administration to recover tax debts. The most commonly used is the ratio of aggregate tax arrears to annual net revenue collections of all taxes (cumulative and noncumulative). Some countries seem to have very low inventories based on the values of this ratio—less than 5 percent in countries such as Denmark, Germany, Ireland, Japan, the Netherlands, Republic of Korea, and United Kingdom. It would be premature to draw conclusions based solely on the values of this ratio. Some caveats apply in view of the potential factors involved, including resources devoted to this core function, the scale of enforcement activities granted to the tax administration by the tax procedures code, and write-off policies, considering the fact that some tax procedure codes do not allow the tax administration to write off uncollectible debts, resulting in high debt inventories. However, trends over time in the tax arrears collection performance of a tax administration could be a very useful indicator. A declining trend may point to improved payment compliance and effectiveness by a given tax administration in collecting tax debts.

The functional features and level-specific practices that characterize the different maturity levels of a tax administration in terms of the tax arrears collection function can be classified as follows (USAID 2013):

Maturity level 1: Initial

- The collection function follows up outstanding amounts when advised of such amounts but does not proactively identify delinquent taxpayers. There are no regularized stop-filer and nonfiler programs, but only pursuit of late payers and nonpayers in reaction to pressure on meeting revenue targets.
- Taxpayers are treated separately under each tax for purposes of debt collection, and the legal provisions are not coordinated—there is no offsetting of tax liabilities.
- The tax administration does not have a consistent approach to selecting cases for collection action. No debt is classified as noncollectible and proposed for write-off.
- Notices are paper based and sent by mail, which may not be reliable. Notices require approval by high-level management and may be delayed or not sent.
- Notices that are mailed but returned as undeliverable are not systematically followed up.
- There are no consistent procedures such as a collection log for collections and no procedures for referring cases to audit or fraud investigations.
- Enforced collection tools such as liens and seizures are rarely used and usually would not be successful if the taxpayer challenged them in court, as there is insufficient documentation of past collection actions or there is too much discretion in procedures.
- New employees are subject only to informal on-the-job training on related legal requirements, such as the definition of delinquency, withholding requirements, and related penalties. There is minimal training on collection procedures or on complex collection issues, such as jeopardy cases or departure prevention. Existing employees are not provided refresher courses or other training.
- There is no automation of case selection, and distribution of collection cases is at the discretion of the supervisor.

Maturity level 2: Basic (Practices for Controlled Operations)

- The collection function follows up outstanding amounts but does not systematically identify delinquent taxpayers. Ad hoc stop-filer and nonfiler programs are undertaken, but the focus remains on the pursuit of late payers and nonpayers as a result of pressure on revenue targets.
- Taxpayers are treated separately under each tax for purposes of debt collection, and legal provisions are not coordinated—there is no offsetting of tax liabilities.
- The tax administration uses an ad hoc approach to select cases for collection action. No debt is classified as noncollectible and proposed for write-off.
- Notices to taxpayers are paper based and generally sent by mail, which may be unreliable, although the tax administration begins to research other channels for communication.
- There are some consistent procedures such as a collection log for collections but no procedures for referring cases to audit or to fraud investigations.
- Enforced collection tools such as liens and seizures are used occasionally but would have limited success if the taxpayer challenged them in court, as there is insufficient documentation of past collection actions.
- New tax administration staff receives some formal course training and on-the-job training on collection procedures and related legal requirements, such as the definition of delinquency, withholding requirements, and related penalties. Existing staff is subject to occasional, but irregular, refresher courses. There is still no training on complex collection issues, such as jeopardy cases or departure prevention, bankruptcy, and payment arrangements.
- There is no automation in the selection and distribution of collection cases.

Maturity level 3: Intermediate (Practices for Efficient Operations)

- The collection function follows up outstanding amounts, although they may not use a risk-based approach and, on an ad hoc basis, identifies delinquent taxpayers, including stop-filers and nonfilers. There is an identification of large taxpayers who are stop-filers, although it may not be systematic.
- Even with combined taxpayer accounts, taxpayers are treated separately under each tax for purposes of debt, as the collection provisions for each tax have not been harmonized (there are offsetting debits and credits with other taxes but no offsetting of tax liabilities with other government payments).
- The tax administration uses a systematic approach to identify existing taxpayer cases that are potentially easier to collect, not necessarily the ones that represent the highest risk to revenue. Debt may be classified as noncollectible and submitted for write-off.
- The tax administration employs multiple channels to notify taxpayers of their outstanding tax obligations. Notices are somewhat automated.
- There are consistent procedures for collection and for referring cases to fraud investigations and audit.
- Enforced collection tools such as liens and seizures are used when appropriate and are typically successful when challenged in court, because they are supported by sufficient documentation of past collection actions and there is limited discretion in procedures.
- New and existing tax administration staff are subject to formal courses and on-the-job training on collection procedures and related legal requirements, such as the definition of delinquency, withholding requirements, and related penalties, as part of their individual development plan based on a rigorous training curriculum. However, the curriculum and course content are not updated regularly. Training on complex collection issues, such as jeopardy cases or departure prevention, bankruptcy, and receiverships, is ad hoc and not a part of a curriculum, if it exists at all.
- There is no automation in the selection and distribution of collection cases.

Maturity level 4: Advanced (Practices for Sustainable and Optimized Operations)

- The collection function implements two distinct activities: (a) identifying delinquent taxpayers and (b) following up outstanding amounts. Separate stop-filer and nonfiler programs are an integral part of the collection function.
- The taxpayer is treated as a single entity for purposes of debt. Tax collection powers are harmonized if under separate laws for each tax, or there is a tax code that covers all taxes.
- A cost-benefit or "business" approach to collections is employed, and the tax administration considers potential yield before collection action. Noncollectible debt is classified and written off.
- The tax administration employs multiple channels to notify taxpayers of their outstanding tax obligations. Notices are largely automated.
- A collection log with all collection actions is maintained, and collection cases are referred to audit and fraud investigations, when necessary.
- Enforced collection tools—for example, garnishment, liens, and seizures—are used when appropriate and are typically successful when challenged in court, because they are supported by sufficient documentation and the application of consistent, transparent collection policies and procedures.
- New and existing tax administration staff are provided formal course training and on-the-job training on collection procedures, the use of software, basic accounting, and similar topics as part of their individual development plan and of a rigorous training curriculum. The curriculum and course content are updated regularly. The course curriculum addresses complex collection issues, such as departure prevention and jeopardy cases.
- Collection case selection and distribution to collectors are automated.

Tax disputes

The establishment of independent appeal mechanisms to resolve taxpayers' claims is necessary for tax administrations to ensure a fair application of the tax system. Taxpayers need to be confident that administering tax laws is an objective process that is governed by a strict application of the legal and regulatory framework in place, thereby avoiding opportunities for corruption and abuses. In addition, tax laws are complex and differences in interpretation between tax administration and taxpayers have to be substantiated before independent judicial instances. An appeal system of this kind is a necessary corollary of a tax collection process that hinges on voluntary compliance and self-assessment. In this context, providing assistance to taxpayers to comply with their tax obligations and putting in place settlement mechanisms when differences of criteria arise are key elements to effectively administer the tax system.

Most tax administrations share common features in terms of the elements of these systems to resolve tax disputes. When a tax administration issues an assessment, taxpayers are granted a period of time in which they can contest either facts or interpretation of articles of tax laws or regulations. In cases of self-assessment, taxpayers can submit a request to rectify the content of the tax return if errors in facts or in the application of tax laws are noticed. Once the tax administration has explicitly or tacitly attempted to resolve the matter, taxpayers may have recourse to the judicial system if they disagree with the tax administration's stance. In some countries, independent tax tribunals consisting of specialized staff from the Ministry of Finance and independent tax experts are in place. Key advantages of this arrangement are that usually there are no litigation costs involved in this scenario and that is a very effective filter of cases. This is understood and accepted as an independent process that serves to reduce the workload of the judicial system. Ideally, only the most complex cases and those involving criminal offenses should reach the judicial system.

Since the appeal system is a costly way of resolving tax disputes in terms of both administrative and tax compliance costs, some administrations favor the use of advance rulings. These rulings provide for an interpretation of specific aspects of tax laws before a taxpayer submits a tax return. In some cases, these rulings are binding for taxpayers and for the tax administration. Other mechanisms that can be used are binding arbitration that takes place after a dispute has arisen. When it comes to transfer pricing, advance pricing arrangements (APAs) and arbitration mechanisms to resolve differences between countries are increasingly exploited with a view to avoiding double taxation to companies. Box 4.8 presents conditions for a credible appeal process.

The functional features and level-specific practices that characterize the different maturity levels of a tax administration in terms of tax disputes can be classified as follows (USAID 2013):

BOX 4.8   Conditions for a credible appeal process

1. *Independence of appeal officers.*

2. *Independence of appeal bodies.* A precondition of any credible appeal system is the independence of the appeal bodies, which is difficult in the case when the appeals are heard within the tax authority.

3. *Adherence to principles of natural justice.* The legal principle "hear the other party" is the bedrock of the principle of natural justice.

4. *Reasonable preconditions for filing appeal.* In some countries, taxpayers are expected to pay in advance some or all of the disputed tax. Where this is not required, taxpayers are required to pay the tax amount along with market rates of interest if they lose their appeals.

5. *Time-bound appeal process.* The appeal process must be time bound, thus resulting in speedy resolution of appeals.

6. *Progressive selection.* The tax appeal system must result in effective resolution of the majority of cases at the lowest levels of the dispute resolution structure.

Source: IFC 2011.

Maturity level 1: Initial

- The right of the taxpayer to object at the tax administration level is loosely provided for in the law, in secondary legislation, or by a tradition of appealing to the tax administration to review an assessment.
- Objections are handled in an ad hoc manner without clearly defined procedures. There are no standard forms or accepted time to object or respond. The processes for handling an objection, if published, are vague.
- The taxpayer is not advised if the objection takes longer than anticipated to review. The tax administration does not inform the taxpayer if a decision is subject to the taxpayer's right to appeal.
- The objection, when received, is not communicated to collection staff, and the objection does not stop collection action.
- Objections are reviewed by a committee of high-level managers and tend to involve the same persons that originally handled the case.
- The process for submitting objections is not automated or online, and neither is the workflow for the objection process.

Maturity level 2: Basic (Practices for Controlled Operations)

- The right of the taxpayer to object is defined in the law or secondary legislation, but it is not clear which decisions of the tax administration are subject to reconsideration. The mechanism for submitting an objection is also not clear.
- Objections are handled in an ad hoc manner without clearly defined procedures. There are standard forms and time-to-object requirements but no clear time to respond. Requirements and published processes for handling objections are vague. The process for allowing an extension to the time to object is not clear.
- The objection, when received, is not communicated to collection staff, and the objection does not stop collection action.
- Procedures exist for handling objections, but there is a lack of detailed guidance, such as detailed internal operating manuals regarding, for example, the calculation of elapsed time to respond to an appeal where the taxpayer has been requested to provide additional documentation and whether the time to respond to an appeal is suspended during this response period.
- Objections are reviewed by a committee of high-level managers and tend to involve the persons who originally handled the case. There is limited automation of the submission of objections online and the objection process workflow.
- The taxpayer is not advised if the objection takes longer than anticipated to review. The tax administration does not inform the taxpayer if a decision is not subject to further appeal.

Maturity level 3: Intermediate (Practices for Efficient Operations)

- The right of the taxpayer to object is defined in the law or secondary legislation, and although the mechanism for objection is clear, it is difficult to know which decisions of the tax administration are subject to reconsideration.
- There are clearly defined and sometimes publicized procedures for handling objections. These include standard forms, an established time to object, an established time to respond, processes for submitting and handling objections, and rules for allowing an extension of time to object.
- Procedures may lack certain provisions, such as requirements for the material that should be reviewed (including original case files, objection submissions, and the law) and precise specifications of when legal services staff or the taxpayer should be involved.
- The taxpayer is not advised if the objection takes longer than anticipated to review. The tax administration informs the taxpayer of their further appeal rights should they disagree with the decision.

- Although an objection stops collection action, the communications between the objecting taxpayer and collections staff of the tax administration are not clearly defined and may be ad hoc.
- Objections are handled by internal experts. There are no clear internal requirements to use staff who were not involved in the original case. Although clearly defined, procedures for objections differ across types of decisions and taxes.
- Although the taxpayer may be able to submit objections electronically, the objection process workflow is not automated.

Maturity level 4: Advanced (Practices for Sustainable and Optimized Operations)

- The right of the taxpayer to object is clearly defined in the law or secondary legislation. All tax administration decisions of fact or law are subject to reconsideration, perhaps with very few exceptions, such as a binding ruling.
- There are clearly defined and publicized procedures for handling objections. These include standard forms, an established time to object, an established time to respond, defined processes for submitting and handling objections, and rules for allowing an extension of time to object.
- Procedures require that the tax administration inform taxpayers of incomplete or invalid forms—such forms are not simply ignored; allow the tax administration to request additional information from taxpayers; require the review of key data, including original case files, objection submissions, and the law; allow for meetings between the tax administration and the taxpayer; and allow for the withdrawal of objections, including the tax administration's request that the taxpayer withdraw.
- Procedures exist to allow the taxpayer full access to information in their tax file, except for third-party information and other information barred by statute.
- The taxpayer is advised if the objection takes longer than anticipated to review. The tax administration informs the taxpayer if a decision is not subject to further objection.
- Procedures require that objections be handled by independent internal reviewers, who are experts on the topic but not involved in the original case.
- The procedures for objections are the same across all types of tax administration decisions and types of taxes. All decisions, which are the result of objections, are subject to an appeal.
- The taxpayer can submit objections electronically. The objection process workflow is automated, and collectors are automatically notified of objections.

Box 4.9 provides a summary of all the issues discussed that should be examined in the course of a technical assessment of the tax disputes function of the tax administration.

BOX 4.9   Assessment of tax disputes function of tax administrations

1. Describe mechanisms in place within the tax administration to deal with taxpayers' appeals. Knowledge of the tax disputes process should encompass both the administrative process and the judicial process.

2. Are there independent tax tribunals as a prior step to submitting an appeal to the courts?

3. Do tax laws contemplate binding advance rulings?

4. Do tax laws contemplate binding arbitration?

5. Is the tax administration negotiating advance pricing arrangements?

6. Are taxpayers required to pay in advance all or part of the disputed taxes? Are taxpayers required to provide some collateral when submitting a tax appeal?

7. Does the tax administration control the number of tax appeals that are being addressed by judicial courts?

8. Is there a dedicated unit in the tax administration to deal with tax appeals? Is this unit independent from the unit that issued the assessment?

Bibliography

Bird, Richard. 2014. "Administrative Dimensions of Tax Reform." *Annals of Economics and Finance* 15 (2): 269–304. http://aeconf
.com/Articles/Nov2014/aef150202.pdf.

Borgne, Eric Le, and Katherine Baer. 2008. *Tax Amnesties: Theory, Trends, and Some Alternatives.* Washington, DC: IMF. https://www
.elibrary.imf.org/downloadpdf/book/9781589067363/9781589067363.pdf.

Crotty, John, and Paulo dos Santos. 2001. *Filing of Returns and Payment of Taxes in Banks.* Washington, DC: IMF.

Ebrill, Liam, Michael Keen, Jean-Paul Bodin, and Victoria Summers. 2001. *The Modern VAT.* Washington, DC: IMF. https://www.imf
.org/external/pubs/nft/2001/VAT/.

European Commission. 2006. *Risk Management Guide for Tax Administrations.* Fiscalis Risk Analysis Project Group. Brussels,
Belgium: Directorate-General Taxation and Customs Union, European Commission. https://taxation-customs.ec.europa.eu
/system/files/2016-09/risk_management_guide_for_tax_administrations_en.pdf.

European Commission. 2021. Compliance Risk Management Capability Maturity Model. Fiscalis Risk Analysis Project
Group. Brussels, Belgium: Directorate-General Taxation and Customs Union, European Commission. https://taxation
-customs.ec.europa.eu/system/files/2023-01/Compliance%20Risk%20Management%20Capability%20Maturity%20
Model_2021.pdf.

IFC (International Finance Corporation). 2011. *Tax Perception and Compliance Cost Surveys: A Tool for Tax Reform.* Investment
Climate Advisory Services. Washington, DC: World Bank Group. https://apexconsulting-me.com/wp-content
/uploads/2020/12/TPCCS_Consolidated_Web.pdf.

Junquera-Varela, Raúl Félix. 2011. "An Integrated Assessment Model for Tax Administration: The Diagnostic Tool." Poverty
Reduction and Economic Management. Public Sector and Governance Group. Unpublished draft, World Bank,
Washington, DC.

Khwaja, Munawer, Rajul Awasthi, and Jan Loeprick. 2011. *Risk-Based Tax Audits: Approaches and Country Experiences.* Washington,
DC: World Bank. https://doi.org/10.1596/978-0-8213-8754-2.

Kochanova, Anna, Zahid Hasnain, and Bradley Larson. 2020. "Does E-Government Improve Government Capacity? Evidence from
Tax Compliance Costs, Tax Revenue, and Public Procurement Competitiveness." *World Bank Economic Review* 34 (1): 101–120.
https://doi.org/10.1093/wber/lhx024.

LeBaube, Robert, and Charles Vehorn. 1992. "Assisting Taxpayers in Meeting their Obligations under the Law." In *Improving Tax
Administration in Developing Countries,* edited by Richard Bird and Milka Casanegra de Jantscher. Washington, DC: IMF.
https://doi.org/10.5089/9781557753175.071.

OECD (Organisation for Economic Co-operation and Development). 2004. *Compliance Risk Management: Managing and Improving
Tax Compliance.* Paris: OECD Publishing. https://www.oecd.org/tax/administration/33818656.pdf.

OECD (Organisation for Economic Co-operation and Development). 2007. *Improving Taxpayer Service Delivery: Channel Strategy
Development.* Paris: OECD Publishing. https://www.oecd.org/tax/administration/38528306.pdf.

OECD (Organisation for Economic Co-operation and Development). 2013a. *Tax Administration 2013: Comparative Information on
OECD and Other Advanced and Emerging Economies.* Paris: OECD Publishing. https://www.oecd.org/ctp/administration
/tax-administration-2013.htm.

OECD (Organisation for Economic Co-operation and Development). 2013b. *Managing Service Demand: A Practical Guide to
Help Revenue Bodies Better Meet Taxpayers' Service Expectations.* Paris: OECD Publishing. https://doi.org/10.1787
/9789264200821-en.

OECD (Organisation for Economic Co-operation and Development). 2014a. *Tax Compliance by Design: Achieving Improved SME Tax
Compliance by Adopting a System Perspective.* Paris: OECD Publishing. https://doi.org/10.1787/9789264223219-en.

OECD (Organisation for Economic Co-operation and Development). 2014b. *Working Smarter in Tax Debt Management.* Paris: OECD
Publishing. https://doi.org/10.1787/9789264223257-en.

OECD (Organisation for Economic Co-operation and Development). 2014c. Increasing Taxpayers' Use of Self-Service Channels. Paris:
OECD Publishing. https://doi.org/10.1787/9789264223288-en.

OECD (Organisation for Economic Co-operation and Development). 2015. *Tax Administration 2015: Comparative Information on
OECD and Other Advanced and Emerging Economies.* Paris: OECD Publishing. https://www.oecd-ilibrary.org/taxation
/tax-administration-2015_tax_admin-2015-en.

OECD (Organisation for Economic Co-operation and Development). 2016. *Co-operative Tax Compliance: Building Better Tax Control
Frameworks.* Paris: OECD Publishing. https://doi.org/10.1787/9789264253384-en.

OECD (Organisation for Economic Co-operation and Development). 2017a. *The Changing Tax Compliance Environment and the Role
of Audit.* Paris: OECD Publishing. https://doi.org/10.1787/9789264282186-en.

OECD (Organisation for Economic Co-operation and Development). 2017b. *Tax Administration 2017: Comparative Information on
OECD and Other Advanced and Emerging Economies.* Paris: OECD Publishing. https://doi.org/10.1787/db6a9062-zh.

OECD (Organisation for Economic Co-operation and Development). 2019a. *Tax Administration 2019: Comparative Information on
OECD and Other Advanced and Emerging Economies.* Paris: OECD Publishing. https://doi.org/10.1787/74d162b6-en.

OECD (Organisation for Economic Co-operation and Development). 2019b. *The Sharing and Gig Economy: Effective Taxation of Platform Sellers: Forum on Tax Administration.* Paris: OECD Publishing. https://doi.org/10.1787/574b61f8-en.

OECD (Organisation for Economic Co-operation and Development). 2021a. *Tax Administration 2021: Comparative Information on OECD and Other Advanced and Emerging Economies.* Paris: OECD Publishing. https://doi.org/10.1787/cef472b9-en.

OECD (Organisation for Economic Co-operation and Development). 2021b. *The Digital Transformation of SMEs. OECD Studies on SMEs and Entrepreneurship.* Paris: OECD Publishing. https://doi.org/10.1787/bdb9256a-en.

OECD (Organisation for Economic Co-operation and Development). 2021c. *Enterprise Risk Management Maturity Model.* Paris: OECD Publishing. https://www.oecd.org/tax/forum-on-tax-administration/publications-and-products/enterprise-risk-management-maturity-model.htm.

USAID (United States Agency for International Development). 2013. *Detailed Guidelines for Improved Tax Administration in Latin America and the Caribbean.* USAID's Leadership in Public Financial Management. Washington, DC: USAID. https://pdf.usaid.gov/pdf_docs/PNAED062.pdf.

CHAPTER 5

Guidelines for a framework on tax sanctions

Challenges and misconceptions of tax sanctions systems

Tax enforcement would not be possible without institutional mechanisms that make noncompliance costly. There may be some (probably few) altruistic taxpayers with a very high motivation to voluntarily comply with their tax obligations. However, the reality is that the motivation for voluntary tax compliance is highly correlated to the threat of being caught (effective enforcement) and consequently punished at the administrative or criminal level, depending on the tax violation. Therefore, when taxpayers do not fulfill their tax obligations, it is necessary to enforce the appropriate institutional mechanisms that help ensure that they face the consequences of their violation. Such mechanisms are known as tax sanctions and comprise different types of tools. The function or objective of these tools is to impose a cost on the noncompliant taxpayer by being punitive, deterring, and sometimes compensatory. This chapter analyzes challenges and misconceptions of tax sanctions systems; guidelines on tax penalties, surcharges, and interests; and guidance on reforming tax sanctions systems.

This chapter reviews the framework governing tax sanctions and provides some basic guidelines on best practices for their design. As a starting point, this section analyzes the challenges and faulty constructions of tax sanctions systems and addresses those features that are desirable. For example, an excessively strict and complex tax sanctions system may discourage tax compliance with the consequent negative effect on the tax base of a country. Also, the ability to implement a tax sanction regime depends on the quality of tax institutions. Consequently, any reform of a tax sanctions system must aim at achieving greater levels of uniformity, coherence, publicity, consistency, proportionality, progressivity, and balance in the application of tax penalties, surcharges, and interests. To this end, it is basic to clearly define the notion, nature, and purposes of penalties, surcharges, and interests to prevent any misconceptions and properly align tax offenses and sanctions.

The notion of tax penalty can be defined as a punitive measure that the tax law imposes for the performance of an act that is proscribed or for the failure to perform a required act. A surcharge can be defined as an additional levy for spontaneous but late voluntary compliance behavior by taxpayers, whose amount usually depends on the period of delay. For example, to avoid penalties for breaching declaratory and payment duties, taxpayers have the option to file the tax return or to pay at any time before the beginning of the administrative audit or collection procedure, but a surcharge is imposed. Surcharges fulfill both a deterring function and a purpose of compensatory damages. As to interests, they are not a sanction but a financial compensation for late payment. Interests are due whenever the taxpayer has retained a sum that should be in the possession of the tax administration. To complete this chapter, the last section offers tax design considerations and recommendations for reforming tax sanctions systems and is complemented by appendix D.

Transparency and simplicity

Transparency, simplicity, consistency, and fairness are some of the key characteristics of a good tax system that also should be applied to the framework governing tax penalties, surcharges, and interests. Uncertainty about the notion, nature, and purpose of each type of sanction can lead to overlapping and discretion in their application. Simplicity may also prevent uneven and discriminatory tax treatment of similar offenses, while still preserving the punitive, deterrent, and compensatory functions of sanctions. Moreover, the severity and quantification of the sanctions should ensure that the costs of rigorously sanctioning tax misconduct do not outweigh the benefits. It is of the utmost importance to educate taxpayers and provide them with the opportunity to amend their mistakes.

In some jurisdictions, tax sanctions are imposed on a tax-by-tax basis and spread across different tax norms, which makes it very difficult for taxpayers to be fully informed about the tax consequences of their actions. Hence, for simplicity purposes and for greater clarity and certainty, it is highly recommended that all tax sanctions (penalties, surcharges, and interests) applicable to all taxes are compiled and consolidated into one single legal body, in the form of a general tax sanctions code. Along the same lines, it is very important to ensure that all information relevant to tax sanctions is consistent and available on one single official website of the tax administration. Otherwise, where multiple websites containing contradictory, outdated, and inaccurate information exist, this could lead to misinformation and create confusion among taxpayers. Another scenario that should be avoided is when the effectiveness of some sanctions is suspended, either formally or de facto, which may create opportunities for asymmetrical enforcement of tax laws in the country.

Hence, the lack of available information and the limited access to updated legislation and administrative regulations in the area of tax sanctions create a high degree of legal insecurity for taxpayers, who may find it hard to know their duties and rights, and the legal consequences of their acts in the tax field. So, it is very important to keep open all communication channels between the tax authority and the taxpayers and, in the case of the website, properly updated. Any sanctions system, to be effective, needs to be known and understood beforehand by all parties involved. Consequently, a general sanctions code should be released and widely publicized among taxpayers for general awareness. Also, the severity of each type of tax penalty should be proportional to the level of difficulty in properly assessing the tax due arising from the violation of the specific duty. Following this logic, predeclaratory offenses should be sanctioned more heavily than nonpayment, since the former may even prevent the very own assessment, and the existence, of the tax debt; the latter behavior is just a tax collection issue, but it does not jeopardize the recognition of the tax liability.

Consistency

Some tax sanctions systems are itemized by tax type instead of by type and nature of tax offense; for example, tax penalties, surcharges, and interests differ from tax to tax, and similar misbehaviors or tax offenses may be treated differently depending on the tax involved. Moreover, even within the same tax type, inconsistencies and unbalanced application of tax sanctions may exist. Obviously, such an approach is highly discouraged and not recommended.

Analogously, late filing and late payment tax penalties should not be used as a substitute for surcharges. The traditional functions of surcharges are sometimes performed by tax penalties, and in some cases, there is an overlapping of both. Moreover, in some instances, the use of surcharges may be limited to a few taxes. This is a clear misunderstanding of the nature and purpose of surcharges, which should be reviewed to clearly draw the line between both sanctions to avoid confusion and overlapping and to guarantee the general application of a revised and comprehensive surcharge system.

Also, a uniform computation mechanism, including a single unpaid tax base, is highly advisable for calculating interest payments. In some countries, various interest computation options may apply, for example, interest on tax due only, interest on both tax due and penalties, or interest on the amount of tax due, penalties, and surcharges. These options, added to the different mechanisms for determining the applicable interest rate, result in a wide and irregular framework for the application of interests, which lacks a uniform rationale and is therefore highly discouraged.

Fairness

Another challenge that has been identified by tax compliance surveys is the need to reduce tax sanctions in cases where fraud is not involved to allow businesses and entrepreneurs that have unwillingly made a mistake to be able to afford to restore their full tax compliance. In this case, the analysis must take a holistic vision of the framework governing tax sanctions, rather than approaching the work from a tax-by-tax perspective.

Furthermore, a proportional, nonregressive, unpaid-tax percentage-based approach helps relieve the excessive economic burden of tax penalties. Tax penalties may become a heavy burden to low-income taxpayers if established as a fixed amount. The adoption of a percentage-based tax penalty model may help solve this problem: the economic burden from fines should be proportional to the unpaid tax, which would significantly reduce the impact of tax penalties on low-income taxpayers. This approach allows noncompliant taxpayers to be reinstated in the tax system and facilitates restoring their full compliance. Table 5.1 summarizes, by type of tax sanction, the challenges and best practices for the design of tax sanctions that will be analyzed in the following sections.

TABLE 5.1 Challenges and best practices for the design of tax sanctions

Tax sanctions	Challenges	Best practices
Penalties	Lack of proper categorization linking offenses and penalties	Clear categorization of tax penalties based on types of taxpayers' duties
	Penalties that are neither consistent across nor within taxes	Uniform inner logic of tax penalties across and within tax types
	Legal insecurity from lack of rules to modulate penalties	Public, objective, and proportionate method to modulate tax penalties
	Need for fairer penalties and equal treatment to taxpayers	Economically nonregressive approach to the design of tax penalties
	Uneven use and application of imprisonment penalties	Balanced use of cumulative and alternative tax penalties
	Confusing and discretionary use of criminal tax penalties	Clear distinction between administrative and criminal tax penalties
	Need for additional sanctions	Nonpecuniary tax sanctions system
Surcharges	Late filing and late payment penalties to replace surcharges	Proper characterization and purpose of surcharges
	Late voluntary compliance	Uniform system of surcharges
	Application of surcharges on a one-time basis	Comprehensive system to compute and apply surcharges

(continued)

TABLE 5.1 Challenges and best practices for the design of tax sanctions (*Continued*)

Tax sanctions	Challenges	Best practices
Interests	Confusion about the function and purpose of interests	Clear idea about the purpose of interests
	Multiple interest rates across and within tax types	Unique interest rate across and within tax types
	Unjust enrichment by the tax administration versus taxpayers	Consistent and fair interest rates across tax procedures
	Various interest computation and determination options	Uniform mechanism to compute interests
	Lack of updated information about applicable interest rate	Transparency on procedure to periodically update interest rates

Source: World Bank data.

Tax penalties

Tax penalties may vary widely from tax to tax and from offense to offense. In recent years, the global tendency has shifted toward significantly increasing tax penalties, especially the amount of fines. Tax penalties may take different forms: capped economic fines, fixed-amount fines, amounts calculated as multiples of the unpaid tax, amounts calculated as percentages of the unpaid tax, periods of imprisonment in case of default of payment, daily fixed amounts for each day default continues, or a combination of some of them.

In many countries, tax penalties are dispersed and lack internal consistency, being different from offense to offense, without any specific rationale for the distinction. For example, some offenses may be sanctioned with cumulative tax penalties while others may be subject to imprisonment only in default of payment of the fine. In other cases, some taxes may impose minimum fines for late filing, combined with fixed-amount fines, applying whichever is greater, or alternatively, some tax penalties may be computed as interest, thereby calculating the proportional part of a fine based on the default time, either on a daily or a monthly basis. Such situations should be avoided to ensure a uniform framework for imposing tax penalties.

Surcharges

As regards surcharges, they may vary widely from tax to tax, and in many countries, there is no generally applicable surcharge regime. In such jurisdictions, surcharges do not follow a uniform configuration and usually take two forms: capped amounts to be fixed by the commissioner according to their best judgment and percentages of the unpaid tax. The spread of percentages often bears no relationship to the period of delay or the nature of the offense; even more, alike offenses may be subject to different surcharges. Generally, a serious challenge exists when there is no general surcharge system that applies equally to all offenses or that distinguishes between types of offenses such as late filing or late payment.

Another misconception may be the reason for the limited application of surcharges to a handful of taxes. For example, in some countries, surcharges apply to offenses in connection with a limited number of taxes, without any connection among such taxes and their respective surcharges, which indicates the lack of a common notion and nature. This may also have an impact on fairness. As a consequence, surcharges become residual tax sanctions that overlap with existing tax penalties applicable to the same offenses, lacking a clear purpose and resulting in uneven application.

Interests

Generally, interests should apply to all tax liabilities pending. Unfortunately, this is not the case everywhere, since some systems only apply interests to some tax debts and are set and computed

TABLE 5.2 Defining traits of tax sanctions

Defining trait	Penalty	Surcharge	Interest
Punitive function	Yes	No	No
Deterring purpose	Yes	Yes	No
Compensatory aim	No	Yes	Yes
Tax deductible	No	No	Yes
Late compliance	No	Yes	Yes
Cooperative reduction	Yes	No	No

Source: World Bank data.

in different ways, varying from tax to tax. Traditionally, taxes have used fixed annual interest rates, although some other systems have adopted an alternative mechanism to set interest rates by linking them to the annual, or even monthly, official bank average lending rates, updating them from year to year. Moreover, interests are applied in diverse manners throughout systems. For example, interests are applied not only to tax liabilities but, in some instances, also to penalties and surcharges. Although interests usually apply to tax due only, on a daily- or monthly-basis computation, in some cases, interests are applied to both tax due and penalties or even to the sum of tax due, penalties, and surcharges.

The several computation options, combined with the different ways to determine the applicable interest rate, result in a wide and irregular framework for the application of interests, which lacks a uniform rationale that needs to be revised. Table 5.2 summarizes some of the defining traits of tax sanctions.

Guidelines on tax penalties

The notion of a tax penalty can be defined as a punitive measure that the tax law imposes for the performance of an act that is proscribed, or for the failure to comply with a tax obligation, such as failure to timely file a return or filing wrong or undervalued returns. Tax penalties have to be painful enough to discourage noncompliant behavior, while at the same time they need to be acceptable, fair, and not repressive. The punitive effect should more than offset any cost–benefit calculations on the taxpayer's side. Hence, limits for tax penalties are difficult to set. Fulfillment of a tax obligation must be more advantageous for taxpayers than the option of being noncompliant. Therefore, it is widely accepted that taxpayers may not use unpaid taxes as a source of revenue for financing their business activity.

Concerning the purposes of tax penalties, it is important to identify the punitive function and the deterring aim. Regarding the punitive function, the amount of the fine, the time of imprisonment, or other penalties are intended to make the offender assume the consequences of their illegal action. On the other hand, more than the punitive effect, there is also a deterring purpose that is based on the prevention of future behaviors not only by the offender but also by people in general. In general, both types of penalties, criminal and administrative, fulfill both purposes: punitive and deterrent. Hence, as a general rule, penalties must be compatible with interest to repair the damages.[1]

Some studies have found that taxpayers are more sensitive to the magnitude of the penalty than to the probability of detection when the probability is very low—4 percent or less (Jackson and Jones 1985). Other researchers (Schwartz and Orleans 1967) have observed a significant relationship between the severity of the criminal sanctions and compliance by high-income self-employed taxpayers; this has also been supported by similar work on sanctions that showed that legal sanctions were most effective for the higher class and the better educated. These studies also found that the threat of guilty feelings was a greater deterrent to tax evasion than the threats or stigma of legal sanctions.

However, studies (Allingham and Sandmo 1972) have provided evidence that in reaching a threshold probability of detection, mild punishment may be as effective a deterrent as a more severe one. The severity of the tax penalty does not necessarily produce a linear effect with tax compliance. Jackson and Milliron (1986) submit that the social cost of sanctions could outweigh the benefits. Taxpayers as a group may become alienated if sanctions are perceived as too severe, resulting in general antagonism and disrespect for the law. On the other hand, the positive effect of increased sanction levels on taxpayer compliance has been found to hold up even where relatively low and realistic penalty levels are used (Carnes and Eglebrecht 1995).

Most studies, including Keinan (2006) and Alm (2013), have found that compliance increases only slightly with increases in the penalty rate on unpaid taxes. The estimated reported income–penalty rate elasticity is typically less than 0.1. Also, penalties need not be limited to financial penalties. The point here is that the threat of public disclosure of one's own compliance behavior may affect compliance due to concerns that one's information may be viewed by others, and the observation of others' compliance or lack of compliance) may also affect one's own reporting behavior. Experimental evidence (Alm 2013) suggests that public disclosure of noncompliance increases compliance. Other studies (Oladipupo and Obazee 2016) have shown that tax knowledge[2] has a higher tendency to promote tax compliance than tax penalties. Governments should therefore do everything possible to increase public knowledge on tax matters, and tax education should be included in high school–level curricula at all times. Small- and medium-scale business owners should also seek to advance their tax knowledge and awareness for the mutual benefits of the governments and taxpayers.

In designing a new penalty system, it is appropriate to consider taxpayer motivations. If taxpayers always behave virtuously without legal incentives, penalties to deter wrongful actions are superfluous. Often, penalty design begins with a contrary assumption—that economic considerations are the sole determinant of behavior. But other factors may intervene, such as normative factors that influence taxpayer behavior.

Clear categorization of tax penalties based on types of taxpayers' duties

Many tax penalty systems lack categorization that clearly links types of taxpayers' duties, offenses, and penalties. It is necessary to have a correlation between the gravity of each type of tax offense and the severity of the tax penalty imposed. To properly design a framework for tax penalties, a categorization based on types of taxpayers' duties must first be established; some options are analyzed below.

By nature of tax obligations

One categorization focuses on the pecuniary or nonpecuniary nature of tax obligations. This distinguishes between tax penalties arising from noncompliance of material obligations and tax penalties derived from noncompliance of formal obligations. The tax legal relationship covers all obligations and duties, rights, and powers arising from the application of taxes. Hence, from the tax relationship can be derived material and formal obligations to the taxpayer and the tax administration, and the imposition of tax penalties for noncompliance. Material obligations are quantified in the form of taxes, while formal obligations refer to those that, without pecuniary component, are imposed by the tax and customs legislation on taxpayers.[3]

By duties of tax procedures

Another categorization classifies tax penalties according to the different duties of taxpayers within the tax procedure, whose noncompliance gives rise to the imposition of the penalties. Thus, tax penalties may arise from the violation of predeclaratory duties such as bookkeeping, audit trails, and documentation duties, declaration duties, and payment duties. In general, predeclaratory duties are intrinsically connected to declaration duties, since the noncompliance of formal obligations has a direct impact on the information available to properly assess, quantify, and declare the tax due. The severity of each type of tax penalty should be proportional to the level of difficulty in accurately assessing the tax due arising from the breach of the specific duty. Following this logic, predeclaratory offenses should be sanctioned harsher than nonpayment, since the former may even prevent its very own assessment, and existence, of the tax liability. The latter behavior is just a tax collection issue, but it does not jeopardize the recognition of the tax debt.

Preparatory penalties cover fines for failure of notifications, failure to cooperate, and failure to prepare and/or submit appropriate documentation.[4] Indeed, breach of predeclaratory duties and declaratory duties should give rise to the imposition of administrative tax penalties, or even criminal, since such violations prevent the correct assessment of the tax debt, or even worse, it denies its own existence; yet, penalties should be replaced by surcharges in case of late voluntary compliance of declaratory duties. Likewise, the noncompliance of payment duties should not be punished by way of penalties but should instead be solved through the imposition of surcharges, as discussed in the "Guidelines on surcharges" section of this chapter.

In case of self-assessment, if the taxpayer does not fill out the tax return, obviously they cannot pay for it, and the declaratory duty is breached. In these cases, the tax administration cannot collect this debt coercively because it is not known. Therefore, the tax administration, when aware of it, shall open an audit procedure to determine the amount and different aspects of the tax debt. As the lack of self-assessment is considered an administrative contravention, an infraction procedure could be open to impose a penalty, usually a fine. To avoid the penalties, the taxpayer has the chance to file the tax return and to pay for it at any time before the beginning of the administrative procedure. This spontaneous but late payment will consequently attract the imposition of different surcharges whose amount will depend on the period of delay.

Uniform inner logic of tax penalties across and within tax types

Tax penalty regimes should follow a uniform inner logic across and within taxes to ensure consistency—same penalties for same offenses. In some cases, in search for greater simplicity, a consistent rationale is neglected when imposing penalties. Hence, whenever possible, the wide array of tax penalties applicable to income tax offenses should be extended to other taxes, since many offenses may be fully applicable to behaviors conducted in the context of other taxes, especially indirect taxes. Indeed, their application should be general, since these offenses contravene legal duties by reason of the behavior itself and irrespective of the tax involved. Some examples are: failing to furnish a tax return or to provide required documents, failing to deliver a true and correct return, failing to provide information upon request, giving inaccurate or incomplete information, knowingly making a false statement or false representation in any tax return or tax declaration, and knowingly and willfully aiding, abetting, or inciting another person to make or deliver a false or fraudulent account, statement, or declaration. Therefore, the design of tax penalties should focus on the types of offenses and tax behaviors, rather than on the types of taxes, since the former determine the latter.

Public, objective, and proportionate method to modulate tax penalties

In some jurisdictions, many tax penalties are capped, using the legal term "not exceeding" for monetary fines and terms of imprisonment, or contain a valid range for application. Often, this wording enables tax authorities to modulate tax penalties in their application, which may create legal uncertainty to taxpayers in the absence of specific legal guidelines. Moreover, in some instances, the scope of application of tax penalties is significantly broadened. Even more important, terms of imprisonment are usually quite high and do not bear any relationship to the amount of the monetary fines they substitute in case of payment default, which makes it very difficult to determine the corresponding term of imprisonment for lower monetary fines.

Therefore, it is recommended that countries enact legislation that standardizes a transparent, objective, and proportionate method to modulate the application of tax penalties. For example, in some common law jurisdictions, such application is entirely entrusted to the courts of justice, which may require an in-depth analysis of their case law to extract the applicable criteria to each scenario.

First, once enacted, legal provisions should be published for the common knowledge. Publicizing these norms is very important so that taxpayers may know in advance the consequences of their actions. Second, the method of determining the applicable tax penalty or penalties must be based on objective criteria that minimize the discretionary power of tax authorities. Such criteria should rely on the abovementioned categorization of infraction, the economic damage derived from the taxpayer's infringement, the quantification of the tax liability, the level of voluntary tax compliance, the stage of the tax procedure, and any other factors relevant for the decision that may be objectively assessed. Third, the mechanism must be proportionate, which means that tax penalties must bear a direct numerical relationship with respect to the offense committed and also to other tax penalties that may be alternatively applied.

Tax penalties should consider the degree of voluntary compliance and cooperation of taxpayers. Accordingly, tax offenses should be classified on the basis of the nature and impact of the underlying misbehaviors, infringements, and violations of taxpayers. Specifically, a clear distinction should be made between late voluntary compliance behaviors and the absence of any compliance-driven behavior. In this sense, those taxpayers who commit an offense but voluntarily choose to restore their compliance, even after the deadline but before a tax audit process is initiated, should benefit from lower or attenuated tax penalties. On the other hand, those noncompliant offenders who opt for persisting in their illegal behaviors should be subject to more burdensome and aggravated tax penalties.

Cooperation is also rewarded by lower penalties at the enforcement stage, to reflect the savings in terms of public money. In some countries, administrative tax penalties may be reduced when the taxpayer agrees with the tax inspector on the amount of the tax debt as a consequence of an inspection procedure[5] or when the taxpayer signs the audit report accepting the proposal of the tax officer. In addition, but only for the second case, if the payment is made during the voluntary period, and no appeal is brought by the taxpayer, one more reduction may be applied.[6] The rationale for this reduction is the joint savings in terms of time and money arising from preventing litigation, apart from eliminating the risk of an eventual court decision that might overrule the decision of the tax administration; therefore, such anticipated savings are shared between the taxpayer and the tax authorities.

An optimal tax penalty system would not require any penalty modulation, eliminating any opportunity for arbitrariness. Such an ideal system would most probably resort to percentage-based tax penalties, since this modality does not require any modulation—the next subsection will analyze this option. Also, as will be further discussed, administrative tax penalties should do away with incarceration. Yet, for criminal tax penalties, a standardized equivalence between monetary fines and default terms of imprisonment should be established and made public. This equivalence could be objectively set by assigning a monetary value per day of imprisonment; consequently, high-income taxpayers would not have any advantage over low-income taxpayers, since they all would have to serve the same term period in case of defaulting on the payment of their economic fines.

Economically nonregressive approach to tax penalty design

Penalties should be fair and treat all taxpayers equally, without any distortion or discrimination, including economic circumstances. Hence, the equity of the system is reduced by tax penalties that adopt the form of either a fixed monthly amount—for example, for late filing for income tax—or a capped fine for most income tax penalties. This poses an important issue: fixed-quantity penalties have a regressive impact on taxpayers in two ways. The first is from an economic viewpoint, since lower-income taxpayers bear a higher burden in percentage terms than higher-income taxpayers. Second, these fixed-amount penalties are also regressive when compared to the underlying tax liability—the higher the amount of tax due, the less burdensome the penalty, in percentage terms. Therefore, a proportional, nonregressive, "unpaid-tax percentage-based" approach would help relieve the excessive economic burden of tax penalties.

Tax penalties should be reviewed to eliminate their regressive impact by introducing an unpaid-tax percentage-based approach. Although tax penalties do not need to be progressive, as income taxes do, they should not be regressive either, as already explained. Therefore, embracing a percentage-based approach is recommended when designing tax penalties, at least for those arising from noncompliance of material obligations that have a direct impact on the tax liability assessment.[7] Yet, the noncompliance of formal obligations may also impede the accurate calculation of the tax due, which may justify extending the unpaid-tax percentage-based approach to the tax penalties arising from formal obligations as well.

Assessing penalties on the basis of the amount of unpaid taxes makes sense within the logic of deterrence theory. A penalty designed to deter should raise the average cost of noncompliance so that it exceeds any average savings from noncompliance. Therefore, a monetary sanction should be equal to an appropriate percentage of the benefit of noncompliance, although what percentage is appropriate is not always clear (Gordon 1996). Although the size of penalties may vary from jurisdiction to jurisdiction, in most cases, penalties should probably not exceed 25 percent of the amount of underpayment for negligence or 50 percent for intentional underpayment.[8] But in some instances, it may be appropriate to apply flat-rate penalties to make them easier, more predictable, and more automatic in their application. This could be the case for those penalties arising from behaviors that have no economic impact on the tax liability—for example, failure to obtain prior approval before accepting deposits and other investments of money.

As already discussed, tax penalties may become a heavy burden to low-income taxpayers, especially when there is a significant increase in the amount of fines. The adoption of a percentage-based tax penalty model would solve this problem. The economic burden from fines would be proportional to the unpaid tax, which would significantly reduce the regressive impact of tax penalties on low-income taxpayers; this approach would allow noncompliant taxpayers to restore their full compliance. In fact, the use of unpaid-tax percentage-based penalties is already present in most tax sanctions systems, but it may be worth expanding its scope to other taxes and offenses; such an approach would avoid rewarding tax offenses that result in higher tax liabilities.

Balanced use of cumulative and alternative tax penalties

The uneven use and application of imprisonment in case of default of payment of monetary fines is a common practice in many jurisdictions—for example, imposing the same period of imprisonment for first-time offenders as a default sanction, irrespective of the amount of the primary monetary fine. This practice creates confusion about whether or not there is a correlation or correspondence between the monetary fine and the default imprisonment sanction. Another case is when penalties introduce cumulative tax sanctions that resemble more a surcharge or an interest than a penalty. Another approach used by some countries is the use of alternative monetary sanctions combined with imprisonment,[9] or even minimum monetary fines to be quantified by comparing different amounts.[10]

Monetary sanctions are not always effective deterrents. One example is where the noncompliant taxpayer has no resources to pay any amount due, including underpaid tax, interest, and any monetary sanction. Although the rules of priority, bankruptcy, lien, attachment, execution, and fraudulent conveyance are designed to protect the government's claim, there may still be instances where the taxpayer is relatively judgment proof. Gordon (1996) suggested that in these cases, non-financial penalties, such as prison terms, should be added. But most legal systems do not tolerate the imposition of prison terms for civil offenses. Civil sanctions could, however, include the temporary suspension of certain privileges, which are discussed in a later subsection.

Notwithstanding the above, it is unclear if there is a rationale or logic behind the use of cumulative and alternative tax penalties. Consequently, introducing mechanisms that may guarantee a balanced design and application of these multiple and combined tax penalties is recommended, not only within a tax but also across taxes. Also, it should be evaluated whether this tax penalty scheme is the most appropriate for each specific tax compliance level and the resources available to noncompliant taxpayers.

Administrative versus criminal tax penalties

It is necessary to clearly establish a distinction between administrative and criminal tax offenses. Once such a distinction is set, tax penalties then need to be differentiated accordingly, based on the administrative or criminal nature of their originating offenses. Furthermore, as already discussed, this framework may justify redefining the content and consequences of both types of tax penalties and, following international best practices, limit the use of imprisonment only to criminal tax offenses and preferably to second or subsequent criminal offenders. The difference between administrative and criminal offenses shall be based on generally admitted principles, which shall translate into the corresponding distinction, notion, and content of administrative and criminal tax penalties.

Following the European Court of Human Rights definition (Gordon 1996), administrative penalties shall compensate caused damages and not be of a punitive or deterring nature. However, the Czech Republic, Italy, Spain, and the United States explicitly define administrative penalties as having the same character and purpose as criminal penalties. Therefore, there is no international consensus. Administrative contraventions can be imprudently committed. Accordingly, any degree of negligence satisfies the culpability requirement, but the penalty cannot be imposed if it is completely absent. This is the case when the taxpayer has observed due diligence in fulfilling their tax obligations.[11]

Simply put, a criminal penalty arises from a criminal offense. In most countries, the subjective element of intent and the objective element of a tax evasion amounting to a certain threshold must be existent to qualify as a criminal tax offense. The criminal aspect shall be defined according to the so-called Engel criteria.[12] According to the prevailing opinion, the concept of fraud implies deceiving the tax administration;[13] consequently, it cannot be recklessly committed. Imposed criminal penalties are usually financial fines or imprisonment sentences.[14]

Fraud or evasion is usually considered a crime, but it is often a difficult crime to prove. Some countries have therefore set forth other acts that may be part of a scheme of fraud, but those acts, in themselves, constitute crimes that may be easier to prove than a fraudulent scheme. The crimes include submitting false documents and interference with tax administration through libel, slander, or other means designed to influence official action, either positively or negatively.[15]

TABLE 5.3 Additional nonpecuniary sanctions

Types of nonpecuniary sanctions	Examples of nonpecuniary sanctions
Indirect sanctions	• Temporary suspension of professional licenses • Loss of privileges to practice professional trade • Revocation of business or professional licenses • Voiding of agreements • Shutdown of business if taxes are not paid • Exclusion from access to public contracts • Publication or prohibition from certain activities • Exclusion from grants or public aids • Exclusion from fiscal and social security benefits • Exclusion from incentives for a period of time • Inclusion in penalty registry affecting credit scores
Hidden sanctions	• No deduction of costs if not recorded correctly • No credit for taxes paid if not documented • No tax exemption if activity is not registered • No access to simplified regimes if not registered

Source: Original table for this publication.

Additional nonpecuniary sanctions

Tax sanctions systems worldwide could benefit from introducing additional nonpecuniary sanctions. This measure would expand the scope of consequences arising from tax offenses beyond the mere traditional economic sanction in the form of fines. Without this, low-income tax offenders may have few opportunities and incentives to restore their full compliance: first, because they may lack the necessary economic resources, given the current highly burdensome tax penalties, and, second, because those taxpayers without economic resources may feel they have nothing to lose and therefore relapse into their illegal behaviors.

Noncompliant taxpayers must be brought back to legality by means other than financial sanctions and imprisonment, whenever possible. As previously mentioned, civil nonfinancial sanctions may include the temporary suspension of certain privileges, such as to practice as a chartered accountant. Some jurisdictions revoke business or other licenses from delinquent taxpayers.[16] However, revoking such privileges, while acting as a deterrent, may actually reduce the ability of the taxpayer to pay off their government debt and may have the undesired effect of damaging the economy and increasing unemployment, by essentially prohibiting a business from operating. For this reason, these measures must be carefully adopted, although they may still be beneficial.

Also, indirect and hidden sanctions, which exist in some countries, should be considered. Indirect sanctions are those that produce disadvantageous consequences—for example, voiding of agreements, shutdown of business if the respective taxes are not paid, or exclusion from access to public contracts. In contrast, hidden sanctions can have the same effect but are not categorized as a typical sanction—for example, there is no deduction of costs if they are not recorded as required.[17] Table 5.3 provides a list of frequently used nonpecuniary sanctions.

Guidelines on surcharges

A surcharge is levied when taxpayers spontaneously act to amend an unintended offense. For example, to avoid penalties for breaching declaratory and payment duties, the taxpayer has the option to file the tax return or to pay at any time before the beginning of the administrative audit or collection procedure. This spontaneous but late filing or late payment should have, as a consequence, the imposition of a surcharge whose amount would depend on the period of delay.[18] Surcharges, as well as interests, are not dependent on fault because, in general terms, they are not authentic penalties. So the procedure to impose them takes only into account the facts, whether or not it is the offender's fault. Yet, surcharges are not tax deductible from the tax base of the income tax or corporate tax, which is another sign of the residual criminal character of these payments.

Surcharges have both a deterring function and a purpose of compensatory damages. The deterring aim is based on the prevention of future behaviors, such as late voluntary filing and late payment, and in some circumstances, it is compatible with the enforcement of interests. The compensatory function aims to cover the expenses incurred by the tax administration for such coercive collection; in this case, interests are also due for compensatory purposes. Therefore, surcharges aim at safeguarding the tax procedure system through incremental costs of noncompliance for the obligated taxpayer.

Proper characterization and purpose of surcharges

Many tax sanctions systems use late filing and late payment tax penalties as substitutes for surcharges. The traditional functions of surcharges are often performed by tax penalties, and in some cases, they overlap. In other instances, the use of surcharges is limited to a few selected taxes such as income tax, indirect taxes, and some administrative licenses. In such cases, the surcharge regime and late filing and late payment tax penalties should be reviewed to clearly draw the line between both figures, to avoid any confusion and overlapping, and to guarantee the general application of a revised and complete surcharge system.

In addition to declaring and quantifying, the taxpayer must pay the amount due within the time provided by law. However, the breach of duty to make the corresponding deposit does not constitute an administrative offense, but it enables the tax administration to enforce collection. Therefore, tax penalties should not be imposed for late payment because the taxpayer has declared and quantified their tax due; in other words, the taxpayer has voluntarily acknowledged their debt with the tax administration. Yet, the taxpayer should face surcharges[19] plus default interest.

The justification for this surcharge is to act as a deterrent from late payment and as a compensation for the expenses incurred by the tax administration for the coercive collection. The same applies to late filing surcharges, which extend to predeclaratory duties like keeping proper books and records, as well as providing documentation as requested by the law; for example, violations of transfer pricing documentation provisions show high diversity regarding the surcharges applied for noncompliance.[20]

Uniform system of surcharges

Surcharges can be defined as an additional levy for spontaneous but late voluntary compliance behavior by taxpayers, whose amount usually depends on the period of delay. A uniform system of surcharges should be established and generally applied to all late voluntary compliance behaviors. As mentioned earlier, late filing and late payment tax penalties should be replaced by surcharges. With regard to declaratory surcharges, late filling surcharges are either applied by a fixed percentage of the assessed tax or of the taxable income or via a provided fixed amount.[21] Surcharges should apply in the presence of late voluntary compliance, not in the absence of any compliance or failure to act, as it wrongly happens still in many countries. Also, in some countries, there is no strict distinction and separation of surcharges according to the respective duties.[22] Surcharges should be carefully designed following international best practices, which are very broad and wide in terms of modalities.[23]

Comprehensive system to compute and apply surcharges

Currently, in many jurisdictions, surcharges are applied on a one-time basis, either as a fixed amount or as a percentage of the unpaid tax, which may encourage late compliance behaviors. To prevent this, international best practice suggests (a) applying surcharges on a variable scale of rates or percentages that increase over time, to discourage late compliance behaviors, and (b) establishing a unique and general system that applies to all surcharges across tax types, for simplicity and fairness.

Guidelines on interests

Interests are not a sanction per se but a financial compensation to the tax administration for late payment. Interests are due whenever the taxpayer has retained a sum that should be in possession of the tax administration. This occurs in the following cases: late payment of taxes due or withheld, when the taxpayer has obtained an unlawful refund, when the execution of the assessment resolution has been suspended as a result of a remedy, or when payment of the tax has been postponed at the taxpayer's request. Yet, as protection against administrative delay, the computation of the interest should cease if the tax administration wrongly exceeds the legal time limit to approve a resolution or decide an appeal.

Clear idea about the purpose of interests

Most countries use some type of interest to safeguard tax assessment and tax collection; their main purpose is to compensate for the cost of money. Interests are surcharges in a broader sense and have the purpose of absorbing liquidity benefits. They, therefore, secure the real value of tax claims or refunds across different time periods and aim at safeguarding timely payment of taxes or refunds. Accordingly, interests are usually deductible in most countries.

There are different scenarios that may trigger the imposition of interests, resulting in several types of interests, including (a) for deferment, (b) on evaded tax, (c) on refund amounts during legal proceedings, (d) while implementation is suspended, or (e) on subsequent tax claims and tax refunds. But interests for late filing are not often applied in self-assessment systems because the elapsed time for filing will be the same as the time for payment. In this case, late filing must not be linked with a specific interest rule, because interests for late payments have to be computed from the same day onward.

Unique interest rate across and within tax types

Due to the nature of interests, a unique interest rate should be set across and within tax types. However, depending on the jurisdiction, interests are set and computed in different ways and vary from tax to tax. Traditionally, fixed annual interest rates were used, but in recent years, annual or even monthly official average lending rates from national banks are also being used. Furthermore, there are significant variations across countries in the determination approach and the level of interest rate.

In general, there are two different approaches to determine interests. The first one is the method of fixed interest rates. The second one follows the idea of a variable interest rate regime, which is determined by a flexible reference rate.[24] Some countries determine interest rates by budget acts or by means of ministerial decrees.[25] The interest level may vary not only between countries but also within. To begin with, the capital market interest may differ. Therefore, if the capital market interest decreases and the interest rate for tax purposes is not adjusted accordingly, the excess of interest rate will no longer be a sole financial compensation for the cost of money but may become a hidden penalty. This hidden penalty may accumulate with other surcharges and result in a disproportional burden to the taxpayer.

However, interests for tax offenses higher than capital market interest may also be justified to prevent the use of arbitrage margins by the taxpayer. The interest level may be led by the benchmark of a taxpayer as a debtor who would alternatively refinance their tax debt at the capital market. In this case, it must be guaranteed that the taxpayer who owns enough liquid equity to pay the taxes is entitled to prevent the accounting of interest by paying a sufficient tax amount in advance before the final tax will be assessed and due.

Consistent and fair interest rates across tax procedures

When a unique interest rate is established for both taxpayers and tax authorities, and across the same tax procedures, it prevents unjust enrichment by the tax administration. Therefore, interest rate charged to taxpayers on late collection of taxes should be the same as tax authorities apply to reimbursements made to taxpayers on income improperly retained or adjusted. Moreover, applying the same interest rate across the same tax procedures means that payments within the tax system should be neutral in overall terms. Unfortunately, there are still countries that apply different interest rates, without any rationale for it.

Uniform mechanism to compute interests

A uniform computation mechanism, including a single unpaid tax base, should be established for calculating interest payments. Currently, various interest computation options are applied in different countries—for example, to tax due only, on a daily or monthly basis, to both tax due and penalties, or to the sum of tax due, penalties, and surcharges. These, combined with the different ways to determine the applicable interest rate, result in a wide and irregular framework for the application of interest and lack of a uniform rationale. Therefore, it is recommended to unify, simplify, and standardize a single computation formula for all interest calculations and adopt a consensus on the base against which interest must apply. The standard practice is to apply interest only to the unpaid tax. However, in some countries, it is acceptable to apply interest to the pending tax penalties or surcharges, from the moment the offense takes place or once the deadline for voluntary compliance expires. In any case, whichever option is chosen should be applied across all taxes and tax procedures, to avoid any asymmetries and to increase simplicity in compliance and in tax administration.

Transparency on procedure to periodically update interest rates

Should a variable interest rate regime be applied, it will be necessary to establish a publicly known procedure to periodically update the interest rate. Transparency requires that applicable interest rates are known by taxpayers at all times. More important, taxpayers are entitled to know the procedure by which variable interest rates are to be updated and the dates on which they change.

Reforming tax sanctions systems

Any reform process of a tax sanctions system should follow a methodology that takes into account (a) the philosophy that should inform the tax sanctions system; (b) the available options to design the code; (c) the scope of tax offenses to be covered; (d) the objectives to be achieved by the new framework governing tax penalties, surcharges, and interests; and (e) the recommendations summarized herein.

Philosophy

Any working process followed to draft a tax reform proposal should be guided by the following principles, values, and beliefs:

1. Respect and recognition for the domestic tax system and legal heritage.
2. Acknowledgment of the value of the national tax legislation and tax practice.
3. Trust in the professionalism of the tax administration and the courts of justice.
4. Awareness of the importance of the social, cultural, and economic local reality.
5. Need for greater simplicity, fairness, and certainty, which foster voluntary tax compliance.
6. Tax knowledge and tax education are key to promote tax compliance.
7. All tax misconducts are conducive to or contribute to evading tax.
8. Public disclosure of noncompliance increases voluntary tax compliance.
9. A rehabilitated taxpayer contributes more than a noncompliant taxpayer.
10. Tax sanctions are as effective as their capacity to deter tax misconducts.
11. Effectiveness of tax sanctions depends on its proportionality (to offense) and enforcement.
12. Tax sanctions must render tax evasion more costly than voluntary compliance.

13. Tax penalties must be commensurate with taxpayers' economic capacity.
14. Sanctions perceived as too severe result in taxpayers' disrespect for tax laws.
15. A good tax sanctions code must bring taxpayers back into the tax system, not expel them permanently from it.
16. Tax education must be stressed to prevent mistakes that happen due to the complexity of the tax system.

These statements summarize the philosophy that should inform the design in terms of policy options and the drafting of the provisions of any proposed tax sanctions code.

Methodology

When faced with the task of designing and drafting a tax sanctions code, countries should codify in a systematic manner only those tax offenses that are common to the administration of all taxes and to provide the code with an inner logic that eliminates penalty mismatches across taxes and other deficiencies. This methodology reflects the philosophy of respect and recognition for the country's tax system and legal heritage. At the same time, it addresses equity and solves most deficiencies and mismatches, providing a coherent structure, an inner logic, a systematic approach to the regulation of tax offenses, and certainty and transparency.

Furthermore, it would be respectful of existing tax acts, but minor amendments would be required for the resulting code to be fully operational. Offenses in tax acts would remain unchanged, and sanctions would only be imposed by reference to the new code, which would group tax offenses by type into main categories, to make it simpler. Greater fairness and certainty would be attained by uniformly sanctioning the same offense across and within taxes. Also, the types of sanctions and their application would be drastically simplified, to ease taxpayers' voluntary compliance, as well as to facilitate enforcement by tax officers and courts.

An alternative approach would be to replicate existing international best practices, preferably from jurisdictions that share the same law tradition (either common or civil) as the country; this makes for the most state-of-the-art and technically advanced tax sanctions code.[26] But this methodology should be discarded because of its many challenges. Another methodology would be to compile, into a single norm, the tax sanction code, all the tax offenses and corresponding sanctions currently spread throughout domestic tax acts, and centralize them without making any changes, thus perpetuating all penalty mismatches across taxes.[27] Hence, this option should also be rejected because it would be a mere aggregation of provisions without any system or inner logic.

Scope

The following types of tax offenses should be identified, systematized, and compiled in any proposal to develop or reform a tax sanctions code:

1. Registration and change of status-related offenses
2. Recordkeeping-related offenses
3. Failure to furnish documents and information
4. Failure to produce a license permit or registration certificate
5. Obstructing of the inspection of books and records
6. Offenses relating to invoices and consignment notes
7. Misrepresentation and impersonation-related offenses
8. Hindering of authorized persons in execution of duties

9. Noncompliance with official orders and notices
10. Offenses involving dishonesty
11. Making of false or misleading statements
12. Refusal to answer questions from authorized persons
13. Providing or fabricating of any false evidence
14. Breach of secrecy and confidentiality duties
15. Failure to make or deliver complete and correct returns
16. Deliberate or careless making of incorrect returns
17. Late filing of return or declaration
18. Failure to pay tax due and payable
19. Failure to account for and pay over tax deducted at source
20. Failure to pay tax due from employed persons
21. Breach of duty to declare estimated tax
22. Improper obtaining of tax refund
23. Unlawful collection of tax
24. Refund of tax paid in excess
25. Fraudulent conversion of property
26. Making of fraudulent statements
27. Fraudulent action with intent to defraud and evade tax
28. Offenses committed by body corporate

For simplicity and practical reasons, those misconducts specific to the administration of certain taxes should be outside the scope of the tax sanctions code—for example, smuggling in connection with customs and excise duties, or offenses related to betting, gaming, and lottery activities. Also, tax-specific offenses should be outside the scope of the sanction code, as well as the amount of some fines that may be insignificant, virtually divesting the sanction from its punitive effect. Similarly, in other cases, the terms of imprisonment may be disproportionate to both the offense and the alternative economic penalty.

Objectives

Any proposal to reform a tax sanctions system should aim at meeting the following objectives:

1. Increase simplicity, fairness, and certainty of the tax sanctions system.
2. Codify tax offenses and tax sanctions into a single body of norms (code).
3. Make a clear distinction between penalties, surcharges, and interests.
4. Eliminate tax sanction mismatches across taxes and offenses.
5. Standardize or unify tax sanctions across tax types.
6. Establish clear rules for simultaneous application of multiple sanctions.
7. Eliminate imprisonment penalty for civil offenses.
8. Eliminate aggravated penalties for second or subsequent tax offenses.
9. Establish a comprehensive system to compute and apply surcharges.
10. Introduce community service penalty as an alternative sentence option.
11. Introduce gender-neutral language in the provisions that regulate tax offenses.
12. Introduce separate sanctions for individual and body corporate offenders.
13. Enact legislation that standardizes a public, objective, and proportionate method to modulate the application of tax sanctions.

14. For criminal tax penalties, establish and make public a standardized equivalence between monetary fines and default terms of imprisonment.
15. Whenever possible, bring noncompliant taxpayers back to legality by means other than financial sanctions and imprisonment.

Principles

When reforming tax sanctions systems, depending on the degree of political will and tax administration involvement, the results may range from minor cosmetic reform to a groundbreaking modernization of the tax sanctions system.

The following principles should inform the development of a new sanctions framework:

1. Design categorization that clearly links types of taxpayers' duties, offenses, and penalties.
2. Make the severity of each type of tax penalty proportional to the level of difficulty in properly assessing the tax due arising from the breach of the specific duty.
3. Extend to other taxes the wide array of tax penalties applicable to income tax offenses when possible.
4. Distinguish and modulate tax penalties accordingly, between late voluntary compliant behaviors and noncompliant behaviors.
5. Review tax penalties to eliminate their economically regressive impact by introducing an unpaid-tax percentage-based approach.
6. Include mechanisms to guarantee a balanced design and application of multiple and combined tax penalties, not only within a tax but also across taxes.
7. Differentiate tax penalties based on the administrative or criminal nature of their originating offenses.
8. Replace fixed-amount fines for unpaid-tax proportional penalties.
9. Create a generally applicable surcharge system.
10. Review the surcharge regime (if existing) and late filing and late payment tax penalties to clearly draw the line between both figures, to avoid any confusion and overlapping, and guarantee the general application of a revised surcharge system.
11. Establish and apply generally a new and uniform system of surcharges to all late voluntary compliance behaviors.
12. Apply surcharges in the presence of late voluntary compliance, not in the absence of any compliance or failure to act, as it wrongly happens sometimes.
13. Establish a comprehensive system to compute and apply surcharges.
14. Set a unique interest rate across and within tax types, as well as for both taxpayers and tax authorities, and across tax procedures.
15. Unify, simplify, and standardized a single computation formula for all interest calculations and adopt a consensus on the base against which interest must apply.
16. Should a variable interest rate regime be adopted, set a publicly known procedure to periodically update it.
17. Standardize or unify interest rates across taxes and procedures.
18. Establish a uniform mechanism to compute interest payments.

Top 10 core legislative measures for reforming tax sanctions systems

This subsection aims at facilitating the task of legislators and tax officials faced with the challenging task of addressing such reform. Table 5.4 provides a preliminary list of the top 10 core legislative measures to address the most pressing issues identified in this chapter, while minimizing the impact on existing tax sanctions systems.

TABLE 5.4 Top 10 core legislative measures for reforming tax sanctions systems

Top 10 legislative measures	Rationale
1. Eliminate imprisonment penalty for administrative offenses.	Imprisonment should be reserved for criminal offenses.
2. Replace fines for unpaid-tax percentage-based penalties.	It eliminates the economically regressive nature of penalties.
3. Eliminate aggravated penalties for second or subsequent offenses.	Administrative penalties cannot be aggravated by this reason.
4. Introduce criminal penalties as a separate category from administrative penalties.	Criminal offenses must be sanctioned differently than ordinary administrative offenses.
5. Create a generally applicable surcharge system.	Penalties must be clearly differentiated from surcharges.
6. Replace current penalties for surcharges, whenever appropriate.	Penalties and surcharges have different notions and functions.
7. Establish a uniform mechanism to compute interest payments. Preferably, use a national bank annual average lending rate, or similar.	Interest rates must apply across taxes to payments and refunds. Also, uniform computation methods must be publicized.
8. Establish clear and uniform rules on simultaneous application (compatibility) of penalties, surcharges, and interests. Same for basis of computation.	Penalties may or may not be compatible with surcharges. Interests may always apply, though on a different basis for computation purposes.
9. Introduce indirect sanctions—neither financial nor imprisonment.	Noncompliant taxpayers must be brought back to legality by means other than financial sanctions and imprisonment.
10. Eliminate incongruities among sanctions across taxes and offenses; standardize and unify sanctions' rates.	Tax sanctions must be consistent across offenses and taxes and applied equally.

Source: Original table for this publication.

Notes

1 | For a summary of the economics of penalties, tax accuracy–related penalties, cost–benefit analysis, and tax penalties and deterrence models, see Keinan (2006).

2 | Tax knowledge is the level of awareness or sensitivity of the taxpayers to tax legislation. It refers to the processes by which taxpayers become aware of tax legislation and other tax-related information. The level of formal general education received by taxpayers is an important factor that contributes to the understanding of tax requirements, especially regarding registration and filing requirements.

3 | Following the Spanish tax legislation, formal tax obligations can be systematized as follows:
- The obligation to register for individuals or entities that develop professional activities or business operations in the territory or may receive income subject to withholding tax.
- The obligation to apply for and use the tax identification number and their relationships with fiscal significance.
- The obligation to submit tax returns, self-assessed tax returns, and communications.
- The requirement to keep and maintain books and records, as well as programs, paper files, and computer files that support them and coding systems used to enable the interpretation of the data when the obligation is fulfilled with the use of electronic devices.
- The obligation to issue and deliver invoices or equivalent documents and to keep invoices, documents, and evidence relevant to their tax obligations.
- The obligation to provide to the tax authorities books, records, documents, or information that the taxpayer is required to maintain in relation to the performance of tax obligations themselves or others, and any data, reports, backgrounds, and proof of taxation at the request of the tax administration or on periodic statements. Where the required information is kept in digital format, it should be provided on said support when so requested.
- The obligation to provide the practice of administrative checking and inspections.
- The obligation to submit a certificate of withholding or proof of payment by taxpayers who are recipients of income subject to withholding or payment on account.
- The formal obligations established by the customs legislation.

4 | For example, in Germany, failure of notification of pension has a charge of €10 per day. Belgium and Hungary have general administrative penalties for not complying with the duties of the tax code that range from €50 to €1,250 in Belgium, while in Hungary, fines can reach up to the equivalent of €660 for private individuals and €1,600 for other taxpayers. France applies a fine of €1,500 for nonprovision of documents. Spain charges formal infringements with no tax evasion with fines ranging from

€150 to €600,000. Fines for minor infractions in Turkey are applied according to the person who commits the contravention and range from the equivalent of €1 to €40. On the other hand, not cooperating in tax audits is generally charged at a higher rate—for example, 100 percent of the concerned tax amount in France and up to €250,000 in Germany.

5 | In Spain, the tax penalty may be reduced by 50 percent in this case.

6 | In Spain, the tax penalty may be reduced by 30 percent in this case. Additionally, one more reduction of 25 percent will be applied if the payment is made during the voluntary period.

7 | In Spain, tax penalties are defined as a percentage of the tax debt.

8 | For example, the U.S. Internal Revenue Service Commissioner's Executive Task Force on Civil Tax Penalties concluded that the civil penalty for underpayment owing to negligence—no reasonable care—should be 20 percent, with a de minimis rule, while the penalty for intentionally underpaying, although without fraud, should be 50 percent, and the civil penalty for underpayment due to fraud should be 100 percent.

9 | This is the case when tax offenses are sanctioned with a fine not exceeding a certain amount, a fine amounting to a multiple (double, treble) of the unpaid tax, or imprisonment.

10 | For example, when the formula "whichever is greater" is used to fix a minimum tax penalty.

11 | This is assumed when they have acted on the basis of a reasonable interpretation of the law or following the tax administration's published criteria. Liability is also excluded when the infringement is caused by a technical defect of software for the assessment of taxes provided by the tax administration.

12 | The Engel criteria consist of the following three-step approach:
- Does the offense charged belong to criminal law according to your national law? Is it a criminal penalty according to your national law?
- If not, can the very nature of the offense be characterized as being of criminal nature?
- If the very nature of the offense cannot be characterized as being criminal, does the degree of severity of the penalty make the European Court of Human Rights applicable? Here, not only the actual penalty imposed but also the penalty the taxpayer is risking to incur has to be considered.

13 | In Austria, Germany, Greece, the Netherlands, Norway, and Poland, the Engel criteria explicitly apply regarding characterization of criminal surcharges. Within the United States, the categorization is made solely by statute; no other criteria are applied.

14 | Maximum periods for imprisonment range from 2 to 10 years, and the thresholds, if existent, to classify an evasion as criminal and not an administrative offense range from the equivalent of €2,000 (Czech Republic) to €120,000 (Spain). According to French law, a tax fraud is either committed through a willful default of filing a tax return or to conceal an amount that exceeds 10 percent of the taxable amount, or (only) €153. In Denmark, according to case law, tax evasion amounting to €33,500 will lead to a 1.5-year imprisonment, but in Germany, only evasions above €100,000 will lead to imprisonment. In the latter case, a sentence can be served on probation, but regularly fines go up to an amount of €1 million. In France, fines up to €2 million are possible. Spanish tax law does not provide fixed fines but correlates the fine to the amount of evaded tax (from 100 to 600 percent). The imposed fines are applied according to the evaded tax amount and the degree of intent or negligence with which the taxpayer committed the evasion or fraud. In some states, the financial and economic situation of the taxpayer is also considered. The U.S. sentencing guidelines provide several factors that can be considered to determine criminal penalties—for example, amount of the tax loss, criminal history, and various upward and downward adjustments—to produce tables setting recommended sentencing ranges.

15 | For example, in the United States, the Internal Revenue Code includes the following acts as crimes punishable by fines and prison: making fraudulent statements in a tax return or information return, making fraudulent statements under penalty of perjury, and removing or concealing information with intent to defraud.

16 | For example, in the United Kingdom and the United States, tax deficiencies may result in a loss of privileges, including the ability of attorneys and accountants to practice their trade.

17 | Other examples can be found in France, where there is a penalty of publication or prohibition from participation in certain activities; also, in Spain, there is an exclusion from grants or public aids and fiscal and social security benefits and incentives for a certain period of time.

18 | In Spain, these surcharges are 5 percent if the delay is less than 3 months, 10 percent if the delay is from 3 to 6 months, 15 percent if the delay is from 6 to 12 months, and 20 percent if it is more than 12 months; only in this latter case is interest also required.

19 | In Spain, these surcharges range from 5 to 20 percent of the unpaid debt, as mentioned above.

20 | Finland applies a maximum surcharge of €25,000, whereas other states impose surcharges referring to the nondeclared income (as in Germany and in Poland) or the overall gross income (as in Greece). In Germany, the surcharge amounts to 5 to 10 percent

of the additional income with a minimum of €5,000 to a maximum of €1 million. Poland applies a much higher rate of 50 percent of the additional income.

21 | It can be seen that rather low surcharges exist (Czech Republic, Denmark, Greece, Norway, Turkey), which range from a maximum €40 (as in Turkey) to a maximum €12,000 (as in Czech Republic). Countries such as Austria and Germany apply a maximum 10 percent of assessed tax (in Germany: limited by a maximum amount of €25,000). Some other countries, such as Finland, France, and the United Kingdom, apply late filing surcharges according to a certain scale of occurred intent or gross negligence. Sole late filing is charged with a comparable low surcharge (France: 10 percent of assessed tax and 40 percent if the return is not filed within 30 days of notification; Finland: € 150–800; United Kingdom: 5 percent of the due tax, if six months of delay, with a minimum surcharge of £300), whereas late filing with a certain degree of severity is charged with up to 80 percent (in France) and up to 100 percent (in the United Kingdom) of the assessed tax and 30 percent of the taxable income (in Finland). In the United Kingdom, it can be seen that surcharges are applied according to several indicators, such as intention, (un)prompted disclosure, and the time period of nonfiling. Submitted tax returns with errors, which lead to lower tax payments, are charged with amounts from 10 to 200 percent depending on the level of intentional behavior the taxpayer may be accused of.

22 | For instance, in Germany and the United States, there is no distinction of surcharges according to the respective duties. Belgium, Italy, and Portugal, for instance, provide a scale of administrative surcharges either according to ranges of fixed amounts (as in Portugal) or according to proportional amounts of the due or evaded tax, as in Belgium and Italy. The amount of the imposed administrative surcharge or of the applied proportional amount depends on the culpability of the taxpayer. The administrative sanctions in Portugal are rather lower (€50 to €165,000), compared to the possible amounts of up to 200 percent in Belgium or 240 percent for nonfiling of tax returns or 200 percent for evaded tax, as in Italy.

23 | For example, countries like Austria, Germany, and the United States apply late surcharges that range from 0.5 to 2 percent per month. Denmark applies a surcharge based on the market rate plus 0.8 percent points, which amounted to 5 percent in 2014, and is applied without respect to the period of nonpayment. France applies a 10 percent surcharge for compensation of damage. Besides those fixed surcharges, there are also countries that apply variable surcharges. These surcharges are staggered according to the period the surcharge is not paid and/or to the intention of withholding tax payments. In Spain, the late payment surcharge is 5 percent, 10 percent, or 20 percent in ex officio assessments that occur mostly after tax audits, depending on the payment being made before or after notification by the authorities. However, as Spain applies a self-assessment tax procedure, the late payment surcharge in these cases is staggered according to the time of voluntary payment before the administrative procedure is initiated—5 to 20 percent; 20 percent is applied for payment that is overdue for more than 12 months. For long delays, more than a year, the 20 percent surcharge is compatible with the interests. Within the Greek self-assessment regime, a similar surcharge is applied from 10 percent, 20 percent, or 30 percent of the tax according to the delay in payment respectively being less than one year, exceeding one year, and exceeding two years. The United Kingdom applies low surcharges for late payment within 12 months staggered from 3 to 6 to 12 months—£10 per day in the first case and 5 percent in the latter cases, with a minimum of £300. In case of longer and deliberate withholding, the surcharge rises to 70 percent or 100 percent.

24 | Tax interest is calculated by applying the rate that is in force during the period of computation, taking into account its eventual changes; this is the case in Spain.

25 | Italy, Portugal, and Spain determine interest rates by budget acts or by means of a ministerial decree.

26 | This option may seem optimal but it is not. The success of any tax reform highly depends on how easily and fast tax officials and the courts responsible for its application and enforcement may become familiar and master the new rules. Obviously, if the new body of norms bears no relationship whatsoever to the previous tax sanctions framework, the learning and adaptation processes will be more challenging and the transition period lengthier, thereby hindering the objectives of the reform and the effectiveness of the tax sanctions code. Besides, when dealing with compliance and sanctions, sociological and cultural aspects tend to be more relevant than tax and economic considerations. If taxpayers feel disconnected from tax norms, they are less willing to voluntarily comply. To prevent this, legislation must be contextualized to each specific jurisdiction and mindful of taxpayers' particulars. One size does not fit all.

27 | This option would be the least disruptive in terms of implementation, given that the tax sanctions framework would remain unaltered. However, it would lack any added value since the penalty mismatches across taxes, and other deficiencies of the tax sanctions system would remain unaddressed.

Bibliography

Allingham, Michael, and Agnar Sandmo. 1972. "Income Tax Evasion: A Theoretical Analysis." *Journal of Public Economics* 1 (3–4): 323–338. https://doi.org/10.1016/0047-2727(72)90010-2.

Alm, James. 2013. "Designing Responsible Regulatory Policies to Encourage Tax Compliance." Conference on "Reflections on Responsible Regulation," Tulane University, New Orleans, March 2013. http://murphy.tulane.edu/files/events/Alm-Designin gResponsibleRegulatoryPolicies-MurphyInstitute-021113.pdf.

Carnes, G., and T. Eglebrecht. 1995. "An Investigation of the Effect of Detection Risk Perceptions, Penalty Sanctions and Income Visibility on Tax Compliance." *Journal of the American Taxation Association* 17 (1): 26–41.

European Court of Human Rights. 1976. "Engel and Others v. The Netherlands." Judgment given on 8 June 1976, Strasbourg, France. https://bit.ly/3t1EYbo.

Gordon, Richard. 1996. "Law of Tax Administration and Procedure." In *Tax Law Design and Drafting*, Vol. 1, edited by Victor Thuronyi, Chapter 4. https://www.imf.org/external/pubs/nft/1998/tlaw/eng/ch4.pdf.

Jackson, Betty, and Sally Jones. 1985. "Salience of Tax Evasion Penalties Versus Detection Risk." *Journal of the American Taxation Association* 6 (2): 7–17. https://aaahq.org/ATA/Publications/JATA/Spring-85#jackson.

Jackson, Betty, and Valerie Milliron. 1986. "Tax Compliance Research: Findings, Problems, and Prospects." *Journal of Accounting Literature* 5: 125–65.

Keinan, Yoram. 2006. "Playing the Audit Lottery: The Role of Penalties in the U.S. Tax Law in the Aftermath of Long Term Capital Holdings v. United States." *Berkeley Business Law Journal* 3 (2): 381–436. https://doi.org/10.15779/Z38M86R.

Lucas-Mas, Cristian Oliver, and Ana Cebreiro Gómez. 2023. "Guidelines for a Framework on Tax Sanctions: Designing the Framework Governing Tax Penalties, Surcharges and Interests." Unpublished. World Bank, Washington, DC.

Oladipupo, Adesina Olugoke, and Uyioghosa Obazee. 2016. "Tax Knowledge, Penalties and Tax Compliance in Small and Medium Scale Enterprises in Nigeria." *iBusiness* 8 (1): 1–9. https://doi.org/10.4236/ib.2016.81001.

Sandmo, Agnar. 2004. "The Theory of Tax Evasion: A Retrospective View." Nordic Workshop on Tax Policy and Public Economics in Helsinki, November 2004. Discussion Paper 31/04. https://dokumen.tips/documents/sandmo-the-theory-of-tax-evasion -vgeorgiousandmopdftax-evasion-is-a-violation.html.

Schwartz, Richard, and Sonya Orleans. 1967. "On Legal Sanctions." *University of Chicago Law Review* 34 (2): 274–300. https://chicagounbound.uchicago.edu/uclrev/vol34/iss2/3.

CHAPTER 6

Digital transformation of tax and customs administrations

Digitalization as a strategic tool for domestic resource mobilization

Digitalization improves the efficiency of tax collection, helps reduce cost, enables a more efficient fight against corruption, helps trace operations, and fosters transparency. Digitalization allows tax and customs administrations to evolve into a new role and find balance between facilitating tax compliance and maintaining effective control of taxpayers' obligations. This chapter focuses on data analytics and information management, and the role of digitalization as a strategic tool for domestic resource mobilization. This chapter analyzes digitalization as a strategic tool for domestic resource mobilization, tax administration as a business of information management, the impact of information technology systems on domestic resource mobilization, and exploiting of data quality management to its full potential.

In view of the radical changes that have taken place globally, tax systems cannot be administered in the way they were two or three decades ago. This new panorama stems mainly from substantial changes in the economy, globalization and financial integration, rapid development of new technologies, and new approaches to the role of taxation in modern and democratic societies. In the current global context and post–COVID-19 pandemic crisis, domestic resource mobilization (DRM) must be at the center of any development and economic growth strategies. This requires creating a strong analytical framework to help countries to establish productive, efficient, and equitable tax systems at both national and subnational levels. Moreover, taxation must be recognized as a key driver for state building and accountability, and tax reform as a possible contributor to broader gains in state capacity and quality of governance.

In the context of policy process, tax administration is the key to successful tax reform. Policy outcomes depend very much on how policies are administered. One of the key goals of policies is to provide countries with modern tax codes that foster a good business environment and incorporate the technological changes that will facilitate control of compliance and facilitation of taxpayers' obligations. Some good examples are the recently approved tax codes of Tajikistan and Uzbekistan that incorporate specific solutions to tax the digital economy and to digitalize all business processes of the revenue administration (box 6.1). Consequently, it is vital to accelerate the move to a digital revenue administration and to use the new wave of disruptive technologies to radically transform how taxes are administered. To remain relevant and effective, tax administrators must continually invest in scanning the external environment for emerging innovations in technology,

---

BOX 6.1 World Bank support to modernize Tajikistan's tax regime

The government of Tajikistan has made digitalization of the tax administration's processes a priority, which has resulted in the following achievements over the past decade:

2012—The system of reporting and accounting for tax payments advanced with the introduction of state bank and cash registries, and the infrastructure expanded.

2013—The State Tax Committee with World Bank assistance established a data processing center.

2014—The government implemented a file management system for mobile devices and introduced a new terminal to address the problems of taxpayers with internet connection problems.

2015—The e-invoice system was finalized. All value added tax (VAT) returns are now issued automatically. The VAT return also reflects the income, and this allows better monitoring of the whole tax position of the taxpayer.

2016—A postterminal system with transmission devices for data was established for the purpose of prefilling of tax returns. Legislation for prefilling returns was changed. Prefilling allows faster filling and submission—customs and cargo declaration are sent directly to customs authorities and other agencies, which reduces noncompliance. Another priority was to assign Taxpayer Identification Numbers in electronic form. The government was assigned to improve the quality of the services to the taxpayer.

2017—In the area of e-services, tax information systems were created.

2019—Discussions were held with the World Bank on how to ensure the provision of high-quality services. A network with regional offices was later built. Pension funds were integrated, and data exchanges were included. Gradually, more offices were included in the network, which are constantly increasing. In the area of VAT registration, Tajikistan created a single e-registry as a source of electronic information that would be available on an operational basis. Services provided not only to the government but also to businesses and taxpayers are part of the source system, and there is continuous interaction between organizations.

Currently, new programs and technologies are being implemented and the World Bank is providing support in introducing key technological developments, including the following:

(a) Modernization of the tax system through e-services, tax returns, and taxation of the digital economy

(b) Automated crediting of all taxes to the budget and links with the taxpayers' accounts for online payment of taxes

(c) Introduction of an automated collection process

(d) Implementation of digital signature and upgrade of information and communication technology infrastructure in the Tax Committee

(e) Implementation of an automated VAT refund system

(f) Automation of selected taxpayer services

The overall results are very positive. More than 80 percent of taxpayers filed their tax return using an e-form, and 70 percent of them were legal entities; 90 percent of them declared they were satisfied, time was reduced, and the new tax code is under development. The focus is hence on new systems for e-services and simplification of legal processes.

Source: Proceedings from the virtual seminars on tax and technology jointly hosted by the World Bank and the WU Global Tax Policy Center, 2020–22.

---

such as cryptocurrencies and digital currency, and their implications on taxpayers' new ways of managing the risk of tax evasion.

Technological change impacts organizational structure, business processes, and human resources (HR) policies. Beyond the mere adoption of new tools and technologies, real digitalization of the tax administration involves a comprehensive legal and institutional transformation. This process encompasses all the required adjustments to traditional operational models to achieve long-term and sustainable efficiencies, offer new and improved services to taxpayers, and develop new capabilities in key areas like digital invoicing, tax payments, digital fiscalization, advanced data analytics, and value chains and factoring. Such developments allow tax and customs administrations to process huge volumes of information and increase the reliability, accuracy, and timeliness of the information processed, which together reduce administration costs.

Moreover, technology helps to standardize and centralize routine processes and improve effectiveness of control of compliance. Organizational structure to centralize, standardize, and streamline information technology (IT) initiatives is an important aspect in building institutional

IT capacity and effective resource utilization. To this end, it is necessary to develop information and communication technology (ICT) and HR assessment tools that help to understand and assess the human and institutional capacity gaps of a tax administration. Also, as a step prior to digitalization, business process improvement and business model change are extremely relevant to the efficient transition between current and new business models.

The COVID-19 crisis has had a profound impact on digitalization as a strategic tool. Relevant improvements include establishing and maintaining remote work capabilities and adopting technological preparedness and adjustments—many jurisdictions have relied on tax authority registries to identify the recipients of business stimulus payments. For instance, the U.S. Internal Revenue Service continues to face technology challenges in the processing of economic impact payments to eligible recipients and in preventing improper payments, as recently published in its 2021 audit report (U.S. Government Accountability Office 2023). In this respect, public–private partnerships and engagement with open-source communities and consortiums could be beneficial in operationalizing digital transformation initiatives.

Based on experience, key success factors for digital transformation therefore include (a) establishing the transformational strategy and vision; (b) achieving the ideal organizational structure; (c) ensuring that the digital transformation is driven by the strategy, a roadmap, and a clear action plan; (d) recognizing the importance of the human factor; (e) addressing business process improvement; (f) addressing fragmentation, structure, legacy issues,[1] and quality of systems and data; and (g) promoting user adoption and trust through an inclusive change management program.

Tax administration as a business of information management

Today, tax administration is essentially a business of information management. The elements involved in tax administration are strongly supported by ICT. The use of ICT is not a choice; it is a necessity. It is important to support e-governance initiatives aimed at fully automating business processes of tax administrations and customs in close collaboration with other public sector institutions to improve delivery of services. In recent years, technical assistance (TA) programs on DRM are adopting a holistic approach that combines tax policy advice with support on implementing international good practices in revenue administration. An example of this whole-of-government approach is the single-window initiative for customs or support in developing and implementing strategies to combat the informal economy.

A strong emphasis on information management to ensure the quality of information that can be exploited efficiently by the tax administration can be seen in World Bank tax administration projects. A program of this kind is now being implemented in Uzbekistan, at both customs and tax administration levels, where the quality of data contained in electronic invoices is being analyzed to ensure that this information can effectively be used for tax audit purposes. Business intelligence[2]—through a variety of tools and mechanisms such as machine learning, Big Data, or exploration of the potential of blockchain—is now taking center stage in tax programs. Big Data has proved to be highly effective, for example, in controlling VAT compliance or avoiding fraud schemes coming from fake VAT refunds. In customs, risk analysis tools for trade operators are being implemented to improve control at the border and customs valuation.

Analytical work is vital to better understand a country context and better design future operations and loans. In Tajikistan and Uzbekistan, for example (see box 6.2), the World Bank is managing two TA programs that paved the way for two projects and development loans that have been recently approved. Key objectives are the full automation and digitalization of the revenue administration, streamlining of business processes, effective use of information through business intelligence, and major changes in HR policies. Tax administrations that coped with the COVID-19

BOX 6.2   World Bank support to modernize Uzbekistan's tax regime

The World Bank supported tax policy changes in Uzbekistan during 2019–20 to introduce new information technologies to improve the operational efficiency and effectiveness of its tax administration and to deliver better services to local taxpayers. New legislative acts allowing the use of modern technologies have been enacted to improve tax collection and counter the shadow economy.

The State Tax Committee has developed a strategy regarding the implementation of information and communication technologies (ICT), which includes the modernization of data centers, automation of business processes in tax administration, transfer of tax information to a single platform, implementation of business intelligence and Big Data technology, merging of the databases of tax and customs administrations, and making such databases available to all ministries and national agencies.

This initiative is expected to increase the speed of data processing and level of confidentiality, enhance the protection against security threats, broaden the base of information, and produce secure and reliable data storage. All the above measures are expected to expand the tax base through the reception of more and reliable data and enhance the image of the tax administration acting as a partner and consultant for taxpayers.

With the assistance and technical support of the World Bank and other organizations, a digital tool for the calculation of the value added tax (VAT) will be launched. Software for tracking the movement of assets, merging of companies and capital, purchasing of new assets, and related activities will be developed and deployed.

Source: Proceedings from the virtual seminars on tax and technology jointly hosted by the World Bank and the WU Global Tax Policy Center, 2020–2022.

---

pandemic are those that were better prepared in terms of technology. And this applies not only to the COVID-19 pandemic but also to any potential crisis. This technological element is present in most World Bank–financed DRM projects, as in Nigeria, Pakistan, Tajikistan, Uzbekistan, and finalized projects in Bulgaria and Colombia, to name a few.

Increased attention must be paid to issues related to mass communication—publishing of the form filings, data formats, and structures for electronic filings—and to the handling of information and privacy intrusion, which affect all taxpayers. For instance, collection of massive amounts of information combined with datamining techniques allow tax administrators to find data that are even unknown to a taxpayer and to use this information to profile the taxpayer. Some Organisation for Economic Co-operation and Development (OECD) tax administrations (OECD 2019; 2020a) have identified three emerging risks regarding the access and use of information that may create increasing difficulties for tax administrations over time: (a) changing work patterns, (b) changing business models, and (c) digital transparency issues. These risks are already present to some extent and may be expected to grow over the coming years with the increasing digitalization of the economy.

Impact of information technology systems on domestic resource mobilization

DRM has become a core priority of the sustainable development agenda for tax and customs administrations. Information systems can play a critical role in revenue mobilization, and successful revenue mobilization efforts can create the much-needed fiscal space for the government and allow for more spending on all the things that drive potential growth over the medium term, including infrastructure, health care, and education. More reliable sources of revenue would help avoid volatility in public expenditure and procyclical fiscal policy. Information technology systems can also increase the effectiveness of the internal operation of the tax administration and can reduce costs, as tax administrations improve their capacity to collect revenue with smarter use of the information they collect.

Voluntary compliance is enhanced with the use of taxpayer information services because taxpayers have certainty about the taxes to be paid, have access to online systems that make it easy to file a tax return, and make paying more convenient. When the tax administration can implement effective and sustainable taxpayer information services, revenue mobilization is enhanced. Taxpayer information systems can also contribute to the reduction in malpractice and corruption in a tax administration, because taxpayers who interact electronically with the organization do not need to come face-to-face with tax officials on standard operations. Where taxpayers interact with tax officials, effective information systems provide a natural deterrent for abuse since the results of discretionary actions are typically recorded in audit trails, increasing the risk that corrupt tax officials will be caught. With a reduction of malpractice and corruption, tax administrations can expect a subsequent increase in revenue for the organization. An additional benefit is the potential contribution to environmental sustainability, including mitigating the carbon footprint.

Information systems can also increase the effectiveness of the internal operation of the tax administration and can reduce costs. Through information systems, integrated taxpayer registries are created to collect the basic information needed to manage taxpayers. Process-intensive functions such as form and payment processing as well as taxpayer accounting are also automated. Selective monitoring and selective enforcing of compliance to reduce costs of compliance and administration can be implemented with information systems, therefore channeling resources directly to compliance activities and taxpayer services.

By automating manual functions, the tax organization can move to a compliance risk management model that systematically identifies, assesses, ranks, and treats tax compliance risks so that the tax administration can effectively deploy its limited resources. The necessary capabilities for improving recovery of arrears and tax debt, supporting intelligence and fraud detection, and identifying tax gaps are therefore created. Hence, effective implementation of information systems for a tax administration has the potential to significantly increase its efficiency, as ICT provides technological support for all functions of the administration.

In terms of which IT systems are more relevant for tax administrations and customs, recently, the focus is on Big Data[3] and data analytics,[4] artificial intelligence[5] and machine learning,[6] natural language process, cloud computing, and distributed ledger technology[7] represented by blockchain,[8] but these are not the most relevant. In fact, in the IT toolkit to be considered by a tax administration and customs, other technologies should be given priority, such as data visualization,[9] statistical analysis,[10] data mining,[11] graph databases, edge computing, robotic process automation, mobile collaboration and e-learning, predictive analytics, and hyperautomation. Others are DevOps, continuous integration and delivery, XaaS (everything as a service), application containerization, and serverless computing. Unfortunately, tax administrations often tend to neglect basic technical needs in favor of social and political trends. Before applying artificial intelligence or blockchain, for example, tax administrations and customs must ensure that the required underlying structural IT systems are in place and are fully functional.

It is important to properly determine the scope of tax administration functions to be covered by the digital transformation process, which goes beyond the traditional assessment methods, filing duties, and audit inspections. Key functions must also include registration, document management, legal obligations, taxpayer assistance mechanisms, communication channels, notification practices, taxpayer portals, appeals procedures, and any other technical functions like risk management.

Contrary to widespread belief, in practice, there is no transitional period during the digital transformation process since the IT systems evolve constantly. In fact, the optimal and smart strategy is to never "change" the IT infrastructure but instead to create the conditions for a continued and gradual evolution of the IT systems. The outdated model that periodically consists of conducting a full-length renovation has become too risky and unnecessary. Therefore, the new approach that should be adopted by tax administrations and customs is to incorporate an IT strategy based on permanent small-scale improvements that constantly transform the functional practices without creating any disruptions. Technological change cannot be perceived like a start-from-scratch process. IT specialists must stop thinking in terms of "overhauls" but instead integrate an evolutionary perspective into their IT practices. Furthermore, IT strategy should align with the broader government IT strategic plan. This emphasizes the fact that revenue administrations do not work in isolation and, therefore, any IT strategy should be part of a whole-of-government approach to allow for interoperability of systems and data standardization and verification.

Exploiting data quality management to its full potential

Awareness of data quality is important. A lot has changed in the world of data in the past 10 years. The amount of data, which is constantly growing, has increased the possibilities to gain valuable insights from complex data; our dependence on it and the problems caused by poor information have expanded as well.

Today, almost every administration has Big Data at the top of their IT list. The importance of this element deserves focused attention, as it is spawning innovation, uncovering opportunities, and optimizing resources in every institution. However, although administrations are aware of this, very few are taking actions to keep a close eye on exactly what data they are receiving and what kind of shape they are in. Most tax and customs administrations, whether knowingly or unknowingly, do not recognize that they have a significant problem in terms of data quality management, or the potential for one. Even the administrations that do recognize it are often hesitant to allocate financial resources and workforce to improve data quality.

Resistance to invest in data quality may be attributed to the lack of awareness regarding its impact, especially in the core business areas. It is common to see administrations that are too focused on developing automation, getting advance information, signing memorandums of understanding with other government agencies to exchange information, trying to develop comprehensive risk assessment systems, and implementing the most advanced tools in business intelligence. These modernization actions may make it appear that the administration is moving forward, but in practice, there is not much progress happening because the data reliability is not effectively satisfying the administration's needs. Data quality assessments are a helpful tool that provides information on the amount of data that is useful enough to execute operational processes that come from automation or are reliable for business analytics, statistical reporting, and risk management functions. If the amount of reliable and accurate data does not meet a certain minimum, how do administrations realistically expect to improve shortfalls, deter tax evasion, and promote facilitation and compliance by minimizing the impact on taxpayers?

If administrations were more conscious about practical consequences of poor data quality, more resources would be directed to address this issue to avoid data that are not fit-for-purpose. Poor data quality may result in short- or long-term operational issues and failure to provide services correctly. It may also weaken evidence, create mistrust, and cause reputational damage. The absence of data quality may lead to the following instances:

- Evidence-based decisions and policies would be only as good as the data they are based upon.
- Missing or duplicate data could result in bad auditing practices, altered or nonobjective reporting, and poor decision-making, leading to negative outcomes.
- Unreliable or contradictory data can make it difficult to verify irregularities among taxpayers or traders, which can lead them to question the data accuracy, creating mistrust toward the administration.
- There could be missed opportunities or failures in service provision.

- Risk mitigation could be impacted by possible inconsistencies in the risk scoring system and unreliable information to identify risk trends or fraud schemes.
- Automated controls are nonexistent due to the lack of format and structure in the data fields.
- Cross-checks cannot be properly implemented for effective compliance monitoring.
- There would be affectations in any integration process and the interoperability between agencies.
- Administrations are unable to assess their own strategic or operational effectiveness.

Regarding common challenges and solutions, it is not enough to simply identify the consequences of poor data quality. Many times, no matter how simple it may seem, managers are unable to measure what it means not to have quality information. To increase awareness, it is necessary to illustrate in detail the challenges and implications that go along with the quality of information as follows.

1. **Duplicated data.** This is an issue every administration must deal with. A frequent case within tax and customs administrations is that although they are receiving electronic invoice data, there is no standardization in the format of the invoice number. Without a unique number, there can be multiple invoices with the same number or an incorrect format that would not allow the system to identify a match for cross-checks and controls. To avoid this, data duplication tools are completely necessary. These solutions have improved considerably; now they are smart enough to spot even substantially different entries for the same taxpayer.
2. **Inconsistent formats.** This refers to inputting data that covers the same information but is stored in different formats. For example, dates are a complex field to many systems, as there are many potential ways that these could be entered into the system. Other potential difficulties may arise from tax identification format, invoice numbers, addresses, and phone numbers, especially when some have area codes and others do not. Therefore, it is vital to specify the exact format for every piece of data to ensure consistency across every source the administration uses. The most effective solution for this challenge is to define guidelines for lodging information, supporting it with validation rules for data consistency.
3. **Incomplete information.** This refers to the fields that are not completely filled in or are left blank altogether, and those can be a major problem for analytic tools as well as for Big Data algorithms. For example, entries that lack zip codes or invoice numbers are not just a problem when it comes to cross-checking data with other sources; they can also make the key analytics process useless if the analysis is based on geographical information that can help to spot trends and improve targeting efficiency. It is also common to see blank fields, generic or vague information on cargo description, or commercial invoices listing logistics companies as the consignee/importer without letting the authority know who the real entity is. With such data problems, it may seem impossible for the risk analysis units to target something that will not show up in a query because the data were lodged as incomplete, vague, or inconsistent. Validation rules are an effective solution to ensure that records cannot be created unless all essential information is included. If there is one field that does not comply with the predefined format, the system would simply reject the message.
4. **Multiple units and languages.** This is the case for invoices, transport documents, or advanced cargo information. Like the case on formatting, sometimes differences in language script or units of measurement can create difficulties if the analytics tools do not recognize or know how to translate them. Even special characters can wreak havoc if a system has not been configured for them. Therefore, administrations may need to consider these potential issues and program the algorithms accordingly. As a first step, it is important to define as many fields as possible as coded identifiers. For instance, instead of having a text field to input the cargo description, it is better to require just the Harmonized Tariff Schedule (HTS) number, or the code previously defined in a catalog. As a second step, the administration can work on creating a data dictionary to help improve the analysis.

5. **Inaccurate data.** There is no point in running Big Data analytics or conducting a risk assessment based on data that are inaccurate. There could be many reasons for this—from taxpayers giving incorrect information to making a typo when entering data manually, or inputting details into the wrong field. These can often be among the hardest data quality issues to spot, especially if the formatting is still acceptable. Entering an incorrect but valid tax identification number, for example, might go unnoticed by a database that only checks the veracity of that isolated input. Of course, there is no cure for human error, but ensuring that the administration has clear procedures being followed consistently is a good start. Creating validation rules can also help with the quality of the information and with compliance.

Data quality is like a telescope that allows us to see distant objects clearly. The better the telescope, the greater the administration's needs are met. Tax and customs risk management strategies rely on adequate and accurate quality data that enable administrations to make better-informed auditing and cargo processing decisions. Therefore, data management should not be viewed as a project or a program but instead as a strategic discipline. Data quality is crucial in optimizing the availability and value of the data required to meet the administrations' objectives.

Processes and protocols should be in place to ensure an acceptable level of confidence in the data, based on two aspects—the relevance of data for their intended use and their reliability. Validation rules are regulations established by the administration, through a system, which oblige the taxpayer to enter information in the indicated and consistent form when filing an invoice, a tax return, or a customs entry, among others. The type of validation can be implemented based on format and compliance, including the following:

- Form and syntax
- Validations of guidelines that establish specific formalities in the procedures
- Complementary validations, when there are specific requirements that come from certain scenarios or entry fillings
- Rules regarding compliance with the requirements of the tax or customs code.

Validation rules may help "clean" the data before they are inputted into the database. By checking against the validation rules, it is possible to assess whether the data meet the defined criteria and possess the required attributes. A good classification can be based on format, logic, informative data, catalog reference, and conditionals. The rules presented in boxes 6.3, 6.4, and 6.5 are some examples for an electronic invoice file.

BOX 6.3   Examples of form and syntax for an electronic invoice file

Format

- Tax ID structure (individual and legal entity).
- Element length.
- Reject special characters except in email address field.
- Multiple repetitive characters within a string or text field.
- Date format should be DD-MM-YYYY.

(continued)

BOX 6.3   Examples of form and syntax for an electronic invoice file (*Continued*)

- All monetary values must be expressed in positive values.
- All the value amounts should be expressed in a two-digit decimal form.

Logic

- Do not allow duplicated records with the same unique electronic invoice code.
- Reject message if there are any empty mandatory fields.
- The ID number from the issuer must be different from that of the recipient.
- Item attributes must contain some of the key words related to the Harmonized System code.

Conditionals

- If field "List of Invoices" is populated as "1," then more than one invoice must be filed.
- If "Certificate of Origin" is populated as 1, meaning the invoice serves as a certificate of origin, then the goods country of origin field is mandatory.
- If field "Certificate of Origin" is populated as "1", then the Enhanced Compliance Validation (ECV) 12 "goods country of origin" should be part of any of the signed free trade agreements.
- If there is a relationship between the issuer and recipient and there is a price affectation, then the method of customs valuation cannot be "1" (Method for Transaction Value).

Catalog reference

- Existing national tax ID
- Location identifier code
- Country identifier code
- Verify if the postal code is valid
- Verify the correct currency identifier code
- Verify code for supply type: B2B, B2C, SEZWP, SEZWOP, EXPWP, EXPWOP
- The correct exchange rate for the currency has been applied
- Entity's business activity code matches registry data
- Sensitive tariff code numbers

BOX 6.4   Examples of guidelines of validations for compliance

Arithmetic

- The total amount of the invoice must be the sum of item lines, corresponding adjustments of discounts or surcharges (Gross amount – Discount amount).
- The gross price of an item (unit price multiplied by quantity—rounded off to two decimal places).

(continued)

BOX 6.4   Examples of guidelines of validations for compliance (*Continued*)

- The total U.S. dollar amount should be equal to the total invoice amount × exchange rate of the issuing date (±10 percent).

- The sum of the total Item discount amount should be less than the total invoice amount.

Legal requirements

- Unique electronic invoice code structure.

- Issuer's tax ID number must be a valid one from an entity authorized to issue an e-invoice.

- Type of document: INV for invoice, CRN for credit note, DBN for debit note.

- Invoice serves as a certificate of origin.

- Whether the tax liability payable is under reverse charge must be noted.

- Indicates whether there is an invoice subdivision.

- Country of receiver must be different from issuer.

- The "Owner" field must be populated when the value in the "Reason for Transaction" field is equal to "06—Shipment of goods owned by third parties."

- Fields in ECV sections 8 and 9 regarding the "Customs Valuation Method" are mandatory when:

  ✓ The tariff code is in the sensitive tariff codes list.

  ✓ The tax ID is related to a recently created company or with less than 12 months of operation.

  ✓ The invoice value is greater than €20,000.

  ✓ The file cannot be modified once the customs declaration has been submitted.

  ✓ If field "HTS Code" from "Section 7—Item Details" is populated as sensitive goods, then field "Item_Attribute" is a mandatory field that should be populated in accordance with the appendix of sensitive codes attributes.

BOX 6.5   Examples of value risk rules for profiling

Value reference

- The unit price presents variations lower than 10 percent in regard to the rest of the importer's operations within the past 15 days.

- There is a difference of more than a 15 percent decrease in the invoice unit price regarding the last unit price from a previous identical transaction of the same importer.

- The invoice unit price presents variations lower than 20 percent in regard to the importer's unit price average of the same commodity for the past three months.

- Identify price variations over 10 percent with respect to the average incremental expenses.

Entities

- Business activity is related to the imported/exported Harmonized System (HS) code.

- Verify if the importer has a high frequency of transactions regarding high-risk North America Industry Classification System (NAICS) HS codes.

(continued)

BOX 6.5 Examples of value risk rules for profiling *(Continued)*

- Identify if the exporter's percentage of operations filed as consignment sales abroad is greater than 30 percent of operations registered in the past year.

- Verify that the issuer address is the same as the buyer, and verify that no link between entities has been declared.

Origin

- If the invoice is considered as a certificate of origin, verify if the declared country of origin is the same as the issuer's address.

- If the country of origin does not correspond to the country declared in the supplier's address, check if there is a relationship between entities. If not, indicate the inconsistency of origin between supplier and invoice.

- Flag whether it is an unusual country of origin with respect to a sensitive Harmonized Tariff Schedule code declared in the invoice. (Unusual activity is determined by less than 5 percent of the current total imports or first-time transactions regarding the origin.)

It is important to differentiate the distinct roles of core stakeholders—systems developers and vendors, systems managers, internal and external users, and independent oversight—including institutional risk managers, internal auditors, and external auditors. Also, it is useful to separately consider and discuss internally generated vis-à-vis externally sourced data, either from stratified sources, such as taxpayers' formal and informal records, or from "the internet of things" sources—mainly for analytical and business intelligence–based risk management. Similarly, when establishing and maintaining credible intergovernmental data exchange interfaces, it is important to include interfaces with taxpayers, as is widely applied for indirect taxes, mainly for sales and use taxes and excise duty from manufacturers. Maintaining credible historical data is also valuable for accurate revenue projections and trend analyses.

Notes

1 | Widely observed challenges in developing and developed economies can be attributed to the failure of revenue administrations to implement strategies that continually monitor and embrace upgrades in IT. An example is a recent audit report by the U.S. Government Accountability Office (2023) that stated that 33 percent of Internal Revenue Service applications were obsolete, ranging from 25 to 64 years in age. Therefore, it is important to adopt and implement strategies to continually identify and replace legacy IT applications and software and hardware systems.

2 | Business intelligence can be defined as the strategies and technologies used by enterprises for the data analysis of business information, providing historical and current views of business operations.

3 | Big Data is a field that treats ways to analyze, systematically extract information from, or otherwise deal with data sets that are too large or complex to be dealt with by traditional data-processing application software.

4 | Data analytics is the science of analyzing raw data to make conclusions about that information.

5 | Artificial intelligence (AI) is a wide-ranging branch of computer science concerned with building smart machines capable of performing tasks that typically require human intelligence.

6 | Machine learning is an application of AI that provides systems the ability to automatically learn and improve from experience without being explicitly programmed.

7 | Distributed ledger technology is normally referred to as "blockchain."

8 | Blockchain is a decentralized distributed ledger technology, which allows creation, validation, and encrypted transaction of digital assets to take place and get recorded in an incorruptible way.

9 | Data visualization is the graphical representation of information and data. By using visual elements like charts, graphs, and maps, data visualization tools provide an accessible way to see and understand trends, outliers, and patterns in data.

10 | Statistical analysis is the science of collecting, exploring, and presenting large amounts of data to discover underlying patterns and trends.

11 | Data mining consists of extracting and discovering patterns in large data sets involving methods at the intersection of machine learning, statistics, and database systems.

Bibliography

BRITACOM. 2020. "Digital Transformation: BRITACOM Perspective." *Belt and Road Initiative Tax Journal* 1 (2). https://www.britacom.org/gkzljxz/dzqk/202012/P020220526625859260676.pdf.

Butler, Jeff. 2020. "Analytical Challenges in Modern Tax Administration: A Brief History of Analytics at the IRS." *The Ohio State Technology Law Journal* 16 (1): 258–77. http://hdl.handle.net/1811/91830.

CIAT (International Center of Tax Administrations). 2020. *ICT as a Strategic Tool to Leapfrog the Efficiency of Tax Administrations*. Panama City, Panama: CIAT. https://www.ciat.org/Biblioteca/Estudios/2020-ICT_STL_CIAT_FMGB.pdf.

IOTA (Intra-European Organisation of Tax Administrations). 2016. *Transforming Tax Administration and Involving Stakeholders*. Budapest, Hungary: IOTA. https://www.iota-tax.org/system/files/transforming-tax-administration.pdf.

IOTA. 2017. *Disruptive Business Models: Challenges and Opportunities for Tax Administrations*. Budapest, Hungary: IOTA. https://www.iota-tax.org/sites/default/files/publications/public_files/disruptive-business-models.pdf.

Junquera-Varela, Raúl Félix, Daniel Álvarez Estrada, and Cristian Óliver Lucas-Mas. 2021. *COVID-19 and Taxation: Between the Devil and the Deep Blue Sea*. Equitable Growth, Finance and Institutions Insight. Washington, DC: World Bank. http://hdl.handle.net/10986/36155.

Junquera-Varela, Raúl Félix, and Cristian Óliver Lucas-Mas. 2021. *COVID-19: Tax Policy and Revenue Administration Implications*. Equitable Growth, Finance and Institutions Insight. Washington, DC: World Bank. http://hdl.handle.net/10986/35920.

Junquera-Varela, Raúl Félix, Cristian Óliver Lucas-Mas, Ivan Krsul, Vladimir Calderón, and Paola Arce. 2022. *Digital Transformation of Tax and Customs Administrations*. Equitable Growth, Finance and Institutions Insight. Washington, DC: World Bank. http://hdl.handle.net/10986/37629.

Junquera-Varela, Raúl Félix, Marijn Verhoeven, Gangadhar P. Shukla, Bernard Haven, Rajul Awasthi, and Blanca Moreno-Dodson. 2017. *Strengthening Domestic Resource Mobilization: Moving from Theory to Practice in Low- and Middle-Income Countries*. Directions in Development, Public Sector Governance. Washington, DC: World Bank. http://hdl.handle.net/10986/27265.

Kariuki, Elizabeth. 2013. "Towards Sustainable ICT Systems in Tax Administrations." Automation in Tax Administration: Summary Note. Africa Policy Research Institute Limited. https://docplayer.net/14328796-Automation-in-tax-administrations-elizabeth-kariuki-summary-note-september-2013-april-publication-no-4-www-april-ssa-com-public-policy-research.html.

KPMG. 2018. *Transforming the Tax Function Through Technology: A Practical Guide to 2020*. Amstelveen, The Netherlands: KPMG International. https://kpmg.com/xx/en/home/insights/2018/04/transforming-the-tax-function-through-technology.html.

Lucas-Mas, Cristian Óliver, and Raúl Félix Junquera-Varela. 2021. *Tax Theory Applied to the Digital Economy: A Proposal for a Digital Data Tax and a Global Internet Tax Agency*. Washington, DC: World Bank. http://hdl.handle.net/10986/35200.

Microsoft and PwC (PricewaterhouseCoopers). 2017. *Digital Transformation of Tax Administration*. https://info.microsoft.com/rs/157-GQE-382/images/Digital%20Transformation%20of%20Tax%20Administration%20White%20Paper.pdf.

Microsoft and PwC. 2018. *The Data Intelligent Tax Administration: Meeting the Challenges of Big Tax Data and Analytics*. https://www.pwc.nl/en/publicaties/tax-administration-by-pwc-and-microsoft/the-data-intelligent-tax-administration.html.

OECD (Organisation for Economic Co-operation and Development). 2019. *Measuring the Digital Transformation: A Roadmap for the Future*. Paris: OECD Publishing. https://doi.org/10.1787/9789264311992-en.

OECD. 2020a. *Tax Administration 3.0: The Digital Transformation of Tax Administration*. Paris: OECD Publishing. https://www.oecd.org/ctp/administration/tax-administration-3-0-the-digital-transformation-of-tax-administration.htm.

OECD. 2020b. *OECD Digital Economy Outlook 2020*. Paris: OECD Publishing. https://doi.org/10.1787/bb167041-en.

OECD. 2021a. *Tax Administration: Towards Sustainable Remote Working in a Post COVID-19 Environment*. Paris: OECD Publishing. https://www.oecd.org/tax/forum-on-tax-administration/publications-and-products/tax-administration-towards-sustainable-remote-working-in-a-post-covid-19-environment.htm.

OECD. 2021b. *Tax Administration: Digital Resilience in the COVID-19 Environment*. Paris: OECD Publishing. https://www.oecd.org/coronavirus/policy-responses/tax-administration-digital-resilience-in-the-covid-19-environment-2f3cf2fb/.

OECD. 2021c. "The Digital Transformation of SMEs." OECD Studies on SMEs and Entrepreneurship. Paris: OECD Publishing. https://doi.org/10.1787/bdb9256a-en.

Tulácek, Michal. 2019. "Legal Aspects of Tax Administration Electronisation." In *European Financial Law in Times of Crisis of the European Union*, edited by G. Hulko and R. Vybiral, 577–84. Budapest: Dialog Campus. http://hdl.handle.net/20.500.12944/20252.

United States Government Accountability Office. 2023. *IRS Needs to Complete Modernization Plans and Fully Address Cloud Computing Requirements*. Report to the Honorable Gerald E. Connolly, House of Representatives. Washington, DC: U.S. Government Accountability Office. https://www.gao.gov/products/gao-23-104719.

CHAPTER 7

Building data science capabilities in tax and customs administrations

Data management applied to data sciences

Data science and machine learning can significantly improve the efficiency of revenue administrations. This chapter explores what a digital roadmap for building data science capabilities would look like and how to determine the appropriate technology to be applied by tax and customs administrations, taking into account their maturity level. This is helpful not only for tax policymakers and tax officials but also for information technology (IT) experts who need to get an understanding of the needs of tax and customs administrations to better design and implement the most appropriate technology solutions. This chapter analyzes data management applied to data sciences, strategies for creating machine learning capabilities and data science tools, applications of machine learning in tax and customs administrations, feasibility of the use of blockchain initiatives for tax administrations, and best practices in implementing information technology systems.

Although there is no consensus on its definition, data science is generally accepted as an interdisciplinary field that uses scientific methods, processes, algorithms, and systems to extract knowledge and insights from structured and unstructured data. Data science includes techniques from a diverse spectrum, including statistics, Big Data, data management, data visualization, data mining, and machine learning. Revenue administrations have been using a subset of data sciences for many years, focused on the field of data analytics, to generate valuable insights from the available data and to make better-informed decisions. Data analytics is the process of cleaning, inspecting, modeling, and transforming data for finding valuable information to enhance the decision-making process (Brown 2014).

Data science is typically used in tax administration and customs to make sense of the vast amounts of data that are available, so that the organization can become smarter, faster, and more efficient. Of particular interest to revenue administrations is machine learning, a subset of data sciences that can be used to solve difficult problems that arise from the inability of a revenue administration to process massive amounts of data efficiently. In the purview of machine learning are applications such as identifying fraudulent operations, automatically answering questions posed by taxpayers, identifying illegal goods in x-rays, predicting the cost of interventions, identifying the code of a given article in the harmonized system, and identifying potential errors or inconsistencies in declarations or tax returns. Hence, data sciences and machine learning can significantly improve the efficiency of a revenue administration.

Data science and machine learning are analytical tools, optimizations, and enhancements that are typically implemented on top of existing basic IT systems in a revenue administration, since these provide the basic data that are needed. For example, an audit module would be required before attempting to predict the total cost of an audit using machine learning. Typical modules that should be fully implemented in a tax administration before attempting machine learning projects include registration, returns processing, arrears management, payment processing, audit management and tracking, taxpayer assistance, and legal affairs tracking and management. For a customs administration, typical modules that should be fully implemented before attempting machine learning projects include registration, declaration processing, arrears management, payment processing, audit management and tracking, trade partner assistance, legal affairs tracking and management, inspection, passenger processing, warehousing, and transit control.

Data science in general, particularly machine learning, relies on high-quality data and professional analysts who use tools and statistical methods for data cleaning—for example, data acquisition, data manipulation, data wrangling and tidying, managing missing data, and eliminating outliers. The performance of the machine learning algorithm will be directly proportional to the quality of the data. For instance, to train a computer to recognize fraudulent requests such as tax returns or import declarations, a series of examples that are not fraudulent could be fed to the computer, and the computer will build a mathematical model of what "normality" looks like. This will enable computing a probability that a new request is fraudulent, based on how much it deviates from the training data.

If the training data are reliable, the machine learning system will perform well. However, if the training data are of low quality and many examples are misclassified, the computer will develop a skewed model of "normality" in the tax declarations or returns, resulting in a high number of false negatives—cases that are fraudulent but are, in fact, correct. Rather than helping, the algorithm will cause the administration to spend a lot of resources to deal with taxpayers or trade partners that are frustrated because they have been wrongly targeted. If the data used to train the algorithm are faulty, then the machine learning will build an incorrect model of the correlation between all these features and the expected level of income for any individual taxpayer, and the algorithm will incorrectly classify the taxpayer's income bracket.

The greatest difficulty about machine learning models is to implement them, but to start with, it is hard to own a good data set to be trained. Data are of such critical importance that several countries have even started national initiatives for creating high-quality repositories, such as the Data Mining Pipeline (Canada), the Data Lake Project (France), and the Unified Data Platform (Singapore). Hence, one of the most important components of a data science team is a data management unit that can create a curated repository of data, which can be used for machine learning projects. This unit would use statistical methods and special algorithms to analyze existing data, delete features that have errors, deal with missing data, eliminate outliers, label data, and, in general, clean up data that will be used for machine learning algorithms.

Synthetic data for machine learning

Due to privacy and confidentiality constraints, it is usually not feasible to release production data to machine learning developers for the construction of learning algorithms. Information in a tax or customs administration is highly confidential. The development of learning algorithms is an iterative approach that requires experimentation and refinement in multiple iterations, experimenting with multiple parameters and configurations until the performance of the algorithms is acceptable.

Much of machine learning work should be done by a diverse set of developers, including researchers at universities, consultants, and machine learning specialists in other administrations who normally would not have access to the original privileged information collected by revenue administrations.

Since the data in a tax or customs administration are highly confidential—and sometimes it is even difficult to disclose information to be used within an administration—researchers and the IT team frequently find it difficult to experiment with machine learning. To allow these groups to make progress, the data management unit needs to create a parallel data repository that contains realistic data that retain the statistical properties of the original repository but have no real information. This parallel data repository is traditionally created by anonymizing the data and replacing them with random values so that it is not possible to infer real information, but it is possible to train machine learning algorithms on it. The process of anonymizing the data repository is time-consuming and difficult to scale up and can render the information useless. Sometimes it is easier to generate new random data that retain the statistical properties of the original data set rather than anonymizing the existing data. These data are formally called "synthetic data."

Advances in machine learning enable the generation of highly realistic and highly representative synthetic data repositories that resemble the characteristics as well as the diversity of actors in a tax or customs administration. Generating synthetic data boils down to learning the joint probability distribution in an original data set to generate a new data set with the same distribution, but the more complex the data set, the more difficult it is to map dependencies.

Creating a synthetic data repository is a huge challenge that requires full-time staff trained on the mechanisms for anonymizing data and replicating them to the synthetic repository so that they retain their statistical properties but are not connected in any way to real entities or data. The rewards of this effort are equally huge, since the synthetic data can be made available to a large group of researchers who will help develop the algorithms that will improve the effectiveness of the revenue administration.

Strategy for creating machine learning capabilities and data science tools

Machine learning is a branch of data sciences that focuses on the use of data and algorithms to imitate the way that humans learn, deriving structure and rules from data, gradually improving its accuracy over time. Machine learning algorithms build a model based on sample data, known as "training data," to make predictions or decisions without being explicitly programmed to do so. Most revenue administrations are using—or are in the implementation phase of—data sciences and machine learning. As this technology matures, they will see increased efficiencies, given that the technologies can be used to (a) correct deficiencies in the revenue administrations, such as unreliability, slowness, and inaccuracies; (b) detect irregularities and errors; (c) predict fraudulent behavior; (d) proactively assist taxpayers; (e) classify level of trust for compliance purposes; and (f) provide insights for data-driven decision-making.

There are two types of machine learning problems: supervised and unsupervised. Supervised machine learning problems are those where a computer is taught by example so it can construct a model of the problem and apply it to new cases in the future. For example, the machine learning algorithm can be trained to identify examples of tax returns or customs declarations that have issues and those that do not. The system will learn to flag samples with problems so that taxpayers or trade partners can be alerted automatically before they are accepted. Supervised learning requires data that are labeled. Labeled data are a group of samples that have been tagged with one or more labels. The process of labeling typically takes a set of unlabeled data and augments each piece of it with informative tags. For example, a data label might indicate whether a tax return is fraudulent, whether a customs declaration is high risk, whether a tax appeal is rejected, or whether a cargo shipment contains contraband.

Unsupervised learning is where the computer discovers patterns and structure in the data without guidance. With this, previously unknown characteristics can be discovered. For example, the computer can be fed a list of taxpayers or trade partners, and it can group them by similarities so that those grouped together can be analyzed. Hence, unsupervised learning does not require labeling data, and it can create patterns and structure from standard data warehouses.

Machine learning techniques include but are not limited to the following:

- **Classification**. Classification algorithms can explain or predict a class value. For example, classification algorithms can help predict whether a taxpayer should be audited or whether a container should be inspected. The two classes in this case are "yes" and "no." Classification algorithms are not limited to two classes and can be used to classify items into many categories.
- **Regression**. Regression methods are used for training supervised machine learning. The goal of regression techniques is typically to explain or predict a specific numerical value while using a previous data set. For example, regression methods can take historical data to predict the income for a new taxpayer that has similar characteristics to other known taxpayers or predict the import volumes for a new trade partner that has similar characteristics to other known trade partners.
- **Clustering**. Clustering algorithms are unsupervised learning methods that group data points according to similar or shared characteristics. Grouping or clustering techniques are particularly useful in an administration that needs to segment its taxpayers or trade partners by different characteristics to better target risk management or audit programs. Clustering is also effective in discovering patterns in complex data sets that may not be obvious to the human eye, such as discovering groups of taxpayers or trade partners that are linked or related.
- **Decision trees**. Decision tree algorithms learn to classify objects by answering questions about attributes located at nodal points. Depending on the answer, one of the branches is selected, and at the next junction, another question is posed, until the algorithm reaches a tree's leaf, which indicates the final answer. A typical example of decision trees is identifying the action to take once a clearance request is received. The decision tree can define a complex map of criteria, such as location, type of cargo, risk level of the trade partner, history of the trade partner, and amount of the commercial transaction, and then determine risk categories based on the request submitted. The system can then evaluate new clearance requests, categorize them by risk, and decide the appropriate action to take.
- **Neural networks**. These networks mimic the structure of the brain and use artificial neurons that connect to several other neurons and together create a complex cognitive structure in a multilayer structure. The neural network typically learns about how to solve a problem or classify an object by trying a different configuration of the connections between the neurons. Neural networks are used for a wide variety of business applications, such as recognizing a taxpayer or a trade partner that is likely to be defrauding the administration or recognizing a question posed by a taxpayer or a trade partner to offer a known response from a database of previously answered questions.
- **Dimensionality reduction**. This is used to remove the least important information—sometimes redundant columns—from a data set. In practice, the administration uses it to simplify data sets with hundreds or even thousands of columns (also called features) from the vast amount of information collected about a taxpayer or a trade partner to data sets that are manageable.

A tax administration's level of maturity in terms of advanced data analytics and machine learning can be measured in three dimensions: scope, data quality, and type of use (figure 7.1).

- **Scope** refers to who is using advanced data analytics in an organization. At the most basic level, use is sparse, and only a few individuals, if any, use advanced data analytics in isolated pockets.

FIGURE 7.1 Dimensions of maturity levels in terms of advanced data analytics and machine learning

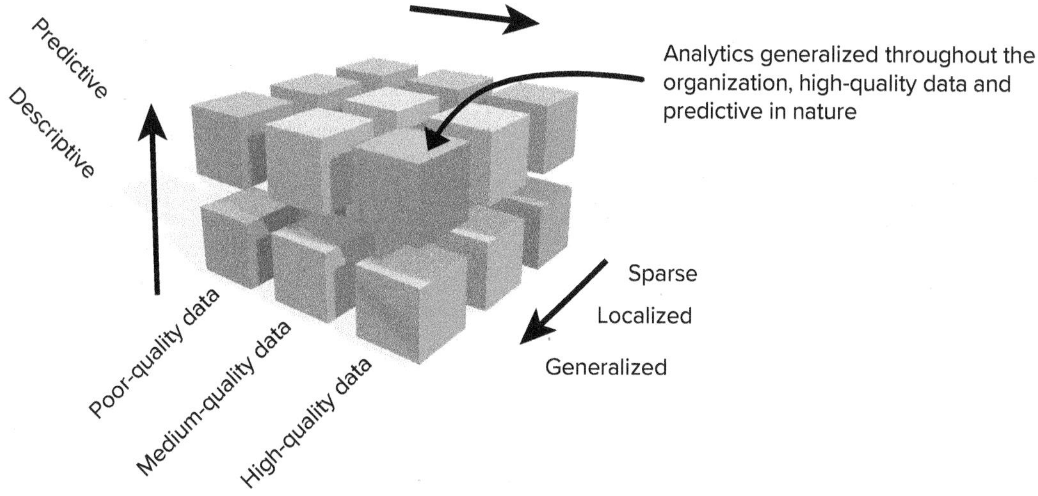

Analytics generalized throughout the organization, high-quality data and predictive in nature

Sparse
Localized
Generalized

Predictive
Descriptive

Poor-quality data
Medium-quality data
High-quality data

Source: Krsul 2021a.

At an intermediate level, localized groups use advanced data analytics in specific areas of a tax administration. In the more advanced level, the use of advanced data analytics is generalized. The optimal and most advanced level is achieved when data analytics is widely used throughout the entire tax administration—by all departments and for all core business processes and functions. Therefore, the goal is to embed data analytics in the general workstream of tax administrations.

- **Data quality** refers to the quality of the data in the tax administration's data repositories—its data warehouse. Advanced data analytics is likely to produce poor results when the data available are of low quality, regardless of the talent of the data analysts. High-quality data enable the data analytics team to obtain exemplary results.
- **Type of use** indicates whether the tax administration is using advanced data analytics to generate reports and statistics about what happened in the past (descriptive) or whether it is using data to change the way it operates in the future (predictive).

The level of maturity of a tax administration, in terms of data analytics, is largely defined by the level of quality of the data that are available (table 7.1). The lowest levels of maturity correspond to low-quality data that are used to describe what happened in the past, and the highest levels of maturity correspond to high-quality data that are used to predict the future behavior of taxpayers and the organization.

The current level of data analytics maturity in most tax administrations is likely to be low. Improvement comes as a result of an iterative process, where the tax administration attempts to build a predictive model and as a result triggers a data-cleansing process that will allow further improvement iteratively—see figure 7.2.

This iterative process also builds talent, as it constitutes a competency framework. As the tax administration completes multiple cycles of this process, it develops a workforce equipped with next-generation skills and advanced tactics in artificial intelligence, resulting in qualified leadership at national and regional levels.

TABLE 7.1 Maturity levels of a tax administration in terms of data analytics

Level of maturity	Scope	Data quality	Level of use
Low	Sparse	Low quality	Descriptive
	Localized	Low quality	Descriptive
	Generalized	Low quality	Descriptive
	Sparse	Medium quality	Descriptive
	Localized	Medium quality	Descriptive
	Generalized	Medium quality	Descriptive
Medium	Sparse	High quality	Descriptive
	Localized	High quality	Descriptive
	Generalized	High quality	Descriptive
	Sparse	Low quality	Predictive
	Localized	Low quality	Predictive
	Generalized	Low quality	Predictive
High	Sparse	Medium quality	Predictive
	Localized	Medium quality	Predictive
	Generalized	Medium quality	Predictive
Very high	Sparse	High quality	Predictive
	Localized	High quality	Predictive
	Generalized	High quality	Predictive

Source: Krsul 2021a.

In most tax administrations, unfortunately, there is a very large disconnect between the functional areas and the IT department that locks the tax administration in the localized scope. The IT department has sufficient knowledge to build basic machine learning algorithms but has no data and no functional demands from the business areas to attempt building a predictive model. The business side of the tax administration is usually completely unaware that the IT department has basic skills to attempt building these predictive models. As a result, it is unlikely that the tax administration will see concrete examples of machine learning in the short term.

To jumpstart this process, the tax administration needs to create specific demands from the business side so that the IT department tries applying machine learning algorithms, with whatever data they currently have. The organization needs to engage senior leaders to work with business process managers so that full executive support can be established. Initially, most machine learning algorithms will have poor performance but will gradually improve. The most successful data science initiatives take small incremental steps rather than pursuing a large and ambitious project. Small, incremental steps help break down skepticism, prove the concept with limited investment, and build trust for wider-scale adoption.

Although every tax administration's eventual goal is automatic fraud detection and intelligent risk management, it needs to identify and promote smaller, less demanding applications where it can make significant progress and gradually strengthen its competency and improve on its level of maturity. In fact, very simple systems with modest goals are likely to pay off handsomely. A system that correctly identifies the economic activity of a taxpayer can save months of manual labor and increase its risk management capabilities. Modest goals indeed add up quickly.

Furthermore, specialized data science professionals in a revenue administration use a variety of tools to manage and analyze the data that are amassed by the organization, internally and

FIGURE 7.2   Iterative data-cleansing process

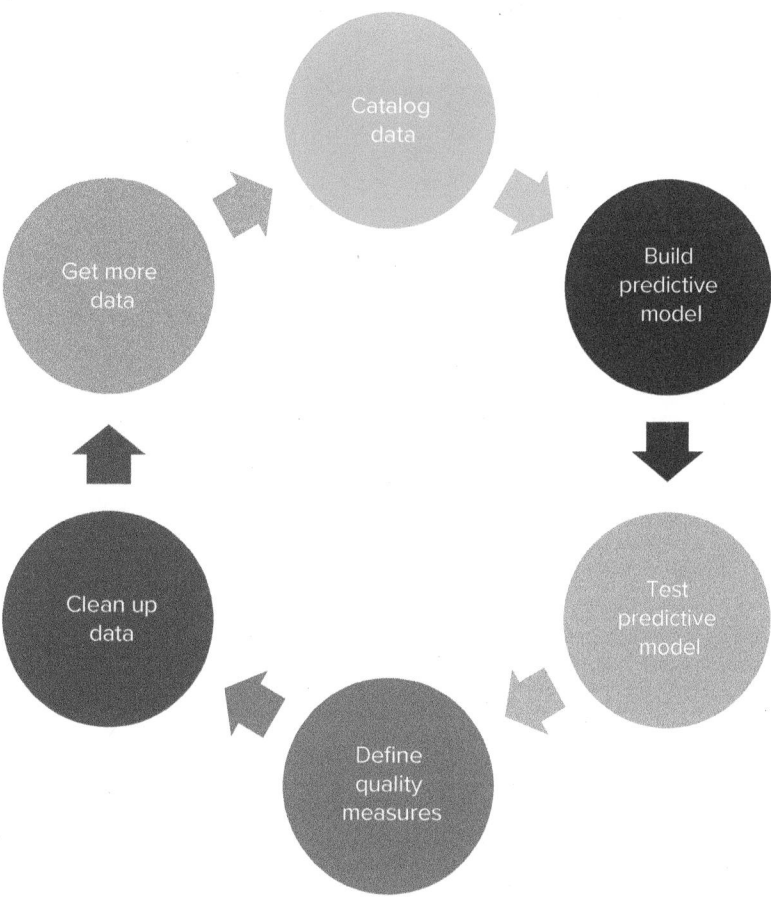

Source: Krsul 2021b.

externally, from data-sharing agreements with other government bodies and financial institutions. The bottom line is that most machine learning solutions currently use publicly available open-source tools, so the revenue administration does not need to invest in software systems. The investment required is in human resources and servers to process the data. The data scientist toolkit includes the notable software systems contained in box 7.1 (Krsul 2021b), with many of them open source and free to use.

All these tools are general-purpose frameworks and platforms for the development of data science solutions for any industry and are not specific solutions for revenue administrations. Each revenue administration is generally responsible for building their customs solutions specifically tailored to their data. There are also some companies that provide data science solutions specifically built for revenue administrations, so it is possible to outsource the task of creating a clean data set and applying data science algorithms, but this does not create a sustainable capacity within the revenue administration. Hence, revenue administrations are typically encouraged to build the required capacity in-house. A revenue administration that will undertake this task requires a dedicated team of at least 5 to 10 people who are appropriately trained. Appendix E provides a sample roadmap for the creation of a data science team.

BOX 7.1   Data scientist toolkit

- **Apache Flink.** A framework and distributed processing engine for stateful computations over unbounded and bounded data streams. Flink has been designed to run in all common cluster environments and perform computations at in-memory speed and at any scale.

- **Apache Spark.** A unified analytics engine for large-scale data processing. It is used for big data workloads and utilizes in-memory caching and optimized query execution for fast queries against data of any size.

- **BigML.** A consumable, programmable, and scalable machine learning platform to solve and automate classification, regression, time-series forecasting, cluster analysis, anomaly detection, association discovery, and topic modeling tasks.

- **Caffe.** A deep learning framework made with expression, speed, and modularity in mind. It is developed by Berkeley AI Research and by community contributors.

- **DataRobot.** A machine learning platform for automating, ensuring, and accelerating predictive analytics, helping data scientists and analysts build and deploy accurate predictive models.

- **GNU Octave.** A high-level language, primarily intended for numerical computations. It provides a convenient command line interface for solving linear and nonlinear problems numerically and for performing other numerical experiments using a language that is mostly compatible with MATLAB. It may also be used as a batch-oriented language.

- **Hadoop.** A software library that provides a framework that allows for the distributed processing of large data sets across clusters of computers using simple programming models.

- **Jupyter.** A nonprofit, open-source project to support interactive data science and scientific computing across all programming languages. The Jupyter Notebook is an open-source web application that allows the creation and sharing of documents that contain live code, equations, visualizations, and narrative text.

- **MATLAB.** A programming platform designed specifically for engineers and scientists to analyze data and design systems. It has extensive support for deep learning techniques.

- **Matplotlib and Seaborn.** Matplotlib is a comprehensive library for creating static, animated, and interactive visualizations in Python. Seaborn is a Python data visualization library based on Matplotlib. It provides a high-level interface for drawing attractive and informative statistical graphics.

- **Neo4J.** A graph database platform that allows enterprise applications such as artificial intelligence, fraud detection, and recommendations.

- **NLTK (Natural Language Toolkit).** A platform for building Python programs to work with human language data, along with a suite of text-processing libraries for classification, tokenization, stemming, tagging, parsing, and semantic reasoning.

- **Pandas.** An open-source library providing high-performance, easy-to-use data structures and data analysis tools for the Python programming language.

- **Python Programming Language.** The most popular language used for machine learning and artificial intelligence.

- **Pytorch.** An open-source machine learning library based on the Torch library, used for applications such as computer vision and natural language processing, primarily developed by Facebook's AI Research lab.

- **R Programming Language.** A language and environment for statistical computing and graphics. R provides a wide variety of statistical (linear and nonlinear modeling, classical statistical tests, time-series analysis, classification, clustering) and graphical techniques and is highly extensible.

- **RStudio.** An integrated development environment for R. It includes a console, a syntax-highlighting editor that supports direct code execution, and tools for plotting, history, debugging, and workspace management.

- **SAS.** A software system used for statistical analysis and data visualization. It has extensive support for visual data mining, data visualization, and machine learning.

- **Tableau.** A data visualization software, also known as visual analytics platform, that focuses on business intelligence.

- **TensorFlow.** An end-to-end open-source platform for machine learning (ML) from Google. It has a comprehensive, flexible ecosystem of tools, libraries, and community resources that lets researchers push the state-of-the-art in ML and developers build and deploy ML-powered applications.

- **Watson Studio.** A software platform for data science from IBM, consisting of a workspace that includes multiple collaboration and open-source tools for use in data science.

As to the prerequisites, data sciences and machine learning are analytical tools, optimizations, and enhancements that are typically implemented on top of existing basic IT systems in a revenue administration, since these provide the basic data that are needed. For example, an audit module would be required before attempting to predict the total cost of an audit using machine learning. Typical modules that should be fully implemented in a tax administration before attempting machine learning projects include registration, returns processing, arrears management, payment processing, audit management and tracking, taxpayer assistance, and legal affairs tracking and management. Similarly, typical modules that should be completely implemented in a customs administration before attempting machine learning projects include registration, declaration processing, arrears management, payment processing, audit management and tracking, trade partner assistance, legal affairs tracking and management, inspection, passenger processing, warehousing, and transit control.

Applications of machine learning in tax and customs administrations

Some applications of the use of machine learning in tax administrations and customs are provided below. Those that are identified with a low level of difficulty are modest applications that can be used to obtain executive support to drive these efforts from the business side of the organization. The general strategy is to encourage the business side of the customs administration to implement machine learning algorithms with low levels of difficulty first and progress incrementally until advanced competencies are developed; the customs administration can then tackle medium- and high-complexity issues. Each level of difficulty is associated with a level of maturity:

- A low level of difficulty is associated with a basic maturity level 2 that comprises practices for controlled operations.
- A medium level of difficulty is associated with an intermediate maturity level 3 that comprises practices for efficient operations.
- A high level of difficulty is associated with an advanced maturity level 4 that comprises practices for sustainable and optimized operations.

Application of machine learning to tax administrations

Low difficulty/basic maturity level 2 (Practices for Controlled Operations). This involves:

- Assign a probable economic activity to unclassified taxpayers (Zambrano and Díaz de Sarralde 2021). The tax administration regularly classifies taxpayers according to their economic activity. This classification is used internally for risk management, outreach, and communication with taxpayers. Some taxpayers may have been misclassified or their classification may have changed since the original registration, and it is possible to deduce the economic activity from financial information using specialized machine learning segmentation models. These can be used to identify taxpayers who may have changed their economic activities or to classify taxpayers in the registry who are lacking economic activity. This application is particularly attractive because it does not require labeling of data since the existing classification for taxpayers is used to train the machine learning algorithms.
- Review the reasonableness of the expenses deducted in the income tax return. Machine learning algorithms can be used to predict the type and amount of expenses that can be detected in an income tax return. This application is useful in assisting taxpayers during the filing phase of the tax return or in assessing the reasonableness of the expenses deducted in an income tax return. This application is particularly attractive, because it does not require labeling of data since existing tax returns are used to train machine learning algorithms as to what is reasonable in terms of expense deductions.
- Automatically classify documents during an audit—for example, Canada (OECD 2021). During an audit, the review team must process thousands of documents, including documents of interest

such as those that mention exports, imports, or financial transactions. Document classification is an area where machine learning can improve overall quality while simultaneously reducing costs. Document classification works through a two-step process. A textual representation of the document is first created by using optical character recognition (OCR), and the output of this process then feeds into another machine learning model that reads the text to determine the context and applies a label to the document that is relevant to the business.

- Use virtual agents to reply to taxpayers' questions—for example, China, Australia, and more than 10 additional countries (García-Herrera 2018; OECD 2021). Machine learning can be used to implement chatbots that enable reducing the size of the taxpayer assistance workforce and ensure taxpayer service to be available 24 hours a day, 7 days a week, and 365 days a year, which can be difficult to achieve with purely human help desk operators. Chatbots can be either voice based or text based—the former involves a taxpayer interacting with the chatbot over the phone, and the latter has the taxpayer interacting through the tax administration's website. These services allow commonly asked questions to be instantly answered as well as prescreen taxpayers so agents can be more targeted on their calls. The implementation of chatbots is already mature and can be implemented with minimal data.

- Estimate cost of supervision activities—for example, audits and desk reviews. Supervision activities are expensive, and past experience can be used to train machine learning algorithms so that the cost of future supervision activities can be estimated from the taxpayer profile and external data available. This cost can be used as a parameter in the prioritization of supervision activities, combining it with additional data to select those activities that will be most cost-effective.

- Estimate probability of success in supervision activities—for example, audits and desk reviews. Supervision activities are expensive and past experience can be used to train machine learning algorithms so that the probability of success of future supervision activities can be estimated from past experiences, the taxpayer profile, and external data available. This probability can be used as a parameter in the prioritization of supervision activities, combining it with additional data to select those activities that will be most cost-effective.

- Answer taxpayer questions—for example, more than 10 countries (García-Herrera 2018). A portion of the questions asked by taxpayers to the help desk are simple questions—for example, "I drive for Uber; is my wait time tax deductible?" or "I drive for Uber, do I need to pay taxes?"— that can be answered by intelligent agents. This frees considerable resources and facilities providing authoritative answers.

- Conduct sentiment analysis in taxpayer communication—for example, Canada (OECD 2021). This is a branch of natural language processing that allows identifying the sentiment, whether positive, neutral, or negative, in text formats, and can be used in taxpayer feedback, such as complaints and suggestions, to route it to the appropriate division for analysis.

- Estimate the probability that the tax administration can recover arrears. Using information from past arrears collection efforts, machine learning algorithms can be trained to estimate the probability that the tax administration can recover arrears, allowing the tax administration to schedule its arrears collection efforts so that more difficult cases are assigned residuary resources or assigned to more experienced teams.

- Estimate the cost of collection for arrears. Using information from past arrears collection efforts, and if the tax administration has recorded the cost of previous collection efforts, machine learning algorithms can be trained to estimate the cost of a future or a planned collection. This allows the tax administration to schedule its arrears collection efforts so that the costliest cases are assigned residuary resources or assigned to more experienced teams.

- Model for estimating the value of real estate—for example, Norway and Brazil (Villalón 2020; OECD 2021). Machine learning algorithms enable creation of a model of the valuation of the market value of real estate to update the value of real estate and determine whether taxpayers are underdeclaring their assets.

Medium difficulty/intermediate maturity level 3 (Practices for Efficient Operations). The key aspects and countries offering good examples follow:

- Detect residents who have emigrated from the country without notifying the tax administration and the central government—for example, Norway (Villalón 2020).
- Conduct data entry of tax forms. Tax administrations frequently need to digitize tax forms that are presented on paper, and poor data capture results in low data quality, with considerable impact on the tax administration's bottom line. Machine learning can be used to improve this process by automating portions of the data entry workflow to ensure that the critical details are captured. This can also increase data entry accuracy while simultaneously making the whole process quicker.
- Generate virtual proposals for tax deduction—for example, Norway (Villalón 2020). Machine learning algorithms can be trained to predict or estimate the individual taxpayer's level of income and its composition, as well as their level of debts and family situation, and estimate the origin of the legal deductions in the annual income tax return. These estimations can be used to cross-reference income tax returns, prefill tax returns, or simply make recommendations to taxpayers during data entry.
- Predict who is entitled to deductions and establish the amount of the deductions. Machine learning algorithms can be trained to predict or estimate the types and amounts of deductions that can be declared by a taxpayer. These estimations can be used to cross-reference income tax returns, prefill tax returns, or simply make recommendations to taxpayers during data entry.
- Deploy automatic risk profiling of taxpayers—for example, Australia and Spain (García-Herrera 2018; Villalón 2020). If the tax administration has a reliable set of curated risk profiles, machine learning algorithms can be trained to assign risk profiles to new taxpayers, even when the systems have never seen them. This process facilitates assigning risk profiles to many taxpayers and can be trained to adapt to new patterns, reclassifying taxpayers, as necessary.
- Discern complex, multilayered relationships between taxpayers. Understanding the relationships between taxpayers and how they are related can substantially improve the risk management system of a tax administration. Machine learning algorithms in combination with graph databases can cluster taxpayers in multidimensional risk groups to enhance our understanding of their relationship and how this relationship influences their behavior.
- Determine deviation from declared income and assets and predicted income and assets from internal and external data. Internal financial information can be grouped with external data to create a comprehensive 360-degree view of the taxpayer, and this fish-eye view can be fed to machine learning algorithms to predict the income and assets of a taxpayer. These predictions can be used to prefill tax-suggested tax statements, identify potential cases for review or audit, or identify taxpayers who have increased their income and assets but have not accordingly adjusted their statements.
- Select the composition of the audit team to match the taxpayer profile. The composition of an audit team can be altered to fit the characteristics of the taxpayer. Machine learning algorithms

can be trained to recognize the composition that is most likely to succeed during an audit, based on the profile of each of the audit team members and the profile of the taxpayer.

- Check tax returns in real time—for example, Norway (Gedde and Sandvik 2020). Machine learning algorithms can be used to check on the reasonableness of a tax return, particularly when the information of the tax return is cross-referenced with the 360-degree view of the taxpayer, including external data.

- Detect singular outliers in tax returns and refund requests—for example, Serbia (Savic et al. 2021). Single outliers, compared with multiple outliers, tend to be better predictors of errors in tax returns and refund requests. On the other hand, multiple outliers tend to represent normal shifts in taxpayers' behaviors. Machine learning algorithms are good at detecting single outliers and can be used effectively as part of the arsenal for filtering incorrect declarations.

- Select tax returns for inspection and review—for example, India (OECD 2021). Tax returns can be examined to determine the probability that the tax return has errors, considering the history of the taxpayer and the historical reviews performed by the tax administration. Taxpayers can be given a chance to review their assessments before they are reviewed by the tax administration.

- Classify taxpayers into risk groups to calculate risk scores—for example, Serbia and Brazil (De Neve et al. 2020; Savic et al. 2021). If the tax administration has a sufficiently large set of previous examples of risk segmentation, machine learning algorithms can be trained to replicate this classification to new taxpayers. A small group of curated classifications can be effectively used to scale up the classification effort into large segments of taxpayers, if the data repository is of high quality.

- Determine whether a taxpayer is making inconsistent tax operations, in terms of its history and its class—for example, Australia (Villalón 2020).

- Segment taxpayers according to the probability of noncompliance—for example, Spain (García-Herrera 2018).

- Process taxpayers' allegations and propose the most likely response—for example, Brazil (OECD 2021). Natural language models can be used to automatically read the taxpayers' allegations, compare them with a knowledge base of previous resolutions, cluster similar allegations, and propose in natural language the most likely outcome.

High difficulty/advanced maturity level 4 (Practices for Sustainable and Optimized Operations). Machine learning algorithms can be trained to do the following:

- Predict accurate tax returns issued by the self-employed and sole proprietorships.
- Identify anomalies in taxpayers' accounts during an audit.
- Identify cases with characteristics that could indicate potential fraud.
- Identify fake invoices—for example, Mexico and India (Zumaya et al. 2021).
- Identify taxpayers who have committed a tax crime—for example, Brazil (Ippolito and García Lozano 2020). Identify taxpayers who omit information, make false declarations, defraud fiscal documents, create false or inexact documents, and deny providing documents or invoices to fiscal authorities.
- Estimate the tax gap, especially for specific segments and sectors.
- Detect enterprises that conduct simulated operations in value added tax (VAT) (enterprises that generate simulated operations and enterprises deducting simulated operations in VAT)—for example, India and Mexico (Mahajan Mittal, and Reich 2018; Zumaya et al. 2021).
- Detect tax fraud for underreporting declarations—for example, Colombia (De Roux 2018).
- Determine violation of transfer pricing guidelines (Laizet 2019).

- Calculate the probability concerning an individual taxpayer's propensity to attempt to evade taxes—for example, Brazil and Spain (De Neve 2020; García-Herrera 2018; Pérez López, Delgado Rodríguez, and de Lucas Santos 2019; De Neve 2020).

Application of machine learning to customs administrations

Low difficulty/basic maturity level 2 (Practices for Controlled Operations):

- Assign a probable economic activity to unclassified trade partners. The customs administration regularly classifies trade partners according to their economic activity, and this classification is used internally for risk management, outreach, and communication with trade partners. Some trade partners may have not been classified or their classification may have changed since the original registration. Specialized machine learning segmentation models can make it possible to deduce the relevant economic activity from the financial information of trade partners. Hence, the models can be used to identify trade partners that may have changed their economic activities or to classify trade partners in the registry that lack economic activity. This application is particularly attractive because it does not require labeling of data since the existing classification for trade partners is used to train the machine learning algorithms.

- Identify declarations with incorrect country of origin. Machine learning models can accurately determine whether the stated country of origin is likely to be correct or not based on the country's history of importations of such types of goods. If the country of origin is considered unusual, the system can list the top five most likely countries of origin, with the corresponding probability of each one being correct. This can be used while preparing a declaration and while examining cargo during inspections.

- Automatically classify documents during an audit. During an audit, the review team must process thousands of documents and find documents of interest. For example, these may be documents that mention exports, imports, or financial transactions. Document classification is an area where machine learning can improve overall quality while simultaneously reducing costs. Document classification works through a two-step process: (a) a textual representation of the document is created by using OCR, and (b) the output of this process then feeds into another machine learning model that reads the text to determine the context and applies a label to the document that is relevant to the business.

- Use virtual agents to reply to trade partner questions. Machine learning can be used to implement chatbots that enable reducing the size of the trade partner assistance workforce and allow trade partner service to be available 24 × 7 × 365, which can be difficult to achieve with purely human help desk operators. Chatbots can be either voice based or text based—the former involves a trade partner interacting with the chatbot over the phone and the latter has the trade partner interact through the customs administration's website. These services ensure that commonly asked questions are instantly answered. They can also prescreen trade partners so that agents can be more targeted on their calls. The implementation of chatbots is already mature and can be implemented with minimal data.

- Estimate cost of supervision activities—audits and desk reviews. Supervision activities are expensive, and past experience can be used to train machine learning algorithms so that the cost of future supervision activities can be estimated from the trade partner profile and external data available. This cost can be used as a parameter in the prioritization of supervision activities, combining it with additional data to select those activities that will be most cost-effective.

- Estimate probability of success in supervision activities—audits and desk reviews. Supervision activities are expensive and past experience can be used to train machine learning algorithms so that the probability of success of future supervision activities can be estimated from past experiences, the trade partner profile, and external data available. This probability can be used as a parameter in the prioritization of supervision activities, combining it with additional data to select those activities that will be most cost-effective.
- Answer trade partner questions. A portion of the questions asked by trade partners in the help desk are simple questions such as "I am thinking of importing iPhones—what are the duties I need to pay?" which can be answered with intelligent agents. This frees considerable resources and allows providing authoritative answers.
- Conduct sentiment analysis in trade partner communication. Sentiment analysis is a branch of natural language processing that allows for identifying the positive, neutral, or negative sentiment in a text. This can be used to analyze trade partner feedback that comes as complaints and suggestions and subsequently to route it to the attention of the appropriate division.
- Estimate the probability that the customs administration can recover arrears. Using information from past arrear collection efforts, machine learning algorithms can be trained to estimate the probability that the customs administration can recover arrears. This enables the customs administration to schedule its arrears collection efforts so that more difficult cases are assigned residuary resources or assigned to more experienced teams.
- Estimate the cost of collection for arrears. Using information from past arrears collection efforts and if the customs administration has recorded the cost of previous collection efforts, machine learning algorithms can be trained to estimate the cost of a planned or future collection. This then guides the customs administration to schedule its arrears collection efforts so that the costliest cases are assigned residuary resources or assigned to more experienced teams.

Medium difficulty/intermediate maturity level 3 (Practices for Efficient Operations). This takes various forms; some countries with good examples are indicated:

- Conduct image analysis of maritime containers to improve efficiency of cargo inspections (Akcay and Breckon 2021). Image analysis is one of the most developed screening technologies that can be effectively used to identify features in x-ray images for cargo with accuracies that exceed that of human reviewers. Deep, convolutional neural networks can be used effectively to identify anomalies in cargo.
- Conduct image analysis of passenger baggage (Akcay et al. 2016; Bhowmik et al. 2019). Similar to the use in cargo inspections cited above, neural networks can be used effectively to accurately identify forbidden goods in passenger baggage.
- Use a Harmonized System goods classification—for example, Indonesia (Paramartha Ardiyanto, and Hidayat 2021). A neural network can be used to classify the products accurately and efficiently according to the Harmonized System based on a given description, and traders are helped because the system can classify goods accurately, save time, and reduce costs. The customs administration also benefits from faster clearance and approval, better compliance from the trading community, and better risk assessment, with the corresponding reduction and prevention of fraud.
- Recommend selections—for example, Brazil. A combination of different machine learning models can be effectively used to recommend potential verifications, considering the history of the trade partner and the characteristics of the operation, helping the customs officer responsible for making those decisions.

- Highlight potential mistakes in declarations. It is common for traders or brokers to make mistakes (human errors) when entering values, weights, and measures on a customs declaration. Machine learning models can identify that a declaration has been populated with incorrect information or an ambiguous or misleading goods description. It can also flag the declaration for document review and possible amendment, listing the item(s) in question and the content that it believes is mistyped.

- Do data entry of customs forms. Customs administrations frequently need to digitize forms that are presented on paper. Poor data capture results in low data quality, with considerable impact on the customs administration's bottom line. Machine learning can be used to improve this process by automating portions of the data entry workflow to ensure that the critical details are captured. This can also increase the data entry accuracy while simultaneously making the whole process quicker.

- Do automatic risk profiling of trade partners. If the customs administration has a reliable set of curated risk profiles, machine learning algorithms can be trained to assign risk profiles to new trade partners, even when the systems have never seen them. This process facilitates assigning risk profiles to many trade partners and can be trained to adapt to new patterns, reclassifying trade partners, as necessary.

- Discern complex, multilayered relationships between trade partners. Understanding the relationships between trade partners and how they are related can substantially improve the risk management system of a customs administration. Machine learning algorithms in combination with graph databases can cluster trade partners in multidimensional risk groups to enhance our understanding of their relationship and how this relationship influences their behavior.

- Select the composition of the audit team to match the trade partner profile. The composition of an audit team can be altered to fit the characteristics of the trade partner. Machine learning algorithms can be trained to recognize the composition that is most likely to succeed during an audit, based on the profile of each of the audit team members and the profile of the trade partner.

- Check customs declarations in real time. Machine learning algorithms can be used to check on the reasonableness of a customs declaration, particularly when the information of the customs declaration is cross-referenced with the 360-degree view of the trade partner, including external data.

- Detect singular outliers in customs declarations and refund requests. Single outliers, compared with multiple outliers, tend to be better predictors of errors in customs declarations. On the other hand, multiple outliers tend to represent normal shifts in trade partners' behaviors. Machine learning algorithms are good at detecting single outliers and can be used effectively as part of the arsenal for filtering incorrect declarations.

- Classify trade partners into risk groups or calculate risk scores. If the customs administration has a sufficiently large set of previous examples of risk segmentation, machine learning algorithms can be trained to replicate this classification to new trade partners. A small group of curated classifications can be effectively used to scale up the classification effort into large segments of trade partners, if the data repository is of high quality.

- Predict the cost, insurance, and freight (CIF) value of each declared item, which is the actual value of the goods when they are shipped and on which duties are calculated. Machine learning models can predict the CIF value of declared items based on the information provided, including on the history of previous importations of such types of goods.

- Automatically identify commercial transactions involving strategic goods such as fuel and other mineral resources, firearms and ammunition, and chemical products including fertilizers for agriculture from broader international trade flows.

High difficulty/advanced maturity level 4 (Practices for Sustainable and Optimized Operations):

- Automatically spot false documents such as invoices.
- Predict fraud associated with declarations—for example, Spain (Giordani 2018). This would involve training a neural network so that it identifies any of these factors when importing or exporting products: falsely declaring the origin of the goods, declaring a lower value on the goods, misclassifying the goods, and smuggling goods.
- Automate the determination of the valuation of goods.

Additional relevant applications of machine learning

The examples presented in the previous subsections are specific to the tax or customs domain but are not the only application cases in a revenue administration. There are many other areas that can effectively use machine learning in the back office to make the revenue administrations more efficient and effective. Appendix F provides additional selected examples of machine learning applications in a revenue administration. Here are some examples of additional uses and benefits of machine learning.

Low difficulty/basic maturity level 2 (Practices for Controlled Operations):

- Increase power usage effectiveness (PUE) of the tax administration's data centers. PUE is an indicator that is used to evaluate the energy performance of the data center by calculating the ratio of the energy used as a whole, compared with the energy used by just the IT equipment alone. Ideally, a PUE value approaching 1.0 would indicate 100 percent efficiency—all energy is used by the IT equipment only. Machine learning models enable data center administrators to effectively use data from monitors and configuration, layout, and parameters to determine the best configuration to lower its PUE and bring it closer to 100 percent efficiency. Lowering the PUE can save the tax administration significant resources and help to create an eco-friendly infrastructure.
- Identify anomalies in the data center to help prevent downtime. Data center administrators need to monitor thousands of parameters to identify anomalies that need to be addressed quickly to prevent downtime. Machine learning models can be trained effectively to identify potential problems and notify human operators so they can perform preventive maintenance.

Medium difficulty/intermediate maturity level 3 (Practices for Efficient Operations):

- Identify uneven application of processes or detect similar treatment of similar tax cases and processes—process drift. Processes should be applied evenly across the tax administration, under the assumption that similar cases should be treated similarly. If the IT systems measure process times and key performance indicators (KPIs), these can be fed into machine learning algorithms to detect process drift. The information is a useful input to internal control to ensure that human resources are trained to apply the process as desired.
- Automate review of resumes for hiring and flagging of biased language in job descriptions. Machine learning can be effectively used in the most time-consuming parts of the hiring process in the organization by shortlisting candidates and removing bias from job descriptions. Machine learning algorithms can effectively detect biased language in documents; this practice is used regularly to review thousands of résumés to identify candidates with skills that match the requirements specified in the job description.

High difficulty/advanced maturity level 4 (Practices for Sustainable and Optimized Operations):

- Automatically process suspense accounts. When a payment is received without identification, the payment goes into a suspense account, and a person must sort out which tax obligation the payment corresponds to and determine what to do with any excess or shortfall. By monitoring existing processes and learning to recognize different situations, machine learning significantly increases the number of payments that can be matched automatically.

Feasibility of the use of blockchain initiatives for tax administrations

Blockchain technology, a type of distributed ledger technology, can be implemented in tax administrations for different types of problems. An essential concept in the blockchain technology is the nonfungible token (NFT), which enables taxpayers to provide proof of ownership of an asset. An NFT is a token that cannot be divided and that, for this purpose, can only be minted once. For example, immutable ledgers can be implemented for the taxpayers' current account, certificates of ownership of movable and immovable properties can be treated as NFTs, and taxpayers' credit or debit can be represented as tokens and safely interchanged to offer new commercial possibilities for taxpayers, especially for small and medium enterprises.

For public administrations, unless otherwise advised, it is suggested to go with permissioned or private blockchains. Depending on the values to be interchanged and the number of participants in the network, a public administration can implement a permissioned (private) or permissionless (public) blockchain. This decision is crucial as the operational procedures for the registration of participants, consensus algorithms, and time to confirm transactions can change drastically in either case. A basic rule of thumb is to consider blockchain technology when multiple parties need to collaborate and exchange information. The business rules associated with the information exchanges are uniform for participants, will not change frequently, and meet at least one of the following conditions is: (a) peers do not trust each other's systems and information, and (b) an objective, immutable log/ledger is needed.

Next, three possibilities of the usage of the blockchain technology will be explored. Each one of these examples will include increasingly complex concepts of the technology. The first example is the implementation of the blockchain principles regarding ledgers that the tax administration wants to keep safe. The second example is the usage of a distributed application to handle tax credit on invoices. The third example is the use of NFTs to handle the property of motor vehicles and use them as a base for tax purposes. These examples show, by increasing complexity, the way blockchain technology can be implemented in tax administrations. There are collateral benefits such as security and trust that come with this implementation—benefits that, depending on the context, can be crucial to the success of the project.

Example 1: Transaction ledger

Starting with a simple structure, which is the taxpayer's current account information, the first thing that needs to be done is to enable the taxpayers to create transactions that are positively associated with them and that have the property of nonrepudiation. To be able to do this, it is necessary to assign to every taxpayer a public and private key. In practice, every taxpayer is provided with a digital certificate known only to them via a strong password (the private key) and the public key of that certificate that is stored in the structure of the taxpayer. From that moment, every transaction generated by the taxpayer can be digitally signed with the taxpayer certificate and therefore inherits the security properties of authentication, integrity, and nonrepudiation (figure 7.3). A blockchain

FIGURE 7.3 Components and properties of the security scheme

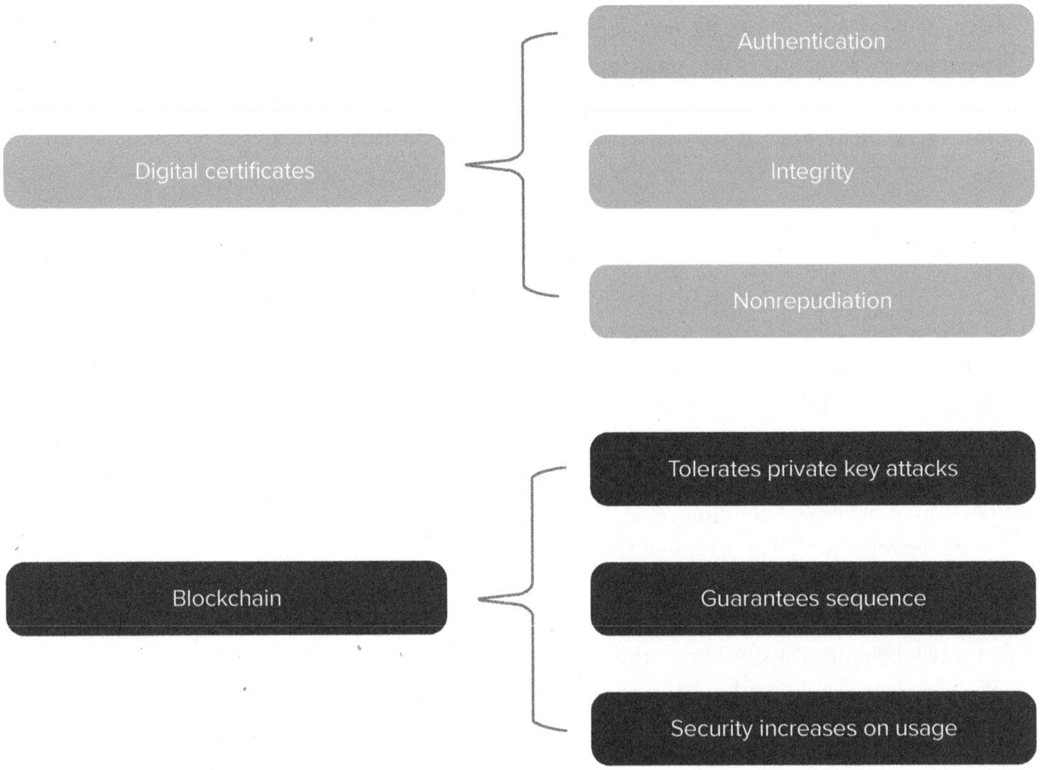

Source: Krsul 2021d.

can be added to increase the scheme's level of security. In the first level, the security properties of a digital certificate involved in the transaction through a digital signature are obtained.

In the second level, other important security properties are acquired. If the transaction is being created with all the needed elements, the blockchain will create the transaction and secure it. This means that if an attacker already has our private key and knows our password, then they can probably use it to create new transactions. But, with the blockchain level of security, the attacker will not be able to change or delete any transaction that has already happened. Also, the attacker cannot change the sequence in which the transactions have occurred. And the older the transaction is, the harder it is to change the blockchain and replace it with other information that is valid.

Example 2: VAT tax credit

A VAT is applied to any invoice, and the tax administration applies the tax to the seller and a credit to the buyer. To enforce the participation of the taxpayers in this scheme, the tax administration usually makes the invoices in the transactions mandatory. However, as small taxpayers do not see the benefits when they act as buyers, the invoices are usually filled in with blank buyers or incorrect taxpayers' identification. The idea is then to pass the ownership of the credit balance to the taxpayer. This is a very important concept, which means that the taxpayers can potentially benefit from the following operations and properties:

- They can cumulate their tax credit to use it to pay taxes whenever they feel comfortable and in the amounts that they feel comfortable with.
- No matter how small or big the invoice is, the tax credit for the buyer is never lost. Taxpayers do not have to worry about the tax administration handling their credit; it is safely up to date and stored without the participation of the tax administration.
- If the tax administration allows, it should be possible to use this credit for other transactions, and its value can be converted in the form of a currency.

The idea is then to implement a decentralized application (DApp) with the following characteristics:

- Provide every taxpayer with a digital certificate to create the wallet for the taxpayer credit.
- Deploy sufficient nodes across the country that will support the blockchain using the tax administration offices and their associated public administration offices.

The information to be stored is mainly the balance of the tax credit of the taxpayers—the blockchain should be sufficient to store this information. The information related to the transactions can stay in the infrastructure of the tax administration, and there is no need to decentralize it.

Example 3: Motor vehicle tax

Contrary to immovable properties, vehicles are movable properties that cannot be physically divided, and ideally, their ownership is represented by an NFT. Changes in the ownership of a movable property can take place very quickly, and it is difficult for the tax administration to stay up to date with this information. A blockchain implementation of this solution could benefit the tax administration with updated information and could give the taxpayers the perception of actual ownership of their property as the blockchain is not owned by one institution. There are other benefits and potential uses to this blockchain:

- The ownership of a vehicle is saved on the blockchain and therefore cannot be forged.
- The complete history of the vehicle owners is also stored in the blockchain; this enables the tax administration to correctly associate the tax with the correct taxpayer. The current owner of a vehicle would know not only all the maintenance work done but also all the events in which the vehicle participated.
- Other networks can use this blockchain to associate other information. For example, all information about vehicle maintenance can be attached to the NFT in a secured, decentralized storage. This enables the whole country to maintain transparency on all the maintenance work done on specific vehicles.
- The police and traffic administration can use another decentralized storage to store all the events related to a specific vehicle.

The implementation of this DApp is quite similar to the previous example. It is important to note that DApps have recognizable templates, which can help public institutions in developing blockchains in a faster and more standardized way. This can help ease the governance of such applications and the information they store.

Best practices in implementing information technology systems

IT systems in tax administrations are often inadequate because many tax administrations fail to implement basic controls and standard international best practices. As a result, the increase in revenue is lower than the investment costs. To reap the benefits of digitalization and maximize the probability of an increase of revenue higher than the investment costs, the tax administration must guarantee that it is capable of sustainably implementing and managing the IT infrastructure and to this effect must implement basic improvements in several areas, as detailed below.

Change management

Digitalization and a sophisticated information technology infrastructure on their own do little for a tax administration that cannot systematically gather, organize, and analyze information. Highly developed information societies have been working on automating their information flows for over 30 years, and current technologies automate evolving information-gathering processes. The information culture for modern societies dates back to the time of telegraphs, wherein train operators reported their status via telegrams and managers had them transcribed into tables to determine the position of every passenger and freight train. Since then, information societies have further evolved to the telephone and currently to the internet. What has changed is the medium used for transmitting data, enabling more timely and sophisticated statistical analysis.

The successful implementation of computer systems for automating the operation of a revenue organization lies in a culture of gathering, sharing, and analyzing information. With it, an organization can use KPIs to measure its performance, the effectiveness of its processes, and the time it takes to execute diverse critical tasks. It can also identify bottlenecks, manage service-level agreements with its providers using numeric and objective levels of service indicators, develop tools to intelligently identify delinquent taxpayers, and generally have an analytical management orientation where decisions are supported by numbers and statistics.

To successfully create and foster a culture of information, the tax administration must invest in knowledge management as well as change management, since successful revenue administrations depend on managing information effectively. Adopting IT systems is not just about buying computers; neither is it about developing or buying the appropriate software. Effective digitalization involves reengineering the entire business model and accompanying processes. Tax organizations without a culture of information therefore need to establish and implement a change management program. Every aspect of the organization must undergo change—the ethos as well as the day-to-day activities.

Change management is an approach to transitioning individuals, teams, and organizations to a desired future state. Rapid organizational change is profoundly difficult because the structure, culture, and routines of organizations often reflect persistent and difficult-to-remove "imprints" of past periods, which are resistant to radical change even as the current environment of the organization changes rapidly.

Without motivation, very little can be done effectively or efficiently, and efforts to modernize will go nowhere as it is difficult to challenge tradition and drive people out of their comfort zones, particularly for an organization that can live comfortably with low performance. Tax administrations have no competitors, cannot go broke, and are not being pressured to compete effectively and hence have no real sense of urgency to digitalize. To make things worse, the status quo has little risk since tax collection has been carried out in the same way for decades. There is even resistance against action because of the fear of possible complications with digitalization, whereas no serious problems happen with traditional, time-honored, paper-based processes.

To effectively promote change, tax administrations—through their change management programs—must convince managers and staff that the current status quo is much more dangerous and limiting than leaping forth and embracing digitalization and control. The change management unit needs to establish a sense of urgency by identifying a series of compelling reasons to pursue digitalization, integrated systems, and intensive information use and analytics; these reasons must be credible and culturally appropriate. The change management program aims to identify the blocks that impede the tax organization from achieving the vision proposed and creatively remove these obstacles by leveraging on leadership and communication campaigns.

A change management program creates a culture of information within an organization, including the habit and discipline needed to collect and analyze information. In this way, a tax administration can minimize the probability of failure in the implementation of its IT systems by establishing essential and necessary administrative structures and correctly implementing basic functionality in the computer systems.

Strategic thinking

A tax administration needs a clear vision that defines what is expected of IT systems over the short, medium, and long term, so that progress can be compared to objective benchmarks. Hence, the tax administration should develop a coherent strategy for implementing its IT infrastructure and the necessary systems and their basic governance structure that will make the acquired technology sustainable, thus decreasing the chances of catastrophic failures. An information and communication technology (ICT) strategic plan not only allows the IT department to align its interest with that of the entire organization but also ensures that the IT systems implemented will fulfill a functional goal. Frequently, tax administrations that do not have adequate ICT strategic plans find themselves at the mercy of technology teams that define the features to be provided rather than those required by the actual business.

Performance management

It is difficult to determine how the organization is performing with respect to the overall objectives and goals defined without the mechanisms for systematically measuring the performance of ICT operations and the IT department. Without such mechanisms, it is even harder to determine the mistakes being performed by members of the organization and their impact. To systematically measure the performance of the organization's IT department, the tax administration must develop a series of KPIs. It is possible to develop KPIs to measure virtually anything. Organizations frequently spend a great deal of time and effort developing a large and sophisticated battery of indicators, only to fail during the data collection phase.

Hence, organizations should carefully choose a smaller set of indicators that help track those aspects of software development, software deployment, and data center operation businesses that truly matter to the organization. More important, organizations should commit to achieving their long-term collection and analysis objectives. With these KPIs, the organization can reduce the number of decisions that are based solely on instinct or gut feeling and make decisions based on objectivity and facts.

The real challenge toward performance-oriented management is not the definition of the KPIs but rather the creation of the necessary organizational maturity level required to collect the necessary data sustainably and accurately. The organization must create, in the short term, capabilities and disciplines on a few indicators and progressively expand the list of indicators to guarantee an analytical and data-driven management style. Box 7.2 provides a long list of typical KPIs as an example, but it is not complete and the organization should seek to construct KPIs that are meaningful with respect to the strategic objectives defined in its strategic plan.

BOX 7.2 Typical key performance indicators

1. **Data center power usage effectiveness (PUE).** Calculated by dividing the total power usage of a data center by the power usage of information technology (IT) equipment, including computer, storage, and network equipment as well as switches, monitors, and workstations to control the data center. PUE = [total power] / [IT power].

2. **Percentage of service desk availability.** A measurement of the service desk availability over a chosen period of time, perhaps monthly.

3. **Percentage of urgent changes.** The size of the potential risk of urgent changes on the quality and performance of the change management process (number of opened urgent changes relative to the total number of changes opened in a given time period).

4. **Percentage of successful software installations.**

5. **Average age of hardware assets in data centers.**

6. **Maximum age of hardware assets in data centers.**

7. **Percentage of software licenses used.** The percentage of software licenses used relative to the total software licenses purchased.

8. **Physical servers versus virtual servers.** The number of servers that are physical—subject to higher costs versus virtual servers.

9. **Mean time to repair in the data center.** The average time—in hours—between the occurrence of an incident and its resolution.

10. **Average percentage of memory utilization for physical servers in the data center.**

11. **Average percentage of central processing unit (CPU) utilization for physical servers in the data center.**

12. **Number of change order requests per project.**

13. **Trouble report closure rate for software development.** Measures the ability of the software development group to answer trouble reports (TRs) within the specified goals. It is based on the deviation between the actual TR answering times and TR goals, set by the assignment owner. It is reported as lost days, averaged across TR priority. The lowest result is zero, indicating that the TRs are answered within the goals. The formula is NLD / (OTR + NTR), where NLD = number of lost days within the time increment for all open new TRs, OTR = number of open TRs at the beginning of the time increment, and NTR = number of new TRs during the time increment.

14. **System Usability Scale.** A simple, 10-item attitude Likert scale giving a global view of subjective assessments of usability and is defined by ISO (International Organization for Standards) 9241—Part 11.

15. **Server availability, excluding planned downtimes.** A percentage of actual uptime in hours of equipment relative to the total numbers of planned uptime in hours.

The planned uptime = service hours minus planned downtime.

16. **Percentage of network bandwidth used.** Measures the gap between actual network usage and maximum capacity of the network.

17. **Percentage of changes that cause incidents.** Number of implemented changes that have caused incidents, relative to all implemented changes within a certain time period (can be monthly).

18. **Percentage of overdue changes.** Number of overdue changes (not closed and not solved within the established time frame) relative to the number of open changes (not closed but still within the established time frame).

19. **Percentage of releases handled within agreed-upon time frame.**

20. **Percentage of changes closed before deadline.**

21. **Time for software bug resolution.** The time taken to resolve bugs in software development process.

22. **Percentage of planned versus unplanned changes.** This KPI can be calculated using urgent or last-minute changes added to the schedule.

23. **Percentage of repeat incidents.** The percentage of incidents that can be classified as a repeat incident, relative to all reported incidents within the measurement period. A repeat incident is an incident that has already occurred (multiple times) in the measurement period.

24. **Problem queue rate.** Measures whether the problem queue is growing faster than the organization can solve the issues. It is the number of problems closed, relative to the number of problems opened in a given time period. So, if the actual value for this KPI is less than 1, the volume of problems in the backlog is growing.

25. **Percentage of incidents resolved without any escalation.**

26. **Percentage of escalated service requests.** The percentage of closed service requests that have been escalated to management, relative to all closed service requests within the measurement period.

27. **Number of open service requests older than 28 days.**

28. **Number of times the corporate website shows a 404 error page.** When a 404 error page of a corporate website is shown more often than a certain target, this might indicate navigation issues within the website, "old" links in the index of search engines or in web directories. To reduce a high rate of 404 page hits, consider redirecting "old" links to new relevant pages.

29. **Production load.** Computed as the total number of users utilizing the server environment and the average peak CPU load. As the user base increases and becomes more demanding on the infrastructure, the peak load

(continued)

BOX 7.2 Typical key performance indicators (*Continued*)

on the servers should steadily increase or hold higher levels for longer periods. Having this type of graph over time showing the increased pressure on the core server environment allows for easier acquisition of capital equipment.

30. **Schedule adherence for software development.** Measures timeliness and "quality" of deliverables relative to the baseline schedule and acceptance criteria and is based on percentage deviation between planned and actual lead times. It is reported as a percentage, where 100 percent is the highest result. The formula used is [1 − ABS (ALT − PLT) / PLT] × 100, where ABS = actual baseline schedule, ALT = actual start date − actual finish date, and PLT = planned start date − planned finish date.

31. **Average number of defects created per man month.**

32. **Corporate average data center efficiency (CADE).** A metric used to rate the overall energy efficiency of an organization's data centers. CADE = facility efficiency × asset efficiency. Facility efficiency = (facility energy efficiency) × (facility utilization). Asset efficiency = (IT energy efficiency) × (IT utilization).

33. **Percentage of service requests due to poor performance of systems, servers, and storage facilities.**

34. **Percentage of delivered changes implemented within budget divided by costs.** The percentage of delivered changes implemented within the set budget divided by defined costs relative to all delivered changes within the measurement period (can be monthly).

35. **Average incident response time for network and data center issues.** The average amount of time, in minutes, between the detection of an incident and the first action taken to repair the incident.

36. **Average cost to solve a problem/incident.** The average costs to solve a problem, calculated by time registration per work performed for problems and applying a cost factor to the work.

37. **Average number of calls or service requests per handler.** The average number of calls or service requests per employee of the call center or service desk within the measurement period.

38. **Taxpayer/Trade Operator Satisfaction Index.** Measures end-user satisfaction and is typically measured through satisfaction surveys and user feedback.

39. **Internal Operator Satisfaction Index.** Measures end-user satisfaction inside the organization and is typically measured via satisfaction surveys and user feedback.

40. **Percentage of services and infrastructure components under automatic availability monitoring.**

41. **Employee turnover rate.** Calculates number of employees who have departed the company divided by the average number of employees in a given period. Typically calculated every six months.

42. **IT employee satisfaction.** Measures IT employee satisfaction and is typically measured by satisfaction surveys.

43. **Salary competitiveness ratio.** A measure of how competitive the current salary is that the institution offers for specific job roles. Salary competitiveness is measured against the general market. The salary competitiveness ratio (competitor) = salary offered by the institution divided by salary offered by other organizations.

44. **Time to hire.** A recruitment indicator that shows how long it takes to fill vacant posts. Time to hire = elapsed time between time of posting and time to start.

Organizational and systems readiness assessment

Implementation of the Systems Readiness Assessment (SRA) can help improve performance management for systems and aid decision-makers in identifying programmatic and technical risk areas. The assessment is a critical part of achieving the goals of improved system performance management and reduced program and technical risk. The SRA enables more effective system development management and integration that can ultimately shorten delivery timelines. The assessment provides decision-makers with awareness of a system's holistic state of maturity and quantifies the level of integration a specific component has attained with other components during system development.

Feedback from users

Effective revenue mobilization, under the terms set herein, requires increasing taxpayer automated systems use for self-servicing their tax returns and corresponding payments. If taxpayers are not satisfied with the electronic services provided, the tax administration must take corrective action. Hence, the tax administration must conduct taxpayer satisfaction or perception surveys and publish the results in the public domain. These actions are extremely important in gauging the effectiveness of the information services being provided to taxpayers. The surveys would also help to determine the effectiveness of the measures taken by the revenue administration to promote voluntary compliance by providing adequate information services.

Basic system features

Whether the tax administration chooses to build a tax system from scratch or buy a ready-made commercial off-the-shelf system, it must ensure that the system correctly performs, at a minimum, the basic operational functions, starting with an integrated registry to collect the basic information needed to manage taxpayers and to facilitate other tax administration functions. The registry should be unique for the entire organization, the registration process should be as easy as possible, and the information contained in the registry must be of high quality, as the registry is the foundation for any other initiative. To facilitate higher levels of service, a high-quality registry should be followed by a system that implements the basic core tasks of processing returns, processing payments, maintaining taxpayers' current accounts, providing tools to identify delinquent taxpayers, automating appeals tracking, and providing staff with access to taxpayer information.

Note

1 | This chapter compiles previous works by Ivan Krsul and Vladimir Calderón, as listed in the bibliography.

Bibliography

Adamov, Abzetdin. 2019. "Machine Learning and Advance Analytics in Tax Fraud Detection." Proceedings from 2019 IEEE 13th International Conference on Application of Information and Communication Technologies (AICT), Baku, Azerbaijan, October 23–25. https://doi.org/10.1109/AICT47866.2019.8981758.

Akcay, Samet, and Toby Breckon. 2021. "Towards Automatic Threat Detection: A Survey of Advances of Deep Learning within X-ray Security Imaging." *Pattern Recognition* 122 (February 2022): 108245. https://doi.org/10.1016/j.patcog.2021.108245.

Akcay, Samet, Mikolaj Kundegorski, Michael Devereux, and Toby P. Breckon. 2016. "Transfer Learning Using Convolutional Neural Networks for Object Classification within X-Ray Baggage Security Imagery." https://www.researchgate.net/publication/307516164_Transfer_learning_using_convolutional_neural_networks_for_object_classification_within_X-ray_baggage_security_imagery.

Atanasijevic', Jasna, Dušan Jakovetic', Nataša Krejic', Nataša Krklec-Jerinkic', and Dragana Markovic'. 2018. "Using Big Data Analytics to Improve Efficiency of Tax Collection in the Tax Administration of the Republic of Serbia." *Ekonomika preduzec'a* 67 (1–2): 115–30. https://doi.org/10.5937/EKOPRE1808115A.

Austin, Marc, and Donald York. 2015. "System Readiness Assessment (SRA): An Illustrative Example." 2015 Conference on Systems Engineering Research. *Procedia Computer Science* 44: 486–496. https://doi.org/10.1016/j.procs.2015.03.031.

Awasthi, Rajul, Hyung Chul Lee, Peter Poulin, Jin Gyu Choi, Woo Cheol Kim, Owen Jae Lee, Myung Jae Sung, and Sun Young Chang. 2019. *The Benefits of Electronic Tax Administration in Developing Economies: A Korean Case Study and Discussion of Key Challenges.* Washington, DC: World Bank. https://documents1.worldbank.org/curated/en/246061561388336942/pdf/The-Benefits-of-Electronic-Tax-Administration-in-Developing-Economies-A-Korean-Case-Study-and-Discussion-of-Key-Challenges.pdf.

Battiston, Pietro, Simona Gamba, and Alessandro Santoro. 2020. "Optimizing Tax Administration Policies with Machine Learning." DEMS Working Paper Series No. 436. Department of Economics, Management and Statistics, University of Milano-Bicocca, Milan, Italy. https://ssrn.com/abstract=3552533.

Bhowmik, Neelanjan, Qian Wang, Yona Falinie A. Gaus, Marcin Szarek, and Toby P. Breckon. 2019. "The Good, the Bad and the Ugly: Evaluating Convolutional Neural Networks for Prohibited Item Detection Using Real and Synthetically Composited X-ray Imagery." British Machine Vision Conference Workshops, September 9, 1–8. https://doi.org/10.48550/arXiv.1909.11508.

Brown, Meta S. 2014. "Transforming Unstructured Data into Useful Information." In *Big Data, Mining, and Analytics: Components of Strategic Decision Making*, edited by Stephan Kudyba, 211–30. New York: Auerbach Publications. https://doi.org/10.1201/b16666.

Collosa, Alfredo. 2022. "How Global Tax Administrations Are Using Blockchain Technology." Bloomberg Tax, March 17, 2022. https://news.bloombergtax.com/daily-tax-report-international/how-global-tax-administrations-are-using-blockchain-technology.

De Neve, Jan-Emmanuel, Clément Imbert, Johannes Spinnewijn, Teodora Tsankova, and Maarten Luts. 2020. "How to Improve Tax Compliance? Evidence from Population-wide Experiments in Belgium." *Journal of Political Economy* 129 (5): 1425–63. https://doi.org/10.1086/713096.

De Roux, Daniel, Boris Pérez, Andrés Moreno, María del Pilar Villamil, and César Figueroa. 2018. "Tax Fraud Detection for Under-Reporting Declarations Using an Unsupervised Machine Learning Approach." Applied Data Science Track Paper. KDD 2018. London, August 19–23. https://doi.org/10.1145/3219819.3219878.

Fatz, Filip, Philip Hake, and Peter Fettke. 2020. "Confidentiality-Preserving Validation of Tax Documents on the Blockchain." 15th International Conference on Wirtschaftsinformatik, Potsdam, Germany, March 8–11. Wirtschaftsinformatik (Zentrale Tracks), 1262–1277. Institute for Information Systems, German Research Center for Artificial Intelligence, Saarbrücken, Germany, https://doi.org/10.30844/wi_2020_l1-fatz.

Flovik, Vegard. 2018. "How to Use Machine Learning for Anomaly Detection and Condition Monitoring." Towards Data Science, December 31, 2018. https://towardsdatascience.com/how-to-use-machine-learning-for-anomaly-detection-and-condition-monitoring-6742f82900d7.

García-Herrera Blanco, Cristina. 2018. "The Use of Artificial Intelligence by Tax Administrations, a Matter of Principles." https://www.ciat.org/the-use-of-artificial-intelligence-by-tax-administrations-a-matterof-principles/?lang=en.

Gedde, Nora, and Ida-Sofie Sandvik. 2020. "Unsupervised Machine Learning on Tax Returns: Investigating Unsupervised and Semisupervised Machine Learning Methods to Uncover Anomalous Faulty Tax Returns." Master's thesis, Economics and Business Administration, Norwegian School of Economics, Bergen, Norway, Spring 2020.

Giordani, Alessandro. 2018. "Artificial Intelligence in Customs Risk Management for e-Commerce." Master's thesis, Delft University of Technology (TU Delft), Delft, Netherlands. https://repository.tudelft.nl/islandora/object/uuid%3Ada9b9c93-eb5f-4954-bdbd-16d2bb61feb5.

Hatfield, Michael. 2019. "Professionally Responsible Artificial Intelligence." Arizona State Law Journal 51 (3): 1057–22. https://arizonastatelawjournal.org/wp-content/uploads/2019/11/05-Hatfield-Final.pdf.

Henman, Paul. 2020. "Improving Public Services Using Artificial Intelligence: Possibilities, Pitfalls, Governance." Asia Pacific Journal of Public Administration 42 (4): 209–21. https://doi.org/10.1080/23276665.2020.1816188.

Hoffer, Stephanie. 2020. "What If Tax Law's Future Is Now? An Introduction to the Symposium on Artificial Intelligence and the Future of Tax Law." The Ohio State Technology Law Journal 16 (1): 68–72. https://scholarworks.iupui.edu/server/api/core/bitstreams/93c2b25b-01fc-43a7-ab8b-9fd24455cbd4/content.

Huang, Zhuowen. 2018. "Discussion on the Development of Artificial Intelligence in Taxation." American Journal of Industrial and Business Management 8 (8): 1817–24. https://doi.org/10.4236/ajibm.2018.88123.

Ippolito, André, and Augusto Cezar García Lozano. 2020. "Tax Crime Prediction with Machine Learning: A Case Study in the Municipality of Sao Paulo." Proceedings of the 22nd International Conference on Enterprise Information Systems (ICEIS 2020) 1: 452–59. https://doi.org/10.5220/0009564704520459.

Junquera-Varela, Raúl Félix, Cristian Óliver Lucas-Mas, Ivan Krsul, Vladimir Calderón, and Paola Arce. 2022. Digital Transformation of Tax and Customs Administrations. Equitable Growth, Finance & Institutions Insight, World Bank, Washington, DC. http://hdl.handle.net/10986/37629.

Kim, Young Ran. 2022. "Blockchain Initiatives for Tax Administration." UCLA Law Review 69: 240–316.

Krsul, Ivan. 2017. "Best Practices for the Implementation of Tax Administration IT Systems. Vol. 2." Working Paper, Unpublished, World Bank, Washington, DC.

Krsul, Ivan. 2021a. "An Incremental Strategy for the Development of Machine Learning Capabilities in a Tax Administration. Vol. 1." Working Paper, unpublished, World Bank, Washington, DC.

Krsul, Ivan. 2021b. "Building Data Science Capabilities in a Tax and/or Customs Administration. Version 7." Working Paper, unpublished, World Bank, Washington, DC.

Krsul, Ivan. 2021c. "Artificial Intelligence and its Application in Tax and Customs Administrations. PowerPoint," unpublished, World Bank, Washington, DC.

Krsul, Ivan. 2021d. "Considerations on the Implementation of Blockchain Technology on Tax Administrations." Working Paper, unpublished, World Bank, Washington, DC.

Laizet, Alexandre. 2019. "Artificial Intelligence and Transfer Pricing: The Future of International Tax Planning." Master's thesis, University of Paris-Saclay ESCP Europe, Paris, France. Unpublished.

Le, James. 2016. "7 Machine Learning Applications at Google." Data Notes. https://data-notes.co/7-machine-learning-applications-at-google-843d49d77bc8.

Lyutova, Olga, and Irina Fialkovskaya. 2021. "Blockchain Technology in Tax Law Theory and Tax Administration." Rudn Journal of Law 25 (3): 693–710. https://doi.org/10.22363/2313-2337-2021-25-3-693-710.

Mahajan, Aprajit, Shekhar Mittal, and Ofir Reich. 2018. "Catching Value Added Tax Evaders in Delhi Using Machine Learning." https://www.theigc.org/wpcontent/uploads/2018/07/Ofir-Delhi-VAT-presentation-IGC-Zambia-website.pdf.

Milner, Cas, and Bjarne Berg. 2017. "Artificial Intelligence and Machine Learning—Level 5." PwC Advanced Tax Analytics & Innovation Series. https://www.pwc.no/no/publikasjoner/Digitalisering/artificial-intelligence-and-machine-learning-final1.pdf.

OECD (Organisation for Economic Co-operation and Development). 2019a. Artificial Intelligence in Society. Paris: OECD Publishing. https://doi.org/10.1787/eedfee77-en.

OECD (Organisation for Economic Co-operation and Development). 2019b. *Hello, World: Artificial Intelligence and Its Use in the Public Sector*. Paris: OECD Publishing. https://doi.org/10.1787/726fd39d-en.

OECD. 2019c. "Scoping the OECD AI Principles: Deliberations of the Expert Group on Artificial Intelligence at the OECD (AIGO)." OECD Digital Economy Papers No. 291, OECD..., Paris. OECD Publishing. https://doi.org/10.1787/20716826.

OECD. 2020a. *The Digitalisation of Science, Technology and Innovation: Key Developments and Policies*. Paris: OECD Publishing. https://doi.org/10.1787/b9e4a2c0-en.

OECD. 2020b. *Identifying and Measuring Developments in Artificial Intelligence: Making the Impossible Possible*. Paris: OECD Publishing. https://doi.org/10.1787/5f65ff7e-en.

OECD. 2021. *Tax Administration 2021: Comparative Information on OECD and other Advanced and Emerging Economies*. Paris: OECD Publishing. https://doi.org/10.1787/cef472b9-en.

Paramartha, G. Y., Igi Ardiyanto, and Risanuri Hidayat. 2021. "Developing Machine Learning Framework to Classify Harmonized System Code. Case Study: Indonesian Customs." In *2021 3rd East Indonesia Conference on Computer and Information Technology (EIConCIT)*, Surabaya, Indonesia, 254–59. https://doi.org/10.1109/EIConCIT50028.2021.9431888.

Pérez López, César, María Jesús Delgado Rodríguez, and Sonia de Lucas Santos. 2019. "Tax Fraud Detection through Neural Networks: An Application Using a Sample of Personal Income Taxpayers." *Future Internet* 11 (4): 86. https://doi.org/10.3390/fi11040086.

Rathi, Ankit, Saurabh Sharma, Gaurav Lodha, and Manoj Srivastava. 2021. "A Study on Application of Artificial Intelligence and Machine Learning in Indian Taxation System." *Psychology and Education* 58 (2): 1226–33. https://doi.org/10.17762/pae.v58i2.2265.

Republic of Serbia. 2020. *Study on the Feasibility of Using Blockchain Technology in Public Administration of the Republic of Serbia*. Republic of Serbia: Ministry of Public Administration and Local Self-Government. https://mduls.gov.rs/wp-content/uploads/Blockchain-study-ENG.pdf.

Saragih, Samuel, and Milla Setyowati. 2019. "E-Readiness of Blockchain Technology in Modernization of Tax Administration in Indonesia." Unpublished.

Savic, Milos, Jasna Atanasijevic', Dušan Jakovetic', and Nataša Krejic'. 2022. "Tax Evasion Risk Management Using a Hybrid Unsupervised Outlier Detection Method." *Expert Systems with Applications* 193: 116409. https://doi.org/10.1016/j.eswa.2021.116409.

Shan, JingJing. 2019. "Optimization Strategy of Tax Planning System in the Context of Artificial Intelligence and Big Data." *Journal of Physics: Conference Series* 1345 (5): 1–7. https://doi.org/10.1088/1742-6596/1345/5/052006.

Villalón Méndez, Víctor Italo. 2020. "Strengthening the Toolkit for Tax Compliance Management: Machine Learning." https://www.ciat.org/fortaleciendo-el-maletin-de-herramientasc'-parac'-lac'-gestion-del-cumplimiento-tributario-machine-learning-1/?lang=en.

Vishnevsky, Valentine, and Viktorija Chekina. 2018. "Robot vs. Tax Inspector or How the Fourth Industrial Revolution Will Change the Tax System: A Review of Problems and Solutions." *Journal of Tax Reform* 4 (1): 6–26. http://dx.doi.org/10.15826/jtr.2018.4.1.042.

Wang, Ying, and Pan Wang. 2020. "New Personal Tax Collection Management System Based on Artificial Intelligence and Its Application in the Middle Class." *Journal of Physics: Conference Series* 1574. https://doi.org/10.1088/1742-6596/1574/1/012105.

World Bank Group. 2020. *Artificial Intelligence in the Public Sector: Maximizing Opportunities, Managing Risks*. EFI Insight-Governance. Washington, DC: World Bank. http://hdl.handle.net/10986/35317.

Zambrano, Raúl, and Santiago Díaz de Sarralde. 2021. "A Very, Very Simple Example on the Use of Artificial Intelligence in Tax Administration." https://www.ciat.org/a-very-very-simple-example-on-the-use-of-artificial-intelligence-in-tax-administration/?lang=en.

Zhou, Lingyan. 2019. "Opportunities and Challenges of Artificial Intelligence in the Application of Taxation System." *Advances in Economics, Business and Management Research* 109. International Conference on Economic Management and Cultural Industry (ICEMCI). doi:10.2991/aebmr.k.191217.038.

Zumaya, Martin, Rita Guerrero, Eduardo Islas, Omar Pineda, Carlos Gershenson, Gerardo Iñiguez, and Carlos Pineda. 2021. "Identifying Tax Evasion in Mexico with Tools from Network Science and Machine Learning." In *Corruption Networks: Understanding Complex Systems*, edited by O. M. Granados and J. R. Nicolas-Carlock. Cham, Switzerland: Springer. https://doi.org/10.1007/978-3-030-81484-7.

Design options for presumptive taxes

Background

The first known case of presumptive taxation in the history of humanity can be found in ancient Egypt.[1] From then and over the thousands of years until today, legislators on fiscal matters have tried to achieve the reconstruction of reality by resorting to presumptive taxation, causing it to become an instrument of widespread use. This is not surprising, if one considers the difficulty involved in knowing the different taxable events even today, despite the instruments and means available to the tax authorities in many countries having been perfected.

The term *presumptive taxation* includes a series of procedures according to which the real tax base is not directly determined but is inferred from some indicators that are easier to quantify than the base itself (Ahmad and Stern 1991). In this way, presumptive taxation entails the use of indirect means of quantifying the tax debt, which differ from the traditional rules based on taxpayers' accounting (Thuronyi 2000). In this appendix, the main features and options for presumptive taxes are studied.

Rebuttable versus nonrebuttable (*iuris tantum* versus *iuris et de iure*)

Presumptive taxes can be classified according to whether they are rebuttable (*iuris tantum* presumption) or not (*iuris et de iure* presumption) (Tanzi and Casanegra de Jantscher 1987). In other words, it is possible to afford the taxpayer a right of choice between the tax on average values and the tax on real values, applying, in each case, the procedure provided for the determination of facts and bases and for payment of the tax (Ferreiro-Lapatza 1996).

When the aforementioned possibility of choice is not granted, these are *iuris et de iure* presumptions, also called fictitious or presumptive valuations. They consist of values ordered by law, regardless of the real value and without the possibility of modification or variation by the tax administration or by the taxpayers. This type of valuation is used for the presumptive estimation system, according to which both the tax administration and the taxpayer are aware that the aim is to tax an approximate quantification of the taxable event that does not have to coincide with the taxpayer's true ability to pay. In fact, this replaces the determination of the real income actually received. Therefore, as long as the tax estimation rules established for this purpose are respected, the result of the valuation cannot be discussed, either by the taxpayer or by the tax administration, regardless of the fact that the real income actually received by the taxpayer has been higher or lower than that resulting from the presumptive or fictitious valuation (Lapidoth 1977). Such extremes may even be demonstrated as convenient for the tax administration or the taxpayer, respectively.

Such *iuris et de iure* presumptions mainly serve two purposes: (a) prevent tax avoidance and (b) set valuation standards in cases where the actual determination entails serious difficulties if the indirect tax pressure is not to be disproportionately increased. On the one hand, those presumptive valuations that pursue the first of the aforementioned purposes should be reduced to the minimum possible while improving the delimitation of the fact and of the tax base. On the other hand, those other presumptive valuations that aspire to comply with the second purpose deserve a positive judgment; they combine the requirements of the principle of capacity with possible, effective, and economic action of the tax administration with that of a minimum intervention in the sphere of taxpayers (Ferreiro-Lapatza 1996). In summary, the quantification of the tax base by means of absolute *iuris et de iure* presumptions reflects the positive note of its neutrality. The legal determination of the tax base is imposed equally on tax administration and administered without changing the position of equality, before and under the law, of the two subjects of the relationship.

The same does not occur, however, with the *iuris tantum* or rebuttable presumptions, which may be contrary to the principle of equality of the parties in the process and to the constitutional right to effective judicial protection when the option of proof to the contrary, or possibility of rebuttal, is granted only to one of the parties (be it the tax administration or the taxpayer) and not equally to both. If this is the case, and there is an asymmetry of this type, its elimination from the tax system should be pursued more vigorously than that of the absolute presumptions and fictitious bases established, as already seen occasionally, on unavoidable reasons to fight against fraud or to eliminate situations of uncertainty that would be difficult to avoid in any other way (Ferreiro-Lapatza 1996). Specifically, as opposed to absolute ones, rebuttable or relative presumptive valuations grant one or both parties in the legal–tax relationship (tax administration and taxpayer) the possibility of proving that the real income actually received by the taxpayer, and calculated in accordance with the rules of direct determination and accounting, was higher or lower than the result of the tax estimate, depending on whether it is the tax administration or the taxpayer, respectively.

Iuris tantum presumptions, also called rebuttable valuations, are a key part of the liquidation procedure in cases of substantial noncompliance with accounting obligations or filing of declarations. Other cases include resistance, excuse, or refusal to the inspection action by the taxpayer. In such cases, the law generally authorizes the tax authority to use indicative methods to quantify the tax base, specifically the real estimate regime. Consequently, in this case, the *iuris tantum* presumptions or rebuttable valuations must be the main and only means to quantify tax bases. This statement can be justified on the basis that the real estimate aims to quantify the taxpayer's income in those cases in which the necessary data are not available for the direct determination of the tax bases or yields, such ignorance being attributable to legally incorrect behavior of the taxpayer. However, if such difficulty is resolved and the aforementioned behavior of the taxpayer disappears, it should be possible to refute the tax estimate and determine the tax base in accordance with the applicable regulations, as long as the taxpayer provides the necessary information for such purposes.

Therefore, one of the determining factors, when differentiating between the "real estimate" and "presumed estimate" regimes, is the rebuttability or admission of evidence to the contrary in relation to the valuations that serve as means of quantifying them. In other words, the "real estimate" will use rebuttable valuations or *iuris tantum* presumptions that will admit evidence to the contrary, preferably by both parties, and that will make it possible to determine the real income when that is in the interest of one of the parties. At the same time, the "presumptive estimate" will make use of presumptive or fictitious valuations, or *iuris et de iure* presumptions, characterized by the nonadmission of evidence to the contrary by either of the two parties to the legal–tax relationship, thus constituting the valuation derived from using the tax estimate as the only reference (Lapidoth 1977).

Also, another defining characteristic of the different regimes is the formal sources in which they must be reflected. Although irrefutable or presumptive valuations must be contained in provisions with the force of law or in delegated regulations, the same is not required of rebuttable valuations or *iuris tantum* presumptions, because they do not veto or prevent the application of the general regime for determining bases contained in the main rule, as happens with fictitious assessments or *iuris et de iure*. In another sense, it can be said that the application of nonrebuttable presumptions can pose problems of unconstitutionality in some countries, especially when their rigidity and lack of mechanisms for adapting to the circumstances of the taxpayer and their environment cause situations of explicit injustice, like the destruction by natural causes of a business and the consequent persistence of the tax debt from the alleged and nonexistent business activity (Bird and Wallace 2003).

These two circumstantial assessment models—rebuttable and nonrebuttable—despite having been presented as two clearly delimited and differentiated conceptions and realities, have given rise to hybrid models that share characteristics and traits of both. Hence, although not advisable, experience has shown that this practice offered a greater variety of alternatives and intermediate approaches; an example is the French *forfait* system.

Minimum tax versus exclusive tax

A "minimum tax" is one that results from applying circumstantial methods and is characterized by determining the minimum threshold in terms of the tax debt to be paid, regardless of whether the actual tax obligation is lower according to the result of the ordinary calculation of the tax determination based on applicable accounting and tax rules. However, if the result of the application of said ordinary accounting and tax regulations results in an amount greater than that obtained from the estimate, the former shall prevail.

Therefore, the establishment of a minimum tax requires a double calculation of tax bases, in accordance with the ordinary rules for determining the tax, and according to the indiciary method (minimum tax *strictu sensu*), considering as a tax debt the greater of the amounts resulting from both calculations. This entails an eminent damage and burden for the taxpayer, which is specified in indirect fiscal pressure consisting of allocating and using resources, not only temporary but also economic, by the taxpayer, to carry out said double quantification of the taxable base when, as is customary in most current tax systems, self-assessment is the general applicable rule.

An "exclusive tax" arises when the tax debt is determined based solely and exclusively on the tax estimation rules, even if the application of the ordinary tax determination rules would result in a higher tax liability (Thuronyi 2000). Moreover, such a result will not be altered if the tax obligation quantified in accordance with the ordinary determination rules yields an amount lower than that derived from the tax estimate. In other words, it is a presumption *iuris et de iure* or presumptive assessment, as previously discussed.

The use of exclusive taxes offers important beneficial effects and incentives with respect to the ordinary income tax. Specifically, exclusive taxes do not generate any type of disincentive to obtain income; if anything, the degree of incentive of the tax will depend on the factors selected and used for the quantification of the presumptive tax. These effects will be minimal when the factors on which the estimate is based have an inelastic supply, land being the quintessential example in this regard (Thuronyi 2000). It can even be argued that an exclusive tax based on estimates does not constitute an income tax but rather a tax on the factors used to quantify the base according to tax estimates. Still, this conclusion is predicable of the majority of taxes whose bases are quantified according to the index method. Exclusive presumptions or assessments are administratively easier to manage than those characterized as minimum taxes, because the latter require, as pointed out before, the comparison of two different tax bases calculated according to two different quantification methods. Against this, the exclusive presumptions present as advantages the simplicity in their quantification and a minimum level of disincentive, without prejudice to suffering from a certain lack of tax equity.

In another sense, it is necessary to treat, albeit tangentially, the legal nature of taxes subject to withholding, which is not generally the same as that of tax presumptions or estimates, given that in the first case, taxpayers usually have the right to file a return and request a refund of the excessive amounts subject to withholding. In the event that taxpayers do not have such power to claim reimbursement, then it is not a tax subject to withholding, but rather a minimum tax collected through withholding, which shares the characteristics of minimum taxes (Thuronyi 2000), already mentioned.

Alternative tax versus nonalternative tax

A distinction should be made between alternative and nonalternative taxes, depending on whether or not their application is based on the amount resulting from calculating the tax using a different quantification method. An alternative tax is understood as one that is quantified by index methods and whose application is an alternative to the result of calculating the base according to different methods. Thus, it is easy to understand the close link between alternative taxes and *iuris tantum* presumptions. Despite this, both classifications and categories should not be confused, since the rebuttal or not of a tax refers to the ability or right to prove otherwise, while its alternativeness reflects the existence or not of alternative ways of calculating the tax. In other words, they are complementary and coincident features of the same characterization and applicability of the tax. Presumptive taxes are characterized as nonalternative taxes when their application is unique, without the possibility of optional or alternative calculations of the base.

Mechanical application versus discretionary application

Presumptive taxes can also be distinguished based on the degree of discretion granted to the tax officers in their application. Some presumptive methods are mechanically applied, leaving no room for any discretion as to their applicability. For example, the methods based on percentages of gross income or company assets stand out (Thuronyi 2000); these methods are analyzed in appendix B.

Other methods, such as the increase in net wealth, offer a greater degree of discretion to tax officials in charge of their application. Generally, those methods that offer greater discretion in terms of their application will tend to be rebuttable to avoid an excessive concentration of power in the hands of the tax administration. This could result in the risk of abuse and the perception of arbitrariness in the application of presumptive methods. In contrast, mechanical application methods may or may not be rebuttable. In certain cases, a method may be mechanical and nonrebuttable once its application is decided, but such prior decision regarding its application may correspond to the tax administration and be discretionary (Thuronyi 2000). As in other areas of tax law, the choice between mechanical and discretionary application methods will depend on considerations of a diverse nature, such as the potential risk of corruption in the case of discretionary regulations, the potential harm derived from the mechanical application of the regulations, and the ability to incorporate the particular circumstance into the mechanical application rule (Thuronyi 2000).

Estimation versus fiction

Although estimation and fiction are similar in many respects, and both fall within the scope of circumstantial quantification, it is necessary to distinguish between both legal figures. Regarding the tax estimate, its use is motivated by the problems involved in the application of a tax rule due to the impossibility of meeting the objective set by legislators through the use of said rule. Therefore, estimation creates a new norm in its place, which supposedly bears some similarity to the first one and its objective and is therefore considered the "next best option," after the original norm (Grapperhaus 1997).

It is generally accepted that tax authorities cannot know or discover at all, or perhaps with excessive difficulty, which is not worth it, the actual taxable events, as they actually occurred. This is the reason a reconstruction of the aforementioned events, say of the taxable event, is carried out based on a "fiction." For example, in Israel, the "tachshiv" method—analyzed in appendix B—is used if the taxpayer does not keep any accounts and consists of reconstructing the benefit obtained based on a series of characteristics and information that can be verified and determined quantitatively, such as the number of workers, the type of business, or its location. Another example of fiction is the possibility of deducting a fixed percentage of the salaries and remuneration, as a proxy for the cost of obtaining them. In this way, in the German-speaking regions, there is a distinction between "Sein-Tax," which takes as a basis to tax the facts as they have happened, and "Sollen-Tax," according to which the legislator creates a fiction. In the same sense, the French term *forfait* expresses, in the context of a quantitative disparity of realities and situations related to sums of money, periods of time, percentages, and so on, the substitution of the same for fictions that are equally applicable to all taxpayers (Grapperhaus 1997).

Individualized estimation versus collective estimation

The tax administration can estimate the tax debt collectively or individually. According to the collective estimate, the tax administration quantifies the income by groups of taxpayers, differentiated according to their activities. The tax administration assigns each taxpayer to a group, and such affiliation will be decisive for the purposes of calculating the taxpayer's tax debt. The affiliation and the taxpayer's classification can be reviewed periodically. Likewise, companies are granted the possibility of discussing the classification of their business activity. In some countries, taxpayers can go to court if they are not satisfied with their treatment and characterization for tax purposes (Bulutoglu 1995).

The individual estimate is characterized by the active participation and central role that the taxpayer acquires in the process of quantifying the tax debt. Thus, several documentary obligations are imposed on taxpayers, who are required to produce to the tax administration the information necessary to calculate their net returns through the application of cost–benefit ratios. In this way, the tax administration evaluates the income subject to taxation of each taxpayer by simply applying the estimation procedure. After the individual estimate, the taxpayer has the opportunity to negotiate with the tax administration or to appeal to the courts, in case of disagreement regarding the result of the tax estimate. In addition, the tax officer can monitor the self-assessment process and advise the taxpayer at different stages. But such a procedure could be time-consuming and costly, apart from being a potential source of corruption on the part of the tax official and harassment of the taxpayer, given that the taxpayer is in a position of inferiority and relatively defenseless in cases where the official of the tax administration is vested with power and discretion (Bulutoglu 1995). Furthermore, the taxpayer can also take advantage of the excessive authority in the hands of the tax official to collude with them. The aforementioned risks are especially acute if the taxpayer does not have the right to effective judicial protection.

Under both the individual and collective types of estimation, the tax administration can update its files and archives only every few years to keep management and administration costs low. As a consequence, there is a multiyear application of the factors used to make the tax estimate, which can be advantageous for businesses in an expansionary phase or during inflationary periods but can prove negative when profits decline (Bulutoglu 1995). The collective estimate has the advantage of greater administrative simplicity, while the individual estimate offers greater precision in calculating the taxpayer's economic capacity. As an emblematic example of collective estimation, apart from France and Turkey, the "global evaluation" that used to be applied in Spain stands out.[2]

The main advantage of the Spanish global evaluation system, and in general of collective estimation, is the possibility for the government to relatively easily increase or decrease tax collection to adjust it to its needs and policies. The government can do so without compromising the simplicity provided by its administration and management, given that the tax administration does not examine the taxpayers' accounts on which they are based to provide the necessary information for distribution. But there are some drawbacks: the lack of equity in the distribution of the tax burden that results from this method and the lack of acceptance of it by those taxpayers who keep adequate accounting, compared to those who do not.

Administrative estimation versus self-estimation

In tax estimation, it is possible to differentiate between the two traditional methods of assessment, the administrative estimate carried out by the tax administration and the self-estimation, which is the one carried out directly by the taxpayer. The transition from a managerial estimation system to self-estimation offers multiple advantages. First, the tax administration can reduce the costs derived from the individual tax assessment. Second, small businesses obtain invoices with which to deduct their expenses and account for their operations, thus promoting voluntary compliance in the tax–business field. Third, the potential collusion derived from taxpayer–tax official relationships is eliminated (Bulutoglu 1995).

Alternative estimation versus additional estimation

Alternative estimation can be defined as the indiciary valuation corresponding to an ordinary tax, the aforementioned tax being the only one, and falling on a taxable event exclusively levied by a tax, the calculation of which may vary depending on the quantification method used. The concept of additional estimation is used as a reflection of the assessment made of an additional or complementary tax, understood as the one that additionally taxes a taxable event already taxed by another tax, which creates a second level of taxation. In this respect, for example, asset-based minimum alternative taxes are different from asset-based minimum add-ons. The latter are not estimates in the strict sense, since their main purpose is not the estimation of an alternative base that has not been able to be quantified through its direct determination, but instead it accrues in addition to the ordinary income tax, without any type of provision that foresees their mutual compensation.[3] Furthermore, it should be noted that asset-based additional minimum taxes are different from property taxes (Rajaraman 1995).

Selection of indicators

The regulations on which the presumptive tax is based establish a link or relationship between economic capacity, which is specified in the tax obligation, and a series of specific indicators of each entity, which are easy to observe and understand. In this sense, for a tax regulation to produce a credible estimate, it is necessary for the indicators to be specifically chosen for each sector or activity, as well as for the regulations themselves to be based on previous studies, surveys, polls, and other tests and objective data. Among the criteria and factors that come into play when choosing the indicators, the following stand out: ease of observation and knowledge; the difficulty of concealment, falsification, or substitution; and income stability. The type of indicator selected determines the form of estimation chosen.

Broadly speaking, three main classes of indicators can be cited, and therefore of estimates: estimation based on flow indicators, estimation based on productive capacity and stocks, and fixed or uniform estimation (Rajaraman 1995). First, the estimation based on flow indicators consists of taking as references for the calculation specific flow measurements of each entity, either at the beginning or at the end of the productive process of the activity carried out. This estimative approach maintains the actual activity as the basis of taxation and simply moves away from conventional income taxation in that the effective income is estimated independent of the self-assessment.

A second category of indicators is the one that takes the form of an estimate based on production capacity and stocks, in terms of what is possible with a normal or average effort, without attempting to define the maximum capacity or production limit—all without any reference to the real and current flows of the activity. This type of estimation can use as indicators either the company's aggregate assets measured in financial terms or the physical measurement of one or a few equity elements indicative of the company's degree of operability. When the factor used is human capital itself, as is the case with self-employed professionals, the indicator must be some representative measure of it, such as the type and level of formal qualification and training, perhaps together with years of professional experience.

The third category of estimation is the uniform one, which is based on the average income of the companies in the sector, due to the impossibility of having specific information from the entity regarding inputs or stocks. This type of fixed estimate results in a flat levy per business. What distinguishes this kind of circumstantial valuation from the traditional figure of the license or other fee or levy of a fixed amount, and deserves the qualification of "estimate," is the previous statistical analysis and survey of the different sectors, coupled with the processing of information and indicative tests of the average taxable income in each sector of activity, which underlie and on which said estimate is based. Yet, the indicators used to estimate the presumed income must be specific to each activity. Additionally, it is worth listing some properties and features of these, of general validity, which are considered desirable and recommendable; these include the prevention of tax avoidance and fraud, the measurement in physical terms or the monetary valuation of the indicator, and the ownership or use of assets (Rajaraman 1995).

Regarding the prevention of tax avoidance and fraud, the stock indicators used to estimate productive capacity generally imply a lower risk of substitution and concealment than inputs, although this applies more to immovable property like land than to movable property. There are also some flow indicators, such as the consumption of utilities—electricity, water, and so on—that offer a limited scope or possibility for substitution and can be easily known if such information is collected in a routine and timely manner for the purpose of fulfilling other objectives, like their billing, and is sent to the tax administration. Within the category of flow indicators, the turnover of the company is prone to concealment and easily manipulated, much more than the factors of production. Regarding the measurement in physical terms or the monetary valuation of the indicator, it is necessary to point out that when faced with an estimate whose indicator consists of the total set of assets, the valuation in monetary terms is inevitable. Still, when only one element of the asset is taken as an indicator (e.g., land), it is advisable to measure it in physical terms, thus avoiding the problems derived from its economic valuation.

When ownership of the asset is taken as the basis of the estimate, the owner becomes the taxpayer of the tax, which may or may not shift the tax burden, in the case of lease of such property, depending on the elasticity of the good in question and the characteristics of the market. However, in general, the choice of the use or operation of the asset or occupation in the case of housing as a tax indicator, instead of its ownership, will be more neutral in terms of its impact on lease and input situations and is therefore preferable.

Notes

1 | As is well known, the Nile Delta owes its fertility to the annual flooding of the Nile River. Thousands of years ago, the population tried to control the level of the river's water, despite there being annual fluctuations in the amount of water that flooded the fields, resulting in different sizes of crop harvests. Thus, the amount of crops that had to be delivered to the treasury as tribute in kind varied from year to year. The tax burden, represented by the quantity of crops to be delivered, was set based on a constant factor and a variable. The constant factor was the area of the farmland, and the variable was the water level of the Nile measured at the beginning of the season; experience had shown that a certain level of water was linked to a certain yield of the crop. The combination of both factors resulted in the estimation of the production of the crops of the farmers-taxpayers individually considered. The advantages of this system were numerous. The use of arable land that is not cultivated as a tax criterion allowed the early development of land surveying in Egypt. Thus, the crop tax became easily manageable. The collectors only needed to know the ownership of the arable land, and they could dispense with the real data regarding the production effectively derived from said arable land. In this way, the tax system offered an incentive to farmers to increase the productivity of their land to obtain the maximum yield from it. After all, the surplus with respect to the estimate made by the treasury was exempt from tax (Grapperhaus 1997).

2 | Under the Spanish global evaluation system, the presumed, not real, income of a group or sector of taxpayers was evaluated. The resulting quota was then distributed among the members of said group according to certain income indicators, which were based on information provided by the taxpayers. This method was applicable only to industrial, commercial, and professional activities, not to investment or agricultural companies. More specifically, the Spanish system of global evaluation was a partial aspect of the regime of objective estimation of tax bases that, in opposition to the direct estimation and the tax juries, which are studied later in appendix B, consisted of the singular or global allocation of tax bases using legally established signs, indices, or modules. Regarding the assessment of the quota, this task was the responsibility of special committees, made up of representatives of the government and taxpayers, and their associations and guilds, who voted on the decisions; if no agreement was reached, the matter was referred to an arbitration committee. Apart from estimating the amount of profits attributable to the sector as a whole, the committee was also entrusted with the task of establishing the factors and indicators on which the quota would be distributed among the different members of the group. As examples of factors used, the invoicing and consumption of raw materials stood out. It is worth mentioning that taxpayers had no obligation to keep accounts. Also, the committee had to establish what factors could be used by the taxpayer to deviate from the use of traditional factors, in the event of exceptional circumstances.

3 | Under the traditional Mexican asset-based alternative minimum tax model, even bases in excess of a year's minimum tax can be retroactively offset by minimum taxes paid in excess of actual returns in the previous year, so that companies aim to achieve the minimum rate as an average of the entire business cycle, rather than in a specific year.

Bibliography

Ahmad, Ehtisham, and Nicholas Stern. 1991. *The Theory and Practice of Tax Reform in Developing Countries*. Cambridge, UK: Cambridge University Press.

Bird, Richard, and Sally Wallace. 2003. "Is It Really So Hard to Tax the Hard-To-Tax? The Context and Role of Presumptive Taxes." Paper prepared for a Conference on the Hard-To-Tax Sector, International Studies Program, Andrew Young School of Policy Studies, May 15–16.

Bulutoglu, Kenan. 1995. "Presumptive Taxation." In *Tax Policy Handbook*, edited by Parthasarathi Shome, 258–262. Washington, DC: IMF. https://doi.org/10.5089/9781557754905.071.

Ferreiro-Lapatza, José Juan. 1996. "El Principio de Legalidad" (The Principle of Legality). Las Facultades de la Administración en Materia de Determinación de Tributos. Ponencia presentada en las XVIII Jornadas Latinoamericanas de Derecho Tributario, Montevideo, ILADT, diciembre 1996.

Grapperhaus, Ferdinand. 1997. "The Trade-Off between Accuracy and Administrability." In *Presumptive Income Taxation. Proceedings of a Seminar Held in New Delhi in 1997 during the 51st Congress of the International Fiscal Association*, edited by Reuven S. Avi-Yonah, Vol. 22. The Hague, Netherlands: Kluwer Law International.

Lapidoth, Arye. 1977. *The Use of Estimation for the Assessment of Taxable Business Income: With Special Emphasis on the Problems of Taxing Small Business*. Vol. 4 of *Selected Monographs on Taxation*. Amsterdam: International Bureau of Fiscal Documentation.

Rajaraman, Indira. 1995. "Presumptive Direct Taxation. Lessons from Experience in Developing Countries." *Economic and Political Weekly* 30 (18–19): 1103–1124. http://www.jstor.org/stable/4402735.

Tanzi, Vito, and Milka Casanegra de Jantscher. 1987. "Presumptive Income Taxation: Administrative, Efficiency, and Equity Aspects." IMF Working Paper 1987/054, IMF, Washington, DC.

Thuronyi, Victor. 2000. "Presumptive Taxation." In *Tax Law Design and Drafting*, edited by Victor Thuronyi, 401–433. The Hague, Netherlands: Kluwer Law International.

Taxonomy of methods of presumptive taxation

Presumptive tax methods

Presumptive taxation comprises any system or method of taxation that taxes based on presumptions and fictions that totally or partially replace the real tax base, without resorting to the ordinary quantification process normally used to determine the total of the income actually received by an individual. In this appendix, all different types of such methods are studied. Box B.1 summarizes the methods of presumptive taxation that are analyzed in this document.

When the method calculates taxable income based on input or output flows, it estimates the real income derived from the real activity by reference to objective external indicators; in this way,

---

BOX B.1   Taxonomy of methods of presumptive taxation

1. Best judgment assessments (or income reconstruction)
   (a) Net worth method
   (b) Bank deposit method
   (c) Expenditures method
2. Percentage of gross receipts
3. Percentage of assets
4. Industry-specific methods for small businesses
   (a) Fixed amounts based on profession or trade (license)
   (b) Contractual method (forfait)
   (c) Turnover-based methods
   (d) Standard assessment guides
   (e) Taxation of agriculture
5. Outward signs of lifestyle
6. Minimum tax
7. Presumptive cost deduction
8. Assessment boards
9. Other methods

Source: Lucas-Mas 2004.

---

the method renders a real estimate. As examples of methods that materialize in a real estimate, the following stand out: two of the income reconstruction modalities—(a) the net worth method and (b) the bank deposit method, (c) certain variants of the method of outward signs of lifestyle, (d) the methods based on standard assessment guides by sectors and industry, and (e) the public evaluation committees.

However, the application of the real estimate system may translate into the use of any tax-presumptive methods that the tax official in charge of the assessment considers appropriate to estimate the taxpayer's real income with greater precision and reliability. Other mechanisms that the tax auditor can resort to and use when applying the real estimate option are comparison with respect to the tax situation of other taxpayers; comparison of previous declarations of the same taxpayer; the use of averages and factors of public knowledge; the official's own judgment, expertise, and experience; the taxpayer's reputation in their community; testimonies from third parties familiar with the taxpayer's tax situation; and any other means that may assist them in estimating the real income (Lapidoth 1977).

But when the presumption bears no relationship to real income, estimation may be done according to two different variants or types of methods. First is estimating according to capacity valuations, in terms of what is potentially obtainable with average effort, which will require specific information regarding physical measurements or economic valuations of assets or other items. The second is applying a fixed presumption, based on the estimate of the average return per company, as derived from studies, statistics, and other samples. In both cases, the method materializes in a presumed estimate.

Examples of methods that materialize in a presumed estimate are (a) the expenditures method, (b) the percentage of gross receipts, (c) the percentage of assets, (d) the contractual method (forfait), (e) the turnover-based methods, (f) the taxation of agriculture, and, in practice, as shown by the Israeli experience, and (g) the method based on standard assessment guides by sectors and industry.

Best judgment assessments (or income reconstruction)

Within the estimative approach aimed at the reconstruction of income, three methods reflect the spirit pursued by the aforementioned approach to presumptive taxation: (a) the net worth method, (b) the bank deposit method, and (c) the expenditures method. The net worth method constitutes the paradigm of the real estimation regime, having been the first manifestation of it in the past.

Net worth method

According to this method, income is estimated by quantifying the change the taxpayer's net wealth has undergone over the year and then adding to this amount the estimated expenses derived from the taxpayer's personal consumption (Rajaraman 1995), which are obtained from an examination of the taxpayer's standard of living (Thuronyi 2000). This method is the realization of the economic definition of income as consumption plus change in net wealth. But the main difficulty with this method lies in the lack of evidence and information and thus the consequent inaccuracy of the resulting estimates.

Generally, this method is rebuttable, in line with its nature of real estimation. In addition, its sense of presumption *iuris tantum* is justified, since it completely replaces the tax base. Also, it implies a degree of discretion that, although limited, is considerable because the reconstruction of net wealth at the beginning and end of the year, and the fixing of the expenses incurred during the same period, each requires a best judgment assessment (Thuronyi 2000). Therefore, the taxpayer normally has the ability to rebut the resulting estimation, either by providing detailed information and evidence of their actual yields or by demonstrating that the expenses plus the increase in net wealth were financed from nonsubject or exempt income—donations, contributions, or, in those countries with a territorial system, income from foreign sources (Thuronyi 2000).

This method entails a large amount of work and resources and qualified staff (auditors), so it is not designed for mass or large-scale application. It requires information on the taxpayer's assets and spending, which is challenging in a noncollaborative environment where the taxpayer is reluctant to provide such information. Because of these difficulties, this method based on the variation of net wealth (dynamic slope) is scarcely applied in developing countries, despite the fact that many of them accept this perspective in their respective regulations. A considerable number of developing countries take net wealth, in its static consideration, as an indicator to estimate the taxpayer's income within the framework of the tax return verification procedure.

Among other technical difficulties posed by this method, it is worth mentioning that, although it is relatively easy to identify the ownership of real estate or registered shares, it is difficult to determine the ownership of bearer securities, foreign currency, and other specific assets. Given that this method is easier to apply with respect to certain types of assets, it can be said that it discriminates against those taxpayers who own the aforementioned assets whose ownership is difficult to determine (Tanzi and Casanegra de Jantscher 1987). Another important problem is the valuation of assets, especially in an inflationary context. Hence, those methods and assumptions that are based on net wealth, both in its static and dynamic dimensions, generate incentives for the taxpayer to increase their obligations (Tanzi and Casanegra de Jantscher 1987).

Bank deposit method

Another method used to estimate income based on the reconstruction of income is that of bank accounts. This involves obtaining and analyzing statements from financial entities, especially movements recorded in the taxpayer's bank accounts (Thuronyi 2000), both national and foreign, and presumes, unless the taxpayer can prove otherwise, that the amounts deposited constitute income. Depending on business practice and the taxpayer's financial situation, this method may result in either an overstated or an understated estimate of net income. The case of undervaluation occurs when the taxpayer's income is received in cash, without ever being registered or reflected in the financial system. A situation of overvaluation or excess occurs when the income or inflows in the bank accounts correspond to gross income or to transfers from other bank accounts of the taxpayer (Thuronyi 2000).

The effectiveness of this method depends on the level of development of the country's financial system. In jurisdictions where most transactions are made in cash, this method will not be very useful or representative (Thuronyi 2000). Furthermore, this method will not be very useful in those cases in which the taxpayer lacks bank information, or presents it for the first time, since it is not possible in that case to make the necessary comparison between bank statements and transactions of the current year and the previous year. Although the tax administration may require the taxpayer to provide an explanation of the origin and reason for the accumulation of his wealth, it will be very difficult for the revenue administration to prove to the contrary that the explanation given by the taxpayer is not true. It should also be stated that all the considerations made in relation to the net worth method are fully applicable to the bank deposit method as well.

Expenditures method

When there is insufficient information on the taxpayer's net wealth, the taxpayer's income can be estimated based on the total of all expenses incurred. In some countries, taxation based on personal expenses has been codified. In such cases, there may be a difference in results derived from the presumed estimate, in the sense that said expenses, instead of constituting an indirect means of proof of taxable income, become the tax base itself in those situations contemplated in the law (Thuronyi 2000). For example, formerly in France, individuals could be taxed based on their "personal, public and notorious expenses," but this method was repealed. As a characteristic feature of this method, it is worth mentioning that it took into account for its computation not only those expenses dedicated to luxury and recreation but also those destined to cover the basic needs of the taxpayer, such as food, housing, and clothing. In addition, it did not include certain assets, such as investments in shares and real estate. A rule similar to the French one was also repealed in Germany in the past (Thuronyi 2000). Prior to this, the tax administration compared the taxpayer's expenses with their declared income, and if those exceeded the latter, the tax administration could estimate the taxable income based on the taxpayer's personal expenses.

In summary, it can be concluded that the presumed tax calculated in accordance with the expenditures method acquires a character more akin to that of a progressive tax on expenses, in accordance with the characterization that Kaldor (1955) made of it, than to that of an income tax. Here again, all the considerations made in relation to the net worth method are fully applicable to the expenditures method.

Percentage of gross receipts

Some countries provide for a method of minimum presumption based on the idea that the taxable income of a business or company cannot be less than a specific percentage of gross receipts from the business activity. For those businesses that are subject to this method, the tax has the same economic effects as a presumptive tax on turnover (Thuronyi 2000), which will be studied later, rather than an income tax. The tax on gross receipts is flawed because it contains an important cascading effect that has two dimensions. First, when most companies are taxed based on their gross income, instead of based on their net income, the tax effectively becomes a sales tax and entails the consequent cascading problem of said tax (Thuronyi 2000). Second, the degree of integration of the company can determine its payment of the tax based on a presumption.

Another problem with this type of minimum tax is the lack of correlation between the net income of a specific year and the gross receipts. Furthermore, net income usually represents different percentages that vary widely over gross income, depending on the industry in question, the degree of integration of the company, and the type of product or service provided. Therefore, the use of the same tax rate for all companies will be considerably inaccurate as a means of estimating net income. Yet, the problem can be addressed, as some countries have done, by classifying taxpayers according to their business activities and setting profit percentages to be applied to gross income, based on studies carried out on the different industries for each type of business (Thuronyi 2000).

To be accurate, this method requires investigation of actual profit margins, which is an effort involving significant resources and may be difficult to achieve in conditions of general economic instability. Another variant of this method consists of estimating, specifically for each industry, the relationship between the assets of a "model" company and its gross income and/or wages paid. Said approach would result in "presumed gross income" or "presumed paid wages" for each company according to a sectorized study (Zodrow and McLure 1991). The amounts would then be used to settle the tax debt, in the event that they exceed the amounts declared by the taxpayer.

The tax estimate based on gross receipts may encounter problems in compliance and result in unequal application. For example, if taxpayers stop declaring their gross income, totally or partially, they will be able to avoid the estimate. Therefore, this method does not seem the ideal method to obtain funds from those taxpayers whose gross income is difficult to know, such as independent professionals. Instead, it will have a greater effect on those taxpayers whose situation prevents them from hiding their gross income, like large companies (Thuronyi 2000).

Also, despite the apparent simplicity of this method, its application presents a great number of difficulties, especially in developing countries. Its administrative feasibility poses drawbacks, given that different rules would be applicable to each of the broad categories of industries (Zodrow and McLure 1991). Furthermore, the system would be arbitrary in most, if not all, cases, and the tax burden of the estimate would vary considerably between sectors and between companies belonging to the same industry. Therefore, this method can be both unfair and distorting, something that would be perceived by the population and would cause political opposition to it. Another drawback is that, if adjustments are not made for those taxpayers who in different years pay their taxes alternating between the estimation system and the general determination system, this method may be disproportionately burdensome for those taxpayers whose income fluctuates substantially from year to year (Thuronyi 2000).

Like estimates based on net wealth or ownership of certain assets, assumptions based on gross receipts are not the optimal solution when seeking to increase voluntary taxpayer compliance. In most developing countries, concealment of gross income is a common method of tax fraud (Tanzi and Casanegra de Jantscher 1987). Additionally, from an objective point of view, access to information related to taxpayers' assets is easier for the tax administration to obtain than information related to the gross income of those businesses that are not large companies. Moreover, it should be noted that many countries currently impose sales taxes at fairly high rates (Tanzi and Casanegra de Jantscher 1987). Therefore, taxpayers would have a double incentive to hide gross receipts: to evade sales tax and income tax.

Countries that have implemented this presumptive tax method or a variant of it in the past include Palestine (during the Ottoman Empire, before 1922) and the British Mandate of the territory (until 1941), periods under which a so-called Usher tax was in force (Wald and Froomkin 1954; Wilkenfeld 1973), and countries of Francophone Africa (Tanzi and Casanegra de Jantscher 1987), Chile, Colombia, Costa Rica, Cuba (Lucas-Mas 2002), Guatemala, India, Madagascar (Malik 1979), Mongolia, Nepal (Khadka 2001), Paraguay, Russian Federation (Herzog 1997; Mikesell 1999; Wallace 2002), Ukraine, Uruguay (Valdés-Costa 1996), and Venezuela (García-Novoa 2002).

Percentage of assets

A version of the tax on assets was applied in the seventeenth century in Italy in the field of agriculture. As with many kinds of tax assessment, one of the main objectives of the tax was to encourage the optimal productive use of taxed assets. More recently, in the twentieth century, renowned European economists such as Luigi Einaudi (Einaudi 1963) and Maurice Allais (Allais 1988) defended the use of a tax on assets in the current context. The theoretical argument on which the tax on assets is based is the belief that an investment must produce a certain return based on the capital invested over a period of time. If said minimum return is not reached, the capital or resources should be put to more productive use. In fact, many countries have adopted the asset tax as an alternative minimum tax.

Asset tax is easier to control than income tax for the following reasons (Byrne 1994): (a) physical assets are more difficult to hide than income; (b) the calculation of the tax liability for each year results from making an adjustment with respect to the calculation and result of the previous year, which facilitates the task of discovering tax fraud and corruption, by simply comparing the results of the years; and (c) the asset tax can be used in conjunction with aggravated sanctions that prevent a cost–benefit analysis of tax evasion.

Several countries, including Argentina, Bolivia, Colombia, Mexico, and Venezuela, have adopted minimum taxes based on a fixed percentage of a business's assets. In Latin America, the tax on assets was not intended to fulfill the function of a tax on the wealth of individuals or on the capital of companies. Instead, it acted as a guarantee and reinforcement of the income tax, especially in those cases in which the country's tax administration is not sufficiently prepared to adequately administer the aforementioned income tax (Byrne 1994). Other minimum taxes on assets have followed an even simpler design than those discussed so far, as in Ecuador and Peru, by not providing concessions for the financial sector, although in the complex case of Nigeria, total assets was one of the four alternative bases.

The tax base of this type of tax varies depending on whether gross assets are taken, as was the case in Argentina, or net assets—understood as assets less the debts associated with them, as in Colombia—being the Mexican system that adopted an intermediate position according to which only certain debts were deductible. The economic justification for this tax is that investors can expect in advance to obtain a specific average return on their assets (Thuronyi 2000). But the imposition could be considered unfair given that the final result may differ from what was originally expected.

Net or gross assets?

Probably one of the most controversial issues in the design of the taxable base of the tax on assets is whether some type of deduction for debts should be allowed. Since the asset tax functions as the base of the income tax, it makes sense to coordinate the rules regarding the deduction of interest between the two taxes. Ultimately, if it is decided that the tax should be levied on gross assets, then it would be necessary to establish an exemption for financial institutions, which would otherwise be subject to an excessive tax burden (Thuronyi 2000); this was the case in Mexico.

Asset valuation rules

Valuation is the Achilles' heel of the asset tax. In fact, the tax would work reasonably well if the base were the market price of the taxpayer's assets. But if, as usual, the value used is the fiscal cost for income tax purposes, then considerable deviations from the market price may appear (Thuronyi 2000).

The practical limitations of property valuation for tax estimation purposes will generally result in a material undervaluation. Taxpayers will complain in the event of an overvaluation and remain silent in the opposite case. If the income tax is explicitly adjusted for inflation, the values adjusted for inflation can be used to calculate the tax on assets. On the other hand, assets could be valued differently for asset tax and income tax purposes, but this would involve considerable complexity (Thuronyi 2000).

Valuation is a specific problem in the case of intangible assets such as goodwill and the results of research and development activities, the cost of which is considered a deductible expense for income tax purposes. It is important to determine if the value to be used should be the average value or, on the contrary, the opening or closing values of the balance sheet. In other words, the moment in time at which the assets should be valued is an essential question. Both the valuation at the beginning of the year and at the end of it can pose problems of inaccuracy if they do not reflect or are not representative of the value of the assets throughout the year. Therefore, in some countries, the average value of the assets during the year has been taken as the tax base; in this way, the application of average values leads to a more precise application of the tax. Fixing the average values of assets entails considerable complexity in its determination, although it is true that it is minimized to the extent that it can later be used for both asset tax and income tax.

Tax base and tax rate

For the tax base, assuming that the tax on assets assumes the function of the minimum tax on corporate income, its base should include all the assets used in the business. First, and despite holding that the base should be as broad as possible, a number of assets should be excluded, such as inventories, accounts receivable, fund provisions, and any other current operating assets of the company. This is because said assets do not contribute directly to the production or commercial process, nor do they integrate the economic activity of the company and therefore cannot be considered a reflection of economic capacity, given that their existence is only circumstantial and dependent on temporary fluctuations of the company's operations (Sadka and Tanzi 1993).

In principal, the inclusion in the base of both tangible and intangible assets such as trademarks, patents, goodwill, and market power is recommendable. However, due to practical valuation issues of the latter, their inclusion is discouraged, receiving a tax treatment similar to that of capital gains, which are only subject to taxation once they are realized. Regarding intangibles, this will happen when they are transferred at normal market values, and those are accounted for and reflected in the purchaser's consolidated accounts; only in this way can their value be determined (Sadka and Tanzi 1993).

Regarding the tax rate, if a tax on gross assets were applied to replace income tax, setting the tax rate would be a task that would require considerable precision to reflect the average level of return on assets. The higher the rate, the greater the number of companies subject to the minimum tax, compared to the normal tax (Thuronyi 2000). The setting of the tax rate will also depend on whether gross assets or net assets are taxed. If the gross assets are taken, this will allow a lower tax rate, compared to the taxation of net assets.

Exceptions for nonproductive periods

In certain periods, assets may not generate returns, for example, during their construction or when they are put into operation. In response to this problem, tax rules often exclude assets from the tax base for specific periods of time before they start to generate income (Thuronyi 2000). For example, in Mexico, the tax on assets provided for certain periods during which the tax is not payable: (a) what the law calls the "preoperational period," (b) the first two years from the beginning of the activity, and (c) the year of liquidation.

Industry-specific methods for small businesses

There is a differentiated tax treatment, allegedly favorable, for small and medium-sized enterprises (SMEs). The two magnitudes that normally allow the tax legislator to classify companies according to their size or dimension are the volume of annual business income and the net amount of turnover. The determination is usually complemented with the so-called specific magnitudes, basically, the weighted average of the number of people employed in the period and the amount of assets on any day of the year. Despite everything, there is no clean and clear border, or an unequivocal division, between large companies and SMEs.

It is important here to define the concept of "business income." This includes income derived from transactions and activities carried out in the normal course of the taxpayer's business or commerce. It may cover income from tangible and intangible property to the extent that the acquisition, management, and alienation of said properties constitute operations that integrate the ordinary business and commercial activity of the taxpayer (Oldman and Brooks 1987).

Fixed amounts based on profession or trade (license)

A fixed estimate can be based fundamentally on two methods, either (a) on the application of a fixed percentage on a fixed amount of taxable income (e.g., a tax on taxi drivers and small merchants) or (b) on a fixed levy without any reference to any kind of base or indicator such as a license that street vendors must pay (Rajaraman 1995). In either case, it is clear that the tax base, or the tax itself, must be updated.

Some countries apply a minimum tax based on the profession or the business or trade carried out. To avoid injustice, the estimated amounts should be set at low levels, but then the method may be ineffective in terms of the taxation of those professionals with high incomes (Thuronyi 2000).

Another somewhat more refined alternative consists of dividing taxpayers belonging to a certain industry or sector into two or more categories, based on their turnover, with a fixed tax according to the turnover within each category. Taxpayers can also be divided into classes based on the type and amount of equipment or capital goods used in the business—for example, owners of gaming machines could be taxed at a fixed amount for each machine they own. Another distinction made sometimes takes into consideration the number of years since a person completed education (Thuronyi 2000). The simplest alternative is to impose a fixed sum on all businesses without distinction, although this approach has serious drawbacks (Bulutoglu 1995). Countries that have implemented this presumptive tax method or a variant of it in the past include Kenya, Lebanon, Morocco, Nepal, the Russian Federation, and Ukraine.

It should be noted that this method has not obtained very encouraging results, whether in terms of collection or in terms of levels of acceptance by taxpayers, as it violates important economic postulates. Also, it violates basic notions of tax equity, since it does not bear any relation to taxpayers' economic capacity or take into account their particular circumstances (Taube and Tadesse 1996).

Contractual method (forfait)

To overcome the problems of administrative practicability posed by direct determination, French law established the forfait regime, with which it attempted to achieve a balance between the principles of convenience and certainty in setting the tax base of certain taxpayers, especially that of small entrepreneurs. The contract (*forfait* in French) estimation method is intended to achieve a high degree of precision. Taxpayers can opt for the system if their annual billing is less than a certain amount. This method differs from other presumptions in that its application is based on an advance agreement between the taxpayer and the tax administration, according to which the tax obligation will be based on the estimated income instead of the real one (Thuronyi 2000).

This method is considered a privilege that the tax administration grants only to certain categories of taxpayers, as long as they meet a series of requirements and do not opt for the general regime. For the latter, it will be necessary that they have appropriate accounting. Among the groups of taxpayers excluded from the application of the contractual method are companies and other legal entities, including personal entities and individuals who carry out a large-scale business activity, as defined by the regulations in terms of the nature of the business and its turnover (Lapidoth 1977). To apply the forfait, the taxpayer must provide the following information regarding the previous year: purchases, sales, closing value of the inventory, number of employees, amount of wages paid, and number of vehicles owned by the taxpayer. The tax administration then calculates the forfait, which is still an estimate of the returns that the company is capable of generating under normal circumstances (Thuronyi 2000).

In summary, the identifying features of the forfait regime are the following: (a) the evaluation of the tax base is carried out in a unique way, that is, with respect to each entrepreneur, and not on a global basis by groups or sectors; (b) the base determination system is made up of internal elements that contribute to the formation of income, previously declared by the taxpayer; (c) the combination of the elements declared and those obtained *ex officio* by the tax administration is produced with a nonrebuttable legal formula; and (d) the taxpayer can appeal the evaluation of the elements not declared and obtained *ex officio*. Similar approaches have been applied in some other countries, including Belgium and Switzerland.

This contractual method, being based on extensive statistical analyses carried out by the tax administration and on a detailed classification of business sectors and productive industries, implies a great deal of sophisticated work. Moreover, its application and management require a highly qualified civil servant body and honest tax auditors (Thuronyi 2000). All of the above may suggest the inadequacy of a system like this in the context of many countries, especially those that lack a well-structured tax administration with solid principles and values.

A characteristic feature of the forfait system is that the indexes established to determine the tax base are based on data or elements internal to the taxable object, that is, on elements such as volume of sales and purchases that intervene in the determination of business profit and decide its amount—for example, if a percentage is applied to the volume of sales, the profit or business performance could be found—and that are, therefore, in relation to the index of economic capacity (income) that the law subjects to taxation. For this reason, the French doctrine, based on the nature and characteristics of these indexes, has emphasized that the objective of the forfait is never the presumptive estimate of the business result but its determination in a simple, objective, and precise manner.

Turnover-based methods

Some countries tax certain types of income from specific sectors of activity based on the company's turnover, with presumed deductions estimated according to ratios developed for each specific sector or type of income. This method is only applicable to small businesses and companies (Thuronyi 2000). It responds to criticism of the percentage of gross receipts method, according to which there are different levels of benefits depending on the industry.

It is also very useful when turnover can be obtained from independent sources; thus, this method can be used to tax exporters in those countries where there is effective control of exports. In such countries, the turnover can easily be determined by checking their export licenses issued by the customs authorities (Lapidoth 1977). Once all the receipts and licenses provide the turnover data, the taxable income may be set either by establishing a fixed rate of net profits or by setting the average rate of gross profits and allowing an average fixed rate of deductible expenses, which is ultimately the same. Alternatively, the taxpayer may be given the option of proving actual expenses and deducting them from gross profits computed at the average rate mentioned above.

This method can also be integrated and applied in the form of a minimum tax on corporate income, constituting the way of estimating its base. However, a turnover-based basis, if applied at a fixed rate common to all sectors, will lack the economic rationale of an asset-based basis (Rajaraman 1995). Countries that have implemented this presumptive tax method or a variant of it in the past include Angola, Bolivia, Brazil, Cameroon, India, Morocco, Nepal, and Uruguay.

Standard assessment guides

The standard assessment guides and lists by companies and sectors were first used in Israel, under the old name of "tachshivim," and was later replaced by the current "tadrihim," in the Republic of Korea, where a model similar to the Israeli one applied, as well as in other countries such as Spain, with the "objective estimate," and in Turkey. This method will now be analyzed through the Israeli experience.

The system originally developed in Israel under the name of *tachshiv*—roughly translated to mean "standard assessment guide"—emphasizes the use of objective indicators and indexes for estimating the income of those taxpayers who do not keep accounts or records of their operations. Physical elements and factors, such as the number of employees, are taken into account for these purposes. Each tachshiv is prepared after detailed research and study, consultations, and visits to representative samples of the different businesses. The average profit level of each sector and its relation to specific factors and indexes emerge from discussion and consultation with representatives of each sector, prior to the approval of the tachshiv (Tanzi and Casanegra de Jantscher 1987).

The original tachshiv, as a specific estimation method for each activity and sector, was based on a selection of input and output flow indicators, and to set the net profit, it used a process consisting of three phases: (a) the setting of the turnover, (b) the gross profits, and (c) the net profit, based on the aforementioned indicators—for example, the number of driving licenses issued with respect to driving schools, by way of output, and fluids, such as electricity or water, as inputs (Rajaraman 1995). Other examples could be taxing a restaurant based on indicators such as its location, its capacity, or the average price of the dishes on the menu or, for an ice-producing company, based on the amount of water consumed—information easily obtainable from the distribution company—and the price lists and profit margins of said industry (Lapidoth 1977).

The credibility of this method derived from the statistics and previous studies that made it possible to draw up the presumed standards and its great acceptance was a reflection of the prior negotiation and consultation process with the professional organizations affected by each of the aforementioned assessment guides, which the tax administration carried out. The agreement affected the tachshiv itself, say the guideline or rule, not its subsequent application to certain taxpayers (Thuronyi 2000). It is worth noting, however, the existence of tachshivim on which an agreement could not be reached, despite which they were issued and approved under the name "tachshiv not agreed upon." In any case, all the tachshivim, agreed or not, were public knowledge and available to those administered. More than 100 tachshivim were developed under this regime (Lapidoth 1977).

This system has been criticized on the grounds that some taxpayers, with income above the averages taken by the tachshiv, pretend not to keep adequate accounting with which to determine their real income and thus be able to apply the tachshiv, which translates into lower tax liability. In other words, the tachshiv is not required bijectively and symmetrically, but unilaterally, with the taxpayers choosing whether or not to avail themselves of the tachshiv, depending on whether their accounting results in a higher or lower tax debt than that established by the guideline. In fact, the excessive importance given by the tachshiv to the precise factors and indicators that serve as its basis ends up transforming the income tax into a tax on the factors on which each tachshiv is based (Tanzi and Casanegra de Jantscher 1987). Despite these drawbacks, the Israeli model has been imitated by other countries, such as the Republic of Korea and Sierra Leone (Malik 1979).

The use of a method such as tachshiv can be very helpful in collecting taxes from small taxpayers in certain sectors, but its application is not an easy task. As pointed out previously, important and rigorous basic work is required to select the appropriate factors and indicators for each industry, as well as indexes and multiplier coefficients for each sector (Thuronyi 2000). Therefore, it requires a significant investment in administrative infrastructure and sufficient preparation time. Nevertheless, after the passage in Israel in 1975 of a law requiring that income tax be based on accounting, the use of tachshivim had to be discontinued. As a result, collections fell, so the system was reinstated with some differences under the new name of "tadrihim." One of the main novelties consisted of the prohibition of prior negotiations with professional associations, following which individual negotiations with the taxpayer acquired a more relevant role. Tadrihim (assessment guides or directives) for more than 140 occupations or activities were introduced, which did not include liberal professionals, such as doctors and lawyers, who are considered to have sufficient capacity to keep records of their activity (Rajaraman 1995).

It would be advisable, in adopting of this system, to avoid the situation of uncertainty that occurred in Israel and ensure that the method is contained in a legal provision. For practical reasons, the details of the system's application should be in regulations, not in a law. Also, the taxpayers to whom these general assessment guides apply should be specified, preferably based on their turnover. An important question is whether for such taxpayers the assessment guides should be optional or mandatory, in other words, whether the method should be rebuttable or not. The preferable solution is to impose a coercive application of the method in the case of those taxpayers with a turnover below the established threshold, allowing said companies the possibility of making an irrevocable choice to use the general accounting standards instead (Thuronyi 2000). Other countries that have implemented this presumptive tax method or a variant of it in the past include Angola, Burkina Faso, Chad, Madagascar, Malawi, Niger, Lesotho, Peru, Spain, Swaziland, Tanzania, Uganda, and Zambia.

Taxation of agriculture

The peculiarity and importance of this sector requires different treatment from that of the other sectors of the economy. This is more important when considering the case of a developing country, because of the extremely strategic role played by the agricultural sector in the most primary phases of economic development.

Throughout history, the taxation of land and agriculture has been present in most of the economic policies and currents of thought of different nations. Thus, there has been an evolution in the conception of what the land tax should be and the role that it should occupy within the tax system, highlighting as main thinkers the Physiocrats (whose greatest exponent was Quesnay), Adam Smith, David Ricardo, James Mill, John R. McCulloch, John Stuart Mill, and Henry George (Tideman 1994). These authors unanimously shared the opinion that a land tax was borne entirely and exclusively by the owners of the same and that it had no negative effects on production, regardless of whether the tax was levied on the sales value, rental value, or, as with the British Land Tax, an arbitrary historical figure for each plot of land (Ortega 1991). All of this was conditional on the tax being less than the rental value of the land and the liquidation process excluding any superstructure and human improvements from the tax base (Tideman 1994).

In many countries, income from agriculture is presumptively taxed. The general approach is to base the tax on the land area and its quality. An estimate is made of the normal yields that can be obtained, depending on the productivity of the type of land, the average production costs, and the price of the products. In turn, aid and remedies can be granted for those cases in which the crops in an area have suffered considerable damage (Thuronyi 2000). Other alternatives to taxing the land are (a) taxation with respect to its area, (b) based on its sale value, (c) according to its estimated rental value, (d) based on of the value of its agricultural production, and (e) according to the decrease or increase in the prices of the products (Tideman 1994).

Generally, the use of presumptive taxation in the agricultural sector seeks to respond to the deficiencies that characterize it, namely (a) the low average productivity of the land, which is sometimes used for pasture cattle or crops of little interest; (b) the very unequal distribution of income typical of agriculture; (c) the tax administration's inability to collect enough from those farmers who receive high levels of income; and (d) the pressing need for revenue by government agencies to cover the costs of providing local services (Berry 1972).

Richard Bird, who was one of the earliest proponents of the need to implement and use presumptive taxation in developing countries, recommended a system for agriculture based on land value, which would automatically incorporate location and quality of the land. He also suggested self-assessment of the tax, applying the expropriation rates, to simplify its management. In his latest works on the subject, Bird opted for using the value of the potential use of the land, with the aim of taxing agricultural income, but with careful attention to the differences with respect to the sale values and with deferral (not exemption) of the taxation of any of the market value on the value of use, until the moment of the sale of the land. Any alternative to estimating the value of potential use will entail the same procedure for updating crop yield values, with the possible drawback of loss of transparency (Rajaraman 1995).

However, the application of presumptive tax methods to agriculture has been criticized from an economic perspective, that tax estimation (a) may increase operating costs of agricultural companies, which will hinder investment and its modernization; (b) will also discourage increased production; and (c) will increase the price of agricultural products. Since the prices of agricultural products are considered to play a major role in calculating inflation, it is important to avoid such increases (Berry 1972).

The most complete model, and in this sense the one that has enjoyed the best results and acceptance, is the French forfait system applied to agricultural land, which taxes the land based on its measurement in physical units at tax rates stratified according to region and agricultural activity. In France, the taxable income derived from agriculture is estimated according to (a) the area of land that is or could be cultivated, (b) the type of crop, and (c) the region. For each region, the average benefit for each type of crop is determined annually by a committee made up of representatives of the tax administration and farmers (Thuronyi 2000). In the event that a natural disaster causes crop failure in a region, individual affected farmers may apply for a tax reduction based on the circumstances. The basic presumptive tax rules applied to agriculture are contained in the law.

Variants of the French forfeiture system on agricultural land have been applied in Morocco and in other Francophone African countries, as well as in Cameroon, Eritrea, Ethiopia, and Mozambique. Other countries that have implemented presumptive tax methods or some variants to the agricultural sector include Bolivia, Chile, Colombia, Costa Rica, Estonia, India, Nepal, Spain, Ukraine, and Uruguay (Malik 1979; Rajaraman 1995; Taube and Tadesse 1996; Dastur 1997; Khadka 2001).

Another relevant aspect of taxation of agriculture is the question of who should be the taxpayer of the presumptive tax on land: should it be the owner or the occupant? The most appropriate answer to this question seems to be the old system in force in the United Kingdom, in accordance with which the tax was collected from the occupant of the land, which reduced the possibilities of tax fraud, since the tax administration could easily know who the occupant of a specific piece of land was, instead of having to find out the owner of the property. In addition, the occupant was more willing to pay the tax, knowing that they could later transfer it to the owner (who ultimately had to bear it) by deducting it from the amount of the lease payment. This system, therefore, considered the occupant as the taxpayer of the land tax, although the one who really had to bear it was the owner. There is also part of the doctrine that defends that the true taxpayer was the owner themselves, and the occupant was only a mere tax agent responsible for collecting the tax and making the payment on behalf of the owner.

The impact of the presumptive tax on production, income, and distribution in the agricultural sector depends on (a) changes in investment; (b) the amount of land leased and alienated, and the resulting changes in land use; (c) the direct impact of the effects on income and equity arising from the land that is not leased or disposed of as a result of the tax; and (d) the demand conditions for various agricultural products and the complementarity or competitiveness in terms of supply between the different types of farms (Berry 1972). Hence, a high land tax, with or without exemption for small farmers, would create an incentive for increased production on larger farms that suffer from low productivity, provide additional income tax revenues, and improve the horizontal equity of the tax system. In addition, a tax that would exempt small farms from paying it would generate an incentive for the division of large-scale plantations and their consequent sale into small plots of land.

To conclude, this system, which seems optimal, ended up failing due to issues of not updating the values. In theory, these values should be updated every five years, unless expressly requested by the taxpayer who was entitled to the annual update, or effected by the tax administration, which at any time could update the values in the event of any structural change in the property that would alter or modify its rating (Lapidoth 1977).

Outward signs of lifestyle

Another presumptive tax method is one that, moving away from real transactions, establishes the tax base by resorting to income indicators, such as personal expenses and wealth accumulation. Specifically, when taxpayers do not comply with their bookkeeping obligations, do not file any return, or file a return and it is rejected because it contains accounting irregularities, many countries allow the use of indirect indexes to set taxable income (Bulutoglu 1995). More precisely, the estimate is based on certain external signs that denote a certain level of personal consumption and quality of life, which are set by law. Both the lifestyle signs of the taxpayer, as well as those of their spouse and their children or dependents, are taken into account. It should be noted that this kind of estimation only applies to individuals.

Additionally, not only ownership is taken into account but also the effective enjoyment of elements such as vacation homes and luxury boats; however, the brief possession of the same for a period equal to or less than one month is normally ignored (Thuronyi 2000). In short, this method assumes the nature of a tax on the imputed income or benefit derived from the ownership or possession of the aforementioned assets. Despite this, it is not a tax on imputed income, or on income in general, or on expenses, but rather a combination of the previous three.

If the presumption is characterized as rebuttable, taxpayers may challenge it before the courts, and most likely the tax administration's position will not prevail unless it has sufficient information about the taxpayer to justify its presumed assessment. If, on the other hand, the presumption is considered nonrebuttable, its application will be unfair in certain cases (Thuronyi 2000). This problem was solved in France by instructing inspectors on the application of the presumption only in justified cases and introducing a requirement that a senior official must approve and authorize the application of the estimate—this last requirement has been maintained even after the presumption has been made nonrebuttable. Estimates of this nature are now seen as a means of ensuring that those taxpayers who enjoy a luxurious lifestyle contribute an adequate amount to the support of government charges, even if they have reliably declared all of their actual income. In other words, this presumption currently serves an objective of fairness and public morality (Tanzi and Casanegra de Jantscher 1987). In turn, depending on its characterization, this type of presumption can take on the nature of a wealth tax, an expense tax, an income tax, or a combination of the above (Lapidoth 1977).

Regarding procedural issues, it may be useful for a more agile application of the method to require taxpayers to include in their returns the information necessary to establish the presumption and even self-assess the resulting tax in countries where the self-assessment regime applies to income tax (Thuronyi 2000). The obligation to include this information in the returns may be limited to those taxpayers whose indicators for the application of the method exceed a specific amount, so that in practice, only a small number of taxpayers would have to provide the aforementioned information.

Practice has shown that presumptions based on visible signs of wealth are difficult to apply. When the signs are set in general terms, tax auditors find themselves in the dilemma of choosing between the application of one sign or another as the basis of the presumption, as well as establishing the income equivalent to each one of them. In those countries where the signs and their income equivalent have been set by law, the rigidity of the rules can generate injustice. In recognition of these kinds of problems, tax departments tend to apply these assumptions cautiously and only when further assessments cannot be made under any other method. One of the areas in which these presumptions have been very useful has been in the quantification of income from illegal sources, say those from drug trafficking, smuggling, or gambling (Tanzi and Casanegra de Jantscher 1987). Likewise, the accumulation of wealth of the taxpayer and their standard of living can be investigated in the course of an administrative investigative procedure.

One of the first manifestations of this type of estimation in history was the "window tax" that was introduced in England in 1696. According to it, the tax rates were progressive and increased as the number of windows increased. It is worth noting that not even such a simple tax guaranteed efficient compliance, and thus practices aimed at tax evasion appeared—for example, bricking up windows before an inspection by tax administration officials and opening them again after his departure, or turning two windows into one by means of a glass that joined them (Sabine 1966). Other examples of taxes of this type in England during this period are the tax introduced in 1777 on all male servants, excluding servants working in industry or agriculture; the tax adopted in 1785 on female servants; pleasure horse tax; racehorse tax and even an additional tax on winning horses; sporting license tax; dog tax; watch tax; powder tax for the hair (Sabine 1966); and so on.

It should be noted that a presumed minimum tax based on external signs of living standards was in operation for many years in France, where it applied to all individuals, regardless of their profession, and took into consideration the following items: rental value of primary home, rental value of second homes, number of household employees, automobiles, motorcycles, recreational boats, airplanes, horses, hunting rights, and golf club memberships. Similar methods and variants have been applied in Belgium, Bolivia (García-Novoa 2002), Brazil, Cuba (Lucas-Mas 2002), Greece (Bird and Wallace 2003), Italy, Lesotho (Thuronyi 2000), Mali, Mauritania, Peru (Tanzi and Casanegra de Jantscher 1987), Spain, Switzerland, Togo, and Turkey. As an example, in 1954, the United Nations Mission in Iran advised that a taxpayer's taxable income should not be less than three times the estimated rental value of their home and recommended other external indicators of wealth, such as the number of servants and motor vehicles based on their cylinder capacity.

Minimum tax

Minimum taxes overlap with several presumptive tax methods already studied, but in turn, they can also be found in an isolated way and even completely unrelated to the tax estimate (Graetz and Sunley 1988). These taxes are normally based on assets, turnover, or any other redefined notion of income and apply to both small and large companies. In fact, presumed or estimated taxes can take the same form as minimum taxes but generally only apply to small businesses that are not able to adjust to the general regime (Stotsky 1995). The purpose of a minimum tax is primarily to ensure that businesses and individuals with income do not avoid or evade paying their taxes. In many developing countries, there are minimum taxes on businesses, but it is rare to find minimum taxes on individuals (Stotsky 1995).

A minimum business tax can be used to increase the fairness (or perceived fairness) and efficiency of corporate income tax. Various kinds of injustices and dysfunctions can arise in relation to this type of tax, with a variety of causes that originate them. These include differences in compliance between sectors and differences in the ability to make use of tax advantages. In many advanced as well as developing countries, corporate income tax is characterized by a proliferation of tax advantages and incentives, granted in the form of exemptions and deferrals (Stotsky 1995). These reliefs can seriously erode the aggregate tax base. In contrast, a minimum tax on business income can reduce this inequity by taxing these entities based on a notion of income independent of what is declared for tax purposes.

A minimum tax can also be justified as a form of fiscal license for business. In fact, the previous existence of these has not prevented the subsequent adoption of minimum taxes in some countries such as France, applying both simultaneously. However, the two taxes must be differentiated (Stotsky 1995). The minimum tax is considered to be payment on account of the general income tax, but if it turns out to be of an amount greater than that, there will be no right to a refund. On the other hand, the deduction of the amount paid for business tax licenses is normally allowed for the purpose of computing the corporate income tax, as a deductible expense, something that is not possible with respect to the minimum tax.

One way to accrue a minimum business tax is to calculate the tax as a percentage of the turnover or gross income of the business; this form is frequently used in countries influenced by France. The advantage of a minimum tax based on turnover is that said financial parameter is easily measurable and must also be known to calculate other taxes, such as value added tax (VAT). Therefore, turnover is a measure available to the tax administration. Likewise, in an economy lacking price regulation, both prices and invoicing are automatically adjusted for the effect of inflation, which does not distort the tax. The drawback of this approach is that turnover is not necessarily related to any measure of income, so this type of tax does not provide a good representation of income tax. Furthermore, it is deficient compared to VAT, since it implies a significant cascading effect (Stotsky 1995).

Another alternative is to accrue the tax as a percentage of the assets (gross, net, or fixed) of the business, an option that has also been the object of prior study. This usage is predominant in Latin America. The use of a tax on assets structured as a minimum tax has superior theoretical support and appeal to the use of turnover, since the economic notion of income seems to bear some systematic relation to assets, not to turnover. Thus, a tax on assets may be a reasonable, although imperfect, representation of the income tax. This form of presumptive taxation is recommended for developing countries (Stotsky 1995). All the considerations made in the previous sections dedicated to the analysis of the percentage methods on assets, gross receipts, and turnover are fully applicable in this context, because ultimately, the minimum tax is no longer an application structure, but rather a method of quantification, and specifically of estimation.

Finally, regarding the minimum taxes on individuals, in a context of full integration of income taxes for individuals and companies, there would be no need for a minimum tax on businesses, since all income would be taxed at the individual level. But even without such absolute integration, the adequacy of this type of minimum business tax is questionable, if the ultimate incidence of it falls on the owners of capital, a question that remains open. On a practical level, the minimum tax on businesses is an essential counterpart to the minimum tax on individuals, and in most countries, it is more relevant (Stotsky 1995).

The use of minimum taxation has found roots not only in Latin America but also in Sub-Saharan Africa, where different variants emerged depending on whether it was applied to legal or natural persons. In the case of individuals, a distinction can be made between those systems that adopted a fixed amount—for example, Burkina Faso, the Central African Republic, Congo, Equatorial Guinea, Ghana, Madagascar, and Malawi, and those that opted for systems based on a percentage of turnover, for example, Cameroon, Chad, Gabon, Gambia, Niger, Nigeria, and Zambia (Taube and Tadesse 1996).

Regarding its application to legal persons, various modalities can be established, depending on whether said minimum taxation is based on (a) a fixed amount, as was the case in Benin, Côte d'Ivoire, Equatorial Guinea, Malawi, and Senegal; (b) gross income, as done in the Central African Republic, Chad, Ghana, Guinea, Niger, Sierra Leone, and Togo; (c) a fixed amount plus a percentage of gross income, as in Madagascar; or (d) the choice between the higher of the fixed amount or the percentage of gross income, prevalent in Burkina Faso, the Comoros, the Republic of Congo, Gabon, and Nigeria (Taube and Tadesse 1996).

Presumptive cost deduction

Halfway between the tax estimate and the self-assessment of the tax, there is the method of deduction of presumptive costs, under which the taxpayer declares income but not expenses. Expenses are estimated by applying assumptions (Bulutoglu 1995). Where costs are presumed deductible, most countries also allow taxpayers the option of deducting actual costs. Thus, a generous presumptive cost deduction will erode taxable income considerably. On the other hand, when there is the option of deducting the actual cost, there is no justification for a generous, or as wide, presumptive cost deduction, since taxpayers who in reality experience high costs may choose to deduct them entirely. On the other hand, when there is an option, the taxpayer can erode the tax base by concentrating all the costs in the year in which the deduction of real costs is made and in the following years to make use of the deduction of presumptive costs (Bulutoglu 1995). A minimum period, say three years, should be required to prevent such abusive changes from one method to another.

From an economic point of view, estimating costs can have the positive effect of encouraging the most efficient taxpayers while discouraging extravagant business expenses. It may also present an administrative advantage by allowing clerks to concentrate on checking and inspecting large taxpayer returns. However, this method also has drawbacks typical of presumptive taxation, such as the fact that there will always be taxpayers whose costs will be lower than the averages used, who will benefit from the estimation, for example, writers who are authors of bestsellers (Lapidoth 1977). Then also, companies that incur expenses higher than those estimated may prove said situation through their accounting and deduct the actual costs. All this results in an overestimation of the costs to be deducted and, consequently, in a decrease in taxable income and the collection derived from it. Moreover, the administration would also have to deal with the lack of acceptance of the method among those taxpayers who are forced to keep accounts to be able to avoid a greater tax debt derived from the underestimation of the costs incurred. Some countries that have implemented this presumptive tax method or a variant of it in the past include Burundi (Malik 1979), the Dominican Republic (García-Novoa 2002), and Israel.

Assessment boards

The use of assessment boards or public committees in tax administration is quite common. Some of the functions they can perform are the resolution of controversies between taxpayers and the tax administration, and the quantification of their taxable income, either by determining it or estimating it. For example, the Spanish Tax Administration used public committees in the past within the framework of the global evaluation procedure. In this context was the now disappeared figure of the "tax juries" in Spain, which were committees or arbitration commissions—made up of members of both the tax administration and professional and trade union associations—charged with resolving controversies between tax administration and taxpayers, and to quantify the taxable income of the latter. The result of this assessment was called the "jury estimate." There were also a central tax jury and other territorial delegations of the same. Other examples of this approach existed in Israel, Sweden, and Turkey.

Other methods

Apart from the methods described so far, there are endless variants and hybrids that are or have been applied in different ways in different countries. One example, the Finance Act of 1988 of India, introduced for the first time the application of tax estimation to residents, according to which the benefit derived from a sale instrumented through auction, delivery, or any other way directed by a person or their agent, called sellers, will be estimated as a percentage of the purchase price and considered as the seller's profit. The alleged tax provision applied to the purchase of alcoholic beverages for human consumption and other products. This rule opened a new path in terms of tax estimation, by applying for the first time the concept of estimated benefit based not on the sale price or turnover but on the purchase price paid. The seller of the specified good had to collect the tax from the buyer at specific rates, which ranged between 5 and 15 percent of the amount to be paid by the buyer as the purchase price, and then pay it to the government (Dastur 1997). Another example is the Central Excise and Salt Act of 1944 in India, under which the tax estimate was reflected in a presumptive levy calculated on the basis of installed capacity in an industry or factory, without any reference to the effective or real production of the same (Dastur 1997).

In another example, in France, the so-called normal income method applied to businesses and consisted of setting the average income that the business in question has produced in the past, during a period long enough to be able to consider the established income as an expression of the average results. The agreement regarding the normal income between the tax administration and the taxpayer lasted for two years and could be extended for periods of two years, unless one of the parties opposed it. Another similar system was the one known under the name of "collective estimate," also in France. This method was mainly applied in the field of agriculture and not so much to companies (Lapidoth 1977). It basically consisted of estimating the average income of a group of taxpayers based on the average yield of the different farms during the current year, without any reference to past years, as would happen with the normal income method.

Also noteworthy is the method in force in Cameroon in the 1970s, based on which merchants whose annual turnover was less than a certain amount were liable for a fixed presumptive tax equivalent to 50 percent of the main amount paid in concept of license right and which was collected jointly with it (Malik 1979). Another variant was the advance payment system that was applied during the same period in Gabon.

Other methods that have been applied in Africa are presumptive taxes on imports, withholding schemes designed to capture income from unregistered businesses, and license fees that apply graduated rates (Taube and Tadesse 1996). Each of them is discussed below.

Regarding the presumptive taxes on imports, these are taxes with the intention of capturing income from registered and unregistered importers. For the latter, the payment of the presumptive tax represents a tax on estimated business income; for registered importers, it only implies a payment on account of their subsequent final tax liability. Generally in Africa, the tax takes as its base the value of the imported merchandise, with relatively low tax rates. This type of taxation has been applied in Benin, the Comoros, Côte d'Ivoire, Ethiopia, Niger, and Senegal (Taube and Tadesse 1996).

Withholding schemes designed to capture income from unregistered businesses have been applied in Benin, Côte d'Ivoire, and Senegal and consist mainly of withholding on account a percentage of the value of the transactions on industrial goods and merchandise, with the obligation to withhold falling on producers, wholesalers, and merchants.

License fees with the application of graduated rates seek to substantially tax business income and achieve an increase in revenue. The gradation of the tax rates is set based on indicators such as the area of the business, the rental value of the establishment, the power of the machinery used, or the number of workers. This method has been applied in Benin, the Comoros, Congo, Côte d'Ivoire, and Guinea (Taube and Tadesse 1996).

Bibliography

Allais, Maurice. 1988. *L' Impôt sur le Capital et la Réforme Monétaire*. Paris: Éditions Hermann.

Berry, R. Albert. 1972. "Presumptive Income Tax on Agricultural Land: The Case of Colombia." *National Tax Journal* 25 (2): 169–181. https://doi.org/10.1086/NTJ41791789.

Bulutoglu, Kenan. 1995. "Presumptive Taxation." In *Tax Policy Handbook*, edited by Parthasarathi Shome, 258–262. Washington, DC: IMF. https://doi.org/10.5089/9781557754905.071

Byrne, Peter. 1994. "The Business Assets Tax in Latin America—No Credit Where It Is Due." Development Discussion Paper No. 506, Harvard Institute for International Development, Cambridge, MA.

Dastur, Sohrab Erach. 1997. "The Indian Methodology." In *Presumptive Income Taxation. Proceedings of a Seminar held in New Delhi in 1997 during the 51st Congress of the International Fiscal Association*, edited by Reuven S. Avi-Yonah, Vol. 22. The Hague, Netherlands: Kluwer Law International.

Einaudi, Luigi. 1963. "La Scienza Italiana e la Imposta Ottima" (Italian Science and the Optimum Tax). Original work published in 1924. In Miti e Paradossi della Giustizia Tributaria, chapter X, edited by Giulio Einaudi. Torino, Italy, 1938. Spanish translation: "Mitos y Paradojas de la Justicia Tributaria." Barcelona: Ediciones Ariel.

García-Novoa, César. 2002. "Los Métodos de Simplificación Fiscal en la Experiencia Latinoamericana. Referencia Comparativa a los Casos Brasileños y Argentino" (Tax Simplification Methods in the Latin American Experience. Compared Reference to the Brazilian and Argentinean Cases). Informe Interno del Proyecto sobre "Justicia Tributaria" del Gobierno Español, Barcelona, 2002.

Graetz, Michael, and Emil Sunley. 1988. "Minimum Taxes and Comprehensive Tax Reform." In *Uneasy Compromise: Problems of a Hybrid Income-Consumption Tax*, edited by Henry J. Aaron, Harvey Galper, and Joseph A Pechman. Washington, DC: Brookings Institution.

Herzog, Theodore H. (1997). "Russian Tax System from Soviet Era Needs Reform in Almost Every Phase." *Journal of International Taxation* 8 (3).

Kaldor, Nicholas. 1955. *An Expenditure Tax*. London: George Allen & Unwin.

Khadka, Rup. 2001. "Presumptive Taxes: Assessing Origin & Its Practice." *The Rising Nepal*, February 22, 2001.

Lapidoth, Arye. 1977. *The Use of Estimation for the Assessment of Taxable Business Income: With Special Emphasis on the Problems of Taxing Small Business*. Vol. 4 of *Selected Monographs on Taxation*. Amsterdam: International Bureau of Fiscal Documentation.

Lucas-Mas, Cristian Óliver. 2002. "The Cuban Tax System Through History." *Tax Notes International* 27 (5): 609–630. https://www.taxnotes.com/tax-notes-today-international/corporate-taxation/cuban-tax-system-through-history/2002/07/29/1b95m?highlight=lucas-mas.

Lucas-Mas, Cristian Óliver. 2004. "General Tax Theory on Simplified Methods for the Assessment of Tax Bases: A Study on Presumptive Taxation." Doctoral dissertation, University of Barcelona, Spain. Unpublished.

Malik, I. A. 1979. "Use of Presumptive Tax Assessment Techniques in Taxation of Small Traders and Professionals in Africa." *Bulletin for International Fiscal Documentation* 33 (4): 162–178. https://bit.ly/3ZxDJwR.

Mikesell, John. 1999. "The Unified Tax on Imputed Income in the Russian Federation: Problems with an Alternative Tax Scheme." *Tax Notes International*. https://www.taxnotes.com/tax-notes-international/unified-tax-imputed-income-russian-federation-problems-alternative-tax-scheme/1999/12/27/1tr2m.

Oldman, Oliver, and Jennifer Brooks. 1987. "The Unitary Method and the Less Developed Countries: Preliminary Thoughts." *Revue de Droit Des Affaires Internationales*, France, and *International Business Law Journal* 45 (1): 45–61.

Ortega, Luis. 1991. "La Nacionalización del Suelo en Gran Bretaña (The Community Land Act 1975)." *Revista Española de Derecho Administrativo* 14: 459–478.

Rajaraman, Indira. 1995. "Presumptive Direct Taxation. Lessons from Experience in Developing Countries." *Economic and Political Weekly* 30 (18–19): 1103–1124. http://www.jstor.org/stable/4402735.

Sabine, B. E. V. 1966. *A History of Income Tax*. London: George Allen & Unwin.

Sadka, Efraim, and Vito Tanzi. 1993. "A Tax on Gross Assets of Enterprises as a Form of Presumptive Taxation." Working Paper 1992/016, IMF, Washington, DC. https://www.imf.org/en/Publications/WP/Issues/2016/12/30/A-Taxon-Gross -Assets-of-Enterprises-as-a-Form-of-Presumptive-Taxation-767.

Stotsky, Janet. 1995. "Minimum Taxes." In *Tax Policy Handbook*, edited by Parthasarathi Shome, 263–266. Washington, DC: IMF.

Tanzi, Vito, and Milka Casanegra de Jantscher. 1987. "Presumptive Income Taxation: Administrative, Efficiency, and Equity Aspects." IMF Working Paper 1987/054, IMF, Washington, DC.

Taube, Günther, and Helaway Tadesse. 1996. "Presumptive Taxation in Sub-Saharan Africa: Experiences and Prospects." IMF Working Paper 96/5, IMF, Washington, DC.

Thuronyi, Victor. 2000. "Presumptive Taxation." In *Tax Law Design and Drafting*, edited by Victor Thuronyi, 401–433. The Hague, Netherlands: Kluwer Law International.

Tideman, Nicolaus, ed. 1994. *Land and Taxation*. Georgist Paradigm Series. London: Shepheard-Walwyn (Publishers) Ltd.

Valdés-Costa, R. 1996. *Curso de Derecho Tributario* (Course on Taxation Law). Depalma-Temis-Marcial Pons, Buenos Aires, Santa Fe de Bogotá: Brazil.

Wald, Haskell, and Joseph Froomkin, eds. 1954. "Papers and Proceedings of the Conference on Agricultural Taxation and Economic Development." International Program in Taxation. Cambridge, MA: Harvard Law School.

Wallace, Sally. 2002. "Imputed and Presumptive Taxes: International Experiences and Lessons for Russia." Working Paper 02–03, Andrew Young School of Policy Studies, International Studies Program, Georgia State University.

Wilkenfeld, Harold. 1973. *Taxes and People in Israel*. Cambridge, MA: Harvard University Press.

Zodrow, George, and Charles McLure, Jr. 1991. "Implementing Direct Consumption Taxes in Developing Countries." Policy, Planning, and Research Working Paper WPS 131, World Bank, Washington, DC. https://documents1.worldbank.org/curated /en/231021468740958491/pdf/multi-page.pdf.

Political economy considerations for tax reform

Tax reform and political economy

Improving state capacity to generate domestic resources through tax and nontax mechanisms has become a core priority of the international community's sustainable development agenda.

Increasing tax collection through a broader and deeper tax base, improved compliance, and lower evasion can help reduce dependence on official development assistance and foreign lending. Internal resources have the potential to eclipse external aid in terms of scale and importance to development. Many lower-income countries could increase their tax collection by at least 2 to 4 percent of gross domestic product (GDP), without sacrificing equity or development. And for some countries, increasing domestic resource mobilization (DRM) could help them pass the 15 percent threshold of taxes/GDP, which is viewed as the minimum required to fund basic state functions. Ultimately, the goal of the sustainable development agenda is for all recipient countries to leverage billions of external public aid into unlocking trillions of funding from private sources, internal and external—for example, domestic taxpayers, internal capital, and foreign investors.

Given this imperative of the international community, what is the best path toward tax reform? What is the relative importance of external funding, technical assistance, systemic economic factors, domestic institutional structures, and political will? Although there is limited research on the effectiveness of tax reform itself, studies on policy reform in other areas can provide meaningful insights as to which factors—both technical and nontechnical—are significant.

Spending and collecting resources are characterized by similar dynamics, so the factors dominant in public financial management (PFM) reforms are also likely to characterize tax reform. Several key implications from this research on PFM reform are likely to be applicable to tax administration reform:

- **Sequencing.** It is important to continuously keep some focus on the basics while supporting or enabling those "advanced" reforms that have the strongest internal demand and the relative best fit with existing bottlenecks and opportunities for improvements.
- **Persistence.** Transformational—rapid and substantial—reform is rare and slow, and incremental improvements are common, but risks of backsliding also exist.
- **Institutions.** Being clear about institutional arrangements and roles is essential for assessing bottlenecks and likely difficulties, as well as for identifying priorities for engagement on institutional changes.
- **Monitoring.** Tracking what functional improvements are being made and sustained is critical in terms of incentivizing real reforms and for planning further steps.

Operationally, effective benchmarking and diagnostics can help those directly involved in reform to identify opportunities and strategic directions, while providing useful benchmarks against which to judge reform progress. Internationally comparable information about national tax systems may further help to identify possible areas for reform and the sharing of experiences. While these benefits are significant, understanding the potential risks associated with benchmarking and diagnostic exercises is equally important. This begins with recognizing the two substantially different sets of goals that may motivate such exercises.

The primary goal of diagnostic and benchmarking exercises is to better understand the strengths and limitations of existing systems and practices to guide reform efforts. However, benchmarking and diagnostic exercises can also become focused on ranking tax systems to facilitate cross-country comparison and quantitative judgments about system effectiveness. These latter possibilities can be a useful additional benefit of such benchmarking processes, but if these goals become predominant, they can distort and undermine the broader effectiveness of diagnostic efforts.

In practice, it is frequently donors and external actors who are more heavily focused on comparison and benchmarking, while local actors are more concerned with targeted diagnostic exercises that can inform reform priorities. This can lead to tension and disengagement if local actors feel that a resource-intensive benchmarking and diagnostic exercise is oriented too heavily toward donor concerns rather than supporting local priorities. These risks are likely to be amplified if local actors are confronted by multiple and contrasting diagnostic exercises that consume valuable resources while primarily serving external agendas. Such tensions can have both short-term and long-term consequences.

In the short term, local actors may choose to disengage from or undermine a benchmarking and diagnostic exercise that they view as holding little value. Effective implementation demands the compiling of extensive data and information by tax administrations, and the quality of that data is likely to be closely linked to the value that local actors place on the process. As Vázquez-Caro and Bird (2011) have written, "If those who must generate most of the critical data needed for a benchmarking exercise are aware that they will be judged by it, and they see no direct benefits for themselves from accurate reporting, accurate reporting is unlikely to ensue."

Over the longer term, the imposition by donors of benchmarking and diagnostic exercises that local actors view as unnecessary and unproductive is likely to undermine the development of the types of strong and open partnerships that are necessary to support reform. Tax administrators in various parts of the world have frequently expressed frustration with such externally mandated processes, which they view as indicative of the absence of genuine partnership. In the worst case, overreliance on externally driven diagnostics can lead to a narrow focus on quantitative targets rather than the development of long-term plans for effective reform.

These challenges do not lend themselves to simple answers but highlight the need to emphasize making diagnostic exercises relevant to local needs, rather than emphasizing primarily the collection of internationally comparable data. Vázquez-Caro and Bird (2011) have argued that benchmarking needs to move away from simple "benchmarking by numbers" in favor of a systemic approach focused on "considering how all aspects of the administrative system function as a whole in the context of the environment within which that system is embedded and operates." The key insight is that tax system performance depends on how the different elements of the tax system fit together, while reform priorities can only be identified and fully understood in light of a broader context of the overall tax system environment.

Seen in this light, a benchmarking exercise focused on gathering discrete pieces of data is likely to be useful to external actors but much less useful to domestic actors. The corresponding challenge is to ensure that the data-gathering exercise forms part of a locally embedded benchmarking and diagnostic process that is closely linked to the immediate reform challenges confronting different tax administrations.

Tax administration reform needs to be customized to the local context, rather than homogeneously applied based on a uniform set of programs. First, the primacy of political will means that effective tax administration reform needs to be customized, systemic and speedy, opportunistic, and attached to broader improvements in governance. The old adage that all politics is local applies par excellence to taxes. And given that local actors will often have the most accurate insight into the internal distribution of power, institutional dynamics, and informal customary practices, tax reform needs to be designed in light of this local knowledge. Internationally driven reform programs without local input or support can result in superficial or formal change that obfuscates the lack of real progress.

Second, expanding a country's DRM is likely to be politically feasible and sustainable only if it is associated with enhanced governance through improved rule of law, accountability, and transparency standards. Taxpayers are unlikely to cooperate with increased tax collection efforts unless they have a better view of their government, confidence in its legitimacy, and trust in how the taxes would be spent. Moreover, increased tax collection capacity can improve the fairness of the tax system in eliminating exceptions or special treatment for those who were able to exploit the inadequacies of the previous system.

Third, since effective tax reform requires political will to overcome vested interests that benefit from the status quo distribution of taxes, it is likely to be more successful if pursued systematically and speedily across all areas, rather than piecemeal and slowly. Any improvement in tax administration, however significant, can be undermined by other parts of the process. For example, new legislation that meets the highest international standards will not increase DRM if the tax system's operations are not concurrently improved to implement the new rules. Likewise, the time horizon for tax reform is likely to be relatively short, for example, 12 to 24 months, as opposition to change eventually emerges and solidifies. Both features, interlinkage and resistance, imply that international engagement through technical assistance and financing needs to be strategic and quickly deployable.

Tax administration reform should also be structured in a systematic manner across time. The idiosyncratic reform challenges due to nontechnical drivers imply that it needs to be opportunistic. Therefore, the optimal sequencing of basic and advanced reforms may need to be ordered based on political feasibility rather than substantive priority; for instance, information technology (IT) improvements may need to precede institutional or human resources reform. World Bank research on PFM reform demonstrates that incremental improvements are common, with risks of backsliding, and that transformational reform is rare, although possible.

Bibliography

Vázquez-Caro, Jaime, and Richard Bird. 2011. "Benchmarking Tax Administrations in Developing Countries: A Systematic Approach." *eJournal of Tax Research* 9 (1): 5–37.

Full text of a proposal for a revised tax sanctions code

1. Scope of application

This Act shall apply to all offenses described herein that are common across taxes. Those misconducts specific to the administration of certain taxes are outside the scope of this Act and shall be governed in accordance with the enactment under which the offense was imposed. The term *sanction* includes penalties, surcharges, and interests.

2. Registration-related offenses

Any person who—

1. without lawful excuse refuses, fails, or neglects—
    (a) to apply for registration in the prescribed form and manner as required by law; or
    (b) to furnish any information as required by the registration authority; or
    (c) to return to the Tax Commissioner a certificate of registration upon cancellation of his or her registration; or
2. being a registered taxpayer, neglects to inform the Tax Commissioner, within the time required by law, of—
    (a) a change in respect of the transfer of ownership by him or her of his or her taxable activity; or
    (b) the address from where or the name in which the taxable activity is carried out; or
    (c) the cessation of his or her taxable activity as required by law; or
3. not being a registered taxpayer, displays or causes to be displayed at his or her place of business any document purporting to be a certificate of registration, commits an offense, and is liable on summary conviction in a Tax Court—
    (a) in the case of an individual, to a fine not exceeding [amount]; or
    (b) in the case of a body corporate or any other person, to a fine not exceeding [amount].

3. Recordkeeping-related offenses

Any person who—

1. without lawful excuse refuses, fails, or neglects—
    (a) to keep in the official language proper books of accounts, records, and any other documents as necessary to exhibit or explain all transactions and financial positions, and statements of annual stocktaking and accounts of all goods sold and purchased, as prescribed by law; or
    (b) to retain for a period of not less than number of years any books of accounts, records, written notices, records of remuneration, records of earnings, returns, certificates, wages sheets, lists, invoices, contracts, or any other documents and information that are relevant to the tax liability of any person, as required to retain by law; or
    (c) to produce, to furnish, or to deliver any books of accounts, records, written notices, records of remuneration, records of earnings, returns, certificates, wages sheets, lists, invoices, contracts, or any other documents and information that are relevant to the tax liability of any person, as required to produce by law; or
    (d) to attend or to give evidence in accordance with any summons issued or in pursuance of any notice served; or
    (e) to answer any lawful question touching the matters under consideration; or
    (f) to comply within the time required by law with any order or requirement of the authorized person exercising a power conferred by law; or
    (g) to deliver account of any tax deducted from payment to a nonresident, as required by law or by the Tax Commissioner; or
    (h) to comply with a contravention notice or with the requirements of a notice issued by the Tax Commissioner; or
    (i) to honor his or her undertaking to inform the Minister or the Tax Commissioner, as required by law, of any change that would result in the loss of exemption from tax; or
2. aids, abets, assists, counsels, incites, conspires with, or induces another person in the commission of an offense under section (1), commits an offense, and is liable on summary conviction in a Tax Court—
    (a) in the case of an individual, to a fine not exceeding [amount]; or
    (b) in the case of a body corporate or any other person, to a fine not exceeding [amount].

4. Falsehood- and obstruction-related offenses

Any person who—

1. knowingly or willfully—
    (a) gives any false evidence before the Tax Commissioner; or
    (b) makes, utters, produces, delivers, or makes use of any declaration, statement, or account that is false, fraudulent, incorrect, or misleading in any material particular; or
    (c) furnishes a document that contains information that is false, incorrect, or misleading in any material particular; or
    (d) falsifies or amends any information contained in a certificate of registration, books of accounts, records, or any other documents and information as prescribed by law; or
    (e) personates or pretends to be an authorized person; or
    (f) assaults, threatens, intimidates, or uses threatening language or behaves in a threatening manner to any authorized person acting in the execution of duties; or

    (g)   obstructs, molests, prevents, or hinders a Tax Commissioner, a tax officer, any authorized person acting in the execution of duties, or any person acting in the aid of a tax officer or any person so employed; or

    (h)   alters or obliterates any notes, memoranda, or indication of check made by any tax officer during the course of inspection of any records, accounts, or documents; or

    (i)   fails to certify any information as required by law or provides an incorrect or incomplete certificate or return; or

    (j)   does or is a party to the doing of any act or transaction, without the mandatory consent in writing of the Minister, the Tax Commissioner, or the authorized person, as required by law; or

2. knowingly or willfully aids, abets, assists, counsels, incites, conspires with, or induces another person in the commission of an offense under section (1), commits a criminal offense, and is liable on summary conviction in a Tax Court—

    (a)   in the case of an individual, to a fine not exceeding [amount] and, in default of payment, up to [time period] imprisonment; or

    (b)   in the case of a body corporate or any other person, to a fine not exceeding [amount] and, in default of payment, up to [time period] imprisonment.

5. Late-filing-related offenses

Any person who—without lawful excuse—

1. makes, delivers, or has delivered on her or his behalf a complete and correct return in respect of a taxable period; or

2. submits a complete and correct declaration of her or his estimated tax in respect of a taxable period; or

3. notifies of any outstanding balances of tax payable by the body corporate, after the deadline prescribed by law, but before an audit procedure has been initiated in respect of such taxable period, commits an offense, and is liable on summary conviction in a Tax Court—

    (a)   in the case of an individual, to a surcharge of [amount] for each day of delay; or

    (b)   in the case of a body corporate or any other person, to a surcharge of [amount] for each day of delay.

6. Nonfiling-related offenses

Any person who—without lawful excuse refuses, fails, or neglects—

1. to make, or to deliver, or to have delivered on her or his behalf a complete and correct return in respect of a taxable period, as prescribed by law; or

2. to submit a complete and correct declaration of her or his estimated tax in respect of a taxable period, computed as prescribed by law; or

3. to notify of any outstanding balances of tax payable by the body corporate as prescribed by law, commits an offense, and is liable on summary conviction in a Tax Court—

    (a)   in the case of an individual, to a fine of [amount] for each day of default; or

    (b)   in the case of a body corporate or any other person, to a fine of [amount] for each day of default.

7. Late-payment-related offenses

Any person who—without lawful excuse—

1. pays, in whole or in part, any amount of tax due and payable in respect of a taxable period; or
2. complies with the requirements prescribed by law relating to the payment and collection of a tax and the furnishing of information relating thereto; or
3. pays or accounts for, in whole or in part, any amount of tax to be deducted at source by her or him on the payment of any sum, as her or his duty may require, whether or not tax was in fact deducted from that payment; or
4. allows a deduction of tax authorized by law to be made out of any payment, after the deadline prescribed by law, but before an audit procedure has been initiated in respect of such taxable period, commits an offense, and is liable on summary conviction in a Tax Court—
   (a) in the case of an individual, to a surcharge of [percentage] of the amount of chargeable interest; or
   (b) in the case of a body corporate or any other person, to a surcharge of [percentage] of the amount of chargeable interest.

8. Nonpayment-related offenses

Any person who—without lawful excuse refuses, fails, or neglects—

1. to pay, in whole or in part, any amount of tax due and payable in respect of a taxable period, as prescribed by law; or
2. to comply with the requirements prescribed by law relating to the payment and collection of a tax and the furnishing of information relating thereto; or
3. to pay or to account for, in whole or in part, any amount of tax to be deducted at source by her or him on the payment of any sum, as her or his duty may require, whether or not tax was in fact deducted from that payment; or
4. to allow a deduction of tax authorized by law to be made out of any payment, commits an offense, and is liable on summary conviction in a Tax Court—
   (a) in the case of an individual, to a fine of [percentage] of the amount of unpaid tax; or
   (b) in the case of a body corporate or any other person, to a fine of [percentage] of the amount of unpaid tax.

9. Fraud-related offenses

Any person who—with intent to defraud the Tax Commissioner and evade tax in respect of any given taxable period, knowingly or willfully—

1. enters into any fraudulent arrangement or agreement, or practices or is concerned in any fraudulent contrivance, or device, or is party to any willful act or neglect, falsehood, deception, art, or omission; or
2. fraudulently changes the place of residence, or fraudulently converts, releases, assigns, conveys, or renders temporarily unproductive any property that was chargeable, in order to evade the payment of tax thereof; or
3. makes or delivers any declaration, return, statement, or schedule that is false or fraudulent, and charges herself or himself with less tax than she or he is liable to pay under the laws imposing

such tax, or in any other manner evades the payment of tax, commits a criminal offense, and is liable on summary conviction in a Tax Court—

(a) in the case of an individual—

    (i)   to a fine not exceeding [amount]; or

    (ii) to a fine of [multiple] the amount of unpaid tax, whichever is greater; or

    (iii) in default of payment, up to [time period] imprisonment; or

(b) in the case of a body corporate or any other person—

    (i)   to a fine not exceeding [amount]; or

    (ii) to a fine of [multiple] the amount of unpaid tax, whichever is greater; or

    (iii) in default of payment, up to [time period] imprisonment.

10. Misappropriation-related offenses

Any person who—with intent to misappropriate funds, knowingly or willfully—

1. not being a registered taxpayer, collects tax and fails to pay over the tax to the tax commissioner; or
2. being a registered taxpayer, collects tax on behalf of the revenue and neglects to pay over, in whole or in part, any amount of tax to the Tax Commissioner; or
3. being an employer liable to pay tax in respect of a person employed by her or him, deducts or attempts to deduct the whole or any part of such tax from the emoluments of the employee, commits a criminal offense, and is liable on summary conviction in a Tax Court—

(a) in the case of an individual—

    (i)   to a fine not exceeding [amount]; or

    (ii) to a fine of [multiple] the amount of unpaid tax, whichever is greater; or

    (iii) in default of payment, up to [time period] imprisonment; or

(b) in the case of a body corporate or any other person—

    (i)   to a fine not exceeding [amount], or

    (ii) to a fine of [multiple] the amount of unpaid tax, whichever is greater; or

    (iii) in default of payment, up to [time period] imprisonment.

11. Secrecy-related offenses

Any person who—having any official duty or being employed in the administration of any tax, with possession of or control over any documents, records, information, returns, assessment lists, and copies of such lists obtained from the tax commissioner relating to any tax matter, knowingly or willfully—

1. without lawful excuse fails—

    (a) to regard and to deal with all such documents, records, information, returns, lists, and copies, as secret and confidential; or

    (b) to make and subscribe a declaration to that effect before a public official; or

2. communicates or attempts to communicate such information or anything contained in such documents, records, returns, lists, or copies of such lists to any person—

    (a) other than a Tax Commissioner or a tax officer of a revenue department or any other person to whom she or he is authorized by the Minister to communicate it pursuant to any law; or

    (b) otherwise than for the purposes prescribed by law, commits a criminal offense and is liable on summary conviction in a Tax Court to a fine not exceeding [amount] and, in default of payment, up to [time period] imprisonment.

12. Interest

Whenever, without lawful excuse—

1. any tax, penalty, or surcharge being due and payable, remains unpaid after the relevant date or the date authorized by law, interest shall be charged thereon from the next day after the relevant date or that other date, as the case may be, until the date of payment; or
2. any refund is not made within [time period] after the date on which the claim for such refund is received by the Tax Commissioner, interest shall be payable to the taxpayer as respects the period beginning immediately after the end of [time period] aforesaid and ending on the date on which the refund is made, at the annual average lending rate established by the National Bank, which shall be computed on a daily basis.

13. Compatibility of sanctions

Should a person commit two or more offenses of the same or different category, the respective sanctions shall add up. Offenses can be committed simultaneously or even derive from a single action or omission. Consequently, all tax sanctions in this act are compatible and can be applied cumulatively. No combined limits shall apply.

14. Alternative sentence

In default of payment of any penalty adjudged for the commission of a civil offense, the Tax Court may commute the economic fine for mandatory community service. The alternative sentence shall establish the duration of the new penalty in accordance with the equivalence between the amount of the unpaid economic fine and the national minimum wage at which the provision of mandatory community service will be valued.

15. Body corporate as offender

Where an offense is committed by a body corporate, the managing director, manager, designated responsible officer, or other officer concerned in the management of that body corporate is, without prejudice to the liability of the body corporate, deemed to have committed the offense and is jointly and severally liable together with the body corporate for any sanctions in relation thereto, unless at the trial she or he proves that the offense was committed without their knowledge, consent, or connivance or that she or he exercised all due diligence to prevent the commission thereof as she or he ought to have exercised having regard to the nature of her or his functions in the body corporate and the circumstances of the case.

16. Complementary legislation

1. The provisions of the Tax Collection Act concerning payment, collection, and recovery of tax and the enforcement of payment thereof shall apply to any penalty, surcharge, or interest payable under this act, in everything that does not contradict this Act.
2. In addition to any other remedy provided under the Tax Collection Act, any penalty, surcharge, or interest payable may be sued for and recovered in the Revenue Court or in a Tax Court by a Collector of Taxes as a debt due to the Government.
3. Any provisions that contradict this Act shall be amended accordingly to comply with this Act.

Sample roadmap for the creation of a data science team

A robust data science team that can produce meaningful machine learning applications for the revenue administration requires at least two to three specialists dedicated to data management and three to five software developers trained in machine learning algorithms and the required tools. This team can be built incrementally, and the revenue administration can quickly initiate small projects that will produce encouraging results while its team of data scientists is being recruited and/or trained.

Simple techniques, such as linear regression, k-nearest neighbor, or density-based anomaly detection, can quickly be applied to interesting data to augment the capabilities of the revenue administration. As the data science team acquires experience, more complex techniques such as neural networks, natural language processing, and deep learning can be applied.

Short term (6 to 12 months)

Initially, for the first six months, the following short-term activities can be executed to jumpstart a data science program for the revenue administration. These activities should be executed sequentially to maximize the benefit.

Create a dedicated data sciences team. Establish a data science team that will work full-time on the development of data science applications. The assignment should be formal with the mandate of developing advanced automation and data analytics applications for the revenue administration. There is no single best location of the data science team within the organizational hierarchy, but if possible, the data science team should not be within the IT department, although it should be supported by IT. The organization can reap results faster if the business is driving, rather than creating, solutions that are IT-centric.

Identify initial applications. Identify potential application of machine learning techniques that can be implemented initially to demonstrate practical applications of data science. Initially, it is best to identify simple solutions that can quickly produce interesting results without substantial investments in time and/or resources.

Make an inventory of existing data. To enable machine learning applications, the data science team must work with existing database administrators to identify information that can be used, document it, note its location, estimate its quality, and note its provenance. The inventory of existing data is not a data repository, but rather just a map of data assets that are available in the revenue administration, if needed by the data management team.

Acquire and install appropriate data visualization tools. The process of analyzing existing data and preparing them for migration to the data repository requires that the data management team have appropriate tools for data visualization. Data visualization allows the team to visually examine the distribution of data before they are processed. It is one of the most important tools for the development of machine learning.

Create an initial data repository with minimal data. Based on the identification of initial applications, the data management team would create an initial data repository that contains only the information that is required by the machine learning projects identified. This initial repository should contain clean and high-quality data that have been preprocessed to identify missing data and eliminate distortions and outliers where appropriate.

Create an architecture for generating synthetic data. As mentioned before, synthetic data allow working with many developers and researchers without violating privacy and confidentiality constraints, but the generation of synthetic data is far from trivial. The data management team needs to create an architecture and strategy for creating this parallel data repository, deciding initially if the repository will be constructed by anonymizing data or if it will be generated from scratch, replicating the statistical properties of the data in the main production databases.

Identify two core developers who will transition to the data science team. Initially, a small group of talented developers can be used to jumpstart the development of machine learning algorithms, but these developers need to be fully engaged to acquire the necessary skills.

Identify one core data manager who will transition to the data science team. Initially, a small group of talented data managers can be used to jumpstart the creation of a high-quality data repository, but these data managers need to be fully engaged to acquire the necessary skills.

Identify the current level of competencies for the data science team members. To create a meaningful training program, the revenue administration needs to identify the level of proficiency of the assembled data science team with the algorithms, tools, and techniques needed in the production of machine learning algorithms.

Design an initial six-month basic induction program for the data science team. Based on the current level of proficiency of the data centers team, the revenue administration should create a six-month training program that equips the team with the fundamental competencies that are required for the development of machine learning algorithms and data management. This induction program can use the training resources that are specified in this document as a starting point, but it is best to establish agreements with existing local educational institutions.

Design a complete 24-month training program for the data science team. The revenue administration should develop a comprehensive 24-month training program for new personnel, covering all the skills and competencies that are desired by the data science team to produce production-level machine learning algorithms. This induction program can use the training resources that are specified in this document as a starting point, but it is best to establish agreements with existing local educational institutions.

Create a recruitment program to hire at least three additional machine learning developers and two additional data managers. The data science team should have at least five dedicated developers and three data managers, and it is best when the revenue administration hires trained personnel that already possess basic skills. Qualified data scientists are difficult to find, and the revenue administration should establish a formal recruitment program that constantly seeks qualified individuals who can be hired into the data sciences team.

Create collaboration agreements with local universities and research centers to perform applied research in applied machine learning. Artificial intelligence and machine learning are active areas of research in many universities and research centers, and collaborations between revenue administrations and these research centers can provide substantial improvements in the quality of the production-level applications developed. If the revenue administration has a synthetic data repository, collaboration agreements can be established, accelerating the pace at which it will deploy data science solutions.

Create an internship program with local universities to identify potential talent for the data science team. An internship program with local universities can help identify talented resources; this should form part of the general recruitment strategy.

Develop at least two initial prototypes of applications of machine learning within the revenue administration within 12 months. Once established, the data science team should have the mandate to produce at least two production-quality prototypes of applications of artificial intelligence and machine learning within 12 months of the establishment of the data science team.

Medium term (12 to 24 months)

In the medium term (within 24 months), the following activities will consolidate the data sciences team and enable the revenue administration to integrate machine learning and artificial intelligence into its constellation of production systems:

Create a synthetic data repository that can be used to develop and train machine learning algorithms. Build a complete and sustainable synthetic data repository that can be used by developers and researchers to construct meaningful and creative applications of artificial intelligence and machine learning within the revenue administration. It is important to note that sustainability implies that the synthetic data repository will generate data periodically to remain current, mirroring the statistical properties of the data in the main production-level repository. This means that the data in the main repository should be statistically monitored.

Create a mentoring program to train the business domain team (BDT) of the revenue administration on the applications of machine learning. The BDT is a specialized team within the revenue administration in charge of defining, analyzing, and maintaining the business processes in the organization. This team may not have in-depth knowledge of the potential of artificial intelligence and machine learning for identifying possible uses of these technologies within the revenue administration. It is the responsibility of the data science team to create a mentoring program that will create necessary competencies within the BDT, including training sessions, workshops, and seminars that can be executed periodically.

Identify additional applications for machine learning. The BDT needs to identify potential applications for machine learning and artificial intelligence within the revenue administration. The applications constitute a roadmap that the development teams can use to guide their implementation efforts. It is important to note that developing this roadmap should not be the responsibility of the data science team, since it does not have the necessary information about the needs of the revenue administration.

Create at least five production-level applications of machine learning within the revenue administration. Once established, the data science team should have the mandate to produce at least five production-level systems that make use of artificial intelligence and machine learning within 24 months of the establishment of the data science team.

Hire (or incorporate) three additional software developers specialized in machine learning. Incorporate three additional software developers into the data science team.

Hire (or incorporate) two additional data managers specialized in data quality, data management, and data visualization. Add two additional data managers to the data science team.

Selected examples of machine learning applications in a revenue administration

Grouping taxpayers

Unsupervised learning can be applied to find groups of related taxpayers for risk management and profiling. Algorithms such as k-nearest neighbor automatically find structure for the selected features. This means that any n features can be selected and the machine learning algorithm will group taxpayers into selected k groups.

To show the power of this technique, only two dimensions will be selected, so the results can be visualized in two dimensions. For example, if two dimensions are selected—"value added tax paid" and "total income tax paid"— the result may be similar to the image shown in figure F.1. Most taxpayers are grouped into the low-VAT, low–income tax grouping, but selected companies are in the high-VAT, high–income tax grouping.

However, if the "age of the corporation" and the "VAT paid" are chosen as dimensions, the results may resemble the image shown in figure F.2, where older companies clearly pay more VAT than younger companies, except for those companies that are highlighted in green. The risk management group of the tax administration can look at these companies to determine the reasons for this disparity, or these companies can be configured to have higher risk profiles.

These are simple examples containing only two dimensions, but in actual practice, k-nearest neighbor algorithms can be fed hundreds of dimensions. In these cases, visualization of these groups is more challenging but possible, especially using a special technique in machine learning called dimensionality reduction. An example is principal component analysis, where dozens of dimensions can be taken from the k-nearest neighbor result and projected into the most significant two-dimensional or three-dimensional figure, minimizing the projection error.

FIGURE F.1   Grouping taxpayers (result 1)

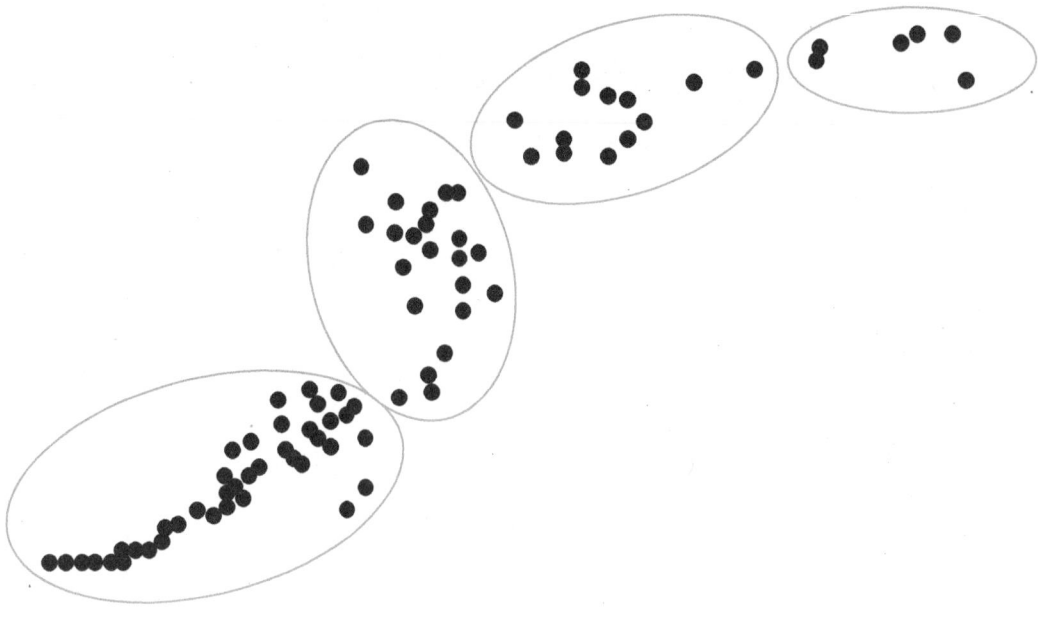

Source: Krsul 2021.

FIGURE F.2   Grouping taxpayers (result 2)

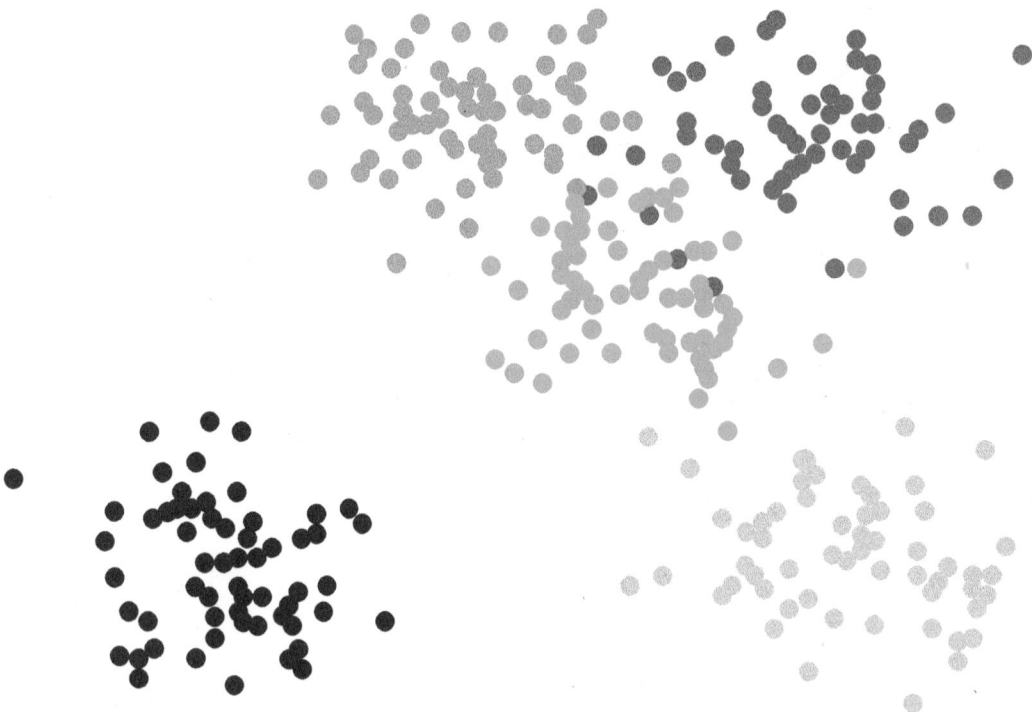

Source: Krsul 2021.

Anomaly detection using multivariate Gaussian distribution

Anomaly detection, using density or multivariate Gaussian distribution, is a technique where developers can feed the machine learning a series of features, and the algorithm can automatically create a model of what normal looks like to identify potential anomalies.

For example, if the algorithm is fed the features "VAT paid" and "size of company," the algorithm will create a series of probability areas based on the data used to train it, as shown in figure F.3. Most companies will fall within the area denoted by the concentric circles, and some companies will clearly fall outside this area. The companies that are shown with the red dots are anomalous and probably deserve close examination or can be flagged as higher risk for the risk management system.

The example provided is simplistic since it uses two dimensions where, in practice, we can feed an anomaly detection thousands of features and the algorithm will construct a probabilistic representation of the data provided to highlight those records that are outside the normal pattern. This technique can be used to identify taxpayers who are performing unusual operations, tax officials who are performing unusual operations, refund requests that are unusual, tax returns that are unusual, financial transactions that are unusual, and so on.

FIGURE F.3 Anomaly detection using multivariate Gaussian distribution

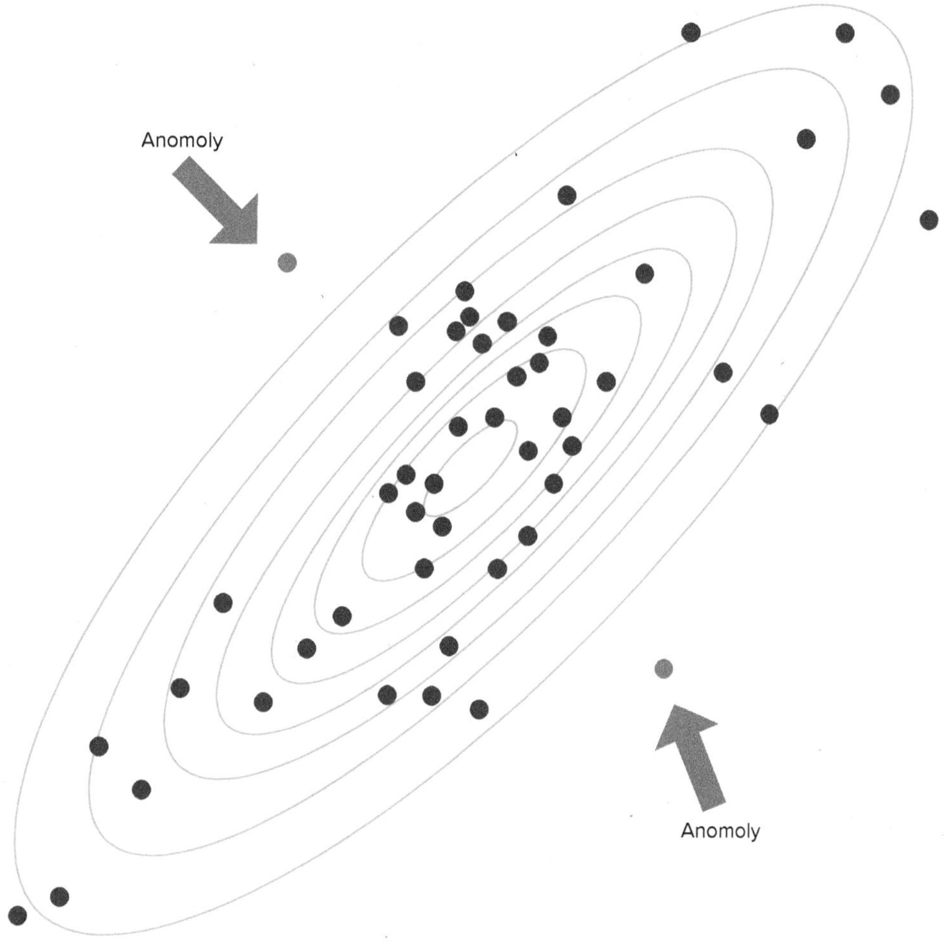

Source: Krsul 2021.

Identification of inquiries using classifiers

One of the most complex problems to automate is the identification of inquiries and their corresponding replies in taxpayer assistance. Most tax administrations receive thousands of inquiries, and most of these questions can be answered from a relatively low number of standard replies. To select the correct answer, somebody from taxpayer assistance needs to read the inquiry, find the correct standard reply, and send it to the taxpayer.

It is possible to train a machine learning algorithm to automatically classify inquiries and match them to standard answers using classification systems such as support vector machines, logistic regression, or neural networks. If we have a historical collection of inquiries and can identify, for each inquiry, a standard reply, then we can train a classification system to automatically identify the correct standard reply that can be applied, forwarding this standard reply to the taxpayer automatically. The taxpayer knows that if the answer is not satisfactory, it will be possible to follow up to contact a person who will analyze the request on an individual basis and respond appropriately.

Support vector machines are classification algorithms that allow classifying a set of inputs into classes and work well for small and medium numbers of data samples. As illustrated in figure F.4, this algorithm allows separating the distinct classes by using hyperplanes in nth-dimensional space using special data points called support vectors.

The way to train a support vector machine to recognize inquiries and their corresponding standard replies is similar to the techniques used to identify SPAM in email. First, create a set of features corresponding to each of the most used words in any language (about 5,000). Then, using a technique called "text vectorization," convert a taxpayer inquiry into a vector of numbers that are fed to the support vector machine to train it to recognize the standard reply that applies.

FIGURE F.4 Identification of inquiries using classifiers

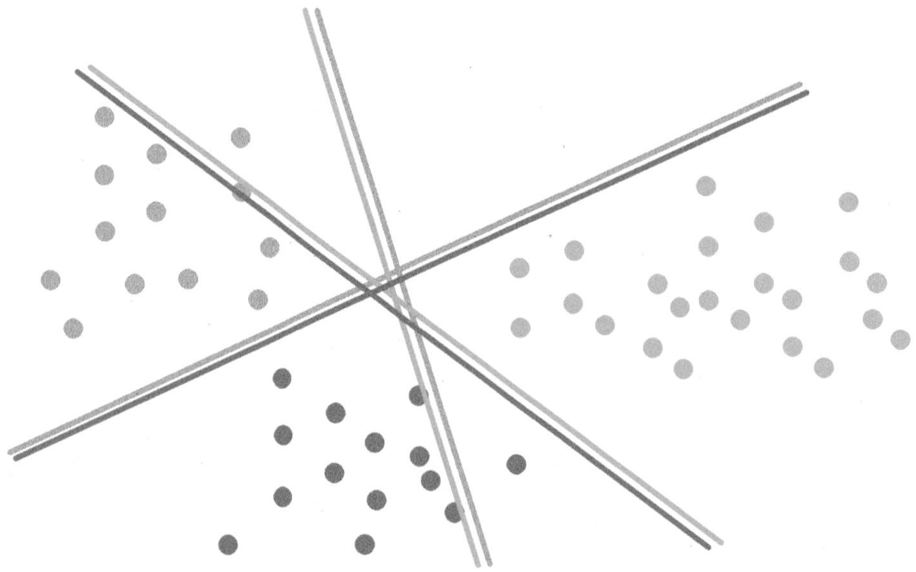

Source: Krsul 2021.

Identification of associated companies

Auditors and risk managers can benefit substantially from identifying linked companies and/or communities of related companies that are somewhat connected because they do business together, import similar products, and have the same individuals on their board of directors; an individual has control of multiple companies; an individual possesses shares in multiple companies; multiple individuals of the same family (spouses and blood relatives) have control of multiple companies; and so on.

Machine learning can discover relationships between companies and create clusters of networks like those shown in figure F.5, where clusters of companies are highlighted in different colors. This can be done using specialized algorithms such as Leiden community detection, surprise community detection, and Walktrap Community Detection 2, or by using k-nearest neighbor. In these cases, the features are the connections between companies, either as edged between nodes in a graph or common features for k-nearest neighbor. This is particularly useful for auditors, because they can run these algorithms to display networks of relations for companies that are associated with the company being audited, or as input to the risk management engine, where companies that are densely connected can have higher risk profiles.

FIGURE F.5 Identification of associated companies

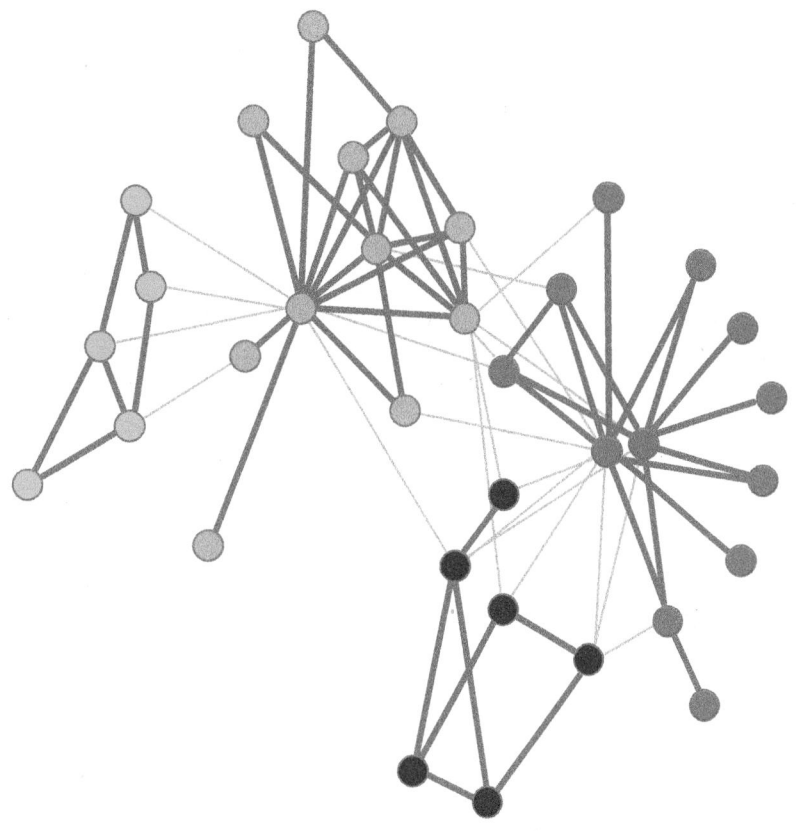

Source: Krsul 2021.

Detection of fraudulent VAT emitters

In some countries, the VAT system allows companies to deduce from their tax obligations the VAT for purchases made, passing the final tax to the end consumer, and fraudulent companies are set up for producing fraudulent VAT receipts. These companies typically do not produce actual services, have no income, have no personnel, and emit VAT receipts that other companies use to deduce the VAT from their tax obligations. After some time, these companies are closed. It is difficult to find these companies because the tax administration does not have the resources to verify by hand the transactions of thousands of small companies, and because these companies hide in the "noise" that is created by legitimate companies.

However, it is possible to train a neural network, as shown in figure F.6, to automatically identify these companies with a high degree of accuracy, especially by cross-referencing information from third parties, such as social security, land registry, and telecommunications registry.

Inputs to the neural network are derived from information from companies, such as total amount of VAT receipts submitted (total expenditures), VAT receipts issued (for 90, 60, and 30 days), property income, deductions claimed, total payroll, social security contributions, telecommunication records, and so on. Output from the neural network is an indication of whether a company is likely to be emitting fraudulent VAT receipts. Neural networks can perform this feat if they have been appropriately trained. This means that the neural network needs to have a history of companies that were identified as fraudulent.

FIGURE F.6   Detection of fraudulent VAT emitters

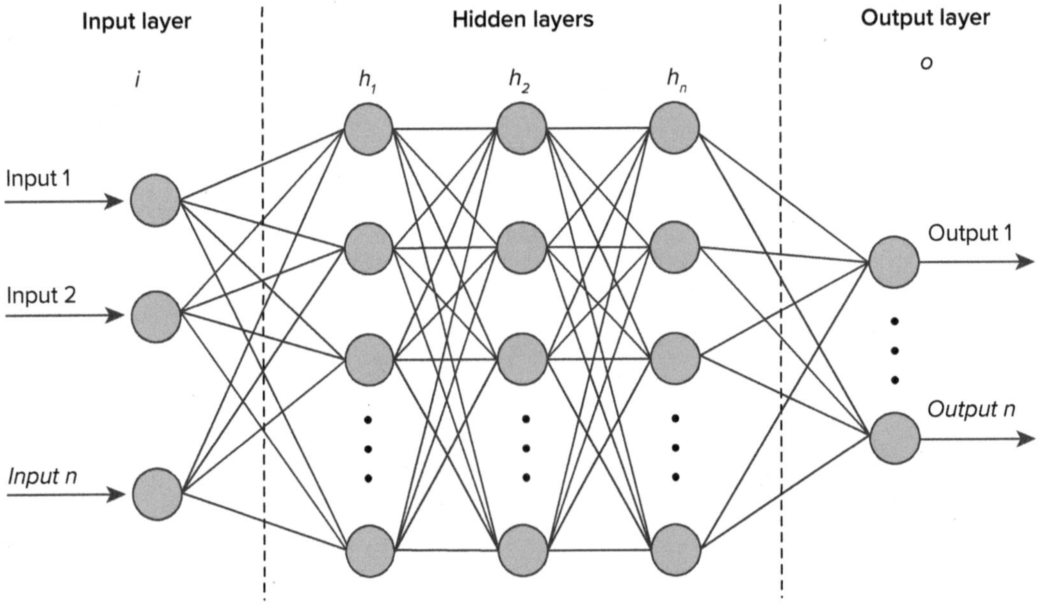

Source: Krsul 2021.

Bibliography

Krsul, Ivan. 2021. "Building Data Science Capabilities in a Tax Administration. Vol. 7." Working Paper, unpublished, World Bank, Washington, DC.